MW00527510

NFL 1970
THE INAUGURAL SEASON OF THE NEW NFL

IAN S. KAHANOWITZ

Mechanicsburg, PA USA

Published by Sunbury Press, Inc.
Mechanicsburg, Pennsylvania

www.sunburypress.com

For information about special discounts for bulk purchases, please contact Sunbury Press Orders Dept. at (855) 338-8359 or orders@sunburypress.com.

To request one of our authors for speaking engagements or book signings, please contact Sunbury Press Publicity Dept. at publicity@sunburypress.com.

FIRST SUNBURY PRESS EDITION: March 2021

Set in Adobe Garamond | Interior design by Crystal Devine | Cover by Terry Kennedy | Edited by Lawrence Knorr.

Publisher's Cataloging-in-Publication Data
Names: Kahanowitz, Ian S., author.
Title: NFL 1970 : the inaugural season of the new NFL / Ian S. Kahanowitz.
Description: First trade paperback edition. | Mechanicsburg, PA : Sunbury Press, 2021.
Summary: The current NFL was formed by its merger with the AFL. This book covers the transactions, key figures, and memorable games from that era, especially the Colts-Cowboys rivalry.
Identifiers: ISBN 978-1-620064-61-0 (softcover).
Subjects: SPORTS & RECREATION / Football | SPORTS & RECREATION / History | HISTORY / United States / 20th Century.

Product of the United States of America
0 1 1 2 3 5 8 13 21 34 55

Continue the Enlightenment!

This book is dedicated to my son Ryan,
whose love for the game of football has
reinvigorated me into following the sport more closely
as I did when I was younger.

To my son Jacob,
who is learning to love the game of football
by watching it with his twin brother, Ryan,
and myself.

CONTENTS

Acknowledgments   vii

Introduction   1

CHAPTERS

1. History of the National Football League—1800s–1960   5

2. History of the American Football League and the War with the NFL—1959–1966   24

3. Anatomy of a Merger: The AFL and NFL Combine—1966   52

4. An Uneasy Peace and the First Four Super Bowls—1966–1969   68

5. The History of the Baltimore Colts—1948–1969   89

6. The History of the Dallas Cowboys—1960–1969   95

7. Year One of the Merger: The 1970 NFL Season   106

8. The Dallas Cowboys in 1970   149

9. The Baltimore Colts in 1970   170

10. The Big Eight Make It into the Playoffs   187

11. The Playoffs   224

12. Super Bowl V, Prelude to the Game   247

13. Super Bowl V, The Game   266

14. Super Bowl V, The Post Game   281

15. The Impact of the 1970 Season   291

Epilogue   298

Bibliography   303

Index   308

About the Author   316

ACKNOWLEDGMENTS

First and foremost, I'd like to thank Lawrence Knorr and the team at Sunbury Press for taking on my manuscript and publishing my book. I'd like to also thank the following people for their love and support: my wife Ann Marie and my two sons, Jacob and Ryan; my mother, Beryl Kahanowitz, and my sister, Shelby Kahanowitz; my friends Vincent Serpico and Andrew Cosentino, who have listened to me talk about the amount of work that goes into creating a book; my friend Irene Hodges whose love and patience means the world to me; to Kim Kushner, who has taken the time to listen to my ideas; to my many followers on social media who always have supported me and have been very kind in buying and reading my published works; and everyone who had bought my works and has enjoyed my storytelling.

INTRODUCTION

It was a Super Bowl like no other before or since. Super Bowl V was the first modern-era National Football League (NFL) championship game, between the first American Football Conference (AFC) champion Baltimore Colts and the first National Football Conference (NFC) champion Dallas Cowboys to decide the NFL champion for the 1970 season. Previously, for the last four seasons, the Super Bowl was dubbed as the AFL-NFL World Championship due to American football having two different pro leagues: The American Football League (AFL) and The National Football League (NFL). Now, in that one vintage season of 1970, the two separate leagues merged into one, and it was the pioneering year for pro football as we know it today. In addition to this new league, this would be the first Super Bowl game played on artificial turf, which was on first-generation Poly-Turf. The game was played on January 17, 1971, at the Orange Bowl in Miami, Florida.

Super Bowl V is sometimes called the "Blunder Bowl" or "Stupor Bowl" because it was filled with poor play, a missed extra-point attempt after a touchdown, penalties, turnovers, and officiating miscues. The two opposing teams, Dallas and Baltimore, combined for a Super Bowl record eleven turnovers, with five coming in the fourth quarter. The Colts' seven turnovers remain the most committed by a Super Bowl champion. The Cowboys also set a Super Bowl record with ten penalties, costing them 133 yards.

At the time, in 1970, the creation of this new league from the two warring leagues brought out record attendance at all the games played during the inaugural season. Fans did not have to choose which league was their favorite. Pro football was now united due to the merger agreement between the AFL and NFL, which was forged four years before in 1966, whereby both leagues agreed to form one new league in 1970. The 1970 pro football season featured all of the 26 teams that comprised both AFL and NFL teams. The two leagues were now divided into two conferences. The National Football League would be placed into the National Football Conference. The American Football League would be placed in the American Football Conference, with thirteen teams in each conference. The American Football League's name would be abandoned as both leagues agreed to be part of the longer-running National Football League brand name. Because the AFL only had ten teams going into the merger, while the NFL had sixteen teams in the merger, it was agreed that three teams from the NFL would join the new AFC Conference to even up both conferences. These teams that traded conferences were the Baltimore Colts, the Cleveland Browns, and the Pittsburgh Steelers.

The Colts were a powerhouse in the NFL for years and represented the older league in Super Bowl III. Now, two years later, they represented the new AFC for Super Bowl V. If there ever was an identity crisis for a team in the history of pro football, the 1970 Baltimore Colts was that team. Meanwhile, the Dallas Cowboys were making their first Super Bowl appearance from many years of disappointing losses after having many good seasons.

The new 26-team league began to use an eight-team playoff format, four from each conference, that included the three division winners and a wild card team (the second-place team in each conference with the best record in any one of the three divisions) in knockout rounds played after the season was over, in a quest to get to the championship or now known as the "Super Bowl." Beginning with this Super Bowl and continuing to the present day, the Super Bowl has served as the NFL's league championship game, with the winner of the AFC Championship Game and the winner of the NFC Championship Game facing off after two, then later three rounds, of divisional and conference series comprising of the new NFL playoff system.

Things on the football fields were changing as well. The year 1970 saw seven teams play their home games on artificial turf. This was five more than just two teams who had artificial turf back in 1969. Now, artificial turf was present in Cincinnati, Dallas, Miami, Pittsburgh, and St. Louis, in addition to the two teams who had artificial turf in 1969, which were Houston in the AFL and Philadelphia in the NFL.

Also, pro football was growing by leaps and bounds, besides the merger of the two leagues. Cincinnati and Pittsburgh opened new stadiums: Riverfront Stadium in Cincinnati and Three Rivers Stadium in Pittsburgh. Due to record-breaking ticket sales in the last few years, there was a need for more stadium capacity to hold the expanding fan base than there had been before. With the expansion of stadiums, pro football followed major league baseball in embracing artificial turf playing fields.

To televise their games, the newly combined league contracted with CBS and NBC, who were previously the primary broadcasters of the NFL and the AFL, respectively. It was then decided that CBS would televise all NFC teams (including playoff games) while NBC would televise all AFC teams. For inter-conference games during the seasons, CBS would broadcast games if the visiting team was from the NFC, and NBC would carry the games when the visitors were from the AFC. At the time, all NFL games were blacked out in the home team's market, so this arrangement meant that fans in each team's home market would see all their team's televised Sunday afternoon games on the same network (CBS for NFC teams and NBC for AFC teams). The two networks also divided up the Super Bowl on a yearly rotation.

Meanwhile, with the debut of *Monday Night Football* on ABC, which was first televised on September 21, 1970, the league became the first professional sports league in the United States to have a regular series of nationally televised games in prime-time. In 1970, the NFL became the only league ever to have its games televised on all the then-three major broadcast networks at the same time. Ironically, both teams that advanced to the Super Bowl, the Baltimore Colts and the Dallas Cowboys, had suffered humiliating defeats at home on *Monday Night Football* in front of a nationwide audience. By adding ABC as a broadcasting outlet in prime time, the NFL would reap the rewards of earning massive television revenue that was never seen before by the prior two leagues before they merged.

NFL 1970 is also the story of the Dallas Cowboys, who were an elite team in the NFL since 1966 but could never win the big game. The Dallas Cowboys were longing to be the brides and not the bride's maids as in previous years. They had a championship-caliber team, and they were ready to be on the biggest stage of all sports, the Super Bowl. This is also the story of the Baltimore Colts, who lost Super Bowl III two years earlier to an under-rated New York Jets team and looked for redemption as the loss still hung over the team like a dark cloud. This time the Colts were in a different conference and with a different coach, but many questioned if they had the fire to win. This is also the story of two leagues, that had their separate traditions and fans, and how the war between the leagues ended in a truce that created the modern era of pro football as we know it today.

So, let us step back in time as we celebrate the 50th anniversary of the season of 1970, ending in Super Bowl V, and the events that led up to that one vintage season in pro football.

1

HISTORY OF THE NATIONAL FOOTBALL LEAGUE – 1800s-1960

The National Football League. Just the name by itself evokes images of large crowds, exciting plays, and amazing history in American sports. It is a sport that transcended throughout the decades from its humble beginnings to become firmly supplanted in the American culture. In 2021, we fans take it for granted that every July begins the ritual of the start of the professional football season, beginning with the opening of training camps for all the teams in the NFL. August arrives shortly thereafter and teases the fans with the pre-season games, making us hungry for the start of the NFL season. We fans wait patiently as summer's heat begins to fade into the cooler and shorter autumn days, and we know that school will start for our kids, television programs will have new episodes, and pro football returns, as our lives shift back to "normal" from the summer mode.

From September to January, millions of fans partake in pro football every Sunday, whether they are at the game, in a sports bar, at home, or listening to the games on the radio in the car. In this modern era of pro football, however, we now have *Thursday Night Football*, and of course, *Monday Night Football*, which has been a fixture on television since 1970.

The game has grown so much since the 1970 season that pre-game shows are no longer limited to Sundays at noon. On almost every cable channel that broadcasts sports, pro football is discussed each day of the week. We get our fill daily on analysis and picks, fantasy football games, and betting odds. Pro football is no longer just a sport in the United States, but it is the national sport and has been that way since the mid-1960s when the sport dethroned baseball as America's national pastime with its popularity. For the first 65 years of the 20th century, baseball was considered the national pastime, with pro football lagging far behind its popularity. College football was even more popular than pro football well into the 1950s. After years of evolving, pro football had achieved this elite status by 1970. The game and its championship, the Super Bowl, fully immersed itself into the American stream of consciousness. Today, pro football is not just a game; it is a religious ritual for many every Sunday during the autumn months.

How pro football got to this point is an amazing story. The game has evolved immensely from its roots going back to the late 1800s and early 20th century. With each passing decade in the 20th century, pro football kept making changes and adjustments to the game in both its rules and style of play to maximize its appeal to the fans in American society. As the popularity of the game grew, so did the investors, and pro football would eventually become big business in addition to being a sport. Sponsors, radio and television rights, advertising, and the excitement of pro football propelled the NFL to be an economic juggernaut it is today.

BIRTH OF THE GAME AND THE COLLEGE EXPERIENCE

American football history can be traced to early versions of rugby-type football and association football, which Americans call soccer. Both games have their origins in varieties of football style games played in Britain, usually at school, in the mid–19th century. Gameplay usually consisted of a ball kicked at a goal or run over a line.

The name "football" referred to any number of ball games played on foot. However, these games' rules differed from one another, some allowing the use of hands in the "running games," others forbidding it in the "kicking games."[1]

American football's ancestor leans more towards the game of Rugby rather than soccer. Rugby was claimed to be invented when an Englishman grew tired of the no-hands restriction, picked the ball up, and ran. Out of interest to enforce the rules of the game, the other players could tackle a player with the ball. This looked like a lot of fun to people, and it was this diversion from the kicking games that running football games were born in the games that were played by pre-colonial European peasants.

No one truly knows who had the first football team, but most sports historians point to the Oneida Football Club, a Boston club founded in 1861. History has not recorded what rules this club used, whether they played a running, kicking, or hybrid version. Simultaneously, the sport of rugby was taking off in Canada around the same time. Records indicate that the Montreal Football club was formed in 1868 and is said to have played a variant of English rugby. This became the root of Canadian football, which is important here for it later had a large influence on American football's development.[2]

It is not clear what the rules and regulations most of these early football games followed. However, the *Rutgers v. Princeton* game in 1869 gives historians some relevant evidence that this was the first football game. Two teams played the game with 25 players on each side. Each team was composed of 11 "fielders," 12 "bulldogs," and two "peanutters" whose job was to hang out near the opposing team's goal to score from unguarded positions.[3] Such being the case, there was no such thing as an "offsides" rule at this time, as hanging out by the opposing goal posts constitutes a major infraction in the modern game. At this point, American football closely resembled soccer, in the sense that a team scored goals instead of touchdowns, and throwing or running with the ball was not allowed. While the NFL states that this early game was based on soccer

1. "A Brief History of Football," accessed September 28, 2017, http://www.historyoffootball.net/.
2. Ibid.
3. Ibid.

and not rugby, colleges began instituting this as a major collegiate sport. Thus, intercollegiate football games were catching on with the public, which increased the sport's popularity. In 1873, Yale, Columbia, Princeton, and Rutgers codified the first-ever set of intercollegiate football rules. However, these rules did not let players throw the ball or run with it. It was soccer or something like soccer.

While that codified brand of soccer took hold, Harvard University had other ideas about what constituted "football." Harvard representatives knew in advance that Yale, Columbia, Princeton, and Rutgers were planning to codify the rules forbidding aggressive physical contact and carrying the ball, so they refused to participate in the games. Thus, Harvard's stubbornness in failing to recognize the codifying of rugby rules led shortly after that to the *McGill v. Harvard* match of 1874 and the *Harvard v. Yale* game of 1875. Due to the popularity of these matches, other American universities began to field rugby teams. Finally, in 1876, a meeting was held between Harvard, Columbia, Princeton, and Yale, where all four schools adopted England's Rugby Union rules, but with two key changes. No longer would the scoring of a touchdown be nullified if the opposing team kicked a field goal.[4]

American football resulted from several significant changes from association football and rugby football, most notably the rule changes instituted by Walter Camp, a Yale University and Hopkins School graduate considered the "father of gridiron football."[5] Between 1880 and 1883, Camp came up with several major adjustments to the game: an eleven player team, a smaller field, and the introduction of the line of scrimmage, whereby a player hands the ball back to begin the play. An even more important alteration created was that if the offensive team failed to gain five yards after three downs, they were forced to surrender the ball. Camp also established the norm of a seven-man line, a quarterback, two halfbacks, and a fullback.[6] Camp was also responsible for introducing the "safety," awarding two points to the defensive side for tackling a ball

4. Ibid.
5. "Camp and His Followers: American Football 1876–1889," Professional Football Researchers Association, OHIO TIGER TRAP (profootballresearchers.org), accessed September 17, 2018.
6. "A Brief History of Football," accessed September 28, 2017, http://www.historyoffootball.net/.

carrier in his end zone followed by a free-kick by the offense from its 20-yard line to restart play. This is significant as the rugby union has no point value award for this action but instead awards a scrum (a method of restarting play in rugby that involves players packing closely together with their heads down and attempting to gain possession of the ball) to the attacking side five meters from the goal line.

The field that the men played on also began to take shape into what we know as a "football field." Over the years, the field's size has been changed from 120 yards, not including the field's end zone areas on either side of the field, to a length of no more than 100 yards, not including the end zone regions. The football field's width has been regulated to 55 1/3 yards, where it was 100 yards wide at one time.[7]

Even the ball itself changed. The first footballs used in college football gaming were 23 inches in diameter at their widest point, and they were shaped like an oval. Today's footballs are more circular spherical balls measuring 20.75 inches around its widest part. Also, a touchdown in football was worth two points for a team, and five points were earned for a field goal. The points applied changed too due to the game's evolution and new regulations changing the points for a field goal to three and the points for a touchdown to six.[8]

PRO FOOTBALL AND THE BIRTH OF A NEW LEAGUE

Pro football officially began in 1892 in Pittsburgh, Pennsylvania, when former Yale All-American guard William "Pudge" Heffelfinger was paid a notable sum of $500 to play in a single game for the Allegheny Athletic Association on November 12th. This game was against Allegheny's rival, the Pittsburgh Athletic Club.[9] Three years later, the first professional game was played in Pennsylvania between the Latrobe YMCA and the Jeannette Athletic Club. By 1896, the Allegheny Athletic Association was made up entirely of paid players, making it the sport's first-ever professional team. As football became more and

---

7. Ibid.

8. Ibid.

9. "NFL founded in Canton," NFL Pro Football Hall of Fame, January 1, 2005, accessed September 17, 2018, http://www.profootballhof.com/news/nfl-founded-in-canton/.

more popular, local semi-pro and pro teams were also organized across the country.[10]

For nearly the next three decades, pro football faced its ups and downs as it was played primarily in small towns throughout western Pennsylvania and the Midwest. One of the players' challenges was that football was a brutal game that contributed to many injuries and players' deaths. Eighteen players were killed in 1905 alone. This was partly due to a lack of protective gear and the use of interlocking defensive formations, and a tendency for teammates to drag ball-carrying players forward to gain extra yards.[11]

Organizers of these local and semi-pro leagues began to see a need to institute safeguards, seeing how chaotic and dangerous the game was to the players. Although 1905 saw the most deaths from football-related injuries, at the time, there began a period of reform by the game's organizers. The biggest part of the playing field that needed the most adjustments was the line of scrimmage. The organizers now developed a neutral zone between scrimmage lines to streamline the game more effectively. With the institution of this new "neutral zone," it was now mandatory that six players from each team were positioned at this neutral zone. Also, the forward pass was now instituted into the game as a legalized play. Putting the forward pass into the game marked a distinct break from rugby, and it became a signature style of play that only American football had.

Even with these reforms, these changes were not enough to protect the players from injury or death. Three years later, in 1908, 33 more players were killed on the field. Seeing a need for more reform, between 1910 and 1912, interlocking formations were finally banned, and more protective padding was introduced. Both measures helped reduce the death and injury toll. Also, changes to the rules were made to add a fourth down and the six-point touchdown, instead of two.[12]

Professional football first established itself as a viable spectator sport in the 1910s with the establishment of the Ohio League. The city of

10. "Professional Football is Born," History.com, accessed September 17, 2018, https://www.history .com/this-day-in-history/professional-football-is-born.

11. "A Brief History of Football," accessed September 28, 2017, http://www.historyoffootball.net/.

12. Ibid.

Canton was the premiere team in the league and featured legendary decathlete and football star Jim Thorpe. From his play with the Carlisle School to his gold medal in the decathlon in Stockholm in 1912, and his time in the outfield with John McGraw's New York Giants in Major League Baseball, Thorpe was an international star who brought legitimacy to professional football.[13] The crowds that Thorpe and the Canton team drew created a market for professional football in Ohio and beyond. Still, the league was struggling due to escalating player salaries, a reliance on college players who then had to forfeit their college eligibility, players continually jumping from one team to another following the highest offer, and a general lack of organization of play. Seeing the financial growth and popularity of their rival sport of major league baseball, professional football realized that they were in dire need of organizing itself.

The organization of pro football began on August 20, 1920, when the owners of four Ohio League teams—the Akron Pros, Canton Bulldogs, Cleveland Indians, and Dayton Triangles—met to form a new professional league. Jim Thorpe was nominated as president of the new league, as it was hoped Thorpe's fame would help the league be taken seriously. A month later, on September 17, the league met again, this time with eleven teams (Akron Pros, Canton Bulldogs, Decatur Staleys, Chicago Cardinals, Cleveland Indians Dayton Triangles, Hammond Pros, Massillon Tigers, Muncie Flyers, Rock Island Independents, Rochester Jeffersons) that were present. At the meeting, the owners agreed to change its name to the American Professional Football Association (APFA) and officially elected Jim Thorpe as the league's first president.[14]

The first matter of business was Massillon's withdrawal from professional football for the 1920 season. The team never joined the new league. However, by season's start, the membership also included the Buffalo All-Americans, Chicago Tigers, Columbus Panhandles, and

---

13. "Professional Football is born," History.com, accessed September 17, 2018, https://www.history .com/this-day-in-history/professional-football-is-born.

14. Ibid.

Detroit Heralds. Only two of the franchises still exist today. The Decatur Staleys moved to Chicago in 1921 and were renamed the Bears one year later. The Chicago Cardinals franchise now calls Arizona home.

A year later, the owners changed its name to the National Football League (NFL) in 1922, the same year the league started to release official rankings. From its ambitious organization as a major sport, the early NFL was not a tightly run organization. Teams often came and went, depending on a club's finances. Because of the league's early struggles, college football was still the dominant form of the game. However, as college football stars like Benny Friedman and Red Grange joined the league after graduation, pro football gained popularity.

THE DEPRESSION YEARS AND THE EVOLUTION OF
MODERN FOOTBALL - 1930-1940

Even with an organized league, the decade of the 1930s began with college football being more popular than pro football. This was due to the inter-collegiate games having a bigger fan base in every state and pro football being seen as an inferior league. The collegiate games also had great rivalries among schools and had championships in bowl games for many years. Pro football was still in its infancy and not as organized as the collegiate leagues due to the frequency of teams coming and going and the unorganized way the league was run year by year. To make matters worse for pro football, the global economy tanked in 1929, and thus the Great Depression took hold of American society. As the depression hit the country, teams struggled to stay afloat financially, and the eight-team league in 1932 was the lowest membership in its history. Despite the low numbers, however, the 1932 season became a catalyst for change in the NFL. Out of that season came two significant updates to the game.

The first of these updates was a series of rule changes designed to improve the NFL's offensive output. In 1932, scoring had become a serious problem in the league. In the 48 games played that season, there were twenty shutouts and ten ties; four were scoreless.[15] In response, George

---

15. Brandon J. Smith, "Football Origins, Growth, and History of the Game," accessed September 17, 2018, The People History, http://www.thepeoplehistory.com/footballhistory.html.

Halas, owner of the Chicago Bears, spearheaded three rules change at the end of the season. First, the goalposts were moved from the back of the end zone to the front, increasing field goals.[16] Second, the NFL instituted hash marks, which, if a play ended near the sideline, allowed the ball to be moved back towards the middle of the field.[17] The goalposts stayed that way until 1974 when the NFL moved it back to the end of the end zone, but the hash mark rules are still in effect. Third, and lastly, a pass could now be thrown anywhere behind the line of scrimmage (before this rule change, a player had to be five yards behind the line to throw it forward). Like the hash mark rule, this was also a permanent change. These new alterations to the rules had an immediate impact. In 58 games played, the next season ties were reduced by five (from 10 to five), and there were only two scoreless draws. The number of shutouts went up, from 20 to 23, but the percentage of shutouts went down, from 41.7% in 1932 to 39.7% in 1933. Additionally, the average score went up: in 1932, the average final score totaled just over 16 points, while in 1933, the average final score was just under 20 points.[18]

Besides the rule changes after the 1932 season, a championship postseason game was created that year. Two teams, the Chicago Bears and the Portsmouth Spartans, ended the season tied atop the standings. The teams played an extra game to decide the champion, with the Bears winning 9–0.[19] Based on this concept, the league split into two divisions in the 1933 season, the Eastern and Western divisions. At the end of the 1933 season, each division's winners would play each other in the newly inaugurated NFL Championship game. And so, an annual championship game was begun in 1933, and by the next year, almost every small-town football team in the NFL had moved to a major metropolitan area, as the game grew in its popularity. Metropolitan cities were more feasible for fans to congregate from many places to watch a game, rather than being played at smaller venues only with a local following.[20] As a result,

16. Ibid.
17. Ibid.
18. Ibid.
19. Ibid.
20. "A Brief History of Football," accessed September 28, 2017, http://www.historyoffootball.net/.

revenues spiked, and fan bases were expanded to different areas to teams closest to their towns.

The Chicago Bears were the NFL's first championship game-winner in 1933, beating the New York Giants 23–21 at Wrigley Field in Chicago behind all-time great running back Bronko Nagurski. The 1933 season also saw the addition of two NFL franchises, the Philadelphia Eagles and the Pittsburgh Pirates. The Pirates would later change their name to the Steelers. A year later, the Portsmouth Spartans were purchased by a new owner, moved to Detroit, and renamed the Lions. The modern NFL was slowly taking shape.[21]

The equipment also changed during the 1930s as the game continued to evolve. The actual football itself changed in the '30s with a 1934 rule change that tapered the ball at the ends more and reduced the size around the middle. This new, sleeker ball made it much easier to handle, particularly for passers.[22] Additionally, with the Great Depression, teams sought ways to save money on equipment, which led to synthetic materials in uniforms instead of the standard cloth. Lastly, helmets were made more protective in the '30s, with a hard leather version becoming popular (instead of the old soft leather). Riddell, a sporting goods company, even debuted a plastic helmet in 1939, though it would take years to catch on.[23]

The 1930s also saw the recording of statistics. 1932 was the first season the NFL recorded official statistics. The draft was also instituted in 1934, when Philadelphia Eagles owner, Bert Bell, came up with the idea of a draft at the end of the season, and the other owners agreed. The draft went into effect in 1936. The order of the draft was determined by a team's previous season's record. This was a process where the team with the worse record could choose a pick first with the other teams following in line until the team with the best record picked last. The first-ever NFL draft pick was Jay Berwanger, the Heisman Trophy winner out of Chicago, chosen by the Eagles. Due to the Eagles' dismay, Berwanger, however, chose not to play professional football.[24]

---

21. Smith, "Football Origins," accessed September 17, 2018.
22. Ibid.
23. Ibid.
24. Ibid.

THE 1940S, WORLD WAR II, AND THE POST-WAR PERIOD

As the 1940s dawned, the world was engaged in war. In Asia, Japan had been invading various parts of China since 1931 and now was eyeing an empire in the Pacific. In Europe, Germany had annexed Austria and Czechoslovakia and had invaded Poland. England and France declared war on Germany in 1939, but very little happened over the winter of 1939 to 1940 in the war's Western European theater. In the east, Russia had invaded Finland for the territory that Josef Stalin wanted for the motherland. Although the United States remained neutral, Americans had the sense that war was looming for them.

By 1940, pro football had the stability it needed to maintain an organized league. From an operational standpoint, the NFL was the strongest it had ever been up to that point. Since 1936, there had been no franchise shifts. The league's popularity was slowly rising as well. Then Pearl Harbor was attacked on December 7, 1941, and the United States now entered the Second World War. With the United States' entrance into World War II, pro football's continuous growth was slowed, as attendance significantly decreased during the war. The 1942 attendance figures were the lowest since 1936. Roster limits for each team dropped from 33 to 28; the free substitution rule was put in place (then eliminated in 1946, only to be put back in 1949 for good).[25]

The quality of play in pro football suffered as the draft (and volunteers) sent many players into the war. This greatly depleted the already reduced rosters. Now that the NFL had established franchise stability that it fought so hard to get by the end of the 1930s, it was now taking a step backward due to the war. It got so bad that pro football looked as if it would eventually wither away at one point. Many teams merged just to keep finances afloat during the war. In Pennsylvania, the Pittsburgh Steelers and Philadelphia Eagles had to combine teams to survive financially, becoming the Phil-Pitt Steeler-Eagles (known to fans as the Steagles) in the 1943 season. The Chicago Cardinals and Steelers did the same thing the next season, becoming Card-Pitt (known derisively as the Carpets).

---

25. Ibid.

In 1945, the franchises in Brooklyn and Boston combined to become the Yanks. None of those mergers, however, lasted more than a season.[26]

During the 1940s, as American society was changing due to the war, pro football was also changing even with its challenges. Thus, the game was becoming more exciting and mobile. The 1940s saw the burgeoning of the passing game for the NFL. The new passing game in the NFL surpassed college football in gameplay, but the pros still had a long way to go to be at the same level of popularity as the college games had. The passing game's aerial attack was due to several factors, including its quarterbacks' maturing talents and the rule changes instituted. Sammy Baugh exemplified this new maturing talent for the quarterback position. No-one saw anything like him before or since.

Baugh was a very talented athlete. He played his college football career for the Texas Christian University (TCU) Horn Frogs. Baugh's collegiate career was nothing less than phenomenal. He was named All-American in 1935 and 1936.

Baugh was drafted by the Washington Redskins in the first round, sixth overall, in the 1937 NFL Draft.[27] As Baugh came into the NFL, pro football was still a very primitive sport and was still evolving with the rule changes and the equipment changes. The gameplay itself was a grueling game of war, where the offense employed a pound it forward running game. Teams ran the ball mostly on every play. Essentially, teams would only pass the ball as a form of desperation. Even when a team did pass, the ball was thrown only within 30 yards of the line of scrimmage.[28] Long passes, or bombs, were not instituted as a strategic offensive weapon by NFL coaches. This would change with Sammy Baugh's entrance into the NFL.

Sammy Baugh was the stimulus that brought about the forward pass and changed the game plans instituted by teams. His athleticism, and strong arm, made the forward pass a more potent strategy in offensive

---

26. Ibid.

27. "Sammy Baugh: The Greatest Overall Football Player Of All Time" (March 15, 2009), Bleacher Report, accessed September 19, 2018, https://bleacherreport.com/articles/139513-sammy-baugh-the -greatest-football-player-of-all-time.

28. Ibid.

play calling. The NFL had never seen such a prolific passer when Baugh came into the league. His accuracy as a passer was unheralded for his time.[29]

Baugh's style of play was a model for all quarterbacks, and it changed the offensive strategy forever in the NFL. In addition to the changing dynamics of the passing game, the growing importance of the receiver was needed to catch those passes.[30] Until 1940, no receiver caught more than 41 passes in a season due to the pound it in the style of play on the ground. In 1940, however, Don Looney of the Philadelphia Eagles caught 58 passes that season. Two years later, in the 1942 season, Don Hutson of the Packers caught 74 passes. Big-play receivers were slowly becoming more a part of the sport, helping take the passing game to new heights.[31]

OTHER LEAGUE RIVALS

"There is a great public demand to see the game." Those were the words of W.H. "Big Bill" Edwards, the commissioner of the American Football League in 1926.[32] The American Football League was the first attempt to set up a rival league opposite the National Football League. It was founded in 1926 when Harold "Red" Grange was denied a franchise with the NFL in New York City.[33] Grange was blocked by Tim Mara, owner of the year-old New York Giants. Although most of the NFL teams were willing to approve Grange purchasing a franchise in New York City, Mara would not sanction another team in the Giants' area. He was thinking of the bottom line and how profits would be lost to another local team.

Grange was not daunted by the NFL shunning him to buy a franchise because he had a manager in C.C. Pyle who believed Grange's popularity could foster the creation of a new league. Grange signed with Chicago Bears in 1925 and soon was the best player in the National Football

---

29. Ibid.
30. Smith, "Football Origins," accessed September 17, 2018.
31. Ibid.
32. Stephen Hensley, "NFL Competitors 1926–1975," Professional Football Research Association, https://web.archive.org/web/20060319233552/http://www.footballresearch.com/articles/frpage.cfm?topic =nfl-comp
33. Ibid.

League. His popularity soared, and the gate receipts for fans coming to see Grange play were staggering. The owners reaped huge profits from Grange's success. But when Grange's manager, C. C. Pyle had a fallen out with the Chicago Bears' owners, who did not let him buy into the club as a partner, Pyle believed that buying a team could be profitable with Grange's popularity. So, when the NFL denied Grange a franchise in New York, Pyle went ahead with the idea of starting a new league, as he believed a whole league could be built around the popularity of Grange.

And so, the AFL was born in 1926. Pyle formed a nine-team league that included: the Boston Bulldogs, Brooklyn Horsemen, Chicago Bulls, Cleveland Panthers, New York Yankees (Grange's team), Newark Bears, Philadelphia Quakers, Rock Island Independents (who jumped from the NFL), and the Los Angeles West Coast Wildcats (a road team led by George "Wildcat" Wilson).[34] Big Bill Edwards became the commissioner with a salary of $25,000. Edwards was a former Internal Revenue Service Collector and Street Cleaning Commissioner of New York, and a famous football player at Princeton. He was heavy into rhetoric in his promotion of the league with such quotes as "I want to help preserve the high-class football as it is played in the colleges . . . Our slogan is football for all and all for football. We want to let the public in on the greatest of all red-blooded American sports!"[35] However, Edwards' enthusiasm didn't equate to the league's bottom line, and the league was not successful. Not all the teams that started that 1926 season finished it. In the end, the Philadelphia Quakers won the championship over Grange's Yankees. With the championship game in the books, the AFL was disbanded. The next year, the NFL absorbed the players from the AFL, and the New York Yankees was merged into the league. Another New York team was added to the NFL after all, just not by design.

Other attempts were made in 1936 and 1940 to create a rival league to the NFL, but both failed. Then, in September of 1944, a group of millionaires announced they would create the All-American Football Conference ("AAFC"). This new league was the most successful attempt

---

34. Ibid.
35. Ibid.

at capturing some of the NFL markets at the time. Its popularity kept the league afloat for three years, from 1946 to 1949.

Part of this new league's mystique is that many famous names were announced as connected with the AAFC. Mrs. Lou Gehrig was to be the owner of the New York club. Former world heavyweight champion Gene Tunney supported Baltimore. The Los Angeles team boasted such backers as Don Ameche, Bing Crosby, and Bob Hope. "Sleepy Jim" Crowley, one of the Four Horsemen of Notre Dame, was named commissioner with a five-year contract of $25,000 per year.[36]

The league started with two rules concerning their operation: no team was to have a player or coach who had an existing contract with an NFL team, and they were to sign no player with college eligibility left. As the league was forming in 1945, the league went to work to get talent for the teams.[37] Paul Brown, the Great Lakes Naval Center coach and former coach of Ohio State's 1942 National Champions, was named to coach Cleveland. In another deal, Dan Topping, owner of the Brooklyn team in the NFL, "jumped" his NFL team to the AAFC, giving the new league an established team in New York. It turned out that Topping had been paid $100,000 to join the new league. Additional help was that Topping had contract rights to many players from his years in the NFL. These players were to be divided over the league.[38]

The new league was formed at a good time, as the United States was recovering in the post-war and was trying to get back to normal. This worked in favor of the new league, as people's leisure time increased, and many went to spectator sports to pass the time. Many college stars were just ending their terms in the service, so there was a lot of available talent to sign. Such former college and service team stars as Glenn Dobbs, Frankie Sinkwich, Otto Graham, Norm Standlee, Frankie Albert, and Elroy Hirsch signed with AAFC teams.[39]

There appeared to be acceptance for the brand of football that was played by the All-American Football Conference. The largest crowd in

36. Ibid.
37. Ibid.
38. Ibid.
39. Ibid.

pro football history attended the opening game between the Cleveland Browns and the Miami Seahawks in September of 1946. The Browns proved to be the class of the league by winning the championship in each of the four seasons that the AAFC operated. Each year, the Browns challenged the NFL champ to a playoff game but were ignored by the NFL. They refused to deal with the new league that they dubbed as being inferior to the NFL.

Even with all the new league's momentum, the All-American Football Conference had its growing pains. It had three commissioners in the brief span for which it operated, and although some teams were very successful, the Miami franchise lasted only one year, and the Brooklyn franchise was disbanded before the last season.[40] Like the NFL in its infancy, twenty-six years before, there was a lack of stability on the AAFC. People wondered if the league could survive by competing with the NFL. By 1948, it could not float financially anymore. The war between the two professional leagues continued into the next year, in 1949. Early that year, eight of ten NFL owners were willing to accept the All-American Conference teams of Cleveland, San Francisco, Baltimore, and Buffalo into the NFL. There was one problem with this. The vote had to be unanimous by all the NFL owners. At the time, eight of the owners were for the merger, and it looked bleak on a merger.

But by the end of the year, the NFL owners agreed, and the leagues did merge. The two naysayers sided with the other owners. Dan Topping was persuaded to sell his Yankees, and Washington agreed to let Baltimore operate in their area. These were important contributing factors in the merger. In the end, only Cleveland, San Francisco, and Baltimore became members of the NFL. The remaining teams' players ended up in a pool to be drafted by the teams in the new National Football League.

In a divine twist of delicious irony, the quality of play in the AAFC was showcased in the 1950 season in the NFL. The Browns, in their first NFL season, won the championship. After all those years of trying to challenge the NFL Champions while they were on top in the AAFC, the Browns were now champs of the NFL.

---

40. Ibid.

THE GOLDEN AGE OF FOOTBALL: THE 1950S

The turbulence of the 1940s for pro football would not be repeated in the 1950s. It would be the exact opposite, as the sport grew to all new heights. Many have called the decade of the 1950s "The Golden Age of Football." Beginning with the merger in 1949 with the AAFC, and the inclusion of Cleveland, San Francisco, and Baltimore, the NFL expanded. Also, for the rest of the AAFC players that were drafted by the NFL from that draft pool, it just made the league better with a considerable increase in the quality of players now all under one roof in the NFL. Along with the free substitution rule (put back in place just before 1950, which allows players to enter and leave the game for other players many times during the game, and for coaches to bring in and take out players an unlimited number of times), pro football was quite simply getting better.[41]

With the advent of the new medium of television, pro football was now brought into millions of homes across the United States. This had an immense impact on the growing popularity of the sport. Pro football was first televised by NBC, the first major television network to cover an NFL game. That game was played on October 22, 1939, and it was between the Philadelphia Eagles and the Brooklyn Dodgers. Television and NBC were still only in their infancy, having only two affiliates, the modern-day WRGB (now a CBS affiliate) in Schenectady, New York, and W2XBS in New York City.[42] Portions of that game still survive via films, but the film is not footage from the telecast (recordings of television broadcasts did not begin until 1948). The use of a sideline camera, the sole camera used in the 1939 broadcast, would become the standard for all future NFL broadcasts until 2017. The angle is particularly suited for estimating yardage compared to more mobile camera angles that began to appear in the 21st century.[43] Regular broadcasts of pro football games began after World War II, and the first NFL championship to be televised was the 1948 match between the Eagles and Cardinals.

41. Smith, "Football Origins," accessed September 17, 2018.
42. Geoffrey C, Arnold, "NBC's 'SkyCam' will provide Madden-like view of tonight's Titans-Steelers game" (November 16, 2017), accessed September 20, 2018, https://www.oregonlive.com/nfl/index .ssf/2017/11/nbcs_skycam_will_provide_madde.html.
43. Ibid.

In 1950, the Los Angeles Rams and the Washington Redskins became the first NFL teams to have all of their games, home and away, televised. In the same year, other teams made deals to have selected games telecast. The DuMont Network then paid a rights fee of $75,000 to broadcast the 1951 NFL Championship Game across the entire nation.[44]

From 1953 to 1955, DuMont also televised Saturday night NFL games. It was the first time that NFL fixtures were broadcast live, coast-to-coast, in prime time, for the entire season. The broadcasts ended after the 1955 season when the DuMont Network folded. DuMont was a less than ideal partner for NFL broadcasts. With only eighteen affiliates in 1954, DuMont was dwarfed by the amount of coverage the "Big Four" had with its contract on NBC, which had 120 affiliates at the time.[45] By 1955, NBC became the televised home of the NFL Championship Game, paying $100,000 to the league for broadcast rights.[46]

What transformed pro football into the limelight from just being a niche sport for some, happened on December 28, 1958, at an icy Yankee Stadium in the Bronx, where the Baltimore Colts defeated the New York Giants, 23–17, to win the NFL championship.[47] This was dubbed the "Greatest Game Ever." It was the first NFL game to go into sudden-death overtime and featured 12 players and three coaches who were eventually elected to the Hall of Fame. The "Greatest Game Ever" changed everything about pro football, setting it on a path to become the most successful pro sport in America. Most importantly, the dramatic contest was broadcast to a national television audience. Since then, football and television were a staple on Sunday afternoons from September to December in the United States. Pro football became a lucrative juggernaut from the medium of television and expanded the sport's marketability beyond game receipts as its major source of revenue.

---

44. Ibid.

45. Mark Ford, "'54, 40 or Fight Canada's 1954 War With the NFL," *The Coffin Corner* 24, no. 4 (2002), accessed September 20, 2018, https://web.archive.org/web/20101218180121/http://profootball researchers.org/Coffin_Corner/24-04-946.pdf.

46. Ibid.

47. Sean Gregory, "The Football Game That Changed It All," *Time Magazine* (December 29, 2008), accessed September 20, 2018, http://content.time.com/time/specials/packages/article/0,28804,1868793 _1868792_1868802,00.html.

By 1959, big-market teams such as the Chicago Bears and the New York Giants had all their games televised, but small-market teams like the Packers and 49ers still did not. Upon becoming NFL commissioner, Pete Rozelle worked hard to ensure that every team got all its games on TV. This was the genius of Pete Rozelle, and he brought pro football into elite status as a sport, that by the end of the 1960s, it had become America's new pastime, surpassing major league baseball.

On the negative side of fans getting to see televised games at home, attendance receipts at the stadiums went down. An example was the gate receipts of the Los Angeles Rams. In 1949, the Rams' attendance was quite good with 205,109 people coming to the stadium (even with the LA Dons of the AAFC competing with them in the same market). A year later, the Rams became the first pro football team to broadcast all its team's games, both home and away, on television.[48] From the home televised games, attendance dropped to 110,162. The NFL learned a valuable lesson from this, and in 1951, the Rams only televised road games, whereby the home attendance went up to over 234,000 attendees, more than double than the year before.[49] When the NFL was taken to court over the rights to broadcast only road games, the courts upheld the league's right to blackout home games on television in 1953. This led to NFL Commissioner Bert Bell instituting a rule only allowing the broadcast of road games in 1956. In the process, 11 of 12 teams had obtained contracts with CBS. CBS had broadcast rights to some regular-season games to selected TV markets across the nation, blacked out within 50 miles of an NFL stadium.[50]

The 1950s were ending on a high note for the NFL. The love of the sport was now firmly ingrained in the American culture, and along with television contracts and rising attendance gate receipts, the horizon looked promising for further success. The 1950s were smooth sailing for the NFL, as no other football leagues were created to challenge them. Then, in 1959, a wrench was thrown into the woodwork. That wrench was the newly formed American Football League.

---

48. Smith, "Football Origins," accessed September 17, 2018.
49. Ibid.
50. "NFL TV: A History," accessed September 20, 2018, http://www.kenn.com/the_blog/?page_id=5533.

2

HISTORY OF THE AMERICAN FOOTBALL LEAGUE AND THE WAR WITH THE NFL – 1959-1966

LAMAR HUNT AND THE BIRTH OF THE AFL

As shown in the last chapter, all attempts to create another league to challenge the NFL had failed. Now, in 1959, a young oil business executive would create the American Football League to rival the NFL. The history of the AFL begins with twenty-six years old, Lamar Hunt.

Hunt was born in El Dorado, Arkansas, the son of oil tycoon H. L. Hunt who was reportedly the richest man in America by the mid-1940s and had amassed a fortune from his oil revenue with several companies, including the Hunt Oil Company. Hunt was raised in Dallas, Texas. He attended Culver Military Academy and graduated from The Hill School in Pennsylvania in 1951 and Southern Methodist University in Dallas in 1956, with a B.S. degree in geology. Hunt was a college football player who spent his entire career on the bench but embraced all sports during his time in college and throughout his entire childhood. Hunt, however, had a passion for the game of football.[1]

---

1. Craig Sanders and Laurie E. Jasinski, "Hunt, Lamar (1932–2006)," Handbook of Texas Online, accessed September 20, 2018, http://www.tshaonline.org/handbook/online/articles/fhu99.

Hunt's story of how he got into pro football begins with the sale of the Chicago Cardinals in the NFL. During the 1950s, the Cardinals franchise did not flourish in this newfound success of the NFL. The Cardinals franchise was owned by the Bidwill family, but Charles Bidwill had died, leaving his widow, Violet, as the team's owner. She remarried after Charles' death to Walter Wolfner. Realizing that the Cardinals were a financial burden because of the success of their town rivals, the Chicago Bears, Violet hoped to relocate their franchise, preferably to St. Louis, but could not come to terms with the league on a relocation fee.[2] Needing cash, Violet began to talk to would-be investors who would be willing to buy the team. Lamar Hunt was one of those investors who offered to buy the Cardinals and planned to move them to Dallas, where he had grown up. Negotiations fell through with Hunt when Violet insisted on retaining a controlling interest and did not want to sell more than 49% of the franchise's stock. Also, Violet did not want to move to a city where a previous NFL franchise had failed years before in 1952. While Hunt negotiated with Violet, similar offers were made by Bud Adams, Bob Howsam, and Max Winter to also buy the Cardinals.[3] In the end, the franchise moved to St. Louis.

Bud Adams, who grew up in Oklahoma, was a fellow oilman like Hunt and lived in Houston. Bob Howsam was a baseball executive who tried to get a major team to the Denver area, where he was born and raised. Max Winter was from Minnesota and was a part-owner of the Minnesota Lakers basketball team. He sought to bring football to the market in Minnesota. When Hunt, Adams, and Howsam were unable to secure a controlling interest in the Cardinals, the three of them approached NFL commissioner Bert Bell and proposed the addition of expansion teams. The commissioner was cautious and skeptical of expanding the 12-team league and risking its newfound success, rejected the offer from all three men.[4]

---

2. Ibid.

3. Ed Gruver, *The American Football League: A Year-by-Year History, 1960–1969* (NC: McFarland, 1997), 9.

4. Ibid., 13–14.

Heading back to Dallas after his meeting with commissioner Bell and the NFL, Hunt conceived the idea of an entirely new league. He decided to contact the others who had shown interest in purchasing the Cardinals, but like him, they were denied a controlling interest in the Cardinals team. Hunt contacted Adams, Howsam, and Winter (as well as Winter's business partner, Bill Boyer) to gauge their interest in starting a new league. Hunt's first meeting with Adams was held in March 1959.[5] When he met Adams in Houston, Adams recalled: "I didn't know him [Hunt], but we had dinner together, and in the course of the conversation, we reminisced about buying the Cardinals . . . Just before he left for the airport, I told Lamar. 'Maybe we ought to start our league.'"[6]

Of course, that was exactly what Hunt was thinking. Adams and Hunt met three months later, and Hunt told Adams he had lined up four other franchises and asked Adams if he wanted in. Adams agreed. Hunt brought in Jack Steadman as his top business associate. He told Steadman that he had big plans to start a new league and establish a Dallas franchise. Hunt asked Steadman to set up the league offices in Dallas. Steadman would stay on with Hunt after the AFL offices were set up. This took Steadman by surprise as he said years later: "For some reason, I'll never know, he was impressed with me . . . It was the first time I had done anything like that . . . I did research and set up the league offices of the American Football League . . . Then I set up the business operations for the Dallas Texans for Lamar, and I did all that while I was with the [oil] drilling company. And then he asked me to come on full time. So, I was kind of there with him from the beginning."[7]

Eventually, when the Dallas Texans moved to Kansas City, Steadman would become the Kansas City Chief's first general manager and served as executive vice president, president, vice chairman, and chairman in his 47 years with the team. He won four championships as a general manager, including the team's Super Bowl IV title.[8]

---

5. Ibid., 14.
6. Ken Rappoport, *The Little League That Could, A History of the American Football League* (Lanham, MD: Taylor Trade Publishing, 2010), 3.
7. Ibid.
8. Ibid.

Besides Dallas, Hunt chose Houston, Denver, Minneapolis, and Seattle as cities where he wanted to establish franchises. He was interested in Houston because it would set up a Texas rivalry with his own Dallas Texans. Hunt, however, was shrewd enough to see that without the New York and Los Angeles markets, the league wouldn't be complete because of the large fan base along with the revenues both city markets would bring. It wouldn't be a major league without the City of Angels and the Big Apple.

On August 14, 1959, six new owners met to set up the new league's foundation. They agreed that play would begin in 1960, with teams in Dallas, Houston, New York, Denver, Minneapolis, and Los Angeles. Bud Adams was given control of the Houston Oilers, hotel mogul Barron Hilton owned the Los Angeles franchise (the Chargers), sportscaster Harry Wilsmer would own the New York Franchise (the Titans), and Max Winter agreed to start a team in Minneapolis-Saint Paul. Willard Rhodes hoped to bring pro football to Seattle but was having a hard time due to the University of Washington refusing his proposals to use their playing field of Husky Stadium. This was probably due to the excessive wear and tear that playing would cause to the facility's grass surface, which would hinder the University of Washington's own football team's performance (the stadium now has an artificial surface, and Seattle would gain entry into the NFL in 1976 with the Seattle Seahawks). With no place for his team to play, Rhodes's effort to bring a franchise to Seattle failed. With Rhodes's failure to secure a place for a team in the Pacific Northwest, the six teams that were already intact would form the new league. The new league was rolled out on August 22nd, when the league office was named the American Football League at a meeting in Dallas.[9]

Immediately, the NFL felt the pressure of competition with the birth of the new league. The pressure was heightened when NFL Commissioner Bell died on October 11, 1959. Lamar Hunt believed that with Bell as the commissioner, an all-out war could have been avoided with the NFL, due to Bell's position of instituting competitive parity

---

9. Brad Schultz, *The NFL, Year One, The 1970 Season and the Dawn of Modern Football* (Virginia: Potomac Books, 2013), 6.

with outside sources into the NFL, to improve the league's commercial viability and promote its popularity.[10] Hunt believed that the AFL would have made Bell look inward to improve his league, and the competition that the new AFL would bring would only expand the sport. Hunt was right. With the passing of Bell, the NFL went on the attack on the newly minted AFL.

NFL owners first tried to undermine the new league when it offered the AFL owners stakes in new NFL teams. Hunt and Adams declined, citing the NFL already denied them franchises. Hilton also passed on an opportunity to buy into an NFL expansion franchise. Only Max Winter in Minneapolis took them up on the offer (leading to the creation of the Minnesota Vikings in the NFL). This was brought to light at a meeting in Minneapolis on November 22, where it was the first time all eight AFL teams had been assembled. More importantly, it is where the league's first draft would be held the next day. At the meeting, Max Winter announced that his group was pulling out, even though the night before, he told fellow owner Hilton that rumors were not true that he was ready to defect to the NFL. Long-time NFL expansion committee chief, George Halas, persuaded Winter to pull out right before the draft.[11] In an obvious show of force, the NFL had expanded into Dallas and Minneapolis. Even with Commissioner Bell's wariness to put a franchise in Dallas, the NFL wanted direct competition with the AFL in the city. As Steadman recalled: "As soon as Lamar announced the start of the league, then the league expanded . . ."[12] This began the all-out war between the two leagues for the next six years.

The AFL replaced Minnesota with a team from Oakland. Before the league officially began to play in 1960, two other franchises were added in Boston (The Patriots) and Buffalo (The Bills). But even with all their wealth, Oakland managing partner, Wayne Valley, looking back at the time the league started up, called the group the "Foolish Club" for taking

---

10. Bob Carroll, *When The Grass Was Real* (NY: Simon and Schuster, 1993), 22.

11. Mickey Herskowitz, "The Foolish Club," *Pro Football Weekly* (1974), accessed September 21, 2018, https://web.archive.org/web/20070605071618/http://www.kcchiefs.com/media/misc/5_the_foolish_club .pdf.

12. Rappoport, *The Little League That Could*, 4.

on the well-established NFL.[13] Lamar Hunt subsequently used this term on team photographs, which he sent as Christmas gifts.[14]

The AFL owners knew that their initial survival hinged on their ability to outbid the NFL for many star players out of college. The draft on November 23, 1959, afforded the new league this opportunity. The NFL had a secret draft and did not show their lists to keep the AFL from using the lists as a guide. There would be issues with the overlapping of drafting the same players by the AFL and NFL. Case in point was the signing of Billy Cannon, the 1959 Heisman winner from LSU. The newly formed Houston Oilers signed Cannon to a three-year, $100,000 contract (worth $724,000 today). However, the Los Angeles Rams (under then-general manager Pete Rozelle) had already signed Cannon to a contract worth $50,000 but left it undated so Cannon could play in the Sugar Bowl, the final game of his college career.[15] The Oilers, however, used guerrilla tactics to get Cannon signed and went to the Sugar Bowl and inked him. The Rams were outraged, and they took legal action against the Oilers. A judge ruled the Oilers contract valid, and the first shot of the war between the NFL and AFL had been fired.[16]

Even with Cannon's signing, the AFL's first draft was not what the owners hoped for. Hunt knew that he would need "big names" to fill the teams' rosters to draw in the fans into the stadiums for the league to survive. Not surprisingly, most of the draft picks ended up signing with the NFL anyway due to the longevity of the league and its status. What the AFL's presence in the draft did show was that it interfered with the NFL that used the draft to fill gaps, shore up weaknesses, and replace retiring players with the collegiate players.[17] Since the NFL had a monopoly over the draft, there was always a surplus of players for teams. If a team needed a quarterback but could not draft the elite college quarterback because another team drafted him, the team could draft the next best quarterback. Now with the AFL partaking in the draft, this was not the

13. Schultz, *The NFL, Year One.*, 6–7.
14. Herskowitz, "The Foolish Club," accessed September 21, 2018.
15. Smith, "Football Origins," accessed September 17, 2018.
16. Ibid.
17. Carroll, *When The Grass Was Real*, 26.

case anymore. The lack of draftees meant that the NFL teams could not improve as quickly as they did.

Another important item for the AFL's growth was marketing the league. In addition to getting "big names," the AFL looked to obtain a television contract, which would bring in desperately needed revenue and would showcase the AFL into millions of homes across the United States. The American Broadcast Company ("ABC") was willing to partner with the new league, and the AFL signed a five-year contract with ABC worth $10 million ($72.4 million).[18] ABC was excited to have the newly minted league on their station, largely in part that the new AFL style of play seemed more exciting than that of the NFL. The AFL added the two-point conversion (which the NFL still didn't have) and encouraged more passing plays, both of which contributed to higher scoring and was extremely exciting to fans.[19] The big thing about the AFL and the ABC contract is that it adopted television revenue sharing from the start. This was an interesting concept at the time because the NFL did not have revenue sharing from their television contracts. Each separate team was contracting with the networks without the other. It did not bring in much money for the AFL owners, at $25,000 a club, but with some clubs struggling financially, it was much-needed revenue to keep the league afloat. As for the NFL, they were a year away from signing a television deal with CBS for the entire league.[20]

To keep the AFL growing, the league also knew they would need a leader with strong credentials to oversee their operations. They found their man in Joe Foss, who had a stellar resume. He was a former United States Marine Corps major and the leading Marine fighter ace in World War II. He received the Medal of Honor to recognize his role in air combat during the Guadalcanal Campaign in the Pacific. In the postwar years, he was an Air National Guard brigadier general, served as the 20th Governor of South Dakota (1955–1959), and was the president of the National Rifle Association.[21]

---

18. Smith, "Football Origins," accessed September 17, 2018.

19. Ibid.

20. Schultz, *The NFL, Year One*, 7.

21. Joe Foss, "The Telegraph" (January 3, 2003), accessed September 23, 2018, https://www.telegraph .co.uk/news/obituaries/1417707/Joe-Foss.html.

Foss relished in his new position as the first commissioner of the new American Football League, as it battled to compete with the already-established National Football League. Foss loved a good fight, and his military career served him well in this war with the more established league. He also had wonderful insight and creativity and was responsible for several innovations in the sport. This included printing the players' names on their jerseys and making both players and staff more readily available to the television networks. With Foss's hard work and determination, he was able to obtain the lucrative television deals, first with the initial five-year, $10.6 million contracts with ABC in 1960 to broadcast AFL games, and then another five years with NBC for a substantially greater amount of $36 million, starting in 1965. He even encouraged one television station to report on his own league's feuds among the teams.[22]

Like their new rivals, the NFL owners also needed a new commissioner after Bert Bell had died. The NFL owners thought they knew what they were getting in January 1960, when they couldn't decide on a new commissioner and settled for Pete Rozelle. Split between two other candidates after 22 ballots, the owners compromised on Rozelle, the 33-year-old general manager of the Los Angeles Rams.[23] The NFL owners believed they had elected a naive young commissioner who would be a lackey and yield to their wishes. They were dead wrong. In the words of the long-time owner of the Dallas Cowboys, Tex Schramm: "They finally picked Pete as a compromise . . . because both sides thought they could control him. But they were wrong. Pete was a lot stronger than any of them realized."[24]

Rozelle would become one of the most powerful men in the United States. He would forge ahead with good business acumen and turn the NFL into a multi-billion-dollar industry. When Rozelle was elected as commissioner, the NFL had 12 teams worth about $1 million apiece. When he left in 1989, there were 28 teams, most worth more than 100

22. Ibid.
23. Bob Carter, "Rozelle Made The NFL What It Is Today," accessed September 23, 2018, http://www.espn.com/classic/biography/s/rozelle_pete.html.
24. Ibid.

million dollars. Rozelle would also be one of the guiding forces that led
to the merger in 1966 between the AFL and the NFL.

A HARD KNOCKS LEAGUE

On a Friday night, on September 9, 1960, at Boston University field, the
opening kickoff between the Boston Patriots and the Denver Broncos
began the new venture of the American Football League. On that Friday
night, the game was played to avoid competing with the college and NFL
games over the weekend.[25] With a turnout crowd of 21,597, the number
itself was low compared to an NFL turnout for games. Like any new
business venture, growing it from the ground up would not be smooth
sailing. However, the league owners and the players believed in the brand
of football they were selling as an alternative to the NFL. Believing in
the product gave them the will to move forward, but it wasn't pretty by
any means in the beginning. There was a feeling of being inadequate by
many when the league started. This was because the playing fields were
subpar, showers for the players were usually cold with a hot fan blowing,
and unruly fans sometimes made it a dangerous environment as they
would throw things at the players from the stands.

Finding suitable places to play for AFL franchises was not an easy
task. War Memorial Stadium in Buffalo is the perfect example of playing
in substandard stadiums. The stadium itself was outdated since it was
built in the 1930s under the Work Progress Act project of the Roosevelt
Administration's "New Deal." The stadium was nicknamed "The Rock-
pile" for the granite-like surface that both the players and fans hated. If
that wasn't bad enough, the stadium was in a crime-ridden area of the
city. Even the Bills' vice president was mugged after one game. To make
matters worse, there were no public parking lots that the stadium had,
and fans had to park in private driveways and on the street where they
paid the locals to watch their cars from being stolen.[26]

Across the league, players had to put up with inconveniences, such
as showerheads not working or showering in cold water, as well as locker

---

25. Jeff Miller, *Going Long* (NY: The McGraw-Hill Companies, 2003), 33.
26. Carroll, *When The Grass Was Real*, 63.

rooms that were ill-prepared and not suitable. In many of the stadiums, the lighting was poor, and the ball was hard to see at times. In the Boston Patriots case, they didn't even have a home field and used Boston College, Boston University, Harvard University, and Fenway Park interchangeably for their home games. One time, the Patriots had to play a home game in Birmingham, Alabama, because the Red Sox were using Fenway Park in the 1967 World Series.[27] Seeing this as a major problem for the team and the city, Boston's mayor, John Collins, had to persuade Boston University President, Harold Case, to grant their stadium to the Patriots for their home games. With Boston University playing their games on Saturday and most New Englanders tuning into the New York Giants games on Sunday, the Patriots were forced to play their games on Friday nights.[28] Out in Los Angeles, the Chargers had to contend with low turnout at the gigantic Memorial Coliseum, which they shared with the NFL's Rams. The place was always filled with a 100,000-seating capacity for Rams games, but the place looked like a ghost town when the Chargers played. Since the Rams had a television deal, many Los Angelans would rather watch the Rams on television than to see the new AFL Chargers team in person.

Most awkwardly, in Dallas, the Texans had to share the Cotton Bowl, not only with the college team, the Southern Methodist University Mustangs, but also the newly minted Dallas Cowboys of the NFL. Although the Texans beat out the Cowboys in attendance for 1960 at the Cotton Bowl, the stadium remained pretty much empty for both teams, as Dallas didn't embrace pro football as of yet. The Cowboys lost $700,000 that year, but the Texans lost $1,000,000, prompting Lamar Hunt's father, L.H. Hunt, to proclaim: "the boy only has 123 years to go [to make a profit]." Hunt's dad ripped that line out of the movie "Citizens Kane," starring Orson Welles. It might seem funny for Hunt, as he had the capital to sustain these losses, but it was dire for the other AFL teams who couldn't handle the losses and battled the NFL in other markets.

In Denver, the Broncos played in the minor league ballpark of Mile High Stadium, which wasn't accepted yet as a big-league stadium until

27. Rappoport, *The Little League That Could*, 37.
28. Carroll, *When The Grass Was Real*, 64.

years later. In Houston, the Oilers had hoped to play at Rice University, but when they were denied, they had to play at Jeppesen Stadium, which was a high school field.[29] To many, the AFL in Texas took a major hit on respectability due to the Oilers playing in such primitive surroundings. What made matters worse was when the AFL Championship was played at Jeppesen Stadium, it didn't look like a big-league championship for those who watched the game on television. And in Oakland, the Raiders couldn't even play in the city of Oakland. They had to settle for the old and rickety Kezar Stadium, falling apart, across the bay in San Francisco. In Gotham, the New York Titans might have had it the worse out of all the teams. While they waited for the new Shea Stadium to be built in Queens, they had to play in the rundown Polo Grounds, that the baseball Giants abandoned for San Francisco back in 1957. Like War Memorial Stadium in Buffalo, the stadium was a scary place, especially at night. No-one wanted to travel to Coogan's Hollow, to see a game and put their lives in danger. Oakland Raider Center, Jim Otto described the run-down stadium in a nutshell: "When they turned on the lights, the drunks woke up."[30]

A BROADCASTING NIGHTMARE

Decrepit and amateur stadiums, inadequate facilities, and dangerous places to play made the league seem second rate to the NFL. The way that some of the games were broadcast to the public just cemented the idea of the AFL being a primitive league. Longtime New England Patriots radio play-by-play announcer, Gil Santos, described the perils of broadcasting in the AFL:

> Many of these stadiums were not made to broadcast pro
> football games . . . When we had a game at Fenway Park, we
> didn't have a broadcast booth as such . . . They put a wooden
> shack, maybe 12 X 12 feet, up on the roof, down the right-
> field line and put us at midfield . . . There were a couple of

29. Ibid.
30. Ibid.

problems-one being that you had no bathroom facilities. You had to go down to the stands. Oh, it was tough. At halftime, you had to scramble down and get to the fan level to use the bathrooms, then get back upstairs in time to go on for the second half. We cut it close many times. That was one problem. The other problem was that there was no heat there. In the winter, it was cold as hell. And it was windy. If it was a windy day, that booth would shake, rattle, and roll. There were times we'd think, 'Oh my god, this thing is going to blow over, and we are going to go flying off the edge, with no place to go.' Fortunately, it never happened.[31]

NOT TRAVELLING IN STYLE AND THE NFL'S "REJECTS"

Not surprisingly, the travel arrangements for the teams were awful. Bad travel arrangements made going to different stadiums across the United States a huge hassle for teams. Sometimes to save money, a chartered flight might have two teams traveling together on the same flight. In the Patriots case, they chartered a flight and landed in Buffalo to pick up the Bills. Then the plane landed in Denver, dropped off the Patriots, and then flew to the West Coast to drop off the Bills.[32]

Oakland Raiders center Jim Otto remembers that the traveling arrangements were not first class: "We used to play the New England Patriots in Boston. We'd fly to someplace in Rhode Island, get on a bus for five hours, play the game, get back on the bus, and fly out because that was the cheapest way. One time we took a train from New York to Boston, and everybody got off at the wrong stations. So, from New York to Boston, we had football [players] all over the eastern seaboard."[33]

Another problem was that talent was hard to come by at the beginning of the AFL. Many of the star players in the new league were usually castoffs from the NFL. These castoff players that were reduced to minor roles on their teams in the NFL would receive new guidance under the

---

31. Rappoport, *The Little League That Could*, 38.
32. Carroll, *When The Grass Was Real*, 64.
33. Ibid., 65.

AFL's coaches and would eventually become impact players. Perhaps the best example was quarterback Len Dawson. Dawson was a career backup quarterback in the NFL, but he would lead the Texans to the AFL title in 1962 and led the league with 29 touchdown passes.[34]

George Blanda was another quarterback exiled from the NFL. Blanda retired after the 1958 NFL season because of Bears coach George Halas's insistence on only using him as a kicker. When the AFL got up and running, Blanda signed with the Houston Oilers as both a quarterback and kicker. The football media pawned him off as an "NFL Reject." Blanda would prove the media quite wrong, as he went on to lead the Oilers to the first two league titles in AFL history. Not only that, Blanda was voted All-AFL quarterback in 1961 and won AFL Player of the Year honors that same year. During the 1961 season, he led the AFL in passing yards (3,330) and touchdown passes (36). His 36 touchdown passes in 1961 were the most ever thrown by any NFL/AFL quarterback in a single season.[35] Blanda adapted well to the high flying, pass offense that the AFL played. He would remain a football player until 1976. His 26 years as a pro football player are still the most seasons played by anyone in pro football's history.

There are countless other feel-good stories about players that were discarded by the NFL but thrived in the AFL, including Frank Tripucka, Babe Parilli, Cotton Davidson, Jack Kemp, Al Dorrow, Butch Songin, and Lionel Taylor, to name just a few.

COACHES THAT DARED

The AFL also recruited former NFL coaches to coach in the new league. Paul Brown was a coach for the Browns for many years until he was fired by owner Art Modell in 1963. After more than 30 years of coaching, Brown spent the next five years away from the sidelines. In the mid-1960s, the AFL put a new franchise in Cleveland's rival city of Cincinnati in Ohio. Brown was the third-largest investor in the team and was given the title of

---

34. Smith, "Football Origins," accessed September 17, 2018.
35. George Blanda, Hall of Fame, accessed September 24, 2018, http://www.profootballhof.com/players/george-blanda/.

coach and general manager. He was also given the right to represent the team in all league matters, a key element of control for Brown.[36]

Another important coach that came to the AFL was Sid Gillman of the Chargers. Gillman's San Diego teams were some of the most offensively explosive in football, thanks in large part to his wide-open passing game, which today is the standard of pro football. Gillman's legacy to modern football included the use of film and studying the opponents, timing routes where the receiver is to reach a certain spot in time from the throw from the quarterback, using four or five receivers to spread the field, and having quarterback's "bounce" on their feet to survey the defense for a play's development.[37] Gillman's impact on the NFL lasted for decades, as many of his assistants would become football head coaches and carry on his style of play. Al Davis took the scheme to the Oakland Raiders, Chuck Noll took it to Pittsburgh, Jack Faulkner took it to Denver, and Joe Gibbs to Washington.[38]

By far, the most successful coach in the AFL was Hank Stram. Stram was an innovator, a shrewd judge of talent, and an excellent teacher. In 1959, Lamar Hunt recruited Stram to coach the Dallas Texans (the Texans moved to Kansas City in 1963 and were renamed the Chiefs). Hunt had previously been a bench player at SMU when Stram had been coaching there, and the Texans' coaching position had been turned down by Bud Wilkinson and Tom Landry, then an assistant at the New York Giants. Stram was an assistant coach at the University of Miami in 1959 when Hunt inquired about his availability to coach.[39] The Texans played their first game in September 1960 and proved to be successful from the beginning. Stram helped develop Hall of Famers Len Dawson, Bobby Bell, Buck Buchanan, Curley Culp, Willie Lanier, Jan Stenerud, Emmitt Thomas, and many others like Johnny Robinson, Ed Budde, and Otis Taylor.[40] He was also the first coach in professional football to

36. George Cantor, *Paul Brown: The Man Who Invented Modern Football* (Chicago: Triumph Books, 2008), 122.

37. Rappoport, *The Little League That Could*, 52.

38. Smith, "Football Origins," accessed September 17, 2018.

39. Hank Stram, Pro Football Hall of Fame, accessed September 25, 2018, http://www.profootballhof.com/players/hank-stram/.

40. Ibid.

use Gatorade on his sidelines and run both the I formation and two-tight end offense, still used in professional football today. On defense, the Chiefs employed a triple-stack defense, hiding the three linebackers behind defensive linemen.[41]

He was considered a motivational genius, and his emphasis on the Chiefs' wearing of a patch commemorating the AFL in Super Bowl IV was one of his typical ploys, extracting maximum effort from players who had been derided by proponents of the NFL. Stram was inducted into the Pro Football Hall of Fame in 2003, nine years *after* Bud Grant, the man whose Vikings team he had convincingly defeated in Super Bowl IV, had been enshrined.

In New York, Charles "Weeb" Ewbank was hired to coach and be the General Manager of the New York Jets, after the Titans had folded. Ewbank previously led the Baltimore Colts to NFL championships in 1958 ("the greatest game ever") and 1959 and would eventually lead the New York Jets to victory in Super Bowl III in 1969 over his former team. Ewbank is the only coach to win a championship in both the National Football League (NFL) and American Football League (AFL).

Despite limited on-field success in Ewbank's first years, the Jets began to put the pieces of a winning team in place. In 1964, they outbid their cross-town NFL rival, the New York Giants, for Matt Snell, a top running back prospect out of Ohio State University.[42] Linebacker Larry Grantham became a consistent All-Pro selection, and safety Dainard Paulson had twelve interceptions in 1964, which remains a team record. An even bigger coup came in 1965 when the Jets signed Joe Namath, the star quarterback at Alabama under coach Paul "Bear" Bryant.[43] The St. Louis Cardinals selected Namath as the 12th pick in the NFL draft, but Namath later said he chose the Jets because he got along with Ewbank and was impressed by how he had developed John Unitas with the Colts.[44]

---

41. Ibid.
42. Mark Cannizzaro, *New York Jets: The Complete Illustrated History* (Minneapolis: MVP Books, 2011), 20.
43. Ibid. 21.
44. Ibid.

OPENING DOORS TO MINORITY PLAYERS

The AFL was opened to changing with the times. The league fully embraced the 1960's cultural revolution. With blacks lobbying for their equality with whites, led by Dr. Martin King, Jr. and Malcolm X, the AFL was creating opportunities for black athletes, more so than their rivals in the NFL.

A good case study was receiver Lionel Taylor. Taylor had played part of the season for the Chicago Bears in 1959 when he was cut by George Halas. Taylor recalled: "When I was released, Halas said he had players from bigger schools he had to keep, so I left . . . He was telling me I was a good football player, but I was the one getting on a Trailways bus back home."[45] Eventually, Taylor joined the Denver Broncos in the AFL and went on to have a great career. He was the first AFL receiver to catch 100 passes in one season, led the league in receptions for the first six years of its existence, and retired as the AFL's all-time leading receiver with 567 catches.[46]

The AFL gave Taylor a shot to succeed, unlike the NFL. As a black football player, the doors were open wider for him in the AFL than the NFL. According to Taylor: "When I was with Chicago, there were four black players with the Bears. But most teams in the AFL had quite a few black players, a lot more than the NFL teams."[47]

It wasn't that the NFL was discriminating. The problem for black players was that the NFL did most of its recruiting at the bigger schools from the major conferences, which were virtually all white. The AFL did the same, but at the same time, the new league also was pursuing the talent in historically smaller black colleges, while the NFL was generally not as active in this area. The AFL went after those players because they wanted to, and they needed to.

Most of the credit for diversifying belonged to Lamar Hunt. Not only was Hunt was a visionary in starting the AFL, but he also made it

---

45. Rappoport, *The Little League That Could*, 119.
46. Ibid.
47. Ibid.

a point to hire a scout, Lloyd Wells, who concentrated strictly on the smaller black colleges. Jack Steadman, Hunt's right-hand man, recalled: "Lamar had gone to any game that was in the Cotton Bowl, and Grambling would play in the Cotton Bowl every year with other black colleges . . . Lamar felt some great players were overlooked because they were black."[48]

Hunt's Kansas City Chiefs were among the most active in recruiting black athletes. By 1966, Kansas City's starting lineup featured eight black players among the 22 players. The percentage of black players on a team in the AFL and NFL was still worlds apart, as evidenced four years later in 1970. In a comparison between the teams in Super Bowl IV, the official game program showed Kansas City with 19 black players and Minnesota with 10.[49] Steadman further recalled the AFL's mindset at the time: "We focused on scouting the black colleges . . . We found some real talent out of those colleges. I think that started it more than anything. It was just looking for talent. It wasn't a point of, 'Well, we're going to bring in black players,' it was a point of finding players who could compete and play well."[50]

Nasty rumors were circulating that the NFL had quotas limiting a team to having only a few black players. Nothing has ever been confirmed on that point, but it did spark concern. Washington Redskins owner George Preston Marshall may have been part of the reason for the assumption of limiting black players on a team. One of the NFL's more influential figures, he refused to sign a black player until the Kennedy administration pressured him in 1962.[51]

Looking back, it was the open-mindedness of the AFL owners to reach into spots that the NFL did not to grow the league. With the implementation of black players, the AFL helped bring pro football into the modern era.

---

48. Ibid., 120.
49. Ibid.
50. Ibid., 120–121.
51. Ibid., 121.

THE AFL-NFL WAR - 1960-1965

For five years from 1960–1965, the AFL and NFL had been waging war; a financial war. Before the AFL's arrival, player salaries were about $7,000 for veterans and $6,000 for rookies, with quarterbacks getting about $10,000 a season.[52] When the AFL began, the two leagues had a gentleman's agreement not to sign each other veteran players that were still under contract. But college players? That is where the AFL excelled at acquiring young talent, and at the NFL's expense.

One thing that the AFL had that the NFL lacked was owners with deep pockets. They were willing to spend big, even if the franchise endured a loss on the books. Nowhere was it more evident than in the draft, where it had to compete against the NFL for recruits. If the NFL offered a first-round selection of $6,000 a season, the AFL team that drafted the same player offered him $10,000 a year. This meant the NFL club would have to counter with the same or usually more to sign him. This created problems with the veteran players whose contracts came up who were suddenly making the same as a rookie. That didn't sit well in the world of pro football.[53]

Right from the announcement of the AFL, the NFL tried to kill the AFL before it even got started. By placing a team in Dallas to compete with Lamar Hunt's Texans, the NFL showed its dedication to wage war with the AFL. The NFL was even willing to compete in the Dallas market that failed the league miserably a decade earlier. The new NFL team in Dallas, like its predecessor, also had financial losses in their first year of existence, as did the AFL's Dallas Texans. Even with the financial losses, the teams in both leagues stayed put in Dallas because this was a war of attrition to grab the Texas market.

Also noticeable in the war was the NFL owners who opened the door to AFL executives to buy into NFL franchises with their deep pockets.

52. Barry Shuck, "When Al Davis Tried to Sabotage The NFL," SB Nation, accessed September 25, 2018, https://www.bigblueview.com/2017/12/2/16721994/when-al-davis-tried-to-sabotage-the-nfl.

53. Ibid.

This showed that the NFL feared the competition in the financial aspect of pro football.

One thing stood out during the war that would be remembered fondly by the AFL players and owners; the more established NFL had little regard or respect for the new AFL. Even with the high-flying offenses and high scoring games that made the AFL very exciting to watch, the NFL still mocked and thought little of the AFL. Nick Buoniconti, a linebacker for the AFL Boston Patriots and later, for the Miami Dolphins, recalled: "They looked down their noses at us . . . They insulted us calling us 'minor leaguers' and the AFL is a 'Mickey Mouse League.'"[54]

Art Modell, who owned the Browns, didn't even want to do business with the AFL. He hated the AFL for even getting the guts to compete in pro football. Len Dawson recalled coach Paul Brown's stance on the AFL: "I remember Paul Brown had us convinced it was bad for football . . . I can remember sitting in a meeting, and he said 'This league is not going to last. It's a bunch of sons of rich guys. It's a hobby with them. They don't know anything about football. The people playing there are not capable of playing in the National Football League. They'll be nothing but castoffs, and they won't last more than a year or two.'"[55]

Resentment was everywhere by the NFL owners over the new league. In the words of Jets' lineman, John Schmitt, "The NFL was trying to kill us . . . They were trying to put the AFL out of business."[56] For some of the AFL teams, it looked this way because of the terrible losses of money they endured. In Oakland, the Raiders lost a half of a million dollars in the first season of the AFL but was saved as a franchise when Buffalo Bills owner, Ralph Wilson, loaned the Raiders $400,000 to survive. Harry Wismer and the New York Titans had worse problems by failing to get an edge in the New York market dominated by the NFL's New York Giants. Wismer couldn't even afford to meet his payroll. The league took control of the fledgling Titans in 1962, and the New York franchise was bought by Sonny Werblin and renamed the franchise, the Jets.[57]

54. Schultz, *The NFL, Year One*, 9.
55. Michael MacCambridge, *America's Game ... The Epic Story of How Pro Football Captured a Nation"* (NY: Random House, 2004), 195.
56. Schultz, *The NFL, Year One*, 9.
57. Ibid.

With the lagging attendance and the loss of substantial money, Lamar Hunt saw the writing on the wall for the Texans after three seasons and pulled out of Dallas. This left the NFL's Cowboys as the only pro football team in Dallas. Hunt moved the franchise to Kansas City, where it would thrive and become one of the AFL's most successful teams. Even with the Texans' sentimental value to the City of Dallas, Hunt was more concerned about the league succeeding and thought the Midwest held more value for a team in pro football. Even with the protests from his players and staff against the move to Kansas City, Hunt decided to roll the dice in Kansas City.

Though it had many obstacles, the AFL did survive in those early turbulent years. As the years went on, and teams got better, Commissioner Joe Foss felt the league was ready to challenge the NFL in a battle of the champions from both leagues in a World Series type of game between the AFL and NFL. Foss wrote to NFL President Pete Rozelle and asked him to have a game between the leagues' champions at the end of 1964. Like many of his constituents, Rozelle probably felt it would be a mismatch due to the AFL not even fielding a team strong enough to compete with the NFL's champion.[58]

Undeterred by the lack of respect by its older rival league, the AFL trudged on, and by 1965, the war between the AFL and the NFL raised in intensity. Drafting the college players is where the battlefield would be fought. Sonny Werblin, the owner of the New York Jets, was ready to break out the canons and fire them at the NFL. Werblin had a great perception and saw that the rival New York Giants were getting old and that they were not an elite team anymore in the NFL. Now was his chance to build a better team than his rivals in Gotham that were crumbling and aged. Unlike the Giants, who remained faithful to veteran players, Werblin believed in the youth movement to build a winner. He also knew he needed star power and went out and signed the University of Alabama quarterback Joe Namath to a stunning $427,000 contract. It was the league's most high-profile signing since the Oilers signed

---

58. Ibid., 10.

Heisman Trophy winner Billy Cannon to $100,000 in 1960.[59] Part of
the deal that Werblin gave to Namath included a retirement plan that
guaranteed Namath $5,000 a year for life after his playing career ended.
At the signing, and for good measure, a brand-new Lincoln Continental
automobile was given to Namath.[60] With the signing of Namath to this
eye-popping contract, pro football's salaries would skyrocket.

Werblin, who worked in the Hollywood industry for more than 30
years, now had star power in New York to attract paying customers for
his Jets. His investment in Namath was well worth the risk he took, and
Werblin's return on investment on the Alabama graduate would exceed
all his expectations.

Namath, however, arrived in the AFL with a well-known reputation
for mischief. At Alabama, he had been suspended as a junior when coach
Bear Bryant kicked him off the team for drinking and carousing before
the last two season games. Namath came off as something of a playboy
with his good looks and no shortage of female admirers. And there was
a certain star quality about in him that was recognized by others.[61] With
good looks and athleticism, teams demanding more players like Namath
would equate to inflating their bottom lines. Dick Butkus, linebacker
for the Chicago Bears, summed up the AFL-NFL bidding war: "mere
buckets" of money became "wheelbarrows."[62] Pro football was entering
into a phase where buying a championship was necessary, and money
became king.

The war was also fought for television rights, which would give both
leagues extra needed revenue for every team in both leagues. Pete Rozelle
secured a $28.2 million contract for two years with CBS to televise
National Football League games. There was even a bidding war for television rights by all three networks (ABC, NBC, and CBS). As explained
many years later by Pat Summerall, NBC had a higher bid than CBS,

59. Duane Cross, "The AFL, A Football Legacy, Part 2," CNN/SI (January 22, 2001), accessed
September 28, 2018, http://www.remembertheafl.com/CNNSIAFLStoryPartII.htm.
60. Jack Doyle, "I Guarantee It. Joe Namath," (December 23, 2009), accessed September 28, 2018,
PopHistoryDig.com/topics/Joe Namath/.
61. Ibid.
62. Cross, "The AFL," accessed September 28, 2018.

but Rozelle did not want the NFL to be broadcast on NBC.[63] Rozelle won a major coup with the television deal as the fourteen teams would be sharing a million dollars a year in revenue from the television contract. This revenue from television was three times as much as the NFL teams were made in the last deal, which amounted to $365,000 a year.[64] The celebration of the NFL owners' major television contract prompted many to believe that this would be a major blow to the AFL. The NFL owners believed they now had the resources to combat the AFL and that the AFL's demise was imminent because of the NFL's record-breaking contract. This thought was short-lived because the NFL owners didn't know that the AFL had its own plans to secure a very lucrative television contract.

CBS might have outbid NBC for the rights to televise NFL games, but when they lost the bidding, their eyes looked to the AFL. Three days after the NFL and CBS deal, the AFL and NBC unveiled a 36-million-dollar deal to televise AFL games from 1965 to 1969, This would be five times the amount that ABC paid the AFL initially back in 1960. On its face, it looked like the NFL got a better deal with CBS, reaping 14.1 million a year for its contract, whereas the AFL received substantially half of that amount at $7.5 million a year. But if you look at the total breakdown among the teams in each league, the NFL would be splitting up 14.1 million dollars among 14 teams per year at a net share of a little over a million dollars a year. The AFL would be splitting up $7.5 million a year among eight teams for almost a million dollars per team. Both deals were comparable in their scope.[65]

The signing of Namath, and the NBC contract, gave the AFL a booster shot to continue with the war with the NFL. This also helped with maintaining a financial lifeline for AFL teams that were struggling with their balance sheets. It also raised the stakes in the war against the NFL. Now, armed with extra cash to spend, the AFL was able to compete further with the NFL, especially in obtaining the same good quality players the NFL

63. MacCambridge, *America's Game*, 191.
64. Ibid.
65. Ibid., 200–201.

had eyed for signing. Picking up on the intensity of the two leagues' fighting to outdo each other, the press made it possible to exploit the rivalry between the leagues in the papers, which helped escalate the war.

By the mid-1960s, the AFL had not only grown to be a major force in pro football, but now they were at a level where no one could have predicted. In five short years, the league now could hold its own, without fears of shutting down as other previous leagues did in the past. They had established themselves as a "major" league, and we're here to stay.

The league's growth was due in part to Commissioner Joe Foss's leadership in cultivating the AFL from the ground up. Now, with an intensified war with the NFL, many of the AFL owners began to question Foss's leadership in this new phase of turbulence. While the AFL owners liked Foss, they had little confidence in his abilities to continue the struggle between the two leagues. Although Foss had served in the Marines in World War II and was the Governor of South Dakota, the AFL owners believed that Foss mellowed with age. They wanted a warrior who would be willing to win the war. Seeing the writing on the wall, Foss resigned on April 7, 1966.

Although it was his own decision to quit the $50,000 a year job with nearly two years still to go on his contract, Foss feels that he was, in a way, a victim of his success. In an interview with *Sports Illustrated*, Foss elaborated on his line of thinking about the origins of the AFL, how the league grew under him, where it was presently going, the continuing war with the NFL, and the future success of pro football:

> I predicted that when the league got into the black [on the
> balance sheet as making profits], my position would change,
> the league has come to the stage where problems are fewer,
> and the owners have more time to get into mischief. I have
> never been a dancing bear for the owners and never could be.
> This is the time for me to leave.
>
> Phase One for the AFL began at the Beverly Hilton hotel
> in Los Angeles in 1959 when the league's founders, Lamar
> Hunt, Bud Adams, Barron Hilton, Harry Wismer, Bob

Howsam, Max Winter, and H. P. Skoglund, approached [me]
about becoming their commissioner.

I worked for the first six weeks for nothing because the
league had no money. I started traveling around the country.
Some of the owners criticized me for not spending enough
time in league cities, but I realized that people in the small
towns had television sets, and we had to have ratings, or
we could get no sponsors and no big television contracts. I
appeared at conventions, anywhere they'd listen to me. Eventually, we succeeded, but it was a miracle we ever made it.[66]

For Phase One of the AFL, it was the pioneering phase, according to
Foss. The beginning of the end of Phase One was the signing of a five-
year $43 million contract with NBC-TV. Due to the signing, Foss nearly
quit as commissioner the year before, when the contract went into effect.
That was because his role as the leader was diminishing as the league
acquired more wealth. Even though Foss had led the AFL in its infant
stages, through the storm to survive, he saw the writing on the wall. The
direction of Phase Two was yet uncertain but seemed to be escalating the
war with the NFL with the rising salaries. Foss explained to the public:

I'm alarmed about this . . . I'd like to plead with the owners in
both leagues not to follow this crazy route of the big bonuses.
The avarice of owners, coaches, and players is amazing.
They're shooting the whole industry out of the sky. The
veterans are upset and should be. Not merging the leagues is
knocking the bottom out of the barrel. It is creating problems,
hurting the image of the game, and causing some people to
use methods that are not right.

I happen to know that in the last 30 days, the NFL had
a meeting of 100 new scouts to tell them about a program
underway right now for signing college boys for the coming

66. Edwin Shrake, "After Foss, A Hotter War," *Sports Illustrated* (April 18, 1996), accessed November 25,
2019, https://www.si.com/vault/1966/04/18/614489/after-foss-a-hotter-pro-war.

season. One of the NFL scouts made the mistake of writing down the instructions, and I saw them. They intend to sign the kids to open, undated contracts that allow them to play pretty much where they choose, as long as it's in the NFL. 'Get next to the boys right now' is the policy. The AFL, I'm sure, is going to combat that plan with one of its own. The NFL is going to wind up being sorry this ever started.

Last year the NFL spent $300,000 on baby-sitters. This year the figure will be more than $350,000. A merger is the only way to solve these crazy actions. We should take a page from baseball and have one commissioner and two league presidents. Merging, I think, will be Phase Three.[67]

According to Foss, previous rumors that a merger was close had not the slightest element of truth. "The closest we ever came was a few owners in one league talking to a few owners in the other . . . There is no faction in our league that is opposed to a merger, but there is a strong faction against it in the NFL. They feel: Why should they give us additional publicity? They're doing well enough as it is. Pete Rozelle feels that way. He's never made a secret of it. Pete is a fine chap, and we've talked over our mutual problems, but he doesn't want to get near us. Of the 15 NFL owners, I would say six or seven want to merge."[68]

However, the lack of a merger is not what has aroused criticism of Foss by his peers. At various times, especially in the past year, Foss has been blamed for the AFL's loss of Atlanta to the NFL, for never being in his New York office, for traveling too much, forgoing hunting in Africa for a TV series called *The American Sportsman* (on his right wrist Foss wears a bracelet made from the tail hair of an elephant he shot) and several other supposed sins. During that same period, he has ceased to be credited with swinging the NBC-TV deal that assured the AFL of survival. Some reports indicated that Sonny Werblin, owner of the New York Jets, did the television negotiating, which sounded logical, since

67. Ibid.
68. Ibid.

Werblin, as former president of the talent agency, MCA, would certainly have had the knowledge and contacts to do so. Foss, of course, denied it. He explained: "The truth is that I negotiated that contract myself, all alone. Sonny wasn't there. I talked to NBC, and they gave me a figure that our people were willing to accept. Our people told me not to push it. I knew my head was on the line, but I pushed the figure forward by $6 million. At the negotiations, I didn't take Billy Sullivan [then president of the Boston Patriots and the league] or even a lawyer. Some of our people said we ought to do it by committee, but I know you can't negotiate by committee. I wouldn't have gone to the meeting with NBC if I hadn't gone alone."[69]

The whole expansion of the league had become an issue for both the AFL and the NFL. Foss elaborated on how the war affected expanding into other cities: "The Atlanta deal was something else again. A year before we ever granted a franchise to Atlanta, I proposed expanding to Atlanta and Miami, but I couldn't get enough support from the owners. On my own, I went to Atlanta and met with the mayor and Leonard Reinsch, president of Cox Broadcasting Corp. We had many more meetings and phone calls, but I was trying to do it quietly. Finally, our executive committee met with Reinsch. The mistake was that Reinsch didn't come with the stadium lease in his hand. I asked him how soon he could get the lease, and he said 48 hours. Meanwhile, Arthur Montgomery, chairman of the Atlanta Stadium Authority, or someone called Pete Rozelle and said to get down there at once. So, the NFL got the stadium and the franchise. Who dropped the bag? It wasn't Joe Foss."[70]

Foss had some notable battles with every owner in the AFL—which was to be expected to be the leader of the league. In his view of the battles, Foss explained: "But they didn't stay mad at me long . . . We had our fights in the meeting room and left with a united front. I have fined owners and coaches but never made it public. If I was a puppet commissioner, I'd like to hire a puppet like that. Some owners became irritated because I would never be frightened or directed. I wouldn't call

69. Ibid.
70. Ibid.

the owners and report to them all the time just to gain Brownie's points. If I went to a congressional committee, I might write a note to the league about it, and I might not. I guess I could have done a lot better job as commissioner as far as the owners and public are now concerned if I had stayed in my office and done public relations work. But that is not in my nature."[71]

Foss summed up his resignation as follows: "It's time for me to take a rougher and bigger job. I was getting tired of looking at placid waters. Now that the league is prospering, I'm ready to move on. My mission is accomplished."[72]

THE WARRIOR

The warrior the AFL had in mind to continue Phase Two was thirty-six years old Al Davis, who was the Raider's volatile coach out in Oakland. This no-nonsense man from Brooklyn, New York, had a personal distaste for the NFL. He had been with the AFL since its inception and was very angry by the NFL's tactics of undermining the junior circuit and its lack of respect for the league. Davis wasn't shy by any means in his animosity against the NFL and didn't hesitate to show it in public. Davis impressed the owners with his fighting spirit that he would be the warrior they would need to make it through the war. Without hesitation, Davis was voted in as commissioner the following day that Foss resigned. The AFL owners now had their field general, who would bring the NFL to its knees, or at least could put pressure on the NFL and force a favorable settlement. This would only be an illusion to both Davis and the public. The owners secretly had other ideas.

Outwardly, the AFL owners portrayed their ambitions to combat the NFL by making Davis the commissioner. But it was just for show. Author Glenn Dickey noted that the owners deceived Davis, "He thought he had been hired to win the war with the NFL. The owners only wanted to force peace. They were quietly negotiating a merger while Davis was

71. Ibid.
72. Ibid.

fighting a war."[73] Davis would soon find out that he was not the general he thought he was, leading the men into the battle. He was just a pawn in a chess game at the bargaining table between the two leagues.

According to sportswriter Ken Rappoport in his history of the AFL, "Davis had a plan, and, considering the football genius the man would become, no one should have been surprised that it would work—brilliantly."[74] Or so everyone thought.

---

73. Glenn Dickey, *Just Win, Baby: Al Davis & His Raiders* (NY: Harcourt, 1991), 38–39.
74. Rappoport, *The Little League That Could*, 164.

3

ANATOMY OF A MERGER: THE AFL AND NFL COMBINE – 1966

When the Miami Dolphins were created as an expansion team in the AFL in 1965, it signaled to the NFL that the AFL was not folding and would not go away. Besides, with the AFL beginning to raid the NFL players and getting more muscle in the draft, plus throwing around the kind of money that was shocking to many NFL owners, the NFL owners started to see the AFL in a new light. "Teams were getting to the point where they wouldn't ask 'Can he help us?' said Gil Brandt, the NFL's Dallas Cowboys' personnel chief, "but instead, 'Can we sign him?'"[1]

The war between the two leagues was making both sides weary. Thoughts of a peace agreement between the two leagues were beginning to surface on both sides, long before Al Davis became commissioner of the AFL. The AFL had proved to the world that it was not the fledgling league it once was. It had become a force to be reckoned with.

By the autumn of 1965, the football war was taking its financial toll, and the idea of peace was becoming not such a bad idea to both sides. Buffalo Bills owner Ralph Wilson explained: "I don't know how the talk

1. Larry Felser, *Birth of the New NFL: How the 1966 NFL/AFL Merger Transformed Pro Football* (Guilford, CT: Lyons Press, 2008), 536–538, Kindle.

of a merger started, except that it wasn't initiated by us . . . we heard that they might be interested in a merger. It was sort of in the rumor stage when we had an AFL owner meeting in Houston."[2]

Barron Hilton, who moved the Chargers from Los Angeles to San Diego in 1961, began to note the need to stop the bloodshed between the two leagues. Seeing that the war was hitting a point of stagnation on both sides, like a war of attrition in the trenches in France during World War I, Hilton devised a peace plan. He indicated to the other AFL owners, "I'm going to name a committee to talk to a representative of the NFL about merging our two leagues . . . we'll see what comes of it." Hilton named a committee of two, Ralph Wilson of Buffalo and Sonny Werblin, of the New York Jets, to figure out a plan.[3]

Werblin, however, wasn't so keen about peace negotiations. Wilson recalled, "Sonny, who had become one of my best friends, was against a merger because he was operating in New York against the Giants." Wilson also stated that, in addition to Werblin's concerns in New York City, "Wayne Valley, the Raiders' owner, was also against it because Oakland was right across the bay from the San Francisco 49ers. Both cities knew there would be demands over the invasion of the territory."[4]

The AFL commissioner, Joe Foss, was not informed of any merger talk or even the committee's formation. This was a silent coup by the owners, and it was a clear indication that Foss was eventually going out to sea as the leader of the AFL.

Cleveland Browns owner Art Modell summed up the view among the NFL owners at the time in spring of 1966: "We could have done our business for another 30 years, but we sought [a merger] to prolong the success of pro football before things got out of hand and we couldn't control them."[5]

What made the merger theory more of a discussion for NFL owners was the signing of the kicker, Pete Gogolak, by the New York Giants. Gogolak was a free agent from the AFL. This was the first signing ever

2. Ibid., 590–591.
3. Ibid., 591–594.
4. Ibid., 594–598..
5. Schultz, The NFL, Year One, 11.

of another league player by a team. The Giants owner, Wellington Mara, heard all the griping by his fellow owners when he signed the Buffalo Kicker from the AFL. Commissioner Rozelle backed the deal, alluding to the NFL By-Laws, which said nothing about signing a player that was a free agent who had played out his option. It didn't say anything about signing a player from another league either. The other owners thought much differently. They were shocked and bewildered over the signing. This was a game-changer in the war between the leagues. Panic set in among the owners of the NFL because Mara just opened Pandora's box. Now, anything was fair game for both leagues.

As for Commissioner Pete Rozelle, he never wanted a merger. In his mind, the NFL was doing fine. However, the NFL owners under his leadership were now seeing the writing on the wall. The war was going to be escalated further from the signing of Gogolak. They were right.

On the other side, in the AFL, when Al Davis heard of the Gogolak signing, he was more than just livid. Davis knew that the war was escalating, and he was embracing every minute of it. To the upset Buffalo owner, Ralph Wilson, who was disgusted and angry over the signing of his kicker by the Giants, Davis told him what he wanted to hear about a possible peace treaty: "If we go out and sign their players, we'll destroy them, and they'll come to the table."[6] In his blood, Davis didn't want a peace treaty but pitched it to Wilson to calm him down from the loss of Gogolak. Davis instead wanted revenge. With revenge on his mind, Davis lived up to his promise of going after the NFL players. The warrior was ready to conquer.

Tex Schramm, the owner of the Dallas Cowboys, told a different story to *Sports Illustrated* about how the peace between the two sides came together, back on June 20, 1966:

> There has been considerable speculation on what finally
> brought about peace. Some think that when the Giants
> signed Pete Gogolak, the Buffalo kicker and the AFL began to
> retaliate, and the two leagues ran for cover to avoid spending

6. MacCambridge, *America's Game*, 222.

money. Some people think that this happened because of the Roman Gabriel case on the coast or the John Brodie case in Houston. But the negotiations were well underway before Gogolak was signed or Gabriel was approached by Oakland or John Brodie, the San Francisco quarterback, visited Houston. The Gogolak, Gabriel, and Brodie cases were stumbling blocks to negotiation.

There had been serious discussions between individual owners in the two leagues for two or three years. You would hear that Sonny Werblin of New York had been talking to Carroll Rosenbloom of Baltimore or that Ralph Wilson of Buffalo had discussed peace with Art Modell. A certain amount of groundwork had been laid before my meeting with Lamar in Dallas.

I had always thought that if a proper plan could be worked out, peace was feasible. Sometime late in February, in a telephone conversation I had with Dan Reeves, the owner of the Los Angeles Rams, we explored the possibilities of a deal and tried to figure out what might be the essentials acceptable to the NFL owners. After talking it over with Dan, I called Pete Rozelle.

Pete and I decided that we should keep the early stages of a peace plan limited to the people most directly involved—Wellington Mara of the New York Giants and Lou Spadia of the San Francisco 49ers, the NFL owners in two-team cities— until it was developed further. We felt that if the NFL could come up with an acceptable plan that was good for the sport, it could then be presented to the American Football League. If they liked it, fine. If not, we could settle down to an all-out war. At the moment, we were half fighting and a half making love. We wanted the decks cleared.

Pete and I outlined a plan to Mara in a telephone conversation in early March; it was, in rough outline, the same plan that was eventually accepted by both leagues. Wellington was something less than enthusiastic, but he said that if the basics of the plan were strong enough so that the rest of the owners accepted it, the special New York problems could probably be solved.

Then I flew out to San Francisco to try to convince Lou Spadia that a deal could work. Lou's problem in San Francisco was a tough one. New York had shown that it was feasible for two pro clubs to exist in that city since the Giants were sold out on season tickets and the Jets had a healthy season-ticket sale of their own. San Francisco, on the other hand, is not as big as New York and history had raised some questions about the success of a two-team market. Lou met me at the airport, and we drove to Palo Alto for lunch.

Lou pointed out, reasonably enough, that he did not mind competing with the Oakland Raiders in San Francisco as long as they were in the AFL and he was in the NFL with exclusive use of NFL teams as opponents. He was not so sure that two NFL clubs could succeed in that area. He pointed out that San Francisco proper is an area bounded on three sides by water, with very little room for growth. The 49ers played in San Francisco's 41-year-old Kezar; the Raiders played in Oakland across the Bay, and the growth area in northern California was there.

I had arrived at the airport at 11 in the morning, and Lou took me back at 5 in the afternoon. After six hours of discussion, Lou was, to put it mildly, still not enthusiastic. But he understood what we were trying to do, and he agreed not to put any stumbling blocks in our way.

The next step was to discuss the whole thing with the NFL attorneys before approaching anyone in the American Football League. I talked to Hamilton Carothers, a member of the Washington firm of Covington & Burling, on March 30. After he and Pete and I went over the various legal and political aspects of the thing at some length by phone, he said go ahead, informally. Then Pete and I went over the list of American Football League owners, looking for the best one with whom we could negotiate.

We wanted an owner who had prestige, the desire for peace, time to work on the problem, no personal prejudices—and who could keep his mouth shut. Lamar filled the requirements perfectly, and also, he was one of the founders of the league. As a small unpremeditated plus, he lives only a few blocks from me in Dallas—which was to simplify our meetings later on.

So, on Monday, April 4, I called Lamar in Kansas City and asked him if he could meet me in Dallas. He said he would arrange his travel from K.C. to an AFL meeting in Houston so that he would have an hour and a half layover in Dallas. His plane arrived in Dallas a little after 7 in the evening, and we met under the Ranger statue, then went out and sat in my car in the parking lot. I laid out the general plan for him, and he listened intently, asking a question now and then for clarification. I told him that this was not just conversation, that Rozelle knew about it and approved, but I explained that only a few of our owners were aware of it and suggested that he keep it as confidential as possible for a while, at least until we resolved the problem of the two-team market. Pro football owners are individualists and competitors who like to compete in public. At this stage, 24 owners would have made the discussions too unwieldy, so I suggested to Lamar that I be his only direct contact in the NFL, and he would be mine in the AFL.

I did not hear from Lamar before going on a brief vacation. In the meantime, at the AFL meeting in Houston, Joe Foss resigned and was replaced by Al Davis. None of this seemed to be too important at the time. I went to Clint Murchison's island on April 12, with my wife and the Rozelles and four other couples, and stayed there until April 17, when my wife and I flew on to Jamaica.

During this time, another problem had developed. Wellington Mara had come across information that Sonny Werblin was negotiating for the sale of the New York Jets. Also, there were newspaper stories that Barron Hilton would sell the San Diego Chargers. One of the early problems in the peace talks was whether the Jets and Raiders would stay in New York and Oakland. Since these things had a bearing on the situation, Lamar Hunt was informed of them. Lamar investigated the stories and reported to us that they would not affect the talks.

Meanwhile, Spadia in San Francisco was growing more and more unhappy, and Pete and Wellington flew out to San Francisco to talk to him on April 21 or 22. I was supposed to go from Jamaica to Panama on May 1st for some fishing, but I canceled the trip so that I could return to Dallas and resume the talks with Lamar. As it turned out, I came back on April 29 because of a flood that nearly washed my house away.

My next meeting with Lamar was in his home at 9 A.M. on the morning of May 3. His home is not far from the Dallas Cowboy office, so the meeting was convenient and inconspicuous. At this meeting, we discussed the questions as they existed at the time—primarily to resolve the New York and San Francisco-Oakland area problems, and for the first time, I told Lamar how much I thought it might cost the AFL. He didn't show much emotion.

Luckily, he is a very quiet, unruffled personality. I could not have had a better man to negotiate with. I'm emotional, and I tend to lose my temper. The few times I lost it with Lamar, he simply sat quietly and never flared back.

After this meeting, he said he would need another week to think over the proposal. He called me the following Monday, and we met at his home again on Tuesday, May 10. Until this meeting, Lamar had been noncommittal. Now he felt any problems could be solved, and for the first time, I thought we had a good chance for success. I called Pete and told him of Lamar's reaction.

The NFL meeting was scheduled for Washington beginning May 16. Pete suggested that I come to New York early so that we could have a meeting with Wellington and Lou Spadia. The meeting took place at the Plaza on the evening of May 13 at 9 P.M., and it did not go too well. Lou was still unenthusiastic, and Wellington seemed less receptive than he had been previously. I did not know at the time that he was contemplating signing Pete Gogolak.

The next day I had lunch with Rozelle, and we concluded that the time was not ripe to present the idea to the league meeting. We decided that we would approach the owners one or two at a time and sound them out in general terms. This way, we could get a go-ahead without any premature publicity or a big stir.

Then on Tuesday at the meeting, Well dropped his Gogolak bomb. His signing of the Buffalo placekicker was perfectly legal and aboveboard, but it came at a bad time for peace negotiations. Far from triggering an agreement between the leagues, it almost ended the possibility of peace. At a time when we wanted the owners in as harmonious a mood as possible, it created division and anger. And, of course, it created even more problems for Lamar.

I talked to Carroll Rosenbloom and Art Modell, who had talked to AFL owners a year ago, and to Edward Bennett Williams, Vince Lombardi, and Dan Reeves, explaining to them the real prospects for a deal and asking their help in talking to the other owners so that there would be no open division at the meeting. They agreed that the prime objective was peace,

and they did a fine job. I called Lamar and told him not to
panic about the Gogolak thing.

On the last day of the league meeting, Pete told the owners
of the possibility of a deal and named a group to meet in New
York the next day. Its members were Mara, Spadia, Lombardi,
Rosenbloom, Modell, Stormy Bidwill of the St. Louis Cardinals, and me. I was expected back in Dallas that day, so I
called my wife and told her to tell anyone who called that I
had stayed over for the Preakness. I had to remember to watch
the Preakness on TV in case anyone asked me about it.

At this New York discussion, Well said he would go along
with us, and Spadia said he thought it would be agreeable to
the 49ers under certain conditions. But he wanted to review
the entire matter with the controlling stockholders of the
49ers, the widows of club founders Vic and Tony Morabito.
He set up a meeting with them for Tuesday, May 24.

I flew back to Dallas Saturday night, May 21, and started
a string of almost sleepless nights. Pete decided during the
next week to discuss with club presidents the details of the
proposed plan, leading to final approval. Tuesday, May 24,
I flew back to New York, ostensibly to discuss a club TV
problem but actually to meet with Pete and some of the other
owners. He set up meetings with the Rooneys, Jerry Wolman,
Bill Ford, Modell, and Mugs Halas, all of whom came to
New York, and outlined the deal for the other owners on the
telephone. Everything went smoothly until we got to San
Francisco. After his meeting with the widows, Lou Spadia had
renewed reservations.

So, Pete caught a plane to San Francisco Thursday evening,
May 26, and met with Spadia on the 27th. He called me in
Dallas later that day to say everything looked O.K., and I
suggested that he come to Dallas for a couple of days so that
we could finalize the general terms of the plan. Pete came in
that night for a quiet weekend, and I told my daughter not

to mention that he was there. She nicknamed him, "Sneaky Pete." but she kept quiet. She could not help overhearing our talk, though, as Pete called various club presidents, and at one point, she asked incredulously, "Mom, are they talking about peace?" My wife had to threaten her with mayhem if she did not keep quiet.

So, Saturday, Sunday, and Monday, with Pete working on a borrowed typewriter, we made notes on the plan, and Pete called all the owners, developing a common ground everyone agreed on. By Monday—Memorial Day—we had it all squared away. The American Football League had not heard this version yet, so Sunday night I called Lamar Hunt, who was in Indianapolis for the 500, and asked him if he could come directly to my house in Dallas after the end of the race the next day. He said he could.

Lamar was having trouble with some of his people at this time. They seemed to feel that the NFL was setting a booby trap for them. For the first time, Pete talked to Lamar on the phone that Sunday night to reassure him of the good faith of the NFL and to let him know that this was not just a conversation with me. Lamar was delayed the next day when the 500 was held up by the big accident. He was supposed to get to Dallas about 7:30, and I was waiting nervously for him to call. Pete had gone back to New York. About 7:50, the phone rang, and I jumped a foot, but it was Clint Murchison, the Cowboy owner. I told him I was waiting for Lamar's call and that he had startled me. Some 20 minutes later, the phone rang again. It was Clint again, and all he said this time was "Boo!"

Lamar finally called about a quarter after 9, but we were both too tired to meet that night, so he came around the next morning, May 31. I gave him a yellow pad and a pencil and then explained the plan using the five pages of notes that Pete and I had produced. Lamar did not comment as I talked, other than to question points for clarification. When I had finished, I said, "There it is. If you accept, this deal has been approved by every NFL club. If you have to alter it too much, it will blow up."

I ought to make it clear here that Lamar and I, in all the hours we talked about this, never argued bitterly. We were on the same side of the fence, doing our best to reach a reasonable settlement for both leagues.

After this meeting, Lamar went to New York, to the Regency Hotel, with his notes. He was to meet with Ralph Wilson and Billy Sullivan there. This, incidentally, was the first time I knew Lamar had a committee. My discussions were always with him alone. I heard from him again later in the week, by telephone. He gave me a list of 26 points of differences or additions. Some were minor; some were not.

I called Pete in New York, and we went over the 26 points. Either they presented no NFL problems, or Pete took them up with the clubs involved by phone. About a third of Lamar's points were acceptable, another third was not, and that left a third to be worked out. A lot of the differences involved simple problems of wording. Even now, there is no formal written agreement between the two leagues other than a few notations made by the participants.

After I talked to Pete, I called Lamar. It seems a roundabout way to do things, but that's the way it went for a few hours. Pete and Lamar were about ten blocks apart in New York, and they negotiated by phone through me in Dallas.

My next meeting with Lamar in person was on Sunday night, June 5, at my home. We went over the master plan, point by point, and we went over the replies to the AFL's 26 points, and by the time we finished that session, at 11:45 P.M., there were only a few items of disagreement left. The big bone of contention was on a question of expansion. The NFL and the AFL would each add a team during the four years before the actual combining of the leagues. The NFL owners wanted the AFL to provide the players for the new AFL team, but the payment for the new franchise would go directly to the NFL. That was the way it was settled.

Finally, Lamar left to fly to New York early the next morning, and that day, Monday, June 6, we were in almost constant telephone contact, clarifying points. We reached a tentative accord around midnight, Dallas time. I called Pete, and he got the approval of the NFL owners by phone by late morning on Tuesday, June 7. It had been planned to appoint committees from both leagues to clear up details and handle the release of the story in a deliberate fashion, but by now, rumors were flying, and stories were appearing hourly that contained incorrect information. Pete talked to our Washington attorneys, and they advised that we release the news in proper form as soon as possible. They set up dates with Senator Philip Hart and Representative Emanuel Celler for Pete, and the original plan was accelerated. Then we arranged to meet in Washington with attorneys, and I called Lamar in New York.

We tried a little cloak-and-dagger here, reasoning that if all of us showed up in Washington, some alert reporter might discover what was up. "We'll take a suite at the Sheraton-Carlton under a fictitious name," I told Lamar. "When you get there, go right up. Don't register under your name." He agreed and hung up.

Unfortunately, I had forgotten to give him the fictitious name.

A friend of mine made the reservation for us under the name of "Ralph Pittman." Pete arrived in the early afternoon, signed in as Ralph Pitman, and then he went to the league attorney's office, where I joined him that evening. I suddenly realized that Lamar did not know the name under which we registered, so I called the desk at the Sheraton and probably created instant confusion. "If a Lamar Hunt comes in and asks for Pete Rozelle or Tex Schramm," I said, "tell him that they are in the Ralph Pittman suite. I am registered there, but my name is Schramm."

Fortunately for all of us, Lamar's plane was delayed, and by pure coincidence, he arrived in the lobby of the hotel just as Pete and the attorneys and I returned to the hotel, around 9 P.M. Then we all went to the Ralph Pittman suite and worked until 3 A.M. on the wording of the publicity release. Pete, late Tuesday afternoon, had conferred with Senator Hart on the legal and political aspects of the plan, and Wednesday afternoon, he talked with Representative Celler.

We set up the press conference at the Warwick Hotel in New York for 6 P.M. Wednesday, and we were 15 minutes late because of traffic on Sixth Avenue. Maybe we were a long time coming to this peace, too. But I'm sure it is not too late.

After long and difficult negotiations that involved concessions by people in both the American and the National Football leagues and recommendations by our attorneys, we feel the plan devised and announced is one that the public wants. It should bring about a better and more orderly era in professional football.[7]

When history looks back on the merger, peace talks began to get serious on April 6, 1966, when AFL founder and Kansas City Chiefs owner Lamar Hunt met with the Dallas Cowboys' Tex Schramm in the parking lot at Dallas' Love Field as already told by Schramm. The meetings between the AFL and NFL were kept from Al Davis. Davis was not friends with many in his own league, much less those in the NFL. In an issue of *Sports Illustrated,* writer Bud Shrake wrote, "It is not certain where Al Davis would finish in a popularity contest among sharks, the mumps, the income tax and himself. If the voters were the

7. Tex Schramm, "How It Happened," *Sports Illustrated* (June 20, 1966), accessed September 28, 2018, https://www.si.com/vault/1966/06/20/608557/heres-how-it-happened.

other American Football League coaches, Davis probably would be third, edging out income tax in a thriller."[8]

Davis knew how to alienate others and didn't care who got in his way. He wanted to win, and he wanted to win at all costs. He despised the NFL because they publicly minimized the AFL as a viable professional football league and often referred to it as "minor league." He had a military background that pounded that mantra of "win at all costs" into him daily. Win, or die. And he kept that going into any new battleground.[9]

Meanwhile, in May, Schramm and Hunt met once again to iron out details from meetings that they had attended with their league's confidants. The NFL agreed to the merger but insisted that Rozelle would become the commissioner. All AFL clubs would be admitted providing they paid the NFL an entry fee of $2 million per AFL franchise (total $18 million with the expansion Miami club).

While all of this was going on, Commissioner Davis *still was not brought on board* with the merger talks. What happened next almost broke things wide-open in the merger negotiations.

Davis instituted his plan to raid the NFL players. His strategy was to approach the best players in the NFL about signing very high contracts *that would begin the minute their team's contract expired.* Davis called them "future contracts." Right away, the Chargers offered contracts to three Giants' players, but it would be Davis' Raiders who would deliver the first blow. He signed the Los Angeles Rams' starting quarterback Roman Gabriel to a four-year deal worth a king's ransom of $400,000. Next, the Oilers offered San Francisco 49ers QB John Brodie a three-year deal for the unbelievable sum of $500,000. The 49ers had previously offered Brodie $40,000 a season (up from the $38,000 he was making).[10]

Seeing Davis's raids taking effect, Schramm frantically called Hunt to determine if he could stop this impulsive financial avalanche that Davis had created. Hunt called both AFL owners, Davis and Bud Adams, and

---

8. Barry Shuck, "When Al Davis Tried To Sabotage The NFL," *SB Nation* (December 2, 2017), accessed September 28, 2018, https://www.bigblueview.com/2017/12/2/16721994/when-al-davis-tried-to-sabotage-the-nfl.

9. Ibid.

10. Ibid.

asked them not to go through with the signings, although he couldn't tell them why just yet. Other agreements were being worked on with Washington Redskins' quarterback Sonny Jurgensen and Jim Ninowski, the Cleveland Browns' starting quarterback.[11]

Hunt sent word to Davis asking that the signings cease. Davis refused. His rationale was that if someone like Brodie and Gabriel were already signed, the AFL's bargaining power was greater than with blank contracts and no players under wraps. And so, announced signings to exorbitant contracts continued.[12]

On May 30, Hunt and Schramm hammered out almost six pages of notes and a final briefing regarding the merger. Schramm already had the NFL owner's blessing, so all Hunt had to do was to get his fellow AFL owners to approve it. On June 7, the final details had been ironed out, and an approved charter was approved by both leagues.[13]

Later that evening, Boston Patriots' owner, Billy Sullivan, Jr., informed Davis about the merger. The two leagues agreed, and they decided that Pete Rozelle would be commissioner of the imminent 26-team league. Davis was furious on so many levels. His main contention was that he was the AFL commissioner, and how dare the owners to engage in anything as central as a merger without his input and subsequent approval. Secondly, *he was convinced the AFL could take on the NFL as an independent, viable league* and instead grow steadily as it had already done.[14]

Davis's fury didn't stop the process of moving forward for the merging leagues. When it was all said and done, the major points of the merger were as follows:

1. The AFL and NFL agreed to join an expanded professional football league. It will consist of 26 teams in 25 cities. Pete Rozelle will be the commissioner.
2. A championship game this season.
3. All existing franchises are retained.

11. Ibid.
12. Ibid.
13. Ibid.
14. Ibid.

4. No franchises transferred from present locations.
5. Two new franchises no later than 1968. Those teams were the New Orleans Saints in 1967, the Cincinnati Bengals in 1968, (The Atlanta Falcons and the Miami Dolphins were already established and set to start play for the 1966 season before the merger was announced in June.).
6. Two more teams as soon thereafter as practical. The Seattle Seahawks and Tampa Bay Buccaneers were created in 1976.
7. Inter-League pre-season games in 1967.
8. Single league schedule in 1970.
9. A common draft in January of 1967.
10. Continued two network coverage.[15]

Included in the merger was an $18 million indemnity to be paid by the AFL to the NFL over 20 years. This didn't sit well with some of the AFL owners, including Sonny Werblin, who would indicate the NFL should pay the AFL for merging. It was not going to be a happy marriage, but more of a marriage by a shotgun. The circumstances that brought about the merger still is debated to this day. Was it the signing of Gogolak, which started the AFL raids on NFL players? Was it the NBC contract that infused more financial stability into the AFL for them to compete with signing rookies from the draft? Was it Al Davis' strategic offensive to strip the NFL? The short answer was that all these factors contributed to the merger. What is paradoxical to see in this whole merger was that Pete Rozelle, the NFL commissioner, did not want the merger and retained his job. Conversely, Al Davis, who helped bring the NFL to the bargaining table because of his strategic raids, was voted out.

The war was over, at least on paper. But ill feelings and animosity remained going into the peace period. An uneasy peace was developing as the two leagues became one. The next few years would see a forced league of two rival league players who hated each other but moved forward towards unification in four years.

---

15. MacCambridge, *America's Game*, 228.

4

AN UNEASY PEACE AND THE FIRST FOUR SUPER BOWLS – 1966-1969

The AFL had been lobbying for a championship game from the beginning since we had nothing to lose. The NFL had resisted that idea because they had everything to lose. But by 1966, the difference in the quality of the two leagues had narrowed to the point where a playoff game became necessary.[1]

—HANK STRAM, COACH OF THE KANSAS CITY CHIEFS

Now that the merger took place, and an agreement for a national championship was to take place between the two leagues in 1967, both leagues had to learn to deal with the peace that had just been made. Peace would not be easy. A lot of hard feelings built up over the years between the players and owners in both leagues. For those who coached and played in the AFL, it was almost as if they were foot soldiers near the front, who never received word that the war was over. That reflexive competition, the us-against-them mentality that drove the AFL for a decade, did not

1. Frommer, Harvey. *When It Was Just A Game, Remembering The First Super Bowl* (Lanham, MD: Taylor Trade Publishing, 2015), 37.

diminish and go quietly into the years leading up to the merger season of 1970.[2]

Though the AFL-NFL merger had been negotiated and announced in the summer of 1966, three years later, the battle still raged, especially in Oakland. At that time, Al [Davis] was the Raiders' managing partner, but he had two other general partners—Wayne Valley and Ed McGah." Raiders' coach, John Madden recalled. "So, Ed, and Al and I are out to dinner a couple of days after I'm named head coach, and this is before cell phones and stuff, so Al had to go make a phone call and excused himself and left just Ed and me sitting at dinner. Ed turned to me and said, 'Look, there's only one game you have to win, and if you win that game, you'll always have a job here, and you'll never have to worry about it. The only game you have to win is the 49ers game. You have to beat the 49ers. You beat the 49ers, and no matter what else happens, you have a job.' And the thing is, we were only playing them in the preseason. That's how big it was. It was the AFL versus the NFL. It was Oakland versus San Francisco. Hell, I still feel all that. Those feelings still dominate. We can have a Bay Bridge series in baseball, and I still want the A's against the Giants.'"[3]

For the record, John Madden's 1969 Oakland Raiders beat the 49ers 42–28 in their August exhibition game in Oakland that season. But even with small victories over the NFL teams in pre-season games, the NFL still didn't recognize the AFL as being equal to them or even legit. Madden remembers the rivalry to this day: "No, it never did die down, even after the merger was announced, I mean, Al Davis was the commissioner of the AFL for a bit, and then he came back to Oakland after the merger was negotiated. But he still had that feeling of competition with the NFL in everything. People in Oakland, we knew we were good, and the fans knew we were good. We thought we were as good or better than the NFL. We were treated kind of as second-class citizens, but we never really felt that we should be."[4]

2. Don Banks, "Forty-Five Years after last AFL season, rivalry with NFL still resonates," *Sports Illustrated*, accessed September 30, 2018, https://www.si.com/nfl/2014/11/12/afl-history-kansas-city-chiefs-oakland-raiders.

3. Ibid.

4. Ibid.

Being treated as second class citizens was not only evident on the battlefield but was present at the bargaining table when the two leagues sat down to hammer out the details for a single players' union for both leagues. AFL linebacker Nick Buoniconti still remembers the shock he had sitting at the table with NFL players: "We had sort of an informal meeting with the NFL players . . . and they looked down their noses at us. I remember Ken Bowman, the Green Bay Packers' Center, acting like we didn't even belong talking to them. Finally, I asked him, 'Who do you think you are?'"[5]

Fans had been feeling the rift among the leagues' animosity for years. You either liked the AFL or the NFL, but not both. This came to a head post-merger when New Orleans was granted the right to create an expansion team. When talks began to surface that the New Orleans franchise would be in the AFL, rather than the NFL, the fans were shocked and didn't want the team going into a second-rate league. With the Saints getting the right to come into the NFL, another problem surfaced. Another franchise team was being created at the same time in Cincinnati. Coached by Bengals founder, Paul Brown (who was a long-time coach in the NFL), Brown remembered the disappointment he felt going to the AFL: "We were promised that we would be in the NFL, not the AFL . . . I wanted to come into the NFL, where my old friends were."[6]

The obvious situation that needed to be addressed immediately was the upcoming season of 1966 and the name of the championship title game that ensued after the season. When the merger contracts were signed, Pete Rozelle formed a committee that included himself and three owners from the two leagues. For the NFL, the committee consisted of Tex Schramm of the Dallas Cowboys, Carroll Rosenbloom for the Baltimore Colts, and Dan Reeves of the Los Angeles Rams. For the AFL, the committee members were Lamar Hunt of the Kansas City Chiefs, Ralph Wilson of the Buffalo Bills, and Billy Sullivan of the Boston Patriots.[7]

---

5. Schultz, *The NFL, Year One*, 13.
6. Ibid.
7. MacCambridge, *America's Game*. 236.

The committee participants sat at a round conference table whereby they wanted to begin preliminary discussions on a smooth transaction on the merger that had an eighteen-month deadline. At this conference, Lamar Hunt asked about the national championship and asked for a week's break after the season to get ready for the first-ever championship game. Somewhat confused on Hunt's suggestions, one of the members asked Hunt if it was each league's championship or the decisive game between the leagues? Hunt exclaimed: "You know . . . the last game . . . the final game . . . the super bowl."[8]

From his mention of the word "Super Bowl," the committee smiled, and there were a few laughs. Hunt had concocted the idea of the name from watching his small children playing with one of the major toys of the time: The Wham-O company's high bouncing Super Ball. Even with the laughs, the committee went on in discussions about the upcoming 1966 season and distinguished the game that was each league's championship, and the last as they dubbed "The Super Bowl." The Super Bowl name did not get the title of the first last game featuring the two leagues. Rozelle wanted it called the Pro Bowl, but that was the name given to the All-Star Game. In the end, the last game between both leagues would be called "The AFL-NFL World Championship Game."

The Super Bowl name, however, stuck. No matter what the leagues would call the game, the players, the commentators, the writers, and the press were using Hunt's pet name about the championship game. All through that first season, the mention of Super Bowl was catching on, and by January of 1967, the name had become mainstream. Networks began calling the day "Super Sunday." Even the NFL film crew who began filming on game day also called the game "Super Bowl." Although "Super Bowl" was used unofficially by fans and the media alike, the term was not officially adopted until the fourth annual championship in 1970—the year before the now-famous roman numerals were attached to the game.[9] The term "Super Bowl" has been challenged over the years,

---

8. Ibid.
9. Lindsay Rowen, "How The Super Bowl Got Its Name," *The Christian Science Monitor* (January 29, 2015), accessed October 1, 2018, https://www.csmonitor.com/USA/Sports/2015/0129/How-the-Super
-Bowl-got-its-name.

with the first portion being called "ultimate" or the "premier bowl." One thing was for sure, the leagues liked the "bowl" portion of the name, and it stuck due to borrowing from the colleges' last games, all called "bowl games."

THE BUILDUP TO THE AFL-NFL WORLD CHAMPIONSHIP AND THE PRESSURE TO WIN THE GAME BY BOTH LEAGUES.

For the 1966 season, there would be no inter-league games played, but one . . . The AFL-NFL World Championship game. It would be the first time the champions of both leagues would square off in a winner take all game, which would decide which league was more dominant.

In the AFL, the two teams that had the most success in recent years before 1966 were the San Diego Chargers and the Buffalo Bills. The Chargers beat the Boston Patriots in the 1963 AFC Championship and were still a solid team to make the AFL Championship games in 1964 and 1965. But the Buffalo Bills had beaten the Chargers in both 1964 and 1965 and were poised to win again in 1966.

The Kansas City Chiefs were also now in the spotlight led by quarterback Len Dawson. With an 11–2–1 regular-season record, the Chiefs won the Western Division in 1966 and defeated the Eastern Champions, Buffalo Bills, to win their second AFL Championship. This victory was the teams' first championship in Kansas City (their first Championship was 1962 when they were the Dallas Texans). The Chiefs would be the first team to represent the AFL in the final World Championship game.

In the National Football League, the Green Bay Packers were one of three teams that were in an elite class. The Cleveland Browns and Baltimore Colts were the other two elite teams. The Packers had won the NFL Championship in 1961, 1962, and 1965. Before their run of successes during the 1960s, the Packers had lost in the NFL Championship in 1960 to the Philadelphia Eagles. Coached by Vince Lombardi, the Green Bay Packers went from obscurity in the late 1950s to a powerhouse in the 1960s. Lombardi was hired as Packers head coach and general manager on February 2, 1959. Previously, he had been an assistant coach with the New York Giants. Few could have predicted that

Lombardi's hiring would be the beginning of a remarkable, immediate turnaround of the floundering team from Green Bay, Wisconsin. Under Lombardi, the Packers would become the team of the 1960s, winning five World Championships over seven years, including victories in the first two Super Bowls. During the Lombardi era, the stars of the Packers' offense included Bart Starr, Jim Taylor, Carroll Dale, Paul Hornung (as halfback and placekicker), Forrest Gregg, and Jerry Kramer. The defense included Willie Davis, Henry Jordan, Willie Wood, Ray Nitschke, Dave Robinson, and Herb Adderley.[10]

Besides the elite three teams of the Green Bay Packers, the Baltimore Colts, and the Cleveland Browns, down in Texas, the Dallas Cowboys were also becoming a powerhouse team in the NFL. Coached by Tom Landry, another assistant coach of the New York Giants, the team was slowly getting better each year from their 1960 launch as a franchise. Landry was noted for his creative mind when it came to strategy in pro football. Landry pioneered the now-popular "4–3 defense" while serving as the Giants' defensive coordinator. It was called "4–3" because it featured four down lineman (two ends and two defensive tackles on either side of the offensive center) and three linebackers—middle, left, and right. The innovation in this style of defense was the middle linebacker position. Previously, a lineman was placed over the center. But Landry had this person stand up and move back two yards away from the line of scrimmage.[11]

Beginning in 1966, the Cowboys would go on to have 20 consecutive winning seasons that included 18 postseason appearances, 13 division championships, and five NFC titles. Remarkably, the Dallas team vastly improved in just a few short years with their innovative coach.

In the 1966 NFL Championship, which would decide who goes to the first World Championship as the NFL representative team, came down to the Packers and Cowboys. For the Dallas Cowboys, they had their first winning record since entering the league in 1960. They were

10. David Maraniss, "In throes of winter, a team in disarray is reborn," *Milwaukee Journal Sentinel,* Milwaukee, Wisconsin, (September 14, 1999), 2B.

11. Tom Landry, Biography.com (April 2, 2014), accessed October 2, 2018, https://www.biography .com/people/tom-landry-9372692.

champions of the NFL's Eastern Conference with a 10–3–1 record. The Packers won the Western Conference with a 12–2 record, their eighth consecutive winning season under head coach Vince Lombardi. It was the old guard of Green Bay vs. the up-and-coming team from the Lone Star state. In a very competitive match up, the Green Bay Packers beat the up-and-coming Cowboys 34 to 27. With the win, the Packers headed to the first AFL-NFL World Championship, which was to be played on January 15, 1967, against the Kansas City Chiefs.

SUPER BOWL I

Now the stage was set. After all these years, the two leagues would now play a decisive championship game to crown a true champion. The anticipation of the game, and the importance to win, brought pressure to both the Kansas City Chiefs and the Green Bay Packers not only to win for their teams but also for the leagues they represented.

Much has been written about the subject of Super Bowl I. In Brad Schultz's book *The NFL Year One,* Schultz argues that the Chiefs were scared going into the game against the Packers. Schultz indicated that an enormous amount of pressure was put on the Chiefs, not only due to facing an outstanding team that the Packers were, but the fact that they didn't have the playoff experience, nor the championship rings their opponents had. There was also that large cloud that hung around the Chiefs that they were the first AFL champions to play in this important game that the AFL wanted for years.

To make matters worse for the Chiefs, the Packers still looked down at the AFL, calling their Chiefs opponents a "Mickey Mouse Team." Adding injury to insult, Vince Lombardi and his Packers practiced in Southern California before the 1967 championship game not far from Disneyland, because the NFL felt that was the best way to sell tickets to the contest. To Lombardi. The AFL was the Mickey Mouse league and not worthy of being on the same field as the NFL. To break the pressure, the Chiefs acquired Mickey Mouse ears and wore them in the locker room before the big game. Bill Ray, the photographer for *Life* magazine, had exclusive rights inside the Kansas City locker room to photograph the team. The Chiefs thought it was funny if pictures were released with them wearing Mickey Mouse ears, should they win the AFL-NFL World Championship game.

Defensive back Frank Williamson was confident in his fellow Chief teammates going into the game. While playing for the Chiefs, Williamson became one of football's first self-promoters, nurturing the nickname "The Hammer" because he used his forearm to deliver karate-style blows to the heads of opposing players, especially wide receivers. To give his team some confidence, before Super Bowl I, Williamson garnered national headlines by boasting that he would knock the Green Bay Packers starting receivers, Carroll Dale and Boyd Dowler, out of the game. He stated, "Two hammers to (Boyd) Dowler, one to (Carroll) Dale should be enough."[12]

Even though they were heavily favored to win in the upcoming championship game, the Green Bay Packers felt the pressure too. This pressure stemmed from the fact that they felt that they had to win the game to save the NFL's claim of superiority over the AFL. The Packers were the dominating team for years in the more dominating league, and those in the NFL felt that the AFL was still an amateur league. It was up to the Chiefs and the AFL to equalize the playing field with a win. The Packer's legacy and pride of the NFL were on the line, something Packers coach Vince Lombardi was scared to death about going into the game. Losing was not an option.

For all these years that the war between the leagues ensued, Lombardi himself believed and spoke about the NFL's importance as pro football's only elite league. Lombardi felt that if anyone wanted to play pro football, the NFL was the place to be and not the AFL. Now with the big game approaching, Lombardi tried to shield his players from the pressure. He alone absorbed all the well wishes and demands from nearly every big name associated with the National Football League. But the Packers' players knew something was up with their great leader.

---

12. Kevin Jackson, Jeff Merron, & David Schoenfield, "100 Greatest SuperBowl Moments," ESPN, page 2, accessed October 2, 2018, http://www.espn.com/page2/s/superbowlmoments50.html.

Lombardi was always demanding because that was his nature and coaching style, and he didn't like getting advice from the outside world. He could avoid that distraction during the regular season, and even in the NFL title-game victory over the Dallas Cowboys. But this was too big, and Lombardi heard from everyone, including commissioner Pete Rozelle, New York Giants owner Wellington Mara, and Chicago Bears owner George Halas. They all implored him to beat the American Football League champion Kansas City Chiefs and uphold the honor of the NFL.[13]

In many ways, the assignment was not difficult because the Packers were a deeper, better, and more experienced team than the Chiefs. Under Lombardi, the Packers made it a habit of winning the most important games. But this time, the Packers played for more than themselves, their coaches, and their fans. They had to win, or the NFL's embarrassment would be all over the Packers and Lombardi. They would go down in history as losers to an inferior league.

Besides honor and pride and not disgracing their respective league, other outside factions contributed to the pressure for the Packers and Chiefs. Most of the outside pressure came from the networks broadcasting the game. The two television networks, CBS and NBC, would be televising the game using the same television feed, but with different announcers. The promotion of the big game by both networks was a marketing bonanza that helped influence the American public that this was the television event of the year. Besides, commercialization took center stage for companies, who all clamored to get their product advertised on the air viewed by the millions of people watching the game. The networks saw dollar signs by running commercials for major companies and charged a whopping $42,000 for a 30-second commercial. The two networks had paid $9.5 million to televise the game, and they wanted to profit every way they could to recapture that sum of money paid and hopefully earn a profit.[14]

---

13. Steve Silverman, "Vince Lombardi Felt Intense Heat in Super Bowl I," CBS (January 25, 2017), accessed October 2, 2018, https://newyork.cbslocal.com/2017/01/25/lombardi-pressure-super-bowl-i/.

14. Evan Weiner, "Super Bowl XLV, Vince Lombardi Wanted No Part Of The Super Bowl," *The Sport Digest* (February 3, 2011), accessed October 2, 2018, http://thesportdigest.com/2011/02/super-bowl-xlv-vince-lombardi-wanted-no-part-of-the-super-bowl/.

The balls that were used themselves were carefully designed and scrutinized at the highest levels. Both leagues couldn't even agree on which ball to use, so they compromised. When Green Bay was on offense, they used the Wilson "Duke" football. When Kansas City had the ball, they used the AFL sanctioned Spalding J5-V.[15]

The game itself was a mixed bag of highs and lows. Kansas City kept it close for 30 minutes. The Teams went into halftime with the Chiefs down 14 to 10 to the Packers. The second half would be a different story, as the relentless pressure applied by the Packers' defense swarmed the Chiefs' offense. The Packers were simply too much for the Chiefs to handle, as Green Bay outscored the Chiefs 21–0 in the final two quarters and won the game by a comfortable 35–10 margin.[16]

Vince Lombardi was visibly relieved at the end of the afternoon, and he paid the Chiefs a backhanded compliment when he spoke with the media about the game. He called Kansas City "a fine football team" but said several NFL teams were better.[17] Lombardi's fear of losing the game was justified by the media's reaction to the Packers winning the championship game. The game validated the media's contention that the NFL was the better of the two leagues, and the AFL was just second rate, as it was always assumed.[18]

SUPER BOWL II

The Packers began the 1967 pro football season with one thing in mind, which was to win their third consecutive NFL Championship. No team had ever done that before in the history of pro football. However, the task wasn't going to be any easier this year as the Packers were getting old. The 1967 season didn't go as smoothly as the other seasons, as the Packers were beginning to show signs of aging. Also, their heavily relied upon offensive running attack had to be restructured because the Packers' running backs from the previous year, future Pro Football Hall of Famers Paul Hornung and Jim Taylor, had left the team. Their replacements, Elijah

15. Silverman, "Vince Lombardi," accessed October 2, 2018.
16. Ibid.
17. Ibid.
18. Ibid.

Pitts and Jim Grabowski, were both injured early in the season, forcing Green Bay coach Vince Lombardi to use veteran reserve running back Donny Anderson and rookie Travis Williams. Fullbacks Chuck Mercein and Ben Wilson, who were signed as free agents after being discarded by many other teams, were also used to help compensate for the loss of Hornung and Taylor. Meanwhile, the team's 33-year-old veteran quarterback Bart Starr had missed four games during the season with various injuries and finished the season with nearly twice as many interceptions (17) as touchdown passes (9). As a result, the Packers finished 9-4-1.

Simultaneously, the Dallas Cowboys were having a good season in 1967 and finished 9-5. This set up a rematch for the NFL Championship in 1967, except in frozen Lambeau Field, in Green Bay and not in Texas, at the Cotton Bowl, as the year before.

The "Ice Bowl" for the National Football League Championship was played on December 31, 1967. The game itself etched itself long ago in football lore. At game time, the temperature was 15 below zero, with wind chill in today's calculations at minus -48. It was so cold that they even called off an elaborate halftime show, leaving the spectators free to swing their hands and stamp their feet to keep warm in the concrete stands. As referee Norm Schachter blew his metal whistle to signal the start of play, it froze to his lips. As he attempted to free the whistle from his lips, the skin ripped off, and his lips began to bleed. The conditions were so hostile that instead of forming a scab, the blood froze to his lip. Besides, the other officials were unable to use their whistles after the opening kick-off. For the rest of the game, the officials used voice commands and calls to end plays and officiate the game. At one point during the frozen game, CBS announcer Frank Gifford said on air, "I'm going to take a bite of my coffee."[19]

The Game came down to the wire when quarterback Bart Starr dove into the end zone, sealing the game with a 21–17 win for the Packers. They had just won their 3rd straight NFL Championship. Next up was the AFL-NFL World Championship.

---

19. David Maraniss, *When Pride Still Mattered, A Life of Vince Lombardi* (NY: Simon & Schuster, 2000), reprint edition, 420.

In the AFL, the Raiders, led by head coach John Rauch, had stormed to the top of the league with a 13–1 regular-season record (their only defeat was an October 7 loss to the New York Jets, 27–14), and went on to crush the Houston Oilers, 40–7, in the AFL Championship game. They had led all AFL and NFL teams in scoring with 468 points. Starting quarterback Daryle Lamonica had thrown for 3,228 yards, and an AFL best 30 touchdown passes. The main strength of the Raiders was their defense, nicknamed "The 11 Angry Men."

In contrast to the frigid conditions earlier in the day at the NFL championship game in Green Bay, the temperature for the AFL title game in northern California was 47 °F (8 °C). The Raiders were 10½-point favorites as hosts. When the game was finished, Oakland covered the points and won 40–7. They shredded the Oilers with 364 yards of offense, including 263 yards rushing, while allowing just 146 total yards and 38 yards on the ground. The Raiders defense also forced three turnovers and lost none themselves.[20]

The AFL-NFL World Championship was played on January 15, 1968, in the Orange Bowl in Miami, the second year in a row that the stadium hosted the Championship game. Super Bowl II is a long-forgotten contest played by two iconic, old school football teams. Everyone expected the Packers to win over the Raiders.[21]

Even though they won the AFC Championship convincingly over Houston, the Raiders limped into Super Bowl II. The entire team was banged up after a very physically exhausting 13–1 regular season. Their one loss came against the Jets. The high margin of victory (40–7) in the AFL championship game against the Houston Oilers did not reflect the team's fatigue. Getting to this Super Bowl took just about everything they had. Both the Raiders and Packers had three weeks rest before the game. The Raiders' primary loss to injury was running back Clem Daniels. With Daniels in top form, the Raiders running game had the tremendous speed to complement their power with guys like Pete Banaszak and

20. Hal Bock, "Oakland romps past Houston, 40–7; meets Packers in Super Bowl Jan. 14" (January 1, 1968), *Youngstown Vindicator* (Ohio), Associated Press, 55.

21. Al's Wingman, "The Business of the Raiders' is Business" (October 4, 2008), accessed October 2, 2018, http://alswingman.blogspot.com/2008/10/al-davis-fires-his-head-coach-even.html.

Hewritt Dixon. An overall healthier Raiders team may have given the Packers a better game.[22]

The Packers won the game 33–14. The second world championship was an end of an era for pro football for two reasons. One was that rumors that had been flying throughout the NFL, that this would be Vince Lombardi's final game as head coach for the Packers. Two weeks later, Lombardi did indeed resign as the head coach of the Green Bay Packers. That segued into the second reason: the end of the NFL dominance. The next Super Bowl would be the coming of young Joe Namath and a guarantee of victory that seemed ridiculous against a superior opponent in the Baltimore Colts of the NFL.

SUPER BOWL III

Now that the NFL had won two World Championships, they were poised to win another. The Baltimore Colts, coached by Don Shula, had a tremendous 1968 season. Baltimore posted a 13–1 record during the 1968 NFL season before defeating the Cleveland Browns, 34–0, in the 1968 NFL Championship Game. Their rivals, the New York Jets, finished the 1968 AFL season at 11–3 and defeated the Oakland Raiders, 27–23, in the 1968 AFL Championship Game. This was the first time the term "Super Bowl" was used for the AFL-NFL World Championship.

The stigma of the NFL being the superior league still was etched in the minds of many. This was seemingly confirmed by the results of the first two inter-league championship games, in January 1967 and 1968, whereby Green Bay both games by wide margins. Most sportswriters and fans believed that AFL teams were less talented than NFL clubs and expected the Colts to defeat the Jets by a wide margin.

Adding to the pressure of the game was that coach Wilbur Charles "Weeb" Ewbank of the Jets had helped the Baltimore Colts franchise to greatness ten years earlier, as their head coach. The Baltimore Colts had won the 1958 and 1959 NFL championships under Ewbank. In the following years, however, the Colts failed to make the playoffs, and the Colts dismissed Ewbank after a 7–7 record in 1962. He was soon hired by

22. Ibid.

New York's new AFL franchise, which had just changed its name from the Titans to the Jets. In Ewbank's place, Baltimore hired an untested young head coach, Don Shula, who would also become one of the game's greatest coaches. Ewbank's past caught up with him going into Super Bowl III, now getting a chance to exact revenge on the organization that fired him.

Along with the pressure to win the AFL-NFL World Championship, Ewbank knew that the superiority image that the NFL held in the eyes of pro football had to be smashed. The task was a daunting one. It was a golden opportunity for the Jets and the AFL to prove themselves, but it was against a more talented and heavily favored team who had only one loss in the whole season.

Baltimore's dominance of the 1968 NFL season and the overconfidence of the NFL in winning the first two Super Bowls didn't matter to the Jets' quarterback Joe Namath. He "guaranteed" that his team would defeat the much-favored Baltimore Colts in the world championship game that year.[23] What made this bold prediction by Namath seem so ludicrous was that the Colts finished the regular season by winning ten games in a row, four by shutouts. Their quarterback Earl Morrall, who had replaced the legendary Johnny Unitas after an injury, was having a great season with a league-leading passing performance. On their way to meeting the Jets in the Super Bowl, the Colts had decisively beaten the Cleveland Browns 34–0 in the NFL championship game. Given this performance, many regarded Colts as one of the best teams of all time[24]

The Jets were the outsiders in professional football going into Super Bowl III, coming from that "upstart" football league. Even with two AFL-NFL Championships played against the NFL, many still regarded the AFL as lightweight and in no way the equal of NFL. Former NFL star and then Atlanta coach Norm Van Brocklin also ridiculed Namath and the AFL before the game, saying, "This will be Namath's first professional football game." Writers from NFL cities insisted it would take the AFL several more years to be truly competitive with the NFL.[25]

23. Jack Doyle, "I Guarantee It. Joe Namath" (December 23, 2009), accessed October 3, 2018, PopHistoryDig.com/Topics/Je Namath/.

24. Ibid.

25. Ibid.

Much of the game's hype had to do with the worth of each league's level of play—AFL vs. NFL. A merger of the two leagues was then in the air, looming next year in 1970, and many doubted that AFL teams were truly worthy of merging with the NFL. Still, Namath's message was the same whenever he was asked about the game: "We're going to win. I guarantee it." [26]

It would still have to come down to the game itself. On any given Sunday, anything could happen. And it did for the Jets and the AFL that Sunday, on January 12, 1969. From the start, the breaks went the Jets' way. Quarterback Earl Morrall, who won the NFL MVP award filling in for the injured Johnny Unitas, fell apart. Morrall led the Colts inside the Jets' 20-yard line three times in the first half but came away with zero points on a missed field goal and two end-zone interceptions, one tipped and one going off a Colt receiver's shoulder pads. Maybe he felt the pressure after Namath had said at least five AFL quarterbacks, including Jets backup Babe Parilli, were better than Morrall.

Namath engineered an 80-yard drive after Morrall's second interception, culminating in Matt Snell's four-yard TD run midway through the second quarter for the first AFL lead in Super Bowl history.[27]

By the 4th quarter, the Jets were up 16–0. Seeing a need to shake up the offense, Baltimore coach, Don Shula, put in a sore-armed Unitas and benched Earl Morrall to rally the Colts. This seemed to work as the Colts started to rally in the fourth quarter. Baltimore finally scored a touchdown on Hill's 1-yard run to cut their deficit to 16–7, but with only 3:19 left in the game. The Colts then recovered an onside kick and drove to the Jets' 19-yard line with three consecutive completions by Unitas, but his next three passes fell incomplete. Instead of kicking a field goal and attempting another onside kick (which would have been necessary), they opted to throw on 4th down, and the pass fell incomplete, turning the ball over on downs. That ended any chance of a Baltimore comeback, as the Jets ran the ball for six plays before being forced to punt. When the

26. Ibid.
27. Joe Belock, "Super Bowl III: Joe Namath leads NY Jets to arguably the biggest upset in history over Baltimore Colts," *New York Daily News* (December 20, 2013), accessed October 3, 2018, http://www .nydailynews.com/sports/football/super-bowl-iii-namath-jets-shock-baltimore-colts-16-7-article-1.1553628.

Colts got the ball back, only eight seconds remained in the game. The Colts then attempted two more passes before the game ended

The Jets did the impossible and won the Super Bowl 16 -7. Years later, Earl Morrall said, "I thought we would win handily. We'd only lost twice in our last 30 games. I'm still not sure what happened that day at the Orange Bowl; however, it's still hard to account for."[28] Wrote Matt Snell, "The most distinct image I have from that whole game is of Ordell Braase and some other guys—not so much Mike Curtis—having a bewildered look. Namath finished the game having completed 17 of his 28 passes. He is the only quarterback to win Super Bowl MVP without throwing a touchdown pass.[29]

With the victory in Super Bowl III, the AFL finally bested the NFL in a title championship. The Jets had just won an iconic victory, and the AFL found new respect from the pro football world. This would set up the showdown one year later in 1970 when the last AFL-NFL World Championship would be played before the merger would combine both leagues. Could the AFL equalize the score with the NFL and make it two championships each league won before the merger?

SUPER BOWL IV

Super Bowl IV was the fourth and last AFL-NFL World Championship Game between the two leagues, and the second one (after Super Bowl III) that officially bears the name "Super Bowl."The game was played on January 11, 1970.

Despite the AFL's New York Jets winning the previous season's Super Bowl, many sportswriters and fans thought it was a fluke and continued to believe that the NFL was still superior to the AFL. Kansas City returned to the Super Bowl in 1970, but the experts fully expected the more dominant Minnesota Vikings to defeat the Chiefs. The Vikings entered the Super Bowl as 12.5 to 13-point favorites. Minnesota posted a 12–2 record during the 1969 NFL season before defeating the Cleveland

28. Shelby Strother, "It came with a Guarantee," *The Super Bowl: Celebrating a Quarter-Century of America's Greatest Game* (NY: Simon and Schuster, 1990), 8.

29. Peary, Danny, and Matt Snell, "Super Bowl III," *Super Bowl: The Game of Their Lives* (NY: Macmillan, 1997), 85.

Browns, 27–7, in the 1969 NFL Championship Game. The Chiefs finished the 1969 AFL season at 11–3 and defeated the Oakland Raiders,
17–7, in the 1969 AFL Championship Game.[30]

Even though it had been three years since the Chiefs played in Super
Bowl I, they were still viewed as a second-class team because of losing the
first World Championship game to Green Bay in 1967. Adding to the
lack of respect was that the Chiefs had the second-best record in the AFC
in 1969 at 11–3, whereas the Oakland Raiders were 12-1-1. Both the
Chiefs and Raiders were overlooked by many even to win the AFL crown
for the 1969 season. In addition, many still saw the miracle of Super
Bowl III continuing for the New York Jets, even with a 10–4 record. The
afterglow of beating a superior Colts team in Super Bowl III gave the Jets
an image in people's minds that they were still the little engine that could
and that they were going to be back in Super Bowl IV, representing the
AFL. But fate was not kind to the Jets, as the Chiefs beat the defending world champions in the first round of the playoffs. Surprisingly, the
Chiefs then beat a superior Raiders team in the AFL championship, who
had just pummeled the Oilers 56–7 in the first round of the AFL playoffs.
Even with these two very surprising victories to get to the Super Bowl,
Kansas City still could not garner much respect for the big game. It wasn't
Kansas City's fault for the lack of respect. It was just that they were facing
an opponent that was so dominating in the Minnesota Vikings. To many,
it was hard to believe that the Chiefs would win the game; nevertheless,
even make it a competitive match up with the "purple people eaters."

As for the team in the land of 10,000 lakes, the Vikings had a stellar
12–2 record during the regular season. The optimism was understand-
able entering Super Bowl IV, along with the Vikings leading the league
in points scored and fewest points allowed. Hard-nosed quarterback Joe
Kapp led a deep offensive unit, with the "Purple People Eaters" dominating opposing offenses with their vicious defensive line, consisting of Jim
Marshall, Carl Eller, Alan Page, and Gary Larsen.[31]

---

30. Super Bowl IV, Super Bowl I–X Collector's Set, NFL Productions, LLC, 2003.
31. "Super Bowl IV Review," Lootmeister Sports, accessed October 4, 2018, http://www.lootmeister
.com/superbowl/iv.php.

The Chiefs, having lost the first Super Bowl, were looking for redemption. Chiefs quarterback Len Dawson was getting another chance in the Bowl and had an ax to grind, having been dismissed as subpar in the "old league" before finding new life with the AFL and the Chiefs.[32] Dawson played this game under the pressures of a week's harassment from the publicity linking him with a gambling investigation in Detroit, even though pro football's official family had proclaimed him "clean."[33]

The game began with the Vikings looking like they would drive deep into Chiefs territory, only to stall out on the Chiefs' 40-yard line and were forced to punt. The Chiefs then took the ball 42 yards to set up for a 48-yard field goal attempt that Jan Stenerud nailed to give the Chiefs a 3–0 lead. After stopping Minnesota on their next drive, the Chiefs drove downfield and into field goal position again, allowing Stenerud to connect on a 32-yard field goal at the beginning of the second quarter to go up 6–0.[34]

The Chiefs and Vikings then traded turnovers. First, Chiefs' safety Johnny Robinson recovered Vikings' John Henderson's fumble, but then Minnesota interception-machine Paul Krause picked off Len Dawson. After the Chiefs pinned the Vikings down and forced them to punt, they took over on the Minnesota 44-yard line. The Kansas City drive ran out of gas in the Viking's red zone, but they went up 9–0 after Stenerud kicked a 25-yard field goal midway through the second quarter.[35]

More bad news came to the Vikings when their kick returner Charlie West fumbled the ball on the ensuing kickoff, giving Kansas City excellent field possession at the Minnesota 19. After getting sacked by Jim Marshall. Dawson got a critical first down before Mike Garrett ran it in from the 5-yard line to put the Chiefs up 16–0. Super Bowl IV just went from bad to worse for the Vikings. Trying to rebound, the Vikings drove

---

32. Ibid.

33. Norm Miller, "Super Chiefs Wreck Vikings, 23–7," *New York Daily News* (December 21, 2003), accessed October 4, 2018, http://www.nydailynews.com/sports/football/super-bowl-iv-super-chiefs-wreck-vikings-23-7-article-1.1552249.

34. "Super Bowl IV Review," accessed October 4, 2018.

35. Ibid.

again late in the half, but a missed field goal sent the 12.5-point favorite Minnesota Vikings into the locker-room down 16–0.[36]

The second half began optimistically enough for the Vikings, who seemed to wake up, taking their first possession for a touchdown, as Dave Osborn ran it in from 4 yards out to narrow the deficit to 16–7. But as soon as things looked to be getting better for the Vikings, Kansas City immediately answered. Len Dawson connected with Otis Taylor for a 46-yard catch that effectively sealed the Vikings' fate.[37]

In the 4th quarter, Joe Kapp threw two interceptions and was eventually taken out of the game after a crushing sack. His replacement Gary Cuozzo didn't fare well either, as he threw an interception of his own. While the Vikings made key mistakes, Kansas City cruised to their first Super Bowl victory. The Super Bowl MVP award winner was vindicated from his previous showing in Super Bowl I. That man was Kansas City quarterback Len Dawson, who put himself on the map with this monumental win, and furthered the cause of the AFL, which now had to be taken seriously.[38] This victory by the AFL squared the Super Bowl series with the NFL at two games apiece. The two leagues now would merge into one after the game.

One interesting tidbit of Superbowl IV was NFL Films trying a new approach to filming a game. The night before the game, Ed Sabol of NFL Films approached Vikings coach Bud Grant about being miked for the game. Grant declined, but Kansas City head coach Hank Stram accepted. This has led to one of the best-known and most popular of the NFL Films Super Bowl footage due to the constant chatter and wise-cracking of Stram. Ed Sabol had his number one sound man, Jack Newman, who also wired Vince Lombardi in a previous playoff game—place the microphone on Stram. Newman, a multiple Emmy award-winning soundman and cameraman, shot Stram for the entire game as well as monitored the sound to make sure it continued to work. The success and popularity of this first Super Bowl wiring of a winning head coach

---

36. Ibid.
37. Ibid.
38. Ibid.

led to 24 years of Newman continuing to wire players and coaches for NFL Films.

As both the Chiefs and the cameras rolled, Stram clamored for his team to run "65 toss power trap" and to "keep matriculating the ball down the field." The Chiefs used the game as a crusade for the American Football League and wore "AFL-10" patches, which referred to the league's 10-year existence.[39] Some excerpts of Stram include:

- To Len Dawson: "C'mon Lenny! Pump it in there, baby! Just keep matriculating the ball down the field, boys!"
- Observing the confusion in the Vikings' defense: "Kassulke (Viking SS Karl Kassulke) was running around there like it was a Chinese fire drill. They didn't know where Mike (Garrett) was. I didn't know where he was! They look like they're flat as hell."
- Before the Chiefs' first touchdown, Stram sent in the play "65 toss power trap." When the Chiefs scored on the play, Stram laughed while yelling to his players on the bench, "Was it there, boys? Was that there, rats? Nice going, baby! Haaa-ha-ha-hahaha! Haaa! The mentor! 65 toss power trap! Yaaa-haaa-haaa-haha! Yeah-haha! I tell ya that thing was there, yes sir boys! Haa-ha-ha-ha-ha! Wooo!"
- As the referees were spotting the ball before measurement to determine if the Vikings got a first down, Stram yelled to the officials, "Make sure you mark it right! Oh, you lost your place! Measure it, take the chains out there! Oh, they didn't make it! My God, they made that by an inch! He gave them an extra foot. Bad! Very bad!"
- Another time, the refs overruled what looked like a Minnesota fumble. Stram: "Mr. Official, let me ask you something. How can six of you miss a play like that?

---

39. Kansas City Chiefs, Chiefs History, accessed October 19, 2018, https://web.archive.org /web/20070823170852/http://www.kcchiefs.com/history/70s/.

Huh? All six of you! When the ball jumped out of there as soon as we made contact? . . . No. What?"

- After Frank Pitts gained on the reverse in the third quarter, when the chains were stretched, and the Chiefs indeed had the first down, Stram was then heard saying to the refs, "Ya did good, you marked it good. You did a helluva job, nice going!"
- On Otis Taylor's touchdown reception that clinched the game, Stram is heard yelling and laughing.[40]

---

40. Super Bowl IV, Hank Stram, NFL FILMS, NFL - 1970 - NFL Film - Super Bowl IV Memories - Chiefs VS Vikings - Coach Stram's Miked On Sideline, accessed October 19, 2018, https://www.youtube .com/watch?v=Jd0EMw7YMWI.

5

THE HISTORY OF THE BALTIMORE COLTS – 1947-1969

The Baltimore Colts were born in the NFL's rival pro football league, the All-American Football Conference (AAFC). Baltimore was granted a franchise in the AAFC after the Miami Seahawks franchise folded in 1946. The team would be named the Colts in honor of Baltimore's rich history with racing and breeding of horses.[1] Every year, after the Kentucky Derby, in May, the Preakness is run in Maryland. It is the second horse race in the triple crown of racing along with the Kentucky Derby and the Belmont Stakes in New York.

The Colts would incur moderate success in the AAFC and became one of only three teams to join the NFL in 1950 during the merger between the two leagues. However, the team could not make a profit and folded after just one season. At the same time, the New York Yankees, another former AAFC team that had joined the NFL in 1950, also was having financial problems and was about to be sold to Baltimore investors in 1951. This was ironic because in major league baseball, back in 1903, the Baltimore Orioles were moved from Baltimore to New York.

1. Frank Fleming, "Baltimore Colts," *Sports Encyclopedia* (July 5, 2002), accessed October 5, 2018, http://www.sportsecyclopedia.com/nfl/balticolts/baltcolts.html.

However, the NFL bought the team instead and had them play in Dallas under the name "Texans." This, too, was also ironic for two reasons. One, when the AFL was established in 1959, owner Lamar Hunt decided to call his team in Dallas "the Texans," which was the same name as the now defunct team in the NFL, and two, the Dallas Cowboys were established because of the creation of the Texans franchise in the NFL. They would also be the Colts' opponent in Super Bowl V.

However, the 1952 NFL Texans were a miserable failure, and by the middle of the season, they were operating out of Hershey, Pennsylvania, and playing all their games on the road. The team would fold at the end of the season. However, it would open the door for Baltimore to get a second chance to get an NFL franchise and replace the failing Texans. Baltimore was granted a franchise that would pay homage to the former team by carrying the name "Colts."[2]

In 1954, Weeb Ewbank was named the Colts' head coach, and he began a steady building program that put his team over .500 for the first time in 1957. The Colts didn't have another losing season for the next 14 years. Powered by a sensational young quarterback Johnny Unitas, who would play his first full season in 1957, and a strong supporting cast that included such future Pro Football Hall of Famers such as Artie Donovan, Gino Marchetti, Raymond Berry, Lenny Moore, and Jim Parker, the Colts would become an elite team throughout the 1960s. The Colts would win back-to-back NFL championships in both 1958 and 1959, and again in 1968. Eventually, Ewbank would meet his old team in Super Bowl III, as coach of the New York Jets.[3]

The Colts helped pro football gain a more national audience in the 1958 NFL title clash against the New York Giants. The game was played before the largest television audience ever up to that time, and it did much to increase fan enthusiasm and interest for pro football. Television audiences saw the young John Unitas perfect the art of a crafty quarterback who engineered long drives for the Colts that led to the tying field

2. Ibid.

3. "Baltimore Colts: Team History," The Pro Football Hall of Fame, accessed October 5, 2018, https://www.profootballhof.com/teams/indianapolis-colts/team-history/.

goal in the 4th quarter and the winning touchdown in overtime, when running back Alan Ameche barreled into the end zone to propel the Colts to a 23–17 victory.

The Colts remained dominant for five more years, but with injuries and age taking their toll, the Colts struggled in the 1962 season, finishing with a 7–7 record. When the season ended, Weeb Ewbank would be fired as the Colts' head coach and replaced by a young Don Shula, who had played with the Colts in their inaugural season of 1953.

The Don Shula era in Baltimore began with the 1963 season, and the team did better than the year before by winning one more game, and they went on to finish the season with an 8–6 record for third place in the NFL West.[4] Not too bad for a young rookie coach, who was reshaping the Colts. The team was still led by quarterback John Unitas, who was Shula's teammate during his final year as a player in Baltimore. The team's primary receivers were Raymond Berry and tight end John Mackey, while defensive end Gino Marchetti anchored the up and coming defense.

In 1964, after losing the first game of the season in Minnesota to the Vikings, the Colts embarked on a ten-game winning streak on the way to winning the NFL Western Division Championship with a 12–2 record, as quarterback Johnny Unitas won the NFL MVP with 2,824 yards passing[5] In the NFL Championship Game, the Colts faced the Cleveland Browns. However, the Colts would stumble in Cleveland, as they were lambasted 27–0 in the NFL championship game.

Coming off a magical season the year before, the 1965 Colts were poised to be a strong contender for the NFL Western Division Championship. However, injuries to quarterbacks Johnny Unitas and Gary Cuozzo forced the Colts to turn to the third-stringer Tom Matte. In a must-win season-ending game in Los Angeles against the Rams, and wearing a plastic wrist brace that carried the team's list of plays, Matte led Baltimore to a 20–17 victory that gave the Colts a share of the Western Division Title

---

4. "1963 Baltimore Colts Statistics & Players," Pro Football Reference, accessed October 5, 2018, https://www.webcitation.org/6KwWCUXYP?url=http://www.pro-football-reference.com/teams/clt/1963.htm.

5. "Baltimore Colts: Team History," accessed October 5, 2018.

at 10-3-1 with the Green Bay Packers.[6] Although the Packers won both regular-season games over the Colts, no tie-breaking system was put into place at the time in 1965. A playoff game was required to determine the Western Conference champion, who would host the Eastern Conference champion, Cleveland Browns, for the NFL title. The Colts and Packers would battle into overtime with the game tied at 10. However, there was no magic for the Colts this time as the Packers won the game on a field goal with a little over a minute into the second overtime period.

In 1966, the Colts stumbled a bit throughout the season and finished with a 9–5 record. They came in second place and failed to make it to the playoffs, as Green Bay won the division. In 1967, the Colts finished the regular season with 11 wins, 1 loss, and 2 ties, the same record in the Western Conference's Coastal division with the Los Angeles Rams. However, the Colts lost the tiebreaker based on point differential in head-to-head games and thus did not make the playoffs. The Colts' official winning percentage of .917 (based on the NFL's non-counting of ties for such purposes before 1972) is the best in North American professional sports history for a non-playoff-qualifying team.

The 1968 Colts team, of course, is best known for coming up short in Super Bowl III against the AFL's New York Jets. Many historians believe this was the best team that Don Shula ever coached, and one of his defensive assistants was the late Chuck Noll, who would coach the Pittsburgh Steelers to four Super Bowl Championships. This Colts defense held 10 of 14 regular season opponents to 10 or fewer points. Late in the season, they gave up one touchdown over 25 quarters, including a string of 16 straight quarters w/out a touchdown allowed.[7]

But the Colts proved unlucky again in the big game. With Super Bowl III, the AFL-NFL battle for supremacy well etched into the minds of owners, players, the press, and the fans, the Colts were a huge disappointment. With a 13–1 dominating record, they could not score against the Jets until the 4th quarter. In the end, the game was a disaster for the

6. Ibid.
7. *Top Ten Single Season Defense: Honorable Mention*, accessed October 5, 2018, https://taylorblitz times.com/tag/1968-baltimore-colts/.

Colts and their psyche going forward. In the hour after Super Bowl III, the Baltimore dressing room was a scene of sore losers and finger pointers. Most of the fingers were pointed at quarterback Earl Morrall and coach Don Shula. "We played the game like an AFL team, throwing the ball deep all day," wide receiver Willie Richardson said. Veteran defensive end Ordell Braase, outplayed by Winston Hill, the Jets' young left tackle, who had been driven off the Colts' roster by Braase years before, was still resentful of Namath: "Football is a team sport. If he thinks he can go out and do it alone, he's crazy. He had a lot of help . . ."

"We beat ourselves," tight end John Mackey said wearily. Linebacker Dennis Gaubatz remarked about the surprising Jets, "They still don't impress me. The breaks didn't come our way; we're a better ball club." Bill Curry, who would become a big-time college head coach years later, said, "It seems stupid to say, but we played ten or twelve teams better than the Jets." Curry was correct. It did seem stupid to say.[8]

A BROKEN COLTS TEAM, AND THEIR MOVE TO ANOTHER CONFERENCE DURING REALIGNMENT

The loss of Super Bowl III and the 1964 NFL championship overshadowed the Colts' dominance during many regular seasons during the 1960s. They were a superb team who should have won a few championships but won none. Perhaps the biggest effect of the Colts' loss to the Jets is that it shattered the image that the AFL was not strong enough to merge with the NFL. Even as satisfying as the Jets' victory over the Colts had been, Joe Namath and the Jets had still not convinced the NFL owners that they should welcome their AFL counterparts into the newly merged league when their shotgun marriage was to be consummated in time for the 1970 season. The rivalry and hatred were still that strong even after four years of knowing that the merger was coming. That was the atmosphere when the "new" NFL convened in Palm Springs, California, in March of 1969 to start discussing the realignment of the league as outlined in the original merger agreement.

---

8. Felser, *Birth of the New NFL*, 2922–2930, Kindle.

During the many weeks of going back and forth on fusing the two leagues, an agreement was finally settled upon. On Saturday, May 10, 1969, Commissioner Pete Rozelle announced that three NFL teams: the Pittsburgh Steelers, Baltimore Colts, and Cleveland Browns, had agreed to switch to the newly formed AFC. The realignment of the remaining thirteen teams in the NFC would be the subject of a later meeting. As it turned out, there were many more meetings with further wrangling, so the last strings of the great realignment wouldn't be tied until January of 1970. There was one other item about the joining of the Steelers, Colts, and Browns to their former AFL adversaries: each of those teams would receive a nice chunk of change of $3 million each for joining their AFL rivals.[9]

The Colts had to play the entire 1969 season under a cloud of disgrace for giving the AFL some credibility with a Super Bowl victory. If that wasn't bad enough, their agreement in the off-season to jump to the newly formed AFC conference with all of the teams from the rival league of the AFL in 1970 angered the Baltimore faithful. Colts' fans and players alike were shocked and amazed at how the franchise converted to the other league's side. They just took the money and ran away from the NFL and their past.

Whether it was the loss of Super Bowl III or having an identity crisis due to realigning to the enemy in the next year, the 1969 season was a dismal one for the Colts. The team was unable to gel like the year before, and the Colts posted an 8-5-1 record. They were never a factor in the race for the Coastal Division title in the AFL.

Following the tumultuous 1969 season, head coach Don Shula, who fell out of favor with the owner, Carroll Rosenbloom, was allowed to resign to take the coaching job with Miami Dolphins. Assistant Coach Don McCafferty would replace Shula in Baltimore.[10] With the merger and playing in the freshly minted AFC conference, the beginning of a new era was dawning for the Colts. Would they succeed in a new league in a new era of pro football?

---

9. Ibid., 3013–3018.

10. Fleming, "Baltimore Colts," accessed October 5, 2018.

6

THE HISTORY OF THE DALLAS COWBOYS – 1960-1969

UP AND RUNNING IN DALLAS

Like the Baltimore Colts, the Dallas Cowboys franchise got off to a rocky start when they entered the league in 1960. An NFL team had failed in the city of Dallas nearly a decade before, and the prospects did not look good for a team to gain many fans to profit in the Dallas area of the Lone Star State. Clint Murchison, Jr., and Bedford Wynne were awarded an expansion franchise in the NFL at the annual league meeting in Miami Beach in 1959. Murchison and his surviving brother inherited their father's wealth and oil business interests to which Clint Jr. added financial ventures of his own. These included establishing the NFL's Dallas Cowboys franchise, real estate development, construction, home building, restaurants, and financing the offshore pirate radio station called Radio Nord.[1] Bedford Wynne was present as an investor when the Dallas franchise was awarded. At the time, most people believed Wynne was a major partner in the Dallas Cowboys franchise. While he was a co-founder, he only owned five percent of the team. However, he was the

1. Frank Fleming, "The Dallas Cowboys," *Sports Encyclopedia* (July 11, 2002), accessed October 7, 2018, www.sportsecyclopedia.com/nfl/dallas/cowboys.html.

director and secretary of this newly formed team and is the person who announced that Tex Schramm would be the team's general manager. He is pretty much the "forgotten" founder" of the Dallas Cowboys.[2]

There was a snag, however, with putting the team into Dallas. Initially, the formation of an NFL expansion team in Texas was met with strong opposition by Washington Redskins owner George Preston Marshall. This was no surprise because despite being located in the nation's capital, Marshall's Redskins had enjoyed a monopoly as the only NFL team to represent the American South for several decades. This came as little surprise to would-be team owners Clint Murchison Jr. and Bedford Wynne. To ensure the birth of their expansion team, the men bought the rights to the Redskins fight song, "Hail to the Redskins" and threatened to refuse to allow Washington to play the song at games. Needing the song, which had become a staple for his "professional football team of Dixie," Marshall changed his mind, and the city of Dallas was granted an NFL franchise on January 28, 1960. This early confrontation between the two franchises helped trigger what became one of the more heated National Football League rivalries, which continues today.

The NFL, however, was being pressed by their new rival league, the AFL, to set up a team in Dallas. AFL founder, Lamar Hunt, set up the Dallas Texans franchise and had an open market in the city with no competition. The NFL felt the pressure to put a franchise of their own in Texas, as not to lose the Texas market because the AFL also created a market in Houston. The AFL would own Texas if the NFL did not move quickly. The NFL moved quickly, but the new team was hampered with obstacles right in the beginning. The franchise was admitted to the league when it was too late to participate in the 1960 NFL college draft. The consequence was that the Cowboys did not have quality picks from the college level. As a result, majority owner Murchison signed two college players, quarterback Don Meredith from SMU, and running back Don Perkins from New Mexico, to personal services contracts before the draft (and before the franchise was voted into the league). The NFL honored

---

2. Bedford Wynne, Jr., Find A Grave (September 19, 2010), accessed October 7, 2018, https://www .findagrave.com/memorial/58907002/bedford-shelmire-wynne.

both Meredith and Perkins' contracts after the franchise was voted in, although the Baltimore Colts drafted Perkins in the ninth round, and Meredith was also selected by the Chicago Bears in the third round after owner George Halas made the pick to help ensure that the expansion Cowboys got off to a solid start. The franchise was allowed to retain both players but had to give their third-round and ninth-round choices in the 1962 NFL draft to the Bears and Colts, respectively.[3]

On March 13, 1960, the franchise selected 36 players in an expansion draft. Each of the other 12 NFL teams could protect 25 players from their 36-man roster. The new Dallas team was given 24 hours to select three players from those unprotected by each other teams.

The team was first known as the Dallas Steers, then the Dallas Rangers. On March 19, 1960, the organization announced that the team name was the Cowboys to avoid confusion with the American Association Dallas Rangers baseball team.[4] With the addition of General Manager Tex Schramm and Tom Landry as head coach, the pieces were intact for the future in Dallas.

Tex Schramm would be an innovator of the game besides being a great general manager for the Dallas Cowboys. He was known for advocating for many changes and innovations that helped modernize the NFL. These included instant replay, using computer technology in scouting, multi-color striping of the 20- and 50-yard lines, 30-second clock between plays, extra-wide sideline borders, wind-direction stripes on the goal post uprights, the referee's microphone, headsets in the quarterback's helmet for hearing plays, and the Dallas Cowboys Cheerleaders.[5] While leading the league's competition committee, he oversaw rule changes such as using overtime in the regular season, putting the official time on the scoreboard, moving the goalposts from the front of the end zone to the back, and protecting quarterbacks through the in-the-grasp rule. Schramm's desire for a more comprehensive scouting combine led

3. "Dallas Lands Six Players," *Milwaukee Sentinel*, UPI, March 16, 1960, part 2, 4.

4. "Dallas Eleven Changes Made," *New York Times* (March 20, 1960), S4.

5. Gerald Eskenazi, "Tex Schramm Is Dead at 83; Builder of 'America's Team'," *New York Times* (July 16, 2003), accessed October 7, 2018, https://www.nytimes.com/2003/07/16/sports/tex-schramm-is-dead-at-83-builder-of-america-s-team.html.

to the annual offseason NFL Scouting Combine in Indianapolis.[6] Don Shula said of Schramm, "I truly believe he had as much, or more, to do with the success of professional football as anyone who has ever been connected with the league."[7]

TOM LANDRY

Tom Landry, too, was an innovator. He invented the now-popular "4–3 defense" while serving as Giant's defensive coordinator.[8] It was called "4–3" because it featured four down lineman (two ends and two defensive tackles on either side of the offensive center) and three linebackers—middle, left, and right. The innovation was the middle linebacker. Previously, a lineman was placed over the center. But Landry had this person stand up and move back two yards. The Giants' middle linebacker was the legendary Sam Huff. Huff remembered: "Landry built the 4–3 defense around me. It revolutionized defense and opened the door for all the variations of zones and man-to-man coverage, which are used in conjunction with it today."[9]

Landry also invented and popularized the use of keys (analyzing offensive tendencies) to determine what the offense might do.

When Landry was hired by the Dallas Cowboys, he became concerned with the Green Bay Packers Coach Vince Lombardi's "Run to Daylight" idea, in which the running back went to an open space than a specifically assigned hole. Landry reasoned that the best counter was a defense that flowed to daylight and blotted it out. To do this, he refined the 4–3 defense by moving two of the four linemen off the line of scrimmage one yard and varied which linemen did this based on where the Cowboys thought the offense might run. This change was called the "Flex Defense" because it altered its alignment to counter what the offense might do. Thus, three such Flex Defenses were developed, strong, weak, and "tackle"—where both defensive tackles were off the line of scrimmage. The idea with the

---

6. Ibid.
7. Ibid.
8. *The Dallas Morning News* (January 29, 2007), accessed October 7, 2018.
9. "Describing 'The Innovator'," *The Sporting News*, archived from the original on December 1, 2005, accessed October 7, 2018.

flexed linemen was to improve pursuit angles to stop the Green Bay running sweep play—a popular play of the 1960s.[10] The Flex Defense was also innovative in that it was a kind of zone defense against the run. Each defender was responsible for a given gap area and was told to stay in that area before knowing where the play was going.

It has been said, after inventing the Flex Defense, Landry then invented an offense to score on it, reviving the man-in-motion and, starting in the mid-1970s, the shotgun formation. But Landry's most significant contribution in this area was the use of "pre-shifting," where the offense would shift from one formation to the other before the snap of the ball. This tactic was not new. Coach Amos Alonzo Stagg developed it around the turn of the 20th century; Landry was the first coach to use the approach regularly. The idea was to break the keys within the defense used to determine what the offense might do. An unusual feature of this offense was Landry having his offensive linemen get in their squatted pre-stance, stand up while the running backs shifted, and then go back down into their complete "hand down" stance. The purpose of the "up and down" (Landry Shift) movement was to make it more difficult for the defense to see where the backs were shifting (over the tall offensive linemen), thus, to cut down on recognition time. While other NFL teams later employed shifting, few employed this "up and down" technique as much as Landry.[11]

Landry also was ahead of his time in his philosophy of building a team. When the Packers ruled the NFL with a dynasty in the 1960s with 245 lb (111 kg) guards and 250 lb (110 kg) tackles, Landry was busy stockpiling size for the next generation of linemen. Tackles Rayfield Wright stood 6 ft 6 in (1.98 m), and Ralph Neely weighed 265 lb (120 kg). Center Dave Manders weighed 250 lb (110 kg). All went on to block in Pro Bowls and Super Bowls in the 1970s.[12]

The same philosophy applied to the defense as with the offense. The better linemen of the 1960s were the shorter, stockier, leverage players like

10. "Tom Landry," Wikipedia, accessed October 8, 2018, https://en.wikipedia.org/wiki/Tom_Landry.

11. Ibid.

12. Ibid.

Willie Davis, Alex Karras, and Andy Robustelli. But Landry drafted the taller, leaner linemen like 6 ft 7 in (2.01 m) George Andrie and 6 ft 6 in (1.98 m) Jethro Pugh in the 1960s and later 6 ft 9 in (2.06 m) Ed Jones in the 1970s. Long arms allow for increased leverage in the pass rush.[13]

In the days before strength and speed programs, Landry brought in Alvin Roy and Boots Garland in the early 1970s to help make the Cowboys stronger and faster. Roy was a weightlifter, and Garland a college track coach. Now, every NFL team has specialty coaches.

Landry also was one of the first NFL coaches to search outside the traditional college football pipeline for talent. For example, he recruited several soccer players from Latin America, such as Efren Herrera and Rafael Septién, to compete for the job of placekicker for the Cowboys. Landry looked to the world of track and field for speedy skill-position players. For example, Bob Hayes, once considered the fastest man in the world, was drafted by and played wide receiver for the Cowboys under Landry.[14]

Landry also was the first to employ a coach for quality control. Ermal Allen would analyze game films and chart the tendencies of the opposition for the Cowboys in the 1970s. That gave Landry an edge in preparation because he knew what to expect from his opponent based on down and distance. Now, every NFL team has a quality control coach, and most have two.

A WORK IN PROGRESS THROUGH THE 1960s

It could be said that the Dallas Cowboys were a work in progress through the 1960s. The inaugural 1960 season for the Cowboys had them pegged as a "swing" club because they were the league's thirteenth franchise. In addition to being an expansion franchise, it was decided that they would play every team in the league once, instead of playing each team in their conference twice, as the other teams did.[15] They were put in the Western Conference of the NFL.

---

13. Ibid.

14. "Bob Hayes Bio," Dallas Cowboys Fan Club.com, archived from the original on October 19, 2010, accessed October 8, 2018.

15. "Dallas and Twin Cities get NFL franchises; AFL declares war," *Milwaukee Journal*, press dispatches, January 29, 1960, part 2, 11.

The Cowboys would lose their first ten games before earning a tie with the Giants in New York, next to the last game of the season. The Cowboys would lose their final game of the season to close out their inaugural season winless at 0-11-1.[16]

In 1961, Dallas was transferred to the Eastern Conference. They also began playing their home games at the Cotton Bowl. The second season saw the team win back-to-back games. In the first game, the Cowboys scored 10 points in the final 54 seconds to beat the Pittsburgh Steelers 27 to 24. The Cowboys would win their next game vs. the expansion team Minnesota Vikings 21 to 7. Unfortunately, Dallas would lose momentum during the season and finish 4-9-1. While the season wore on, a tale of two Dons was emerging in Dallas, despite the losing record. Don Meredith at quarterback and Don Perkins at running back were elevating their game and would be two future stars in Dallas.[17]

The next year, in 1962, saw the emergence of the Cowboys' offense. Quarterback duties were shared between Don Meredith and Eddie LeBaron. Also, Frank Clarke became the first receiver for the Cowboys to catch over 1,000 receiving yards in a single season for the franchise.[18] The Cowboys also scored the second-most points in the league at 398, on the way to a 4-3-1 start. However, the defense allowed the second-most points in the league, and the Cowboys lost five of their last six to finish with a 5-8-1 record.[19]

By 1963, the Cowboys had Dallas all to themselves. The rival AFL Dallas Texans, despite competing against a Cowboys team that managed only a 9–28–3 record in their first three seasons, and winning the 1962 AFL Championship, moved out of Dallas. Like the Cowboys, the Texans were losing money in the Dallas market. Texans' owner Lamar Hunt decided that the Dallas–Fort Worth media market could not sustain two professional football franchises. He considered moving the Texans to either Atlanta or Miami for the 1963 season. However, he was ultimately

16. Marty Strasen, *Cowboys Chronicles, A Complete History of the Dallas Cowboys* (Chicago:Triumph Books, 2010), 1.

17. Ibid., 8–11.

18. Ibid., 16.

19. Fleming, "The Dallas Cowboys," accessed October 7, 2018.

swayed by an offer from Kansas City Mayor Harold Roe Bartle. Bartle promised to triple the franchise's season ticket sales and expand the seating capacity of Municipal Stadium to accommodate the team.[20] The team was named the Kansas City Chiefs.

The 1963 season remained dismal for the Cowboys. *Sports Illustrated* picked the team to win the Eastern Division. However, the Cowboys got off to a terrible start losing their first four games and six of their first seven. Just as the Cowboys started to play better football, the city of Dallas was thrown into darkness as President John F. Kennedy was assassinated in a motorcade. That darkness of Kennedy's assassination shrouded the Cowboys, and they would go on to lose three games in a row before winning their final game of the season in St. Louis against the Cardinals, to finish with a 4–10 record.[21] During the season, coach Landry picked Don Meredith as the starting quarterback for the team. Meredith would be secure in that position for future seasons to come.

The 1964 draft was the bridge to the team's future, as the Cowboys selected defensive back Mel Renfro in the second round and quarterback Roger Staubach in the tenth. Both would have a significant impact on the club's rise by the 1970s. Despite Staubach winning the 1963 Heisman Trophy while at the US Naval Academy, his selection was a gamble, as he had four years to serve in the Navy before he could even report to the Dallas Cowboys. The Cowboys would struggle again in 1964, finishing with a 5-8-1 record. However, despite calls for his firing, coach Tom Landry was given an unprecedented ten-year contract extension.[22] This was unheard of at the time in all professional sports. On another bright note, the defense was up and coming and gelling as a young unit. They had given up only six rushing touchdowns for the whole year, which was best in the league.

In 1965, the Cowboys were on the move up in the standings. The team got off to a promising start winning their first two games against division rivals. The good start would not last, as the Cowboy's inconsistent

20. Kansas City Chiefs, Wayback Machine, accessed October 9, 2018, http://www.kcchiefs.com/history/60s/.
21. Fleming. "The Dallas Cowboys," accessed October 7, 2018.
22. Ibid.

play reared its ugly head again during five consecutive losses. However, the team would rebound to end the season on a strong note winning five of their last seven games to finish with a 7–7 record. With the addition of "Bullet" Bob Hayes, who just won Olympic gold the year before in track and field, the Cowboys had a receiver who was the fastest man in the world. Hayes caught 12 touchdown passes in his first year, and his quickness showed opposing team defenses that the Cowboys could score from anywhere on the field. Besides, Don Meredith threw 22 touchdown passes, and for the first time in franchise history, the Cowboys outscored their opponents.[23]

1966 was a turning point in the history of the Dallas Cowboys. First and foremost, president and general manager Tex Schramm was heavily involved in the negotiations as the AFL and NFL agree to a merger setting up a season-ending championship game. Second, the Cowboys began an NFL-record streak of 20 consecutive winning seasons. That streak included 18 years in the playoffs, 13 divisional championships, five trips to the Super Bowl, and victories in Super Bowls VI and XII.[24]

As for the 1966 season, the Cowboys looked like a candidate for that first final championship game between the AFL and NFL. From the start of the season, they won their first four games in blowout fashion. After a rough four-game stretch, where the team went 1-2-1, the Cowboys pulled out a one-point victory in Washington over the Redskins to get back on track. A week later, the Cowboys set a record by sacking Pittsburgh Steeler quarterbacks 12 times in Pittsburgh to improve to 6-2-1. Four days later, a tradition would be born, as the Cowboys hosted the Cleveland Browns in the first Thanksgiving game in Dallas. The game would end up being a key game as a 26–14 win put the Cowboys in the driver's seat for the Eastern Division Championship. Dallas went on to claim their first title with a solid 10-3-1 record. In the NFL Championship Game, the Cowboys hosted the Green Bay Packers at the Cotton Bowl in front of 75,504 fans. The Packers would prove to be the better

---

23. Strasen, *Cowboys Chronicles*, 37.
24. "Dallas Cowboys," Pro Football Hall of Fame, accessed October 9, 2018, https://www.profootballhof.com/teams/dallas-cowboys/team-history/.

team that day, but the Cowboys did not go down without a fight, as they gave the Packers all they could handle before a Don Meredith pass was intercepted in the end zone with 28 seconds left in a 34–27 loss.[25]

The 1967 campaign saw another good season for the Cowboys. Despite losing three of their final five games, the Cowboys won the Division Championship in the newly formed Capitol Division by posting a solid 9–5 record. Even though the Cowboys won two games less than the year before, the running game established itself as one of the best in the league when Dan Reeves and Don Perkins both rushed for over 600 yards and outgained their opponents on the ground by more than 800 yards.[26]

In the Eastern Conference Championship, the Cowboys crushed the Cleveland Browns 52–14 for their first-ever playoff win, earning them a trip to the NFL Championship Game in Green Bay for a rematch with the Packers. The game would take on legendary status, as wind chill temperatures dipped to -48 degrees below zero, in what would become instantly known as "The Ice Bowl," Despite the frigid weather, the Cowboys took advantage of Packers turnovers to hold a 17–14 lead late in the 4th Quarter. However, the Packers would drive down the field and break the Cowboy hearts when Bart Starr plunged over the goal line with 16 seconds left to pull out a 21–17 win.[27]

After the heart-wrenching loss at the Ice Bowl, the Cowboys rebounded and looked dominant in 1968, winning their first six games and never looking back, as they captured the Capitol Division with a 12–2 record. Dallas scored a league-high 431 points while the "Doomsday Defense" allowed only 186. The defense was ranked second in the league, and the Cowboys destroyed opponents, winning by more than 17.5 points per game.[28] Now, with the defense being built up by Landry to elite status over the years, the Cowboys now had an extraordinary offensive attack. Don Meredith had grown into one of the best quarterbacks in the league, which gave Dallas a potent aerial attack to compliment their offensive

25. Fleming, "The Dallas Cowboys," accessed October 7, 2018.
26. Strasen, *Cowboys Chronicles*, 53.
27. Ibid.
28. Ibid., 61.

attack on the ground. As a result, the Cowboys were ranked first in the NFL in offense. By season's end, the Cowboys were the only team to pass for over 3,000 yards. Now, the Cowboys were ready to hedge on their season successes and were poised to take this momentum into the play-offs. However, their season would end with a disappointing 31–20 loss in Cleveland to the Browns in the Eastern Conference Championship. For the Browns, it was delicious revenge for last year's crushing defeat by Dallas in the 1967 playoffs

In 1969, Dallas had a setback on offense when both starting quarter-back Don Meredith, and running back Don Perkins retired. Scrambling somewhat to fill their shoes, Craig Morton was brought in to replace Meredith at quarterback, and he did a good job replacing "Dandy Don," and tossed 21 touchdowns for the year. Calvin Hill replaced Perkins at running back and ran for 942 yards and had eight touchdowns; enough offensive fireworks to win the Rookie of The Year Award.

The Cowboys cruised to an 11-2-1 record and again entered the postseason with high hopes. However, once again, the Cowboys season would end in disappointment as the Cowboys were crushed at the Cotton Bowl 38–14 by their familiar nemesis, the Cleveland Browns, in the Eastern Conference Championship.

The 1960s ended with the growth of the Cowboys into a major powerhouse in the NFL. Their losses twice to Green Bay in 1966 and 1967, and the Browns in 1968 and 1969, gave the franchise a label of being "bridesmaids," that were unable to win the big one. The new decade would be more kind to the Cowboys. They would stop being bridesmaids and would-be brides during the 1970s. Dallas would win the Vince Lombardi Trophy twice and be in five Super Bowls during the decade. Their winning ways began in the upcoming season of 1970.

7

YEAR ONE OF THE MERGER: HIGHLIGHTS OF THE 1970 NFL SEASON

With the end of Super Bowl IV, the AFL and NFL were no longer separate leagues. Now pro football was uniform. This uniformity took shape in many ways, and not just a papered event. First, the merger standardized the practice in professionalism, especially for the AFL teams, whereby the players no longer played in high school stadiums, there were no more botched film exchanges, no more playing fields with weird dimensions for an end-zone, and no more players dressing in hotel rooms.[1] Secondly, the new league decided to use the football that was used from the old NFL, but not the ball that the AFL used. However, the new NFL utilized two important AFL innovations: to put the players' names on the backs of their jerseys and use the scoreboard clock as the official game clock.[2]

With the merger completed, the networks were eager to get the television rights for the new league. CBS signed a four-year contract to televise all NFC games, and NBC signed a similar contract to televise all

1. MacCambridge, *America's Game*, 280.
2. Ibid.

AFC games. The NFL also had signed a contract with ABC to televise a weekly Monday night game on the network. These television contracts were an indication that professional football was headed for a very lucrative future. With these television contracts, the NFL was looking to cultivate a larger audience for network television and surpass the gross receipts of $3.8 million for Super Bowl IV, which was the largest amount of revenue taken in for any previous sporting event.[3]

The old NFL had sixteen teams, and the AFL had ten teams that merged into the new league. To even out the newly created NFC and AFC leagues under the newly established NFL, the agreement was to have thirteen teams for each league. Thus, the Pittsburgh Steelers, Baltimore Colts, and Cleveland Browns agreed to defect to the AFC for a sum of $3,000,000 given to each team for switching leagues.[4]

Also, the league broke up each league with three divisions. Then they created a wild card spot for the second-best record in the league that did not win one of the three divisions. Tex Schramm had put forward this idea.[5]

The three divisions in each league were set up as follows:

- NFC East: Dallas, New York (Giants), Philadelphia, St. Louis, Washington
- NFC Central: Chicago, Detroit, Green Bay, Minnesota
- NFC West: Atlanta, Los Angeles, New Orleans, San Francisco
- AFC East: Baltimore, Buffalo, Miami, Boston, New York (Jets)
- AFC Central: Cincinnati, Cleveland, Houston, Pittsburgh
- AFC West: Denver, Kansas City, Oakland, San Diego

---

3. Felser, *Birth of the New NFL*, 3199–3203, Kindle.
4. MacCambridge, *America's Game*, 281.
5. Ibid.

FORMER NFL ALIGNMENT

Before 1966, the NFL had two seven-team conferences:

- Eastern Conference: Cleveland, Dallas, New York, Philadelphia, Pittsburgh, St. Louis, and Washington
- Western Conference: Baltimore, Chicago, Detroit, Green Bay, Los Angeles, Minnesota, and San Francisco.

Atlanta was added as an expansion franchise in 1966 and placed in the Eastern Conference. Every team had a bye week during the 1966 season.

When New Orleans was awarded an expansion franchise for 1967, the NFL divided its teams into two eight-team conferences, with two four-team divisions in each conference as follows:

- Eastern Conference/Capitol Division: Dallas, New Orleans, Philadelphia, and Washington
- Eastern Conference/Century Division: Cleveland, New York, Pittsburgh, and St. Louis
- Western Conference/Central Division: Chicago, Detroit, Green Bay, and Minnesota
- Western Conference/Coastal Division: Baltimore, Atlanta, Los Angeles, and San Francisco.

The Giants and Saints swapped divisions in 1968 and then returned to the 1967 alignment in 1969.

FORMER AFL ALIGNMENT

Meanwhile, the AFL for entire its ten-year existence had:

- Eastern Division: Boston, Buffalo, Houston, and New York (with Miami added in 1966)

- Western Division: Dallas/Kansas City, Denver, Los Angeles/ San Diego, and Oakland (with Cincinnati added in 1968).

A TOUGH START FOR A NEW LEAGUE

Things got off to a rocky start for the NFL even before a game was even played in the 1970 season. In early July of 1970, on the eve of the opening of training camps, the players association for pro football announced a strike over-improved pension, disability insurance, and several other demands. The strike didn't last long and was settled on August 3rd, without much benefit to the players. Marvin Miller, head of the baseball union, who had led the baseball players since 1966, was not impressed with the strike's outcome. Miller had worked in the unions since 1938, including being a lead negotiator for the steelworker's union from 1950–1966. Summing up his thoughts on the NFL strike, Miller proclaimed, "It wasn't a strike, it was a student demonstration . . . the students marched around campus and then went back to class."[6] After being through tough negotiations and strikes throughout the years for unions, Miller just didn't see enough marketable gains for the players, nor did he see much solidarity.

Also, that summer, two tragic events cast their shadows over the newly minted league. On June 16, 1970, Chicago running back Brian Piccolo lost his battle with cancer and had died. His story was told in the 1971 movie, *Brian's Song,* about his friendship with fellow teammate, Gayle Sayers. The next tragic event was the death of the Buffalo Bills' offensive lineman Bob Kalsu. He became the first active pro football player to die in combat duty in Vietnam when his platoon came under heavy fire by the enemy.[7]

The biggest shadow, though, was the death of coach Vince Lombardi, right before the season began. Lombardi had suffered from digestive tract problems for years but refused to see a doctor. On June 24, 1970, Lombardi was admitted to Georgetown University Hospital, and tests "revealed anaplastic carcinoma in the rectal area of his colon, a fast-growing cancer

6. Felser, *Birth of the New NFL*, 3205–3208, Kindle.
7. Schultz, *The NFL, Year One*, 32.

in which the cells barely resemble their normal appearance." On July 27, Lombardi was readmitted to Georgetown, and exploratory surgery found that the cancer was terminal. Lombardi and his wife, Marie, received family, friends, clergy, players, and former players at his hospital bedside. He even received a phone call from President Nixon telling Lombardi that all of America was behind him, to which Lombardi replied that he would never give up his fight against his illness. On his deathbed, Lombardi told the Priest, Father Tim, that he was not afraid to die, but that he regretted he could not have accomplished more in his life. Lombardi passed in Washington, D.C. at 7:12 A.M. on Thursday, September 3, 1970, surrounded by his wife, parents, two children, and six grandchildren. He was only 57. He had coached only one season in Washington, but he brought the franchise to its first winning season since 1955, the year before in 1969. The greatest coach of his generation had left his mark on the game with his success with the Packers and now with an up-and-coming Redskins team. His epitaph was forever etched in history when a week later, the NFL named the Super Bowl trophy after him.[8]

MOVERS AND SHAKERS IN 1970

The 1970 season saw many great moments and players take center stage. It was a new venture with an exciting and uncertain future. The stars shone brightly on some of these players and the game itself in 1970.

GEORGE BLANDA

One of these players was forty-three year old, Oakland Raider kicker/ quarterback George Blanda. He might have been the brightest spotlight of the season. In a sport where the average career lasts less than four years, George Blanda's lasted 26 seasons. Blanda retired after the 1975 season, at the age of forty-eight. He was the oldest man to play in a National Football League game, and at the time, he was the only one to have played in four separate decades. His career record for points scored

---

8. Felser, *Birth of the New NFL*, 3209–3211, Kindle.

(2,002) stood for 25 years, but his reputation as the ultimate clutch player was cemented in one five-week period in 1970.[9]

It all started when Blanda replaced an injured Daryle Lamonica at quarterback and threw three touchdown passes to rally the Oakland Raiders to a 31–14 win over the Pittsburgh Steelers. The next Sunday, he kicked a game-tying field goal with three seconds left, and a week later, he again replaced an injured Lamonica in the final quarter, thus tying the game with a touchdown pass with just over a minute to go. Then Blanda won the game with a 52-yard field goal, the second-longest kick of his career, with three seconds on the clock. The next week he took over quarterback again, and with four minutes to play, Blanda threw a game-winning pass. The next game, Blanda kicked a short field goal for another win. Blanda's streak as a savior was snapped when he failed to rally the team the next week, but his legend was established. Blanda was the magic man who helped the Raiders win the new AFC West and have the best record in the AFC. For his outstanding performances on the football field, Blanda won the Bert Bell Award for the player of the year, even though he threw only 55 passes the entire season.[10] With this remarkable achievement, Blanda became the poster child of endurance and showed all middle-aged men across the United States that age is nothing but only a number.

MONDAY NIGHT FOOTBALL

Another shaker or rather shake-up was the institution of *Monday Night Football* on ABC. This would add another dimension to televising pro football and changed the way fans would watch pro football in the future.

Back in the 1960s, before the merger with the AFL, commissioner Pete Rozelle envisioned the possibility of playing at least one game weekly during prime time that could be viewed by a greater television audience (the NFL had scheduled Saturday night games on the DuMont Television Network in 1953 and 1954 but had low ratings. Eventually, the

---

9. Michael Carlson, "George Blanda: American footballer who played in the NFL at the age of 48," *Independent* (December 3, 2010), accessed October 12, 2018, https://www.independent.co.uk/news/obituaries/george-blanda-american-footballer-who-played-in-the-nfl-at-the-age-of-48-2149823.html.
    10. Ibid.

dissolution of DuMont led to those games being eliminated by the time CBS took over the rights in 1956).[11]

An early bid by the NFL in 1964 to play on Friday nights was not accepted, with critics charging that such telecasts would damage the attendance at high school football games. Changing course on the prime time and date, Rozelle decided to experiment with the concept of playing on Monday night, scheduling the Green Bay Packers and Detroit Lions for a game on September 28, 1964. While the game was not televised, it drew a sellout crowd of 59,203 spectators to Tiger Stadium, the largest crowd ever to watch a professional football game in Detroit up to that point. Two years later, Rozelle would build on this success, and the NFL began a four-year experiment of playing on Monday night, scheduling one game in primetime on CBS during the 1966 and 1967 seasons, and two contests during each of the next two years. NBC followed suit in 1968 and 1969 with games involving American Football League teams.

During subsequent negotiations on a new television contract that would begin in 1970 (coinciding with the merger between the NFL and AFL), Rozelle concentrated on signing a weekly Monday night deal with one of the three major networks. After sensing both NBC and CBS's reluctance in disturbing their regular programming schedules, Rozelle spoke with ABC.

Despite the network's status as the lowest-rated of the three major broadcast networks, ABC was also reluctant to enter the risky venture. After Rozelle used the threat of signing a deal with the independent Hughes Sports Network, an entity bankrolled by reclusive businessman Howard Hughes, ABC signed a contract for the scheduled games. Speculation that Rozelle already signed with Hughes caused panic among the ABC executives because many ABC's affiliates throughout the United States would have pre-empted the network's Monday lineup in favor of the football games. If ABC didn't sign a contract with pro football, it would severely damage potential ratings that added up to dollar signs.

---

11. Maury Brown, "A Look Back On The First ABC *Monday Night Football* On Its 45th Anniversary," *Forbes* (September 21, 2015), accessed October 12, 2018, https://www.forbes.com/sites/maurybrown/ 2015/09/21/a-look-back-on-the-first-abc-monday-night-football-on-its-45th-anniversary/#13d8bc6d111c.

After the final contract for *Monday Night Football* was signed, ABC Sports producer Roone Arledge immediately saw possibilities for the new program. Setting out to create an entertainment "spectacle" as much as a simple sports broadcast, Arledge hired Chet Forte, who would serve as director of the program for over 22 years. With Forte's guidance, *Monday Night Football* would showcase football games as never seen before and would raise the bar to convert sports games into "television events." Arledge also ordered twice the usual number of cameras to cover the game, expanded the regular two-person broadcasting booth to three, and used extensive graphic design within the show as well as instant replay.[12]

Looking for a sportscaster who could jump-start the program, Arledge hired controversial New York City sportscaster Howard Cosell as a commentator and veteran football play-by-play announcer Keith Jackson, the voice of college football for many years. Arledge had tried to lure Curt Gowdy and then Vin Scully to ABC for the *MNF* play-by-play role, but settled for Jackson after they proved unable to break their respective existing contracts with NBC Sports and the Los Angeles Dodgers. Jack Buck, the broadcaster for the St Louis Cardinals baseball team, was also considered. When Arledge's assistant, Chuck Howard, telephoned Buck with the job offer, Buck refused to respond due to anger at his treatment by ABC during an earlier stint with the network. Arledge's original choice for the third member of the trio, Frank Gifford, was unavailable at the time since he was still under contract with CBS Sports. However, Gifford suggested former Dallas Cowboys quarterback, Don Meredith, setting the stage for years of fireworks between the often-pompous Cosell and the laid-back Meredith.[13]

Monday Night Football first aired on ABC on September 21, 1970, with a game between the New York Jets and the Browns in Cleveland. Advertisers were charged $65,000 per minute by ABC during the viewing time, a cost that proved to be a bargain when the contest collected 33% of the viewing audience. The Browns defeated the Jets, 31–21 in a game that featured a 94-yard kickoff return for a touchdown by the

---

12. MacCambridge, *America's Game*, 276–277.
13. Brown, "A Look Back," accessed October 12, 2018.

Browns' Homer Jones and was punctuated when Billy Andrews inter-cepted Joe Namath late in the fourth quarter and returned it 25 yards for the clinching touchdown.[14]

Before 24/7/365 sports networks, Howard Cosell would provide half-time recaps of the games around the league, which often were the weekly capsules for all the games on Sunday many got. Thus, the Monday night game and the half-time show became the regular entertainment we now expect after our workdays.[15]

Success would come quickly for the Monday night games, and just in the first few airings of the games, the ratings showed that *Monday Night Football* would be here to stay. The Nielsen ratings for the first game were 35 percent of television viewers for that time slot. The show continually got excellent ratings and reached about 60 million homes in viewership weekly during the 1970 season. By October, *Monday Night Football* knocked the top-rated talk show, *The Dick Cavett Show*, off Monday nights. It was rescheduled from Tuesday through Friday night until football season ended, and then the show returned on Monday Nights by the end of December.[16]

These Monday night games changed the game visually. From the multiple camera angles, the games were more vivid under the lights, which also gleamed off the players' helmets and made the action more dramatic. Also, showing the replays of the games played the day before on Sunday at halftime replaced the usual halftime show, which consisted of local marching bands entertaining the crowd until halftime was over. The highlights from the day before also benefited NFL Films, who were growing as an institution. Ed Sabol and his son, Steve, would revolution-ize the game with their footage of action in the NFL. Now, with *Monday Night Football's* request to get highlights from the day before, NFL Films put two camera people in each stadium to film the games and then send footage to ABC. The highlights show at halftime proved to be powerful

14. "September 21, 1970, ABC *Monday Night Football* Debuts," Eyes of a Generation, accessed October 19, 2018, http://eyesofageneration.com/september-21-1970-abc-monday-night-football-debuts most-think-this-was-a-m/.

15. Brown, "A Look Back," accessed October 12, 2018.

16. MacCambridge, *America's Game*, 277.

because even if the Monday Night game was lopsided, viewers still tuned in to see the halftime highlights. Otherwise, football fans would have to wait for the NFL Films weekly show called *This Week in Pro Football,* which was broadcast the following Saturday after the games were played the Sunday before.[17]

The reason the NFL is so widely successful in the North American sports landscape can all be attributed to the brilliance of Pete Rozelle. He understood the impact television would have on the sports world and hitched the NFL's wagon to it. In making national television rights deals equally shared by each owner in the league, the NFL has enjoyed parity in the standings and terms of profits gained by all teams and not just one. More than any other league, the NFL owes its successes to television.[18]

A KICK FOR THE AGES IN THE BIG EASY

Another personal highlight of the 1970 season was Saints' placekicker Tom Dempsey's 63-yard field goal against the Detroit Lions on November 8, 1970, at Tulane Stadium in New Orleans. What made this a historical moment was that Dempsey was born without toes on his right (kicking) foot or fingers on his right hand. He wore a modified shoe with a flattened and enlarged toe surface. This generated controversy about whether such a shoe gave a player an unfair advantage. When reporters asked Dempsey if he thought it was unfair, he said, "Unfair, eh? How 'bout you try kicking a 63-yard field goal to win it with 2 seconds left an' yer wearin' a square shoe, oh yeah, and no toes either."[19]

Additionally, when an analysis of his kick was carried out by ESPN *Sport Science,* it was found that his modified shoe had offered him no advantage. It was found that the smaller contact area could have reduced, not increased, the margin for error.[20]

Dempsey's field goal stirred controversy, as many saw the kick as a form of advantage for the disabled kicker. To guard against instances

---

17. Ibid., 279.
18. Brown, "A Look Back," accessed October 12, 2018.
19. "Remembering 'The Kick'," avoyellestoday.com, Avoyelles Journal, Bunkie, Record, Marksville Weekly. Archived from the original on January 4, 2015, accessed October 15, 2018.
20. ESPN Sport Science, espngo.com.

such as this, the league made two rule changes in the subsequent years to discourage further long field goal attempts. The first was in 1974, which moved the goalposts from the goal line to the back of the end zone (adding ten yards to the kick distance) and awarded the ball to the defense on a missed kick at the spot where the ball was snapped (this changed in 1994 to the spot of the kick). Then, in 1977, the NFL added a rule, informally known as the "Tom Dempsey Rule," that "any shoe that is worn by a player with an artificial limb on his kicking leg must have a kicking surface that conforms to that of a normal kicking shoe."[21]

THE STRANGE CASE OF JOE KAPP

Joe Kapp was a unique quarterback who played in both the Canadian Football League and the NFL. He came to the Minnesota Vikings in 1967. Unlike finesse passers of the day, such as Johnny Unitas or Bart Starr, Kapp was a hard-nosed player, who played the game with sheer determination. Playing in the Canadian Football League in his early years out of college, Kapp had proven that he was an elite quarterback and developed the reputation of being a tough player and a great leader. While most quarterbacks disliked being hit, Kapp was the opposite. He relished in physical contact, and when he took off on a run, he'd try to run over defenders.

Born in Santa Fe, New Mexico, to a Mexican-American mother and a father of German heritage, Kapp explained that while his father was blonde haired and blue-eyed, the unique Nuevo Mexicano culture made it so that "in northern New Mexico, everyone spoke Spanish. [My father] spoke Spanish better than he spoke English . . . he spoke street Spanish fluently." From New Mexico, the Kapp family moved to Salinas, California, living in housing projects with lettuce pickers.[22]

---

21. J. Conrad Guest, "The Lions Were Sunk By a 63 Yard Field Goal," Detroit Athletic Company (December 29, 2012), accessed October 15, 2018, https://www.detroitathletic.com/blog/2012/12/29/tom-dempsey-63-yard-field-goal/.

22. Roberto Franco and Jose Andrade, "Why Does No One Remember Joe Kapp, the NFL's First Mexican American Super Bowl Quarterback?" Remezcla (September 29, 2017), accessed October 17, 2018, http://remezcla.com/features/sports/joe-kapp-nfl-latino-pioneer/.

Kapp learned to play football on those lettuce fields, and it was also in those housing projects where Kapp developed a toughness that defined the rest of his life. "If a kid didn't have machismo in the . . . neighborhoods . . . where I grew up, he had it tough," Kapp explained. "Sometimes, the Mexicans would fight the Anglos; sometimes, it would be Mexicans and the blacks from Pacoima. They had gang fights going all the time and even an occasional shoot-out or knifing."[23]

Kapp's athletic talents led him to the University of California in Berkeley, where, besides playing on the basketball team, he quarterbacked the team to a Rose Bowl appearance. After college, in 1959, the NFL's Washington team drafted him in the 18th round but never contacted him. Thus, Kapp signed a contract to play in the Canadian Football League, where he remained for eight seasons before reaching the NFL.[24]

Growing up in an environment that, above all else, valued toughness, it heavily influenced how Kapp played quarterback. He was a barroom brawler, someone who even started fights with teammates. The first fight occurred while playing in Canada; it left him with a scar across the jaw, courtesy of a bottle broken and raked across his face. The gash required 100 stitches and came within a half-inch of severing his jugular. Kapp never pressed charges since, as he explained, "we were teammates, and we'd both been drinking, and it was one of those things." Similarly, in his first year in the NFL—in 1967 as a 29-year-old, third-string rookie quarterback—Kapp fought a Viking defensive teammate after each refused to let the other take blame for a loss. As they drank tequila and expressed that blame should fall on them, the disagreement escalated to a fistfight.[25]

Kapp built a reputation based on that acquired toughness, and as a player that didn't allow others to intimidate him. In football, a sport that values toughness above all, Kapp earned respect from many of his peers, which compensated for his actual ability as a quarterback. Being of Mexican American heritage, Kapp served as a uniting force between white and black players. Kapp explained: "[When] I got to the team, some parties

23. Ibid.
24. Ibid.
25. Ibid.

were going on with the Wall Street gang over here and maybe some over here with the black guys . . . I said, 'Hey man, why don't we have a party together, you know, I'm a Mexican . . . I get invited to both, why don't we all have a party.'"[26]

In 1967, Kapp's first season in the NFL, he started 11 of 14 games for the Minnesota Vikings. That season, the team compiled an unusual record of 3 wins, 5 losses, and 3 ties. Kapp's numbers were not impressive that season, as he completed only 47 percent of his pass attempts with 8 touchdowns and 17 interceptions. However, he did score two rushing touchdowns, showing his toughness of going into the defense headfirst both times. However, even with Kapp's subpar playing, the team was winless without him starting at quarterback.

The next year would prove to be a better year for Kapp and the Vikings. Kapp led the Minnesota Vikings to their first-ever playoff appearance in 1968. However, the Vikings did lose to the Baltimore Colts, 24–14 in the first round at Memorial Stadium in Baltimore. Of course, the Colts would go on to Super Bowl III as the NFL's representative against the New York Jets.

The next year would be stellar for both Kapp and the Vikings. On September 28, 1969, Kapp tied the record for touchdown passes thrown in a single game. On that momentous day, Kapp threw for seven touchdown passes against the Colts. He is tied with seven other players (Sid Luckman, Adrian Burk, George Blanda, Y. A. Tittle, Nick Foles, Peyton Manning, and Drew Brees). Kapp also led the Vikings to a 12–2 record that year and a berth in Super Bowl IV after defeating the Cleveland Browns 27–7 in the last NFL Championship game ever played. Despite Kapp being the team's unquestioned leader, Kapp still was anything but graceful or smooth as a quarterback. Still, his hard-nosed play was effective enough to lead the Vikings to a Super Bowl IV appearance.[27]

Leading up to Super Bowl IV, where the Vikings were 13-point favorites against the Kansas City Chiefs, newspapers across the country wrote about Kapp's unconventional talent. *The Colorado Springs*

26. Ibid.
27. Ibid.

Gazette-Telegraph called him "Minnesota's ugly duckling quarterback," while South Dakota's *The Daily Republic* noted that the "Mighty Mexican" was an "anti-hero." In Rochester, New York's *Democrat and Chronicle*, stated: "Kapp has been labeled half-passer, half-Mexican and half-collision." When a reporter told Kapp he didn't have the classic passing style since his passes wobbled rather than spiraled, he responded, "So I'm not a classic passer. Classics are for Greeks. I'm a winner."[28]

His ability, or inability, to throw the ball, even led a few reporters to theorize why he didn't throw a perfect spiral. In watching Kapp play, it was noticed that he did not use his fingers to grip the football's laces when throwing the ball. From this observation, the reporters deduced that the reason for this was because Kapp learned to pass by "heaving lettuce heads in Salinas, and there are no laces on lettuce."

Whatever theories were created about Kapp, or criticism of his style of play, he is also the only quarterback to have played in the Rose Bowl, Super Bowl, and the Grey Cup—the Canadian Football League's championship—though he lost two out of the three, winning only the Grey Cup.

In one of the Super Bowl's biggest upsets ever, the Chiefs manhandled the Vikings by the score of 23 to 7. The loss included Kapp getting knocked out of the game with a shoulder injury. "Do you know what happens when you lose the Super Bowl?" Kapp asked rhetorically. "The world ends. It just stops. There's been all this build-up, all these bruising games, all this study and preparation, and strain, and then it ends. There's not even a fanfare."[29]

After the Super Bowl loss, Kapp never played with the Minnesota Vikings again. He didn't show up for the 1970 training camp, despite being on the *Sports Illustrated* cover which read, "The Toughest Chicano: Viking quarterback Joe Kapp." Kapp and the Vikings' management disagreed on how much he was worth. The team offered him a 3-year contract at $100,000 per season. Kapp asked for $1.25 million over five years. Kapp would eventually end up on the New England Patriots before sitting out the 1971 season to protest his contract just as he did

---

28. Ibid.
29. Ibid.

in Minnesota. In March of 1972, Kapp filed an antitrust lawsuit against the NFL, arguing the league's "standard contract[s] restricted his freedom in the pro football marketplace." Kapp became a pioneer in the player's fight towards free agency.[30]

Joe Kapp played only four seasons in the NFL, but he was a pioneer in many respects. Long before the NFL celebrated Hispanic Heritage Month and before built themselves a Hispanic fan base in the tens of millions, Joe Kapp became the first Latino quarterback to lead his team to the Super Bowl, and perhaps more importantly, he helped spark the fight against the NFL's ever-present control of players.

Even though he was through in the NFL, Kapp's football career was resurrected in 1982, when he was hired as the head football coach at his alma mater, the University of California, at Berkeley. Kapp had never coached before but was ready to take on the job in his usual head first fashion. In his first year as head coach, he was voted the Pacific-10 Conference Coach of the Year. On a final note, Kapp was the coach during "The Play," the famous five-lateral kickoff return by the Cal team to score the winning touchdown on the final play of the 1982 Big Game against arch-rival Stanford.

TEAMS THAT WERE IN CONTENTION,
BUT MISSED THE PLAYOFFS

The 1970 season saw many teams that vastly improved from the previous years from having losing records. With the new wild card system in each conference, many teams had an opportunity to make the playoffs if they couldn't win their respective divisions. With Detroit winning the Wild Card for the NFC and the Dolphins winning the wild card for the AFC, these other teams were near misses in a very tight race to the first playoffs under the new NFL.

NFC EAST - THE NEW YORK GIANTS

The 1970 Giants were a very good team in the inaugural year of the merger. The Giants' offense was led by Pro Bowl performers, quarterback

---

30. Ibid.

Fran Tarkenton, and running back Ron Johnson. The team was in the top ten in several offensive categories: including points, yards, and first downs. The Giants had over one hundred rushing yards in eleven of its fourteen games, including 202 yards in a week eight win against the Dallas Cowboys. However, the offense struggled when the team failed to run the ball well, as shown in a week fourteen loss to the Los Angeles Rams in which the Giants rushed for only 50 yards. When the team was able to run the ball and play defense, they were able to win games, as shown by the fact that in all their wins, they had a hundred or more rushing yards.[31]

The backbone of New York's defense was a stout front four featuring end Fred Dryer and Jim Kanicki and tackle Bob Lurtsema. Pro Bowl cornerback, Willie Williams, was part of a solid secondary, which also included Tom Longo, Scott Eaton, and Spider Lockhart. First-round draft pick Jim Files moved in at the starting middle linebacker spot for the departed Henry Davis, who moved on to Pittsburgh.[32]

The team was led by second-year head coach Alex Webster, an assistant Giant coach under Allie Sherman, and he was later promoted to head coach (1969–1973). Webster was named UPI NFL Coach of the Year in 1970. However, the Giants finished the season 9–5, missing the playoffs by losing their final game against the Los Angeles Rams by 31–3. The Giants would finish second in the NFC East, a game behind the Dallas Cowboys, who won the division. They were also only one game out of a wild card playoff spot. The future looked bright for the Giants after this great turnaround season.

NFC EAST - ST. LOUIS CARDINALS

The St. Louis Cardinals were another good team in the NFC East that failed to qualify for the playoffs. Led by quarterback Jim Hart and running back MacArthur Lane, plus a bruising defense, the Cardinals were

---

31. "1970 New York Giants," Pro Football Reference, accessed October 18, 2018, https://www.pro-football-reference.com/teams/nyg/1970.htm?redir.
32. Ibid.

able to have some stunning victories en route to a respectable record of 8-5-1.

There were five Pro Bowlers from the team, including tackle Ernie McMillan, tight end Jackie Smith, running back MacArthur Lane, linebacker Larry Stallings, cornerback Roger Wehrli, and free safety Larry Wilson.[33]

Overall, the team improved from the season before, whereby they had a record of 4–9–1. Despite them shutting out three consecutive opponents (and holding a fourth, the defending Super Bowl champion Kansas City Chiefs, without a touchdown in a 6–6 draw), they failed to reach the playoffs for the 22nd straight season, falling part with three consecutive losses in December. Before the season-ending skid, the Cardinals swept the Dallas Cowboys, with the second victory a 38–0 desecration on *Monday Night Football* at the Cotton Bowl in Dallas. However, Dallas did not lose again during the rest of the season and the playoffs until they fell to the Baltimore Colts in Super Bowl V.

NFC WEST - THE LOS ANGELES RAMS

With the completion of the AFL–NFL merger, the Rams were placed in the NFC Western Division with the Atlanta Falcons, New Orleans Saints, and San Francisco 49ers, none of whom had a winning record for any of the prior two seasons. This very good Rams team was poised for a brighter future with the realignment. With the merger, many thought that the Rams would thrive in the new division when the Baltimore Colts, with whom the Rams battled for a division title for the past three seasons, left for the newly minted AFC. Consequently, the Rams were heavy favorites to win the weakest of the new divisions in 1970.

As it turned out, those who predicted the Rams to win the NFC West could not predict that 49ers quarterback John Brodie would have an MVP season and that the 49ers had acquired some skilled young players to take the division.

---

33. "1970 St. Louis Cardinals," Pro Football Reference, accessed October 18, 2018, https://www.pro-football-reference.com/teams/crd/1970.htm.

During the 1970 season, the Rams veteran roster began to show signs of aging and suffered several injuries. Thus, instead of battling the Colts, the Rams would stage a season-long battle for the NFC West with their geographic rivals, the San Francisco 49ers.

The Rams started the season as expected, with easy wins vs. the St. Louis Cardinals 34–13, at the Buffalo Bills 19–0, and against the San Diego Chargers 37–10. The 49ers came to L.A. in week 4 with a 2–1 record, having lost at Atlanta the week before, 21–20. The Rams were the favorites to win, but the 49ers forced 4 turnovers and had 3 sacks to win 20–6 and gain a share of the division lead. The Rams regained the division lead the very next week with a 31–21 win in Green Bay, while the 49ers tied the Saints in New Orleans. The 49ers then won 4 games in a row while the Rams struggled to find consistency. They lost in the mud and rain on a Monday night in Minnesota to the powerful Vikings 13–3 but beat the Saints in New Orleans 30–17 the next week. In a very inconsistent contest vs. Atlanta, the Rams needed a last-second touchdown to tie the Falcons in L.A. 10–10. Sloppy play continued for the Rams and had contributed to the Rams collecting 4 turnovers in an upset loss at home to the New York Jets (playing without an injured Joe Namath), then beat the Falcons in Atlanta 17–7. Week 11 was a show-down in San Francisco between the 7-2-1 49ers and the 6-3-1 Rams. The Rams played perhaps their best game of the season in winning 30–13 and were now tied with the 49ers for 1st place with three games to play. More importantly, the Rams held the tiebreaker over San Francisco due to having a better division record. After beating the Saints 34–16 in week 10, the 8-3-1 Rams faced the 8-4 Detroit Lions on a Monday night game in Los Angeles. The Lions won what would prove to be a pivotal game by the score of 28–23, dropping the Rams one game behind the 49ers and a half-game behind the Lions for the wild card spot. The Rams would come back the week later to crush the New York Giants 31–3 in New York (costing the Giants both the NFC East title and the wild card spot), then awaited the result of the 49ers and Lions games. The

Lions won easily at home vs. Green Bay 20–0, and the 49ers crushed the Oakland Raiders, 38–7 (the Raiders, having already won their division, rested most of their regulars).[34]

The 1970 season was a disappointment for the team as it looked to improve on its 11–3 record from 1969. However, the Rams missed their previous record by two games and finished with a respectable 9-4-1 record. Despite the winning record, the team missed the playoffs for the 2nd time in 3 seasons.

AFC CENTRAL - CLEVELAND BROWNS

With the move to the AFC, Cleveland had new division foes unfamiliar to them after the merger. Looking to capitalize on a string of very good past seasons, including a stellar 10-3-1 record the year before, the team was plagued with issues during the 1970 season. The most glaring issue was their coach, Blanton Collier. Many did not know that this season would be his last because he had severe hearing problems. The 64-year-old coach announced his retirement before the end of the 1970 season, as the Browns finished with a disappointing 7–7 record.[35] Collier told owner Art Modell that he could no longer hear his players, and it was difficult to read their lips through new face masks that obscured their mouths.[36] Modell tried to help by getting Collier to try new hearing aids and even sent him for acupuncture treatment, but nothing worked.[37] Collier struggled during press conferences because he often could not hear what reporters were asking, and his answers didn't even match the questions asked.[38] In eight years as coach, Collier led Cleveland to a championship and a 76-34-2 record. Nick Skorich, who came to the Browns as offensive coordinator in 1964, was named his replacement in 1971. Collier had been on the job since 1963 and guided the Browns to

---

34. "1970 Los Angeles Rams," Pro Football Reference, accessed October 18, 2018, https://www.pro-football-reference.com/teams/ram/1970.htm.

35. "Browns' Blanton Says He's Retiring This Year," *Rochester Sentinel* (December 2, 1970).

36. Terry Pluto, *Fumble: The Browns, Modell, & the Move* (Cleveland: Cleveland Landmarks, 1997), 297.

37. Ibid., 69–70.

38. Ibid., 70.

the NFL championship a year later and made it to the NFL Championship game in 1965, 1968, and 1969.

Another problem for the Browns was that their starting quarterback, Bill Nelsen had knee problems. Seeing a problem down the road at the quarterback position due to Nelsen's situation, the Browns made a blockbuster trade with the Miami Dolphins on the eve of the 1970 NFL Draft to get the rights to select the man they felt would be their passer of the future, Mike Phipps. But it came at a steep price because they had to give up Pro Football Hall of Fame wide receiver Paul Warfield in the process. That loss, coupled with Nelsen's physical condition, contributed to major concerns about their offense going into the 1970 season. Combined with the unfamiliarity of the personnel on the former AFL clubs they were now playing, these obstacles took the wind out of the Browns' sail on offense. The Browns' offense would be just a mere shell of itself in the 1970 season, far from the high caliber offense that was so dominating since 1963. With the offense in tatters, the result was inevitable. The Browns scored 65 fewer points than they had the year before and 108 less than two seasons before.

The Browns' defense, though it gave up 35 fewer points than it had in 1969, just could not make up the difference with their subpar offense. The Browns stumbled all season long and faltered in the playoff chase against the Cincinnati Bengals. It was only the second non-winning mark in club history.

Though the season was an up and down affair with the Browns, two events highlighted the good about the second place Browns. First, the Browns beat Joe Namath and the New York Jets 31–21 at Cleveland Stadium in the opener in the first *Monday Night Football* game in history, and, three games later, edged rival Ohio resident, Cincinnati 30–27, spoiling Bengals' head coach Paul Brown's first official visit to Cleveland since being fired by the Browns eight years before.

As for the first *Monday Night Football* game played on September 21, 1970 on prime time National Television on ABC, the buildup to the game itself was exciting, as millions of Americans were ready to tune in to watch the New York Jets and the Cleveland Browns square off at Municipal Stadium in Cleveland.

There was some concern for playing the first Monday night game at Municipal Stadium. The Stadium was opened in 1931, and was built with pillars, which obstructed the view of the field for many fans. Being built near Lake Erie, the stadium was susceptible to bitter cold winds off the lake in the winter, and the invasion by swarms of insects that plagued the field in the summer. By 1970, the stadium was the epicenter for entertainment in Cleveland. Everything from rock concerts, pro football games with the Browns, major league baseball games with the hometown Indian's baseball team, college football games, and having the circus at the stadium had taken its toll on the field. With so much wear and tear on the field from all of these events, along with Municipal Stadium aging and becoming an outdated ball park, the stadium was called the "Mistake by the Lake."[39]

Browns' owner, Art Modell was well aware of the issues regarding Municipal Stadium. He also knew that new stadiums were beginning to be built to house other cities' sporting teams, and that Cleveland was lagging behind when it came to having their sports teams play in a venue with up to date amenities. Shiny and gleaming, these new poly turf stadiums opened in 1970 for the new NFL season. Three Rivers Stadium in Pittsburgh and Riverfront Stadium in Cincinnati showcased the new modern stadium design, which made Municipal Stadium look like an old and dilapidated ballpark it had become over the years. Although these new stadiums were built with the idea of housing both baseball and football in mind, they not were not very original in design. These concrete donut shaped stadiums were criticized later on as being "cookie cutter" venues, as all of these stadiums looked exactly alike. However, in 1970, these new stadiums were miles ahead in looks and design than the old Cleveland Municipal Stadium. Coincidentally, Three Rivers Stadium and Riverfront Stadium housed two of the Brown's division rivals: The Pittsburgh Steelers and the Cincinnati Bengals.[40]

Seeing his competitors getting new venues, Modell had to do something to showcase Municipal Stadium to the public to bring in more

39. Schultz, *The NFL, Year One*, 48.
40. Ibid.

earnings. Unlike other owners, who had other business ventures that brought in more income than their football teams, the Browns were Art Modell's main source of income. Modell was always looking for ways to market the team so that the Browns could make a profit. Now in 1970, Modell saw a good opportunity for the Browns to host the first *Monday Night Football* game, because he believed that a large national audience would tune into the game on television sets across the country in a prime time slot. Modell was so sure that the program would have high ratings, which would in turn generate large revenue streams to the teams from the network. Modell said:

> No one else wanted the game because they thought it (*Monday Night Football*) would die at the gate . . . But I was willing to take a chance. All I said was 'Give me the Jets,' because I figure having the New York market would give the game a jump.[41]

Modell was hedging big on the game, and he was right about the match up between the Jets and Browns, and the New York market. The New York Jets were still considered an elite team in the old AFL after their victory in Super Bowl III over the more superior Baltimore Colts in the NFL. The Cleveland Browns were also a good team in recent years in the old NFL, beating the Dallas Cowboys twice in the last two years in the playoffs. On this warm Monday night, these two teams were still being billed as an old AFL vs. NFL rivalry to attract an audience, even though they were under one league, and now in one conference. With the Browns moving to the AFC, it was the new AFC Jets team vs. the new AFC Browns team, but it wasn't seen that way by the media or the public. The merger didn't stop old allegiances to the former leagues when it came to the rivalry. Besides, it was a good marketing plan, because the public did not get used to the new merged league yet, as this was the first week of the new season.

---

41. Ibid.

On that warm Monday night, on September 21, 1970, *Monday Night Football* was born. The opening theme song was played, which would become the definitive theme song for the program, if not for all of pro football for the next few decades. Sportscaster Keith Jackson opened the show by stating: "From Municipal Stadium in Cleveland, Ohio . . . two powers in professional football meet for the very first time as members of the American Football Conference of the National Football League . . ."[42]

Advertisers were charged $65,000 per minute by ABC during the clash, a cost that proved to be a bargain when the contest collected 33 percent of the viewing audience. The Browns defeated the Jets, 31-21 in a game which featured a 94-yard kickoff return for a touchdown by the Browns' Homer Jones and was punctuated when Billy Andrews intercepted Joe Namath late in the fourth quarter and returned it 25 yards for the clinching touchdown. However, Cleveland viewers saw different programming on WEWS-TV, because of the NFL's blackout rules for home games at the time which would apply for all games through the end of the 1972 season. Beginning in 1973, home games could be televised if they sold out 72 hours before kickoff.[43]

Art Modell's gamble had paid off. *Monday Night Football* was a huge success that night, and it became the number one prime time program on Monday nights. The revenue streams soared for the NFL in televising the football games on Monday night. 50 years later, *Monday Night Football* is still Monday night's go to program during the autumn months, and is still a staple for football fans.

AFC WEST - THE KANSAS CITY CHIEFS

The Kansas City Chiefs had good reason to be optimistic for the merger and the 1970 NFL season, as they just upset the heavily favored

---

42. Mike Vaccaro, "*Monday Night Football* debut 50 years ago began a television revolution" *New York Post* (September 21, 2020), accessed February 21, 2021, https://nypost.com/2020/09/21/monday-night-football-debut-50-years-ago-began-a-tv-revolution/.

43. Bobby Ellerbee, "September 21, 1970... 'ABC *Monday Night Football*' Debuts" (September 21, 2014), Eyes of a Generation... Television's Living History, accessed February 21, 2021, https://eyesofageneration.com/september-21-1970-abc-monday-night-football-debutsmost-think-this-was-a-m/.

Minnesota Vikings in Super Bowl IV. With the realignment, both the Chiefs and their old nemesis, the Oakland Raiders, were put into the same division. Both teams would remain competitive after the merger and vie for the AFC West crown that year. The year before, in the final game in AFL history, the Chiefs became the league's only three-time champions, defeating the Raiders by a 17–7 score in Oakland. Making the victory even more satisfying for the Chiefs was that the Raiders players had to sheepishly walk out of the stadium with the luggage they had packed for New Orleans and Super Bowl IV.[44] The Raiders, who went 12-1-1, longed for revenge.

In addition to the Raiders wanting revenge on the Super Bowl champs, the Minnesota Vikings also thirsted for revenge on the Chiefs for losing Super Bowl IV. With the realignment and new schedules, there would be a rematch between the Vikings and Chiefs in game one of the new season. The Vikings took the loss to the Chiefs in Super Bowl IV very hard but were further exasperated by their coach, Bud Grant, who showed his team the NFL Films of Chiefs' coach Hank Stram miked up during the game. Seeing Stram gloat on the sidelines as his Chiefs dominated the Vikings rubbed salt into the losing teams' wounds. Also, the footage showed Stram being very critical of the Vikings' defense, which in itself was very embarrassing for the defeated team to see. The Vikings waited eight months for this moment and got their chance for revenge on the Chiefs in the opening week of the 1970 season when they hosted their Super Bowl-winning foes in Minnesota. In the words of Vikings' coach Bud Grant: "We've been lying behind a log for eight months waiting for this game."[45] Minnesota took out those eight months of frustration on the champs and blasted Kansas City 27–10. The Vikings would have another great year like the previous season with the same record of 12–2. Conversely, the Kansas City Chiefs season would not be as successful, as replicating the success of 1969 proved a difficult task for Stram and the Chiefs.

---

44. Kansas City Chiefs, Chiefs History, accessed October 19, 2018, https://web.archive.org/web/200708 23170852/http://www.kcchiefs.com/history/70s/.

45. Schultz, *The NFL, Year One*, 34.

One of the reasons for Kansas City's difficulty was the trading of running back Mike Garrett, who was the club's all-time leading rusher at the time. This was a big blow to the offense. He was traded to San Diego and replaced in the lineup by Ed Podolak. Even with some glimpses of dominance, including a 44–24 win at Baltimore on September 28th in just the second-ever telecast of ABC's *Monday Night Football*, the Chiefs faltered and just had a 3-3-1 record at the season's midpoint.

One of the season's most pivotal games came in a 17–17 tie vs. Oakland on November 1st. The Chiefs were ahead 17–14 when Dawson apparently sealed the win by running for a first down. This would have allowed Kansas City to run out the clock. Circumstances would change that. While on the ground, Dawson was hit late by Raider's defensive end Ben Davidson. Seeing the hit on Dawson, Chiefs' wide receiver Otis Taylor retaliated, and a bench-clearing brawl ensued. Offsetting penalties were called nullifying Dawson's first-down run. This would cost the Chiefs a victory and further inflamed the already heated Chiefs-Raiders rivalry because the Chiefs were forced to punt and Raiders kicker George Blanda eventually booted a game-tying FG with 0:08 remaining. That tie game ultimately set the Chiefs back because Kansas City finished the year with a 7-5-2 record, while the Raiders went 8-4-2 and won the division crown. Had the Chiefs won the game, they would have won the AFC West.[46] Just as the Minnesota Vikings had their revenge on Kansas City by beating them in the first game of the season (after losing to the Chiefs in Super Bowl IV), the Raiders would also get their revenge on Kansas City after losing to the Chiefs in the AFL Championship 17–7 back in January (and not going to Super Bowl IV).

---

46. Ibid.

The newly built Riverfront Stadium in Cincinnati opened in 1970. This new all-purpose, "cookie cutter," artificial turf stadium was the home of the Cincinnati Bengals until 2002. (Pinterest.com)

The newly built Three Rivers Stadium in Pittsburgh in 1970. Like Riverfront Stadium in Cincinnati, this all-purpose, "cookie cutter," artificial turf stadium would be the home of the Pittsburgh Steelers for many years until 2000. (Pinterest.com)

Legendary head coach, Paul Brown, took a Cincinnati Bengals team that was in the cellar of the Central Division of the AFC, by the halfway point of the season (with 1-6 record), and eventually won the division in 1970. (Pinterest.com)

NFL Commissioner, Pete Rozelle, shows the press the merging of the two pro foot-ball leagues. (Blogspot.com)

Lamar Hunt had a vision to create a new pro football league. The American Football League was born from his vision. (Blogsport.com)

Tex Schramm, Pete Rozelle, and Lamar Hunt announce the merger of the AFL and NFL. (Boston.com)

George Blanda gave new meaning to middle age in 1970. (Pinterest.com)

The Raiders' patriarch, Al Davis, was made the Commissioner of the AFL in order to wage war against the rival NFL. He had to settle for a peace agreement instead. (Getty Images)

Joe Namath gets ready to pass against the Cleveland Browns in Monday Night
Fooball's first game televised on September 21, 1970. (Pinterest.com)

John Madden was the youngest coach in the league at 32 years old in 1969, and in
1970 he piloted a resilient Oakland Raiders team to win the Western Division of the
new American Football Conference. (ESPN.com)

49ers veteran quarterback, John Brodie, won the Most Valuable Player award in 1970, and brought the team to the NFC Championship. (Pinterest.com)

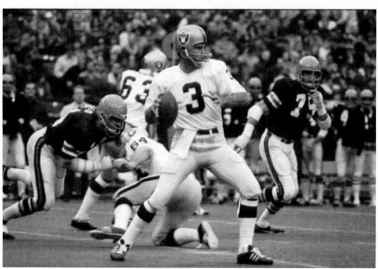

Raiders quarterback, Daryle Lamonica, exemplified the high scoring aerial attack of the AFL and was nicknamed "The Mad Bomber." (Getty Images)

Cowboys coach, Tom Landry, had his hands full in an unpredictable 1970 season for Dallas. With his guidance the team would make it to Super Bowl V. (ESPNgo.com)

Baltimore Coach, Dona Shula, defected to Miami to coach the Dolphins in 1970. Shula coached the Dolphins to a 10-4 record, and was the AFC's first wild card team ever to make it in the playoffs. (Pinterest.com)

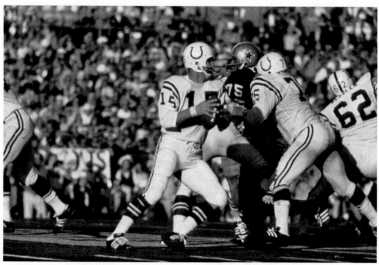

Colt's quarterback, Earl Morrall, tried to erase the bitterness of losing to the underdog New York Jets in Super Bowl III. Morrall would get the opportunity for vindication in Super Bowl V. (Courtesy Houston Chronicle)

One tough player, quarterback Joe Kapp was not a finesse quarteback but played smashmouth football. (Pinterest.com)

Minnesota Vikings coach, Bud Grant, sought redemption in the new merged league in 1970 after the Vikings lost the last AFL-NFL Championship in Super Bowl IV to the Kansas City Chiefs earlier in the year. The Vikings went 12-2 in 1970. (Pinterest.com)

Baltimore Colts' Johnny Unitas was no longer an elite quarterback in the NFL and his play suffered due to many injuries sustained in 1970. (Sports Illustrated)

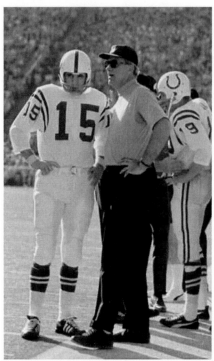

Colt's rookie head coach, Don McCafferty, had big shoes to fill after Don Shula left to coach the Miami Dolphins. Here he is seen talking it over on the sidelines with quarterback Earl Morrall. (Pinterest.com)

Dallas Cowboys' Mel Renfro was stellar as a defensive back during the 1970 season. (ESPNgo.com)

Roger Staubach was too flashy and arrogant to be the starter for the Cowboys in 1970. So he shared the quarterbacking duties with Craig Morton. (Pinterest.com)

Dallas Cowboys' quarterback, Craig Morton, got no respect in the the 1970 season. (FoxNews.com)

Sportscasters Howard Cosell, Keith Jackson, and Don Meredith called it on Monday nights for the new prime time show: Monday Night Football on ABC. (Pinterest.com)

Baltimore Colts' defensive end, Bubba Smith, terrorized offenses with his rough style of play. He refused to wear his Super Bowl V ring because of the disappointment of losing Super Bowl III to the Jets. (Getty Images)

Miami Dolphins head coach, Don Shula, talks it over with his starting quarterback, Bob Griese. (Pinterest.com)

Dolphin's hard-nose fullback, Larry Csonka, scared defenses across the league with his abilities to run over them. (Pinterest.com)

Head coach, Joe Schmidt, took the Detroit Lions into the playoffs as the first wild card seed ever for the NFC in 1970.

Saint's half-footed kicker, Tom Dempsey, kicked the longest field goal in Pro Football history at the time with a 63-yard boot against the Detroit Lions in 1970. (Pinterest.com)

San Francisco 49ers' coach, Dick Nolan, guided his team to the first NFC Championship but could not beat his old teacher and mentor, Tom Landry and the Dallas Cowboys. (Deadspin.com)

Event poster for Super Bowl V. (Pinterest.com)

Super Bowl V featured the first matchup between the winners of the newly formed NFC and AFC Conferences to square off for the Vince Lombardi Trophy. (Youtube.com)

Dallas Cowboys' linebacker, Chuck Howley, had two interceptions and a fumble recovery in Super Bowl V and was named the MVP. He is still the only player from the losing side to win the MVP award. For a long time, it was rumored that Howley refused the MVP honor due to his team's loss. Howley would later admit in 2015 that this was not accurate. (Getty Images)

Action in Super Bowl V between the Colts and the Cowboys. (Pinterest.com)

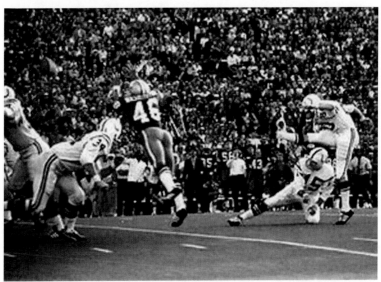

Rookie kicker, Jim O'Brien, kicks the ball for a field goal in the final seconds in Super Bowl V. (*The New York Daily News*)

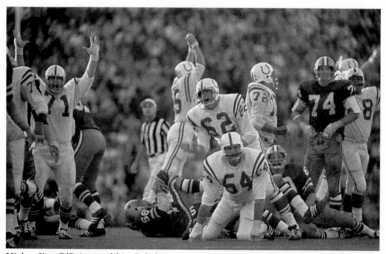

Kicker Jim O'Brien and his Colts'
teammates celebrate his winning field
goal in Super Bowl V. (Pinterest.com)

Super Bowl V Champions Baltimore
Colts on a collector's button,
commemorating their victory.
(Ebay.com)

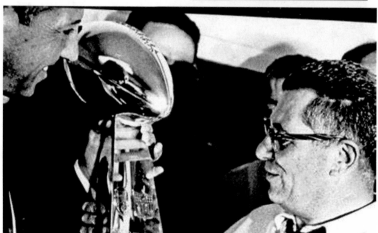

Packers' Coach Vince Lombardi holds the first AFL-NFL Championship trophy after
Green Bay beat the Kansas City Chiefs in Super Bowl I. The trophy would be named
for Lombardi after his death, before the 1970 NFL season began. (Pinterest.com)

8

THE DALLAS COWBOYS IN 1970

The 1970 Dallas Cowboys were unlikely heroes in the newly minted NFL. The season was so topsy-turvey that at one point in October, coach Tom Landry thought the team would not even be in contention for a playoff spot. The Cowboys battled the New York Giants and the St. Louis Cardinals all season long for the NFC East crown. Unlike previous seasons, where the Dallas Cowboys dominated their division, this season was not easy to follow. For the players, the 1970 season was a grueling excursion on many battlefields where the outcome would not be decided until the end of December. It was a season not to be watched . . . but to be lived through.[1] Somehow, the 1970 Cowboys would claw their way to the NFC East crown and then fight the Lions and the 49ers in the playoffs to win the first NFC title, earning them a berth in the Super Bowl, which eluded the team since 1966.

The 1968 Cowboys were 12–2, and in 1969 they were 11-2-1 and easily won their division in both years with ease. However, both seasons ended in disappointment as the Cowboys lost to the Cleveland Browns in the playoffs in both years. Even with the two consecutive playoff losses to

---

1. Gary Beard, "The Decline and Rise of the Dallas Cowboys, 1970 Highlights," published June 18, 2018, accessed October 22, 2018, https://www.youtube.com/watch?v=aaxLuYN73-U.

the Browns, things looked bright for the Cowboys in 1970. The team had so much talent that losing was not an option. Even the Cowboys' second and third stringers were that talented, and they were highly qualified to play as a starter for many of the other teams in the NFL. Calvin Hill and Walt Garrison were the running backs who powered the Cowboys' rushing attack. Hill was the offensive rookie of the year the year before and steamrolled into the record books with 942 rushing yards and 8 touchdowns during the 1969 campaign. As for Garrison, he was known for his toughness and blocking, and he took over at fullback after the retirement of Don Perkins in 1969. Along with Hill, Garrison had a great 1969 season with a career-high 818 rushing yards and 2 touchdowns. His style of play and his ability to play hurt, brought him recognition throughout the league. In 1970, the Cowboys added rookie running back Duane Thomas to create quite a trio in the backfield. Thomas was a quiet man, who didn't talk much, but who did his talking by running over people while carrying a football.[2] In 1970, he would do plenty of running.

The Cowboys had to overcome many obstacles during the 1970 regular season. For starters, fullback Calvin Hill had 577 yards and 4 touchdowns but was lost for the year after suffering a leg injury late in the regular season. More problematic for the team was that the Cowboys had a quarterback controversy between Craig Morton and Roger Staubach. Morton and Staubach alternated as the starting quarterback during the regular season, but Landry eventually chose Morton to start Super Bowl V because he felt less confident that Staubach would follow his game plan (Landry called all of Morton's plays in Super Bowl V).[3] Also, Morton had done exceptionally well in the regular season, throwing for 1,819 yards and 15 touchdowns, with only 7 interceptions, earning him a passer rating of 89.8. In contrast, although a noted scrambler and able to salvage broken plays effectively, Staubach threw for 542 yards and only 2 touchdowns compared to 8 interceptions, giving him a 42.9 rating.[4]

2. John Schaefer, *Dallas Cowboys 1970: A Game-by-Game Guide* (2012), 18–21, Kindle.

3. Bill McGrane, "A Mad, Mad, Mad Super Bowl," in *The Super Bowl: Celebrating a Quarter-Century of America's Greatest Game* (NY: Simon and Schuster, 1990), 56.

4. "1970 Dallas Cowboys," Pro Football Reference, accessed October 22, 2018, https://www.pro-football-reference.com/teams/dal/1970.htm.

Bob Hayes was the main deep threat on the team, catching 34 passes for 889 yards (a 26.1 yards per catch average) and 10 touchdowns, while also rushing four times for 34 yards and another touchdown adding another 116 yards returning punts.[5] Although Hayes had a fine season, he was benched by head coach Tom Landry for poor performances on several occasions. This upset the receiving core of the offense, as the fastest man in the world was forced to sit. On the other side of the field, opposite Hayes, was wide receiver Lance Rentzel, who recorded 28 receptions for 556 yards and 5 touchdowns.[6]

Even with the quarterback controversy, the main strength of the Cowboys' offense was their running game. Rookie running back Duane Thomas rushed 151 times for 803 yards (a 5.1 yards per carrying average) and 5 touchdowns while adding another 416 yards returning kickoffs. Fullback Walt Garrison, who replaced the injured Hill, provided Thomas with excellent blocking and rushed for 507 yards and 3 touchdowns himself. Garrison was also a good receiver out of the backfield, catching 21 passes for 205 yards and 2 touchdowns. On the line, Pro Bowl guard John Niland and future Hall of Famer tackle Rayfield Wright anchored the offensive line.[7]

When rookie safety Cliff Harris arrived in the Cowboys' camp in 1970, he joined a star-studded defensive backfield that included future Hall of Fame members Mel Renfro and Herb Adderley at cornerback, and Cornell Green and fellow rookie Charlie Waters at safety. But Harris would more than hold his own in a standout 10-year career that included six Pro Bowl selections and two Super Bowl titles. Only five players in Cowboys history have been selected to more Pro Bowls than Harris. He was also a four-time All-Pro selection and a member of the NFL's all-decade team for the 1970s.[8]

Coach Tom Landry was very optimistic going into the 1970 season. He even remarked: "I feel better this year than I have ever felt about

---

5. Ibid.
6. Ibid.
7. Ibid.
8. #43 Cliff Harris, Safety, 1970–1979, Dallas Cowboys, accessed October 22, 2018, https://www.dallas cowboys.com/team/ROH-Cliff-Harris.

the potential of this team.[9] Landry instituted his brand of getting tough attitude coupled with his four musts to get to the Super Bowl: technical ability, consistency, dedication, and competitiveness from the get-go.[10] One thing about Landry was that he was not a coach who breathed fire as a dragon on his players like Lombardi did or Shula in Miami. Because he did not instill fear into his players, Landry was criticized for being too lax on his team. Many felt it was this precise reason the Cowboys lost the last four efforts to get to the Super Bowl due to him not being a taskmaster. Being knocked out in the playoffs by Cleveland in the last two years gave Dallas a very unsavory nickname by sportswriters: "Next Year's Champions."[11] Taking notice of the disappointing losses in the last few seasons, Landry doubted his team's desire to win.

Before the season started, Landry instituted his brand of get-tough attitude by sending out lengthy questionnaires to all his players and then followed up with computer-generated evaluations of player performances.[12] Playing time would be determined by those who received the highest grades after each game. This probably did more harm than good on the players' psyches, but Landry remained determined in his resolve. He let the team know at training camp that no one had won a starting position. The 1970 season would test Landry's patience about starting and benching players in what would be the wildest roller coaster ride in Cowboys' history.

Game One of the 1970 season was at Franklin Field in Philadelphia, where the Cowboys met the Eagles. Going into the game, the Cowboys were favored by two touchdowns over the Eagles, who lost all the pre-season games going into the season. Calvin Hill, who rushed 117 yards, provided most of the offense, and starting quarterback Roger Staubach hit most of his passes, completing 11 in 15 attempts.

The game wasn't a blowout as most expected. The Eagles stunned the Cowboys in the first quarter with a 63-yard drive ending when

9. Joe Patoski, *The Dallas Cowboys ... The Outrageous History of the Biggest, Loudest, Most Hated, Best Loved Football Team in America* (Boston: Little Brown and Company, 2012), 236.

10. Ibid.

11. Schultz, *The NFL, Year One*, 96.

12. Ibid.

Philadelphia quarterback, Norm Snead, threw a 10-yard pass to receiver Ben Hawkins for the touchdown, and kicker Mark Moseley converted the extra point for a 7–0 lead.[13] Dallas struck back late in the second quarter when defensive end George Andrie recovered a Philadelphia fumble at the Eagles' 34. It took eight plays for Dallas to march down the field. 227-pound Calvin Hill carried the ball on six of those plays, as the Dallas offense went deep into Eagles' territory. The drive ended when Walt Garrison ran into the end zone from the 1-yard line, and Clark kicked the extra point.[14]

The teams went into halftime with a surprising 7–7 tie. The momentum would swing the Cowboys way for the rest of the game, partly because the Doomsday defense of Dallas held the Eagles scoreless for the rest of the game. This gave the Dallas offense a chance to score, which they did by getting the winning points in the third period on a 31-yard pass from Roger Staubach to split end Lance Rentzel. Mike Clark added three insurance points late in the final quarter with a 13-yard field goal. The Cowboys had won the first game of the 1970 season, but in a lackluster style with a 17–7 victory. The supposed dominance of the Cowboys just was not present in the game. This lack of dominance would follow them all season long.

After their victory over Philadelphia, cracks began to emerge with some of the players' morale. Not everyone in the Dallas locker room was smiling after the victory. Bob Hayes, who was benched by Landry and only used on punt returns after a poor preseason, spoke up and said he was "very, very unhappy. I don't like playing on the second team when I know I'm best." He also said he would rather leave the Cowboys than be a backup.[15]

At their home opener for the second game of the season, the Dallas Cowboys hosted the up-and-coming New York Giants. The Cowboys won the game, highlighted by a trick play that was instituted on the practice field as horseplay, and some sterling defensive gems by rookie

13. Schaefer, *Game-by-Game Guide*, 51–55, Kindle.
14. Ibid., 52.
15. Ibid., 57–61.

safety Cliff Harris were the big contributions to the Cowboys' defeat of the New York Giants 28–10.

As for the trick play, it looked like a normal running play when the Dallas offense called a right end sweep as quarterback Roger Staubach handed off to Calvin Hill, the NFL's leading rusher, at Dallas' 42-yard line. But suddenly, Hill handed off to wide receiver Lance Rentzel, sweeping by toward the left in an apparent double reverse. Rentzel swept wide, to the right, but suddenly stopped, cocked his left arm, and let fly a southpaw pass. Back in the wide receiver position, Bob Hayes streaked under the ball and caught it on the New York 13-yard line and zipped into the end zone to make it 21–10. "It was the first time I've thrown a pass since high school days," Rentzel said later. "I've been throwing passes to Bob Belden (the taxi squad third-string quarterback) while he runs pass patterns in practice, and we've had a lot of fun with it."[16]

As for the Dallas defense, Cliff Harris was the star of Doomsday. The Giants were leading 10–0, and everything the Cowboys did seemed to turn sour until Harris picked off a Fran Tarkenton overthrown pass and streaked 60 yards with it to the New York 8-yard line to set up a three-yard scoring plunge by Hill. Less than three minutes later, Harris stole another Tarkenton pass, but that effort didn't produce any points when Mike Clark missed a 47-yard field goal try. Two plays later, however, Harris was at it again. He pounced on a Ron Johnson fumble at the New York 29 to set up (two plays later) Walt Garrison's 18-yard rumble behind a big block by Rayfield Wright. "He's coming on strong, and he's going to be a comer," Landry said of Harris. "That was a great run by him on the first one (interception)."[17]

The glaring issue during the game was the Cowboys' offense. It was flat. The Giants had also made the most of a string of Dallas errors in the first half to get a 10–0 lead. If not for the Giant turnovers, the game might have had a different outcome.

Game three at Busch Memorial Stadium in St. Louis would be more of the same for the Cowboy offense. It was just anemic. The team would

16. Ibid., 158–162.
17. Ibid., 171–176.

almost be shut out by the Cardinals' stingy defense, who chased Roger Staubach from the game. If not for Calvin Hill's touchdown with 3.06 remaining in the game, the Cowboys would have been shut out for the first time in their history.[18]

The Cardinals were eager for the meeting with the Cowboys as their coach, an ebullient Charley Winner said, put it: "Our objective this week was to gain a share of first place . . . and now that we're there we kind of like the feeling."[19]

Going into the game, the Cardinals had studied film of how the Cowboys beat them a year before and saw some of Dallas' weaknesses. With Charley Winner firing them up, the Cardinals got mentally tough for the game. Their toughness showed, in the finals score, as the Cardinals won 20 to 7.

The Cowboys were overwhelmed by St. Louis and knew it. "We just had a hard time getting going," said Cowboys coach Tom Landry, who yanked an unsteady quarterback, Roger Staubach, after throwing a second interception that set up a 35-yard Jim Bakken field goal for the Cardinals in the first half. Craig Morton, who took over, didn't fare much better against St. Louis. Morton only managed seven completions in 16 attempts, but four were delivered to tight end Mike Ditka. The Cardinals' defense bottled up the other receivers.[20] "I've always said four or five passes are the difference in a ball game," said Winner, whose Cardinals moved into a tie with the Cowboys at 2–1 atop the National Football Conference East standings. "Our defense gave us the opportunities, and we were able to cash them in. Next time we play Dallas in Dallas, it might not be so easy. They're a good, tough club and one that's hard to beat because they usually don't make the mistakes."[21]

With the horrible play from both Staubach and Morton, Landry was under increasing pressure to settle on a quarterback. "The morale is down," linebacker Lee Roy Jordan said. "But once a decision is made at

18. Marty Strasen with Danny White, *Cowboys Chronicles, A Complete History of the Dallas Cowboys* (Chicago, Triumph Books, 2010), 77.
19. Schaefer, *Game-by-Game Guide*, 285, Kindle.
20. Ibid., 298–302.
21. Ibid., 302–306.5.

quarterback, it will help the team get settled." A terse Staubach simply said of his benching, "I'm at my best in a tough game." Later, Landry chimed in by saying, "I think Roger will do a good job. He has a great arm but lacks experience. I would like to go with just one quarterback, but you have to see a trend to warrant doing that."[22]

The sky opened, and the rains came at the Cotton Bowl for game four when the Cowboys hosted the Falcons. The Dallas defense lived up to their reputation by stonewalling the Falcons 13 to 0. Craig Morton was not at his best, hitting three of 10 passes, and the offense continued to flatline. With Bob Lilly leading the way, the defense gave the Falcons fits on a wet afternoon more suited for surfboarding. Heavy rain drove away fans after the game started and handed the synthetic turf a good test. The moist conditions hindered both offensive units.[23]

The Cowboys' defenders paved the way in the muck for two more Dallas scores in the second half. After the second-half kickoff, Atlanta's Cannonball Butler fumbled, and rookie Cliff Harris scooped it up and raced 31 yards before being knocked out at the 7.

The final score pleased Tom Landry with the tough playing of his team. "This is the first good game we've had of 60 minutes of football," Landry said. "Both the offense and the defense hustled today."[24] The Cowboys were at 3–1 with four games played. But even with their good record, the team didn't look strong to be a contender.

The fifth game was in Minnesota, at Metropolitan Stadium, where the Cowboys took on the Vikings, NFL champions from the year before. Going into the game, the Minnesota Vikings were tied for the lead in the Central Division after winning four of their first five starts. The Purple People Eaters would notch another victory under its belt as the Cowboys were decimated and overrun by the Minnesota Vikings' defense. The Vikings' notorious defense scored two touchdowns and set up one more plus one field goal, while quarterback Gary Cuozzo was buzzing with aerials and had 11 completed passes out of 20 attempts for 133 yards and

22. Ibid., 306–311.
23. Ibid., 413.
24. Ibid., 426–430.

one touchdown. "We played nearly perfectly," Cuozzo said. "We had one penalty and no turnovers. It was our best game of the year, even better than Kansas City." The 54 points were a team-high, and it also was the worst beating in Dallas' 10-year history.[25] Even though the Vikings had a good record before the match up with the Cowboys, there was a general feeling by the press and the public that the team's record 54–13 win over Dallas was the first time all season they put it all together.

Coach Bud Grant of the Vikings was typically less exuberant than some of the players about the massive beating his team gave the Cowboys. "It could happen to us next week . . . everything we did fell in the right spot . . . we haven't had much luck against Dallas in the past," Grant added that this was the first time in six regular-season contests that the Vikings beat the Cowboys. "But it all came to us today."[26]

For the Cowboys, the woes on offense continued. Quarterback Craig Morton had a dismal day completing only four passes out of ten attempts, with an interception. Landry shuffled the quarterbacks once more and brought in Roger Staubach, who had to trudge through the game as the Minnesota steamroller plowed their way through. Staubach was intercepted three times, and the Cowboys fell under the heel of the Minnesota juggernaut. More bad news came when running back Calvin Hill got injured during the game and did not play at 100 percent for the rest of the season.[27]

The loss dropped the Cowboys to second place behind the St. Louis Cardinals after retaking the first spot the week before. The schedule would not get any easier for Dallas.

The Cowboys continued their road trip with a stop at Municipal Stadium in Kansas City to play the Super Bowl champion Chiefs. After being dealt a shattering defeat by Super Bowl IV's runner ups the week before, prospects didn't look good facing the Super Bowl Champs. Also, numerous problems plagued the Cowboys going into the game. There was much to consider for Tom Landry: The Army called up regular safety

25. Ibid., 545–552.
26. Ibid., 570–573.
27. Gary Beard, "Decline and Rise of the Dallas Cowboys," accessed October 22, 2018.

Cliff Harris; quarterback Roger Staubach didn't make the trip because of a staph infection, and offensive tackle Tony Liscio was out with an injury. As if that weren't bad enough, running back Calvin Hill was hurt on the first play from scrimmage during the game and carried the ball only once after that against the Chiefs.[28]

Going into the game, the Cowboys' spirits were already broken from the trauma of last week's beating from the Vikings, coupled with the unfortunate circumstances with Harris, Staubach, Liscio, and Hill. Miraculously, the Cowboys' fortunes would change for the better in Kansas City during this roller coaster ride of a season. Rookie running back Duane Thomas stepped in brilliantly for the injured Calvin Hill and rushed for 134 yards and two touchdowns. The fastest man on earth, Bob Hayes, made good on his nickname by catching a touchdown pass for 89 yards from Craig Morton. But it was the defense that bore down on the Chiefs' offense. The defense stifled quarterback Len Dawson all day. Dawson was picked off twice by the Cowboys' Mel Renfro in the secondary.[29] The Doomsday Defense of Dallas hindered the Chief's running game, forcing a very conservative, Len Dawson, to throw the ball 38 times in the game.

In the end, the Cowboys beat the Chiefs 27 to 16. The victory put Dallas in a tie with the Cardinals for first place in the NFC East Division at 4–2. Tom Landry summed up the two-game road trip in Minnesota and Kansas City as follows: "We didn't do anything different against Kansas City," Landry insisted. "We just played football. We didn't play football against Minnesota."[30]

The seventh game of the season marked the halfway point of the 1970 season. Back in the friendly confines of the Cotton Bowl, the Cowboys felt good to be at home against an 0–6 Philadelphia Eagles squad. But these Eagles would not be humble as pigeons as expected. Instead, these birds from Philly would fight the heavily favored Cowboys like Eagles in flight, attacking their prey.

---

28. Schaefer, *Game-by-Game Guide*, 707–711, Kindle.
29. Strasen, *Cowboys Chronicles*, 78.
30. Schaefer, *Game-by-Game Guide*, 733–737, Kindle.

It would take three big plays to unravel rival Philadelphia. Taking away those three big plays, the Cowboys could only muster less than 100 yards of total offense. Also, and what was very impressive, was that the Eagle defense completely shut down the Cowboys' rushing attack. For the first time in the club's history, the Cowboys didn't make a single first down rushing. Even with the potent rushing attack vs. the Chiefs a week before, the Cowboys' backfield never got going.

The first big play came in the second quarter after a stalemated first quarter. Craig Morton threw to receiver Lance Rentzel a picture-perfect pass over the middle for 86 yards and the day's first touchdown.

In the second quarter, Morton connected with Bob Hayes for six points with a 40-yard strike. Finally, in the 3rd quarter, Morton threw a 56-yard pass to Rentzel, who scored his second touchdown of the day.

Philadelphia utilized the bomb also when Norm Snead collaborated with wide receiver Ben Hawkins on a 78-yard pass and run in the third period.

If you took away Philly quarterback Norm Snead's four interceptions on the day, the Eagles would have won the game despite a 14–0 deficit at halftime.

Coach Tom Landry was far from pleased with the victory. "Philadelphia played well. They kept our backs to the wall, and we didn't distinguish ourselves," Landry said. "Our running game didn't look good, basically because we weren't hitting. Philadelphia stacked eight men up on the line, and that, of course, opened them up for the big bombs."[31] That wasn't the Landry style of football. Even Landry would have doubts about the rest of the season with the way his Cowboys played. At the halfway point, the Cowboys were far from a dominating team headed for the playoffs.

In-game eight, which began the second half of the season, the Cowboys traveled to New York, and into the Bronx, at Yankee Stadium to face the rival Giants for the second time this season. The Cowboys were tied with St. Louis for first place in the NFC's Eastern Division going into the game. The Giants, however, began the season with a 0–3 record,

31. Ibid., 881.

including a loss to Dallas in game two. However, the team gathered themselves and rattled off five straight wins and were now jockeying with St. Louis and Dallas for playoff contention in winning the NFC crown.

The Dallas offense got cooking and utilized the bomb effectively again as they had done the week before. Morton hit Bob Hayes for two long touchdown passes in the first half. Dallas jumped to a 17–9 halftime lead as Bob Hayes snared those two bombs from Craig Morton, covering 38 and 80 yards, and Mike Clark kicked a 28-yard field goal to offset three long three-pointers by kicker Pete Gogolak of the Giants.

The second half saw a see-saw battle between the two division rivals. Sloppy play plagued the Cowboys' offense, especially when they were denied big gains due to self-inflicted penalties. Giants kicker, Pete Gogolak, booted 4 field goals in the game and broke a Giants record, hitting a 54-yard field goal, but missed a 29 yarder in the 4th quarter, leaving the Cowboys four points ahead. However, the Giants still would not give up the fight and got the ball back with 5:26 to play in the game. Tarkenton marched his offense 73 yards for the winning touchdown. On the Giants' drive into Cowboys territory, a 32-yard pass from Tarkenton to Clifton McNeil pushed the drive over midfield and into Dallas territory. Then a 22-yard pitch to Johnson carried them to the 17-yard line. Tarkenton then scrambled to the 12-yard line, tossed one incomplete pass, and then hit Johnson, who had gotten a step on Mel Renfro, for the decisive score.[32]

The Giants defense held the number one rushing team to just 28 yards in the first half and 102 yards overall. The excitement of the Giants and their fans in beating the Cowboys was overwhelming. From such a dismal start, the Giants had clawed their way into a three-team race for the NFC East. When asked why the Giants had a resurgence after their 0–3 start, coach Alex Webster said, "We're not making as many mistakes, and when we do, we don't let them bother us."[33] As for the Cowboys, they fell to 3rd place with the loss

32. Ibid., 1006.
33. Ibid., 1020.

In-game nine, the Cowboys came home to the Cotton Bowl for a showdown with the first-place St. Louis Cardinals for a Monday night game. If home cooking was the Cowboys' remedy, they only got the leftovers no-one wanted from the meal. Former Cowboys quarterback Don Meredith, who was now an announcer for *Monday Night Football*, returned to his old team at the Cotton Bowl to cover the game. The Dallas Cowboys' fans who booed Don Meredith from defecting from the NFL as their quarterback to television commentator cried out for help from "Dandy" Don. While the Cardinals were steamrolling the Cowboys, the crowd began chanting, "We Want Meredith, We Want Meredith." Meredith, who retired two years earlier in 1968, was surprised by the crowds' enthusiasm for him, but saw the decimation of the Cowboys by the Cardinals and remarked: "There's no way I'm going down there, folks, I'll tell you that."[34]

In an ironic twist, Don Meredith had contacted Dallas owner, Tex Schramm, earlier in the year before the season to see if he could come back to the Cowboys, but only if he was the starting quarterback. Meredith's private life was quieting down with a divorce from his wife, and he said he was able to come out of retirement. Schramm denied Meredith's offer to return to the team because he saw both Craig Morton and Roger Staubach as the future of Dallas. But on this night, as he was calling the plays, he knew he had been there and done that. If there were any animosity against Meredith by the Dallas fans, it was put to bed this Monday night.

The Cardinals won 38 to 0, and in doing, so became the first team since 1935 to record three shutouts in a row. The team was indeed on fire. For the Cowboys, it was the first time they were shutout in team history. The Cardinals defense forced six turnovers, including intercepting Morton four times and Staubach once. The Cardinals' offensive running backs rushed for 242 yards along with four touchdowns on the ground.[35]

St. Louis had outscored its last three opponents 113–0. It beat Houston 44–0, Boston 31–0, and now Dallas 38–0. From the NFL standpoint,

34. Ibid., 1138.
35. Strasen, *Cowboys Chronicles*, 80.

the Cardinals looked unstoppable in the NFC East. For the Cowboys, they looked lifeless. Even Landry wondered if there was a playoff hope left for the team. With a 5–4 record, and with the losses mounting, it seemed to be getting worse for the Cowboys as the weeks went by. If that wasn't disappointing enough, then this reality was: Dallas would need to win all 5 of their last games to have a chance winning in the NFC East. In looking at the standings, the Cardinals were at 7–2, and the Giants were at 6–3, and both teams beat the Cowboys in consecutive weeks. The way the Cowboys had been playing, this would not be an easy task. If anything, it would be a daunting task.

Going into RFK Stadium in Washington, D.C., to play the Redskins in game ten was not an optimistic time for the Cowboys. The team knew that they would have to break out of their funk and play like the elite team that the experts said they were at the beginning of the season. In Washington, the magic returned to the Cowboys and showed the NFL they still had glimpses of that superiority about which everyone spoke.

The first matchup of the season with the Redskins, saw the Cowboys firing on all cylinders. When the score was 24–14 in favor of the Cowboys in the 3rd quarter, rookie Mark Washington returned a kickoff 100 yards for a touchdown showing the Washington Redskins the spark the Cowboys had at special teams. Substitute running back Duane Thomas rushed for 104 yards and three touchdowns. Craig Morton looked sharp, completing 12 of 15 passes and two touchdown throws.[36]

In the end, the Cowboys crushed the Redskins 45 to 21. The team played as a coherent unit and put life back into their dejected morale from the two previous losses. There were still four games left to the season to make a run at winning the NFC East. Meanwhile, the Cardinals had tied the Chiefs, and the Giants lost that week to the Eagles in Philadelphia. There was still a glimmer of hope for the Cowboys to salvage the season. Next up for the team. were the Packers, who would be at the Cotton Bowl in four days for a Thanksgiving match-up that all the United States would see on live television.

---

36. Ibid.

The Packers' dominance of the Cowboys from the past few seasons still hung over the Cowboys like a dark cloud. The Packers had thwarted the Cowboys in winning the NFL Championship games and advancing to the first two Super Bowls in both the 1966 and 1967 seasons. Also, the Packers won their last six straight over the Cowboys. If the Cowboys were to continue to be a playoff contender, they would have to exorcise their demons quickly. With a crowd of 67,182 packing the Cotton Bowl to root on their beloved Cowboys, the team did just that in-game eleven.

It was a warm, windy day for Thanksgiving festivities in Dallas. Things looked bleak from the start when the Packers marched down the field after the opening kickoff and ran ten minutes off the game clock. Dallas's Doomsday Defense looked helpless against the Packers on the drive but was able to stop the Cheeseheads, and the Packers only got 3 points on a 19-yard field goal by the kicker, Dale Livingston. After the field goal, the Cowboys defense bore down on the Packers for the rest of the game. Although the Cowboys' offense struggled in the first half, there was vindication when Dallas tied the score with two minutes remaining until halftime with a 21-yard field goal by kicker Mike Clark.[37]

Landry called all the offensive plays in the game, trying to spark the offense. He employed a simpler offense and moved away from the big play in this game. They did not try to bomb their opponents as in the last three games. Instead, Morton threw short passes rather than bombs, and the strategy worked.

With the Dallas offense clicking, the Cowboys' defense shined brightly throughout the game. The Cowboys' Doomsday defense held the Packers to 78 yards on the ground and turned the defense around from the recent games when nearly everybody was cramming the rush down their throats.[38] After the game, linebacker Lee Roy Jordan remarked: "I thought we regained our confidence against the run . . . We made some tough plays, and I think people will start thinking twice about us again,"[39]

---

37. Schaefer, *Game-by-Game Guide*, 1432–1436, Kindle.
38. Ibid., 1440–1445.
39. Ibid., 1445.

With Landry calling the plays for quarterback Craig Morton, he responded extremely well by executing the plays that moved Dallas 151 yards on the ground and 201 yards in the air.

As for the defense, the significance of the Packers' opening 68-yard drive was even more pinpointed by the fact that they gained only 61 yards the rest of the game.

The Cowboys played a well-balanced game, as they finally beat the Packers and continued their pursuit for playoff contention. Green Bay was knocked out of playoff contention, leaving the Cotton Bowl with a 5–6 record.

Game twelve saw the Redskins coming to visit Dallas at the Cotton Bowl. The two teams had played two weeks earlier, where the Cowboys' dominating performance was still fresh in the Redskins' minds. There would be no redemption for the Redskins at the Cotton Bowl.

The juggernaut that the critics said the Cowboys were in pre-season showed up in full force to steamroll over the Redskins by a score of 34–0. Rookie Duane Thomas and veteran Walt Garrison gained nearly 200 yards rushing off a banged-up Washington Redskins defense, with Garrison scoring twice. Dallas's rushing total of 276 yards was a team record, surpassing their previous high of 241 set in 1966. The opponent in that game was also Washington.[40]

The defense stifled the Washington offense, who could go as far as the Cowboys' 31-yard line for most of the game.

With both the offense and defense looking like the dominant machine it should have been all season, the Cowboys now looked like the superior ones in the NFC East, and their star was rising. The shutout, the first suffered by the Redskins since the New York Giants did it 53–0 on Nov. 5, 1961, gave the Cowboys their third straight victory and an 8–4 record that pulled them within one-half game of Eastern Division pacesetter St. Louis, which was 8-3-1.

On a side note, this was the first game played without star wide receiver Lance Rentzel, following his arrest on Monday morning that week. Rentzel was charged with indecent exposure and placed on the

40. Ibid., 1570.

inactive list at his request. He was charged in an alleged incident involving a 10-year-old girl. In the original report filed, Rentzel allegedly drove up in his car, talked to the girl, and then exposed himself. Police said a warrant was issued for Rentzel's arrest after an automobile license plate was traced. Rentzel, then a member of the Minnesota Vikings, pleaded guilty to several charges in 1966 after numerous residents in a St. Paul neighborhood complained that he had exposed himself in the presence of small children on three different occasions.[41]

Rentzel was never sentenced, but a judge ordered him to seek psychiatric care. Rentzel's wife, actress Joey Heatherton, divorced him shortly after his 1970 arrest. He would never again play for the Cowboys, who traded him to the Los Angeles Rams before the 1971 season. Rentzel played three years for the Rams before retiring.[42]

The Cowboys' next stop was the Cleveland Browns, at Municipal Stadium in Cleveland, who knocked the Cowboys out of the playoffs in the previous two seasons and beaten the Cowboys in the last three meetings. Game thirteen was eagerly awaited by Cowboys' fans, but they were deprived of viewing the match up by a television blackout in the Dallas area because of the Pecan Bowl game coverage.

The Cowboys wanted to keep the momentum going and felt good about going into the game with a three-game winning streak that solidified the team not only with their play on the football field but also on the psyches. Finally, the Cowboys were acting as a unit, and the last three games showed that Dallas was a force to be reckoned with in the NFL.

On this day, the defenses took over for both the Cleveland Browns and Dallas Cowboys. The conditions were horrible at Municipal Stadium in Cleveland, making it impossible for both offenses to gain any ground. Municipal Stadium was a mud pit in a cold, dreary rain that puddled the field.

Cleveland's only scoring on the day was tackling Bob Hayes in the end zone on a punt return for a safety. Otherwise, the Dallas Doomsday defense stonewalled the Cleveland offense, and cornerback Dave Edwards

41. Ibid., 1605–1609.
42. Ibid., 1613.

had two interceptions. Altogether, the Cleveland Browns turned the ball over four times. Mike Clark supplied the scoring with two field goals from 39 and 31 yards for the Dallas offense.[43] The Cowboys would win 6–2 in the monsoon.

Both Cleveland and Dallas needed to win this game. With a 6–7 record in the AFC's Central Division, Cleveland had to depend on a loss by Cincinnati to have a chance at a playoff berth. The Bengals were 6–6 with two games remaining.

Now 9–4, Dallas was in a tight race with St. Louis (8-3-1) and New York (8–4) in the NFC's Eastern Division. It would all come down to the last week to see who would win the NFC East.

The last game of the season to be played by Dallas was at the Cotton Bowl, where the lowly Houston Oilers visited to play the Cowboys. Houston was not headed to the playoffs but was looking to play spoilers to their cross-state rivals in the quest for the NFC East crown.

The press and the fans were still processing this strange season for Dallas. Going from a heavily favored team by those who analyzed the predictions to fight for their playoff hopes confused everyone. Five weeks ago, no one could have believed that the Cowboys would be in playoff contention with the odds they had to overcome. The Cowboys, however, defied the odds by winning their last four games in a row. Now, it was time to seal the deal against Houston.

If there were any doubters that the Cowboys were an elite team, the team would put these naysayers to rest. It was just about impossible to single out a hero since all the Cowboys performed exceptionally well and destroyed their southern Texas rivals. But if anyone broke the game open, it was Bob Hayes and Reggie Rucker, Lance Rentzel's replacement. Craig Morton, the quarterback who had been booed unmercifully in the season, threw five touchdown passes, four of them to Hayes and the other to Rucker.

Dallas played a near-perfect game and blasted the Houston Oilers 52–10. They also got help from the Rams, who beat the New York Giants

---

43. Strasen, *Cowboys Chronicles*, 81.

31–3 in New York. This, coupled with the Cowboys' win over the Oilers, gave Dallas the title for the fifth straight season.

Summing up the 1970 season for the Cowboys, the turning point in the season was that humiliating 38–0 home loss to the St. Louis Cardinals on that Monday night national telecast. Right after the Monday night game, Landry told the team how disappointed he was. At the beginning of the season, he thought they had a chance to go to the Super Bowl, but after that loss, he had lost all faith in the team. He believed his team had no hope of making the playoffs. Landry took it upon himself to place blame for the predicament the team was in and apologized for not doing a better coaching job. Many players got the distinct impression that he had given up on the season.[44]

The next day, the players braced for a brutal film session. But Landry surprised them. Near tears, he told the team, "Y'all can just play flag football if you want."Then he tossed his clipboard and walked out. Defensive tackle Bob Lilly and linebacker Lee Roy Jordan decided to hold a meeting right then and there. Jordan told the team: "Hey guys, there is no one pulling for us but us, the guys right here in this room. Hell, the coaches aren't pulling for us. They've already given up . . . We know damn well the press has been against us forever, so they're not pulling for us. And most of the fans are not excited about us anymore . . . Guys, it's going to happen right here in this room, or it's not going to happen." Several of us talked. We said, "We are going to do it for us, not for somebody else, not for the coaches or the fans or Tex or anyone else."[45]

Blaine Nye recalls: "After we lost the game to the Cardinals, Tom decided the season was over. He let go and started taking a lighter approach. We'd go out and play touch football or volleyball on Mondays, things like that. Suddenly, it got to be fun, and the team began to do better. For a reason that I still can't explain, there was suddenly the feeling that you were a part of this unified effort . . ."[46]

---

44. "1970: Super Bowl V - Dallas Cowboys vs Baltimore Colts," *Golden Football Magazine*, accessed December 3, 2018, http://goldenrankings.com/SuperBowl5-A.htm.

45. Ibid.

46. Ibid.

Mel Renfro remembers: "People had written us off. The season was over. Coach Landry relaxed his practices a little and kind of threw out the playbook and said, "You guys have some fun the rest of the year."[47]

After the meeting, the intensity at practice changed. Lee Roy Jordan explained: "We got after each other. The next day in practice, we were competing against the offense, and they were competing against us, hard . . . When you don't practice intense against yourself, you don't play intense against somebody else . . . By golly, we beat Washington. It wasn't a real great game, but we played hard, won the game, and then we went to Green Bay and held them to three points, and now all of a sudden, everyone is getting excited about us again. The coaches got to coaching well again . . . We talked about game plans with the coaches, and we were much more involved in expressing our feelings about what we were doing in the game plans."[48]

With this new attitude, the Cowboys won the last five games of the season to finish 10–4, good enough to win the NFC East. Dallas made the playoffs despite both their quarterbacks playing with significant injuries all season. Morton had his right elbow drained before every game and hurt his knee in the Minnesota game. Staubach endured an infected right elbow.

Morton threw four TD passes to the resurrected Bob Hayes in the 52–10 rout of the Houston Oilers in the final game of the regular season.

You can overcome offensive deficiencies if you have a great defense. Lee Roy Jordan & Company gave up just eight points in the last four-game. Tight end Pettis Norman, a nine-year veteran, said he had never enjoyed the final weeks of a season like he had the one that just ended: "It used to be, if you dropped a pass, you'd come back to the bench, and 30 heads would turn away from you. Now you get everybody rushing up to you to tell you it's okay, forget it, don't worry about it. Catch the next one."[49]

---

47. Ibid.
48. Ibid.
49. Ibid.

Defensive tackle Bob Lilly said: "The pressure was removed . . . After the St. Louis game, Landry was still in control but let the assistants use more of their ideas. We started dealing with our coach."[50]

The Cowboys did the impossible. They had won five in a row and vaulted themselves into the playoffs. Now that they made the postseason, the Detroit Lions' high-flying offense awaited them in the first round. This would be the Cowboys' first step in their quest to make it to Super Bowl V.

---

50. Ibid.

9

THE BALTIMORE COLTS
IN 1970

The Baltimore Colts were looking for redemption in 1970, after finishing the National Football League's 1969 season with 8 wins, 5 losses, and 1 tie. They finished second in the Western Conference's Coastal Division and failed to make the playoffs.

Coach Don Shula was let go after the season, a disappointing campaign many attributed to the hangover of losing to the heavy-underdog Jets in the Super Bowl the year before. It was one of the first instances of a Super Bowl hangover, in which the team that played in a Super Bowl the previous season and underperformed the next season. Don McCafferty took over as head coach of the Colts after Don Shula vacated the coaching job to go to the Miami Dolphins and coach in South Florida.

McCafferty could not have been more opposite of Don Shula. That did not mean he was less potent. Shula scared his players with harsh discipline and scathing insults to motivate his teams. The soft spoken McCafferty belonged to a new breed of "good guy" coaches. Hence, McCafferty's coaching style was described as easygoing, pleasant, and open.

Previously, McCafferty had spent 11 seasons as a Baltimore assistant under Shula and Weeb Ewbank, now general manager of the New York Jets, and ten years before that at Kent State University. McCafferty joined the Colts in 1959 and became the offensive backfield coach in 1963.[1] His experience in coaching throughout the years gave him a boost as a rookie head coach.

When McCafferty replaced Don Shula as the coach of the Baltimore Colts for the 1970 National Football League season, many seasoned players were among his biggest backers. Some felt relief from the continuous, relentless insults from Shula. Johnny Unitas described McCafferty as: "[He] is a calm, collected individual. He doesn't shout and scream. He can look at football objectively without getting carried away emotionally."[2] McCafferty even sat in on players' poker games and formed a bond with his players that Shula never had.

The 1970 Baltimore Colts proved to a powerhouse team in the newly created American Football Conference and they transitioned from the former NFL to the new league very comfortably. The Baltimore offense scored the most points in the conference yet went through some mid-season changes. John Williams moved into the starting lineup at guard after an embarrassing 44–24 loss to Kansas City. Hustling Tom Nowatzke filled in as running back when injuries sidelined Tom Matte, and veteran passers Johnny Unitas and Earl Morrall occasionally relieved each other at quarterback. However, the defense was a rock-solid unit, with defensive gems in Bubba Smith, Mike Curtis, Ted Hendricks, Rick Volk, and Jerry Logan leading a quick and mobile unit.[3]

Before the 1970 season, the Colts plugged some glaring holes that needed attention. The wide receiver positions were upgraded with speedy players who gave Unitas and Morrall a potent outside attack, drafting Eddie Hinton in the 1969 draft and trading for Roy Jefferson from Pittsburgh.[4] The 1970 draft brought in running back Norm Bulaich, defensive back Ron Gardin, and running back Jack Maitland, who would contribute to the team's success in the upcoming season.[5]

1. "The Chancellor of Football, Super Bowl V Champion 1970 Baltimore Colts," *Taylor Blitz Times*, accessed October 29, 2018, https://taylorblitztimes.com/2014/05/18/super-bowl-v-champion-1970-baltimore-colts/.

2. Ibid.

3. Schaefer, *Baltimore Colts 1970: A Game-by-Game Guide*, 17–20, Kindle.

4. Schultz, *The NFL, Year One*, 86.

5. Ibid.

The strange thing about the 1970 Colts is that they are a forgotten team to history in the realm of Super Bowl Champions. When you think of the old Baltimore Colts, the first flashback that comes to mind are the black and white films with Johnny Unitas leading the team in the 1950s, with the greatest game against the New York Giants in the NFL Championship in 1958 as the best image. Then another thought stirs up images of Bert Jones, Lydell Mitchell, and the mid-1970s version with Head Coach Ted Marchibroda. Then you fast forward to 1984, with the green and yellow Mayflower trucks moving the team to Indianapolis in the middle of the night. Yet sandwiched between the first and second of these events is the most forgotten champion in modern football history. The 1970 Baltimore Colts.[6]

A few things stand out for the 1970 Baltimore Colts being under-appreciated by history. After they won the Super Bowl in 1971, the team was sold a year later after the 1971 season. Before the 1972 season, Robert Irsay (Los Angeles Rams) and Colts owner Carroll Rosenbloom swapped franchises. Rosenbloom had one of the most successful tenures as an owner in NFL history. However, the loss of head coach Don Shula to the Miami Dolphins the year after the loss of Super Bowl III also cemented the notion that the Colts were still a cursed team.[7]

These champions are not remembered because there wasn't a power-ful main character in the clubhouse. The Colts still had aged and fading, John Unitas at quarterback, whose determination and competitiveness were an example to the younger players. The team, however, lacked a fierce motivator who could fire up their spirits. In 1970, Unitas finished the season with a career-low 51.7% completion percentage, and he threw more interceptions (18–14) than touchdowns.[8] This was not a motivat-ing factor to the team, especially when backup Earl Morrall was utilized when Unitas got injured, showing that age was catching up with him. Unitas was not the quarterback he used to be. For the last three seasons, Unitas failed to be elected to the Pro Bowl, after 11 straight Pro Bowl

---

6. "The Chancellor of Football," accessed October 29, 2018.

7. Ibid.

8. Unitas was the only quarterback to win the Super Bowl in a year when he threw more interceptions than touchdown passes.

appearances. No longer a Pro Bowl quarterback who won five player of the year awards, Unitas was just as an inner shell of his former greatness.[9]

Whatever their shortcomings to history or lack of dominant personalities, the 1970 Colts were a resilient bunch. Not only did they have to contend with their opponents on the football field, but they still had to contend with the shadow of their loss to the New York Jets Super Bowl III, which contributed to a dismal season the year before. With a dominating 15–1 record (including the two wins in the playoffs) and the heavy favorite to win Super Bowl III, they had every reason to be embarrassed. Bubba Smith, the giant defensive end, who played most of his career in Baltimore summed it up best in 2007, "Super Bowl III, I still haven't gotten over it."[10]

Now two seasons later, the Baltimore Colts were part of the former AFL, with a three-million-dollar payout to switch leagues with the merger. But memories of the old days still were conjured up even though they were in a new league. They still felt the pain from Super Bowl III, and they left the NFL for the AFC still with their heads hung in shame. With a new identity, a new coach, and a new league, 1970 would bring redemption to these wounded warriors.

Game One saw the Baltimore Colts open the 1970 season at San Diego Stadium to meet the San Diego Chargers. The Chargers went 8–6 in the last year of the AFL before the merger. Replacing the Chargers' venerable head coach, Sid Gillman (who was still general manager of the team), was Charlie Waller. Waller's Chargers proved to be a worthy opponent for the Colts in opening the season.

The game was a seesaw battle throughout. No-one scored until the second quarter when rookie kicker Jim O'Brien hit a 25-yard field goal, which would be the only point for either team in the first half. O'Brien had just graduated from the University of Cincinnati, where he led the nation in scoring as a football senior. A gifted athlete, O'Brien also played basketball for the Bearcats in his freshman year. However, he was not akin to discipline or being told what to do by his superiors. Hence, when

9. "The Chancellor of Football," accessed October 29, 2018.
10. Ibid.

he was a cadet in the Air Force, he developed ulcers because he didn't like being told what to do. He certainly looked the part of a rebel, with long flowing hair. His teammates called him "Lassie" after the famous collie dog and O'Brien went through freshman hazing by the veterans who even threatened to cut his hair if the team made the Super Bowl.[11]

In the 3rd quarter, the Chargers struck back, with a pass to wide receiver Gary Garrison from quarterback John Hadl, electrifying the crowd of 47,782 and gaining the edge for San Diego in the third period.[12]

Baltimore came back on Norm Bulaich's 1-yard touchdown set up by a 43-yard punt return by rookie Ron Gardin. The Colts increased the lead on a 34-yard field goal by O'Brien early in the fourth quarter.[13]

The Chargers came back on a 43-yard touchdown play on a pass from Hadl to Garrison again, with 4:50 remaining in the game. Garrison made a leaping catch on the Baltimore 23 and raced into the end zone. Mike Mercer added his second extra point. The Colts then drove from their 30-yard line to San Diego's 21, with a pass interference call on San Diego's 26, the key play of the drive, before O'Brien's game-winning boot.[14]

Colts quarterback Johnny Unitas had completed 15 of 31 passes for 202 yards. Tom Matte had 12 carries for 43 yards for the Colts but was lost for five weeks until the sixth game of the season with an injury in the game. Matte's injury would be a big blow to the Colts, for he had led the league the year before in combined passing and rushing yards.

With coach Don McCafferty's first victory of the season, the team returned home to Baltimore at Memorial Stadium to take on the Super Bowl Champion, Kansas City Chiefs, for their home opener.

This was the second *Monday Night Football* game of the season, and the Kansas City Chiefs were coming off a loss to the Minnesota Vikings the week before. The Vikings were a hungry team in 1970, trying to make up for their embarrassing loss in Super Bowl IV. Like the Colts the year before, the Vikings hung their heads in shame, as they were also an overwhelming favorite to win the game, but the Chiefs foiled them. They

11. Schultz, *The NFL, Year One*, 86–87.
12. Schaefer, *Game-by-Game Guide*, 52, Kindle.
13. Ibid., 52–56.
14. Ibid., 56.

got their revenge, sort of, on the Chiefs by beating them in a rematch the week before.

The Chiefs came into Memorial Stadium with an urgency to rebound from the loss in the first game and show that they were still a dominating team that won Super Bowl IV. Kansas City didn't disappoint. The Chiefs got things going in the first quarter with a touchdown pass from quarterback Len Dawson to Gloster Richardson to take a 7–0 lead. Kicker Jan Stenerud would add 3 more points to finish off the first quarter with a 10–0 lead over the home team. The Chiefs added to their lead when Robert Holmes caught a 13-yard pass from Len Dawson to make it 17–0. Things got predominately worse for the Colts as running back Norm Bulaich fumbled the ball and the Chiefs' safety, Johnny Robinson ran 46 yards the other way for a touchdown. Robinson would contribute more to the defense with 3 interceptions in the game that set up 10 points for the hot Chiefs offense that scored off his picks.

The drubbing continued late into the second quarter, as Len Dawson found wide receiver Frank Pitts for a 54-yard score. With minutes before halftime, Earl Morrall replaced John Unitas, due to Unitas playing with an injured knee from the week before against San Diego. "When things got going so bad, I took him out because I didn't want to take any chances," Coach Don McCafferty said.[15] Morrall was an older player like Unitas and was in this situation before when he was asked to fill in for Unitas. Two years earlier, an arm injury kept Unitas out of the 1968 season, and Morrall guided the team to the Super Bowl.

Morrall got the Colts rejuvenated, and Baltimore got on the board with an aerial strike from Morrall to Roy Jefferson for 3 yards with time running out in the first half. The teams went into halftime with a 31–7 lead in favor of the visiting Chiefs. Baltimore put up somewhat of a fight, but in the end, they would lose the game to the Super Bowl champs, 44 to 24.

The Kansas City defense had glimpses of that spark that dominated the overpowering Vikings in the Super Bowl. Besides the fumble recovery return for a touchdown by the Chiefs' defense, they also sacked Unitas

15. Ibid., 187.

and Morrall seven times for a total loss of 73 yards. Johnny Unitas was horrible due to injury and didn't play the last 35 minutes due to injury. Unitas had the worst day of his 15-year storied career, only completing 5 out of-15 passing attempts for 58 yards with no touchdown passes thrown and two interceptions. Morrall fared a little better throwing three more interceptions but did have 3 touchdown passes in this miserable contest for Baltimore.

"We stunk out the place in the first half," said Baltimore's rookie head coach, Don McCafferty. "That includes all phases of the game—offense, defense, the special teams . . . and even the coaching."[16]

What was sad to see was that the fans started to leave the game long before it ended. The beating was really bad for the proud Colts, who held the best record of any team in the NFL for 12 years at 112-48-3. Previously, they had lost badly 70–27 to the Rams back in their first season as a franchise in the NFL in 1950. They also endured a 57–0 loss to the Bears in 1962. But the sting of this loss seemed to morph those losses. They had just played their first two games against two AFL squads that were supposed to be inferior to them. However, both the Chargers and the Chiefs proved to be formidable foes for the supposed superior Colts. With the first two games in the books, speculation by many wondered if the Colts were even a good team or were they as bad as they had looked against the Chiefs.

The dejected Colts traveled to Harvard Stadium in Massachusetts for game three, hoping to rebound from the devastating loss to the Chiefs. The game against the Patriots would be a hard-fought grudge match between the two teams.

Earl Morrall directed the Colts for three periods, firing a 13-yard touchdown pass to Ed Hinton in the second period to get the Colts on the board with a 7-0 lead. With Boston's top running backs, Jim Nance and Carl Garrett, on the bench, the Colts' defense repeatedly held off the Patriots except for a field goal by Gino Cappelletti in the second to make the score 7–3 in favor of the Colts going into halftime. But the Colts' offense was anemic that day, and the Patriots kept it close. Cappelletti

16. Ibid., 166.

would boot another field goal in the 4th quarter to bring the Patriots within a point at 7–6. A hobbling Johnny Unitas came off the bench and hit receiver Roy Jefferson for 55 yards in the Colts' clinching touchdown.[17] The Colts would win 14 to 6 over the Patriots. For the Colts, the win was still not convincing that they were a good team.

On a side note, the Boston Patriots had just signed former Minnesota quarterback Joe Kapp to a 4-year contract, but he did not play in the game against the Colts.

Game four saw the Colts heading to the Astrodome in Houston to take on the Houston Oilers. With a thunderstorm raging outside the dome, many fans used umbrellas inside the stadium due to the cracks and leaks the Astrodome had. But the fans who braved the storm would be treated to a competitive contest between the two teams.

Jack Maitland got the Colts on the board early with a 2-yard run in the first quarter. The Colts scored again in the second quarter when receiver Roy Jefferson caught a 17-yard sling from John Unitas to put the Colts up 14–0. But the Oilers scored later in the second with a strike from quarterback Charley Johnson to receiver Jerry LeVias. But the Colts got some insurance when kicker, Jim O'Brien, booted a 43-yard field goal for Baltimore. The teams went into halftime with the Colts up 17–7.

The second half would get more interesting as the Oilers stormed back in the third quarter with a one-yard run touchdown by running back Roy Hopkins. A field goal by the Oilers' Roy Gerela in the 4th quarter would tie the game at 17. When the Oilers were stopped by the Colts defense, as they drove down the field into Colts territory, Gerela hit another field goal to make it 20–17 in favor of the Oilers.

With their backs against the wall, that old magic of John Unitas emerged. Unitas was well known for leading fourth-quarter comebacks, and he did so in the Astrodome by driving the Colts 80 yards in six plays, finishing the drive with a 31-yard scoring pass to Roy Jefferson with just 46 seconds remaining.[18] The Colts would win the game 24–20 over the surprising Oilers and their comeback effort.

---

17. Ibid., 325–329.
18. Ibid., 434.

With a 3-1 record, the Colts returned home to Baltimore to play the
Jets in game five. The Colts had waited for this moment for two years
since they lost in Super Bowl III to Broadway Joe and the New York
faithful. It wasn't the type of redemption the Colts dreamed of as the
game was marked by turnovers by both sides. Namath would throw for a
stellar 397 yards and a touchdown. Broadway Joe also threw six interceptions that day. For Baltimore, Unitas would toss three interceptions of his
own in this dismally played game.

Besides getting their revenge on the Jets from Super Bowl III, another
thing was egging the Colts on in this game against New York. The Colts
wanted to keep the euphoria going in Baltimore as the Orioles just beat
the Big Red Machine in the World Series four days before.

The Colts took a 17–3 lead into the second quarter when kicker Jim
O'Brien added another three points with an eighteen-yard field goal. The
Jets stopped Colts running back Jack Maitland for a safety as the teams
went into halftime with the Colts went up with a 20–5 lead.

In the third quarter, the Colts scored on Bob Grant's interception,
but O'Brien missed the extra point. Even with the missed extra point,
the Colts defense played a stellar game. Also, the Colts' offense would
remain dormant for the 3rd and 4th quarters with only a field goal by
Jim O'Brien in the 4th quarter.

Even with all the turnovers, the Jets mounted a comeback but fell
short. The Colts would win 29–19. The highlight of the game was the
Colts' safety, Jerry Logan, who resembled his baseball counterpart at
third base, Brooks Robinson. Robinson had made fantastic plays at third
base throughout the 1970 World Series, robbing the Reds batters of base
hits.[19] On this day, Logan would rob Broadway Joe as he intercepted
Namath three different times. The day after the game, it was revealed
that Namath had suffered a broken right wrist when the Colts' Billy Ray
Smith sacked him during the fourth quarter. He was projected to be out
for six weeks but ended up missing the rest of the season as the Jets fell to
a 4–10 record for the 1970 campaign.

19. Ibid., 536–556.

As for the Colts, it was a lackluster win. The soft-spoken Logan, who was the hero of the game, with his three interceptions, remarked about the win over the Jets in comparison to the Super Bowl III loss: "Any victory is a sweet victory . . . that was 1968, and this is 1970. It's all water under the bridge. All we're thinking about is now."[20] Even with the win, the stigma of the loss in the Super Bowl remained. The Colts still had something to prove. Although their record was good, the team was far from firing on all cylinders.

Game six featured the second matchup of the season between the Colts and Patriots, this time at Memorial Stadium. The first game between these two teams was a hard-fought grudge match, where the Colts barely eked out a victory. This game would be different for the Colts.

Quarterback Joe Kapp, who didn't play in the matchup in the first game, played this time around. The hard-nosed quarterback who led the Vikings to the Super Bowl the year before was a huge pickup for the Patriots. His bruising style of play was a morale booster for the club. However, Kapp got a heavy dosage of tough football dealt to him as the punishing Colts defense brutalized him. The Colts picked him off three times and sacked him seven times. The year before, when he was with the Minnesota Vikings, Kapp ripped Baltimore apart and stunned the Colts with an NFL record-tying seven touchdown passes in a 52–14 victory.[21]

John Unitas threw three touchdown passes, and the Colts rolled over the Patriots 27–3. However, all was not good news in this dominating win. The Colts again lost running back Tom Matte when he re-injured a knee on the game's first play. It was his first appearance since being in the season opener.[22] This time he would be lost for the season.

The team turned their eyes to the next game, with the trumpets of war sounded in Baltimore, as former coach Don Shula led his up-and-coming Miami Dolphins into Memorial Stadium for the seventh game of the season. His departure came with controversy, as Colts owner Carroll

20. Ibid., 577.
21. Ibid., 710.
22. Ibid., 714.

Rosenbloom accused the Dolphins of tampering with Shula when he was still under contract with Baltimore. With the seeds for a hot new rivalry planted, the teams met for the first time as AFC East foes.

The Dolphins would not be fortunate on this day in Baltimore. Although the Dolphins attacked with a ball-controlled run offense and gained many yards, the Colts did all the scoring. Miami held a whopping 373–239 edge in total yardage while getting off 73 offensive plays to just 44 for Baltimore.[23]

For the Colts, it was the special teams and the punishing defense that propelled the momentum in this contest, compiling 297 yards in returns of kicks and pass interceptions, scoring on a 99-yard kickoff return by Jim Duncan and an 80-yard punt return by rookie Ron Gardin. Baltimore also sacked Miami quarterbacks twice for 21 yards in losses, recovered a fumble, and picked off three interceptions—running its total for the last three games to 13. Linebacker Mike Curtis returned two interceptions to the Miami 42 and 10-yard lines. John Unitas and Earl Morrall each threw a touchdown pass and turned the heat up high on the Dolphins, blasting them 35–0.

The Colts earned their fifth straight win and improved to 6–1, while the runner-up Dolphins fell to 4–3 following their second straight shut-out. The rematch was scheduled in Miami on November 22.

Whatever animosity the Colts players had against their former coach was on full display for the hometown fans to see in this glorious victory. The team looked like it was starting to gel, especially with their defense holding their opponents in their last two games to only three points. Whatever criticism of the Colts lacking fire and intensity was slowly being stamped out with the last few wins.

At the midpoint of the 1970 season, the Colts were seemingly coasting along and brimming with confidence. The eighth game would be at County Stadium in Milwaukee to play the Green Bay Packers. However, these were not the dominant Packers that won the first two Super Bowls. These Packers looked like a skeleton of their former selves, with glaring weaknesses and a poor style of play that did not justify a dominant Packer

23. Ibid., 826.

team in Green Bay. The quarterback comparison between the two teams were stark contrasts. John Unitas still was a player who persevered even at his advanced age, even without all his abilities. However, Bart Starr was fading fast for the Packers, so the Packers turned to backup quarterback Don Horn to carry the team on this Monday Night game.

The decision to start Horn came after the Green Bay coaching staff, with the Baltimore staff watching just as intently, closely checked out Starr in the pregame warm-ups. Starr threw the ball but could put little zip on it. "He couldn't have thrown the ball," Packers coach Phil Bengtson said. "He's got tendinitis just below his elbow. I honestly did not know before the game what his condition was. He didn't throw at all until Sunday, and we just had to wait and see."[24]

Horn's day against the Colts was dismal. Nothing much had changed for the quarterback from his first pass of the game and his last. Rick Volk intercepted his first pass. His last pass, with less than a minute to play, was picked off by Jerry Logan. Two more interceptions spelled disaster for the young quarterback who got his first start of the season ruined by the Colts' dominating defense.

However, the game itself remained close for much of the game. Green Bay took the lead with a field goal by their kicker, Dale Livingston, in the first quarter. A rushing touchdown by running back Jerry Hill put the Colts back on top 7–3 going into the locker room at halftime. Two more field goals by Jim O'Brien in the 3rd and 4th quarter distanced the score to 13 to 3 in the 4th quarter. But the Packers scored when Jim Grabowski ran a yard in the end zone to move closer to the Colts, being down 13–10. When it looked like the Colts were in deep trouble when Green Bay downed a punt on Baltimore 3-yard line, John Unitas completed a 26-yard third-down pass to Ray Perkins with 8 1/2 minutes to play to keep the clock moving. The game ended with the Colts beating the Packers 13–10.

The second half of the season saw the Colts returning home to play another old-time AFL team, the Buffalo Bills, in week 9. The last game against the Packers was a good matchup, but things might have been

24. Ibid., 963.

different had Bart Starr played and not the inexperienced Don Horn. The Colts' offense looked feeble and did not get enough steam against the Packers. Now the Bills came to town looking for a victory of its own.

Bills quarterback Dennis Shaw got the ball rolling for the Bills, throwing two touchdown passes in the first and second quarters to put the Bills up 14–0. In the second quarter, the Colts struck back when Unitas hit receiver John Mackey for a 25-yard touchdown reception. The teams would go into halftime with the Bills up 14–7.

The Colts would tie it up in the 3rd quarter when Eddie Hinton rushed in for 16 yards, and the Colts tied the game up at 14. A Jim O'Brien field goal in the 4th quarter would put the Colts up 17–14. The Bills would mount a comeback as quarterback Dennis Shaw led the Bills' offense 52 yards into Baltimore territory with under 5 minutes to play in the game. The Bills brought in their rookie kicker, Grant Guthrie, for a 36-yard field goal attempt. Earlier, the rookie missed from 58 yards out. The rookie also had problems with this kick, too, as he didn't get a good foot on the ball. However, Guthrie's weak kick was aided by a stiff breeze from the left side, which blew the ball toward the right upright. The ball stayed within the uprights with 1:09 to play and earned the Buffalo Bills a tie with the heavily favored Baltimore Colts.[25]

With the surprising see-saw game against the Bills, culminating with a disappointing tie, the Colts took the tie and went to the Orange Bowl in Miami, where they faced off against Don Shula's Dolphins again. The up-and-coming Dolphins had revenge on their mind from the week seven drubbing they got from the Colts in Baltimore. This time, the Dolphins wreaked havoc on the Colts in week 10.

A sign that hung from the upper deck railing of the Orange Bowl that read, "Griese is no kid stuff," proved to be prophetic. The Dolphin quarterback would run a touchdown in and pass for two more against the Colts defense. Also, Miami's defense was stellar that day. Bob Petrella and Larry Seiple each recovered Baltimore fumbles, defensive tackle Frank Cornish blocked one of Jim O'Brien's three field goal attempts, and Jake

25. Ibid., 1083–1106.

Scott stopped the Colts at the Dolphins' 8-yard line by intercepting Baltimore quarterback Johnny Unitas. [26]

Unitas threw for 206 yards with two touchdown passes but also threw two interceptions. Miami's Bob Griese only had 16 attempted throws but completed 10 of them, including bombs into the Colts secondary with a 27-yard touchdown pass to the newly required receiver Paul Warfield and a 51-yard strike for another touchdown to receiver Karl Noonan.

Special teams also helped the Dolphins when safety/punt returner Jake Scott ran a 77-yard punt back for a touchdown in the second.

Don Shula was pleased with his team's all-around play and acknowledged that his Dolphins made the big plays when they needed it. The Dolphins won by a score of 34 to 17. Shula got sweet revenge on his old team as his Dolphins moved on towards their quest for a playoff berth.

The Colts were still up in first place over the Dolphins and acknowledged this setback. The Colts moved on with their 8-2-1 record back to Memorial Stadium to face an old foe, the Chicago Bears.

Things did not look much brighter in Baltimore for the Colts in week 11 than it did a week earlier. The Bears got out to a 17–0 lead over the Colts, until the Colts scored two touchdowns in the second quarter, one by Jerry Hill who leaped a yard in for a touchdown and a pass from John Unitas to Roy Jefferson for seven yards to pull within three by halftime. The score would remain 17–14 in favor of the Bears until the 4th quarter when Bears' kicker Mac Percival hit a 27-yard field goal to put the Bears up by six. But Unitas was resilient late in the game and tossed a 54-yard pass to John Mackey, who sat on the bench for most of the game, for the winning score with 3 minutes and 47 seconds on the clock to barely beat the Bears 21–20. Unitas threw two touchdown passes but was intercepted 5 times by the Bears' defense. However, the big plays with the touchdown to Jefferson with 44 seconds before the half and the final strike to Mackey redeemed Unitas on the day.

Week 12 saw the Colts staying home in Baltimore to host the Eagles, another rival from the former NFL. The game was not much of a contest as the Colts' defense smothered the Eagles' offense.

---

26. Ibid., 1235.

The Colts scored twice in the first quarter, first when John Mackey caught a 14-yard pass from Johnny Unitas, and then Eddie Hinton ran 9 yards for a touchdown (O'Brien missed the extra point). Taking a 13–0 lead into the second quarter, Jim O'Brien hit a 45-yard field goal, answered by the Eagles' Mark Moseley, who connected with a 38-yard field goal, making the score 16–3 in favor of the Colts. The Colts would get another touchdown in the second with a 33-yard interception return by Jerry Logan to send the teams into halftime with a 23–3 Colts lead. In the second half, Jim O'Brien would hit two field goals, and the Eagles would score a touchdown on a one-yard rush by quarterback Norm Snead. The Colts would eventually win the game 29–10.

Unitas passed for a measly 113 yards with a touchdown pass and an interception. However, the offense clicked on the ground with the rushing game. The Colts gained over 150 yards from four different backs, and the defense picked off the Eagles' Norm Snead three times and had only 60-yard passing yards, and held backup quarterback Rick Arrington to only 34 yards passing.

Week 13 saw the 9-2-1 Colts traveling to Buffalo for a second match up with the Bills at War Memorial Stadium. The last time the two teams met, they settled for a tie. This time, the two teams had to deal with snow on the ground and slippery turf for field conditions.

The first half was a back-and-forth affair, tit for tat, scoring match for both teams. The Colts struck first with a Jim O'Brien field goal from 32 yards. The Bills answered with running back Lloyd Pate's 1-yard rush later in the first quarter, putting the Bills up 7–3. Later in the first quarter, Tom Nowatzke ran in a 1-yard score for the Colts, putting the Colts up 10–7 at the end of the first quarter.

Bills quarterback Dennis Shaw found Marlin Briscoe for a 10-yard strike that put the Bills up 14–10, which was the score the teams took into halftime.

The Bills were proving to be a formidable rival again to the Colts in keeping the game close. However, the Colts defense took over in the second half and held the Bills scoreless for the rest of the game. The Colts scored in the third with their brand of power rushing when Norm

Bulaich ran in the end zone on a 2-yard rush, giving the Colts at 17–14 lead going into the 4th quarter. The Colts would score once more with a Jim O'Brien 38-yard field goal in the 4th quarter, making it 20–14 in favor of the Colts, and that's the score by which the game ended with the Colts clinching the AFC East division for the playoffs.

Unitas had a less than stellar day with the hampering conditions, only completing 13 of 31 passes, but had 236 yards passing. The running game was grounded by the weather conditions, and the slippery, snow-covered field limited the Colts to only 49 yards rushing.[27]

The Baltimore Colts didn't bother to award a game ball after becoming Eastern Division champions of the NFL's American Football Conference. "None of us were pleased with our performance," said coach Don McCafferty. After the Colts defeated the Buffalo Bills, he admitted that the game "scared the hell out of me."[28]McCafferty knew if his team was to survive in the playoffs, they had to play better than this.

The season's final game saw the New York Jets coming into Baltimore for the second matchup between these two teams. Revenge for their Super Bowl loss by the Colts was achieved earlier, including knocking out Joe Namath for the season.

Now that the playoffs were a lock for the Colts, coach McCafferty said he might pull John Unitas out early to rest his ailing body. That meant the call would go to Earl Morrall, who was in a familiar role and was up to the challenge. The lackluster Jets came into Baltimore with a 4–9 record and was finishing a dismal season. Morrall indeed got the call after McCafferty pulled Unitas early.

For most of the game, the Jets gave the Colts a run for their money. Even in the fourth quarter, the score was 21–20 in favor of the Colts until Earl Morrall found Ray Perkins for a 41-yard strike, putting the Colts up 28–20. A block kick recovery in the end zone by Ted Hendricks sealed the Jets' fate, as the Colts won 35–20.

Morrall was incredible, tossing for four touchdowns and putting up 348 passing yards after Unitas was pulled in the first quarter. Morrall

27. Ibid., 1633.
28. Ibid., 1603–1625.

played like a man possessed against the Jets. The game was an air battle between the two teams as both teams' running game never got off the ground.

With an 11-2-1 record, the Colts went into the playoffs with an emotional high from this last performance for the regular season. Up next would be Paul Brown's Cincinnati Bengals, who just made an amazing run of their own to gain a spot in the AFC playoffs.

For the Baltimore Colts, 1970 was a very good season for the club in the new NFL. They adjusted to playing their new foes in the AFC from the AFL and were successful, even with the injuries that plagued them throughout the season. The defense was the main reason the Colts got this far, and coach McCafferty knew he would need more out of his offense going into the playoffs against the other elite teams of the AFC.

10

THE BIG EIGHT MAKE IT INTO THE PLAYOFFS

Besides the Baltimore Colts winning the AFC division, the Cincinnati Bengals won the AFC Central, the Oakland Raiders won the AFC West, and the Miami Dolphins would be the first Wild Card team for the AFC in the newly aligned conference. In the NFC, the Minnesota Vikings won the NFC Central, the San Francisco 49ers won the NFC West, and the Detroit Lions were the first Wild Card team in the new NFC Conference. The standings for the 1970 NFL season were as follows in both conferences[1]:

THE AFC

Team	W	L	T	W-L%	PF	PA	PD	MoV	SoS	SRS	OSRS	DSRS
AFC East												
Baltimore Colts*	11	2	1	.846	321	234	87	6.2	-5.8	0.4	0.9	-0.5
Miami Dolphins+	10	4	0	.714	297	228	69	4.9	-6.3	-1.3	-1.3	0.0
New York Jets	4	10	0	.286	255	286	-31	-2.2	-2.7	-4.9	-2.2	-2.7
Buffalo Bills	3	10	1	.231	204	337	-133	-9.5	-2.8	-12.3	-5.8	-6.5
Boston Patriots	2	12	0	.143	149	361	-212	-15.1	-0.7	-15.9	-9.1	-6.8
AFC Central												
Cincinnati Bengals*	8	6	0	.571	312	255	57	4.1	-3.5	0.5	1.2	-0.6
Cleveland Browns	7	7	0	.500	286	265	21	1.5	-0.9	0.6	0.5	0.1

1. Pro Football Reference, Season 1970, accessed November 5, 2018, https://www.pro-football-reference.com/years/1970/index.htm.

Team	W	L	T	W-L%	PF	PA	PD	MoV	SoS	SRS	OSRS	DSRS
Pittsburgh Steelers	5	9	0	.357	210	272	-62	-4.4	-3.0	-7.4	-5.9	-1.5
Houston Oilers	3	10	1	.231	217	352	-135	-9.6	0.4	-9.2	-3.5	-5.8
AFC West												
Oakland Raiders*	8	4	2	.667	300	293	7	0.5	0.5	1.0	2.3	-1.3
Kansas City Chiefs	7	5	2	.583	272	244	28	2.0	-0.5	1.5	-0.1	1.6
San Diego Chargers	5	6	3	.455	282	278	4	0.3	-1.0	-0.7	0.5	-1.2
Denver Broncos	5	8	1	.385	253	264	-11	-0.8	-1.8	-2.6	-2.5	-0.1

THE NFC

Team	W	L	T	W-L%	PF	PA	PD	MoV	SoS	SRS	OSRS	DSRS
NFC East												
Dallas Cowboys*	10	4	0	.714	299	221	78	5.6	1.4	7.0	2.5	4.5
New York Giants	9	5	0	.643	301	270	31	2.2	-0.2	2.0	1.9	0.1
St. Louis Cardinals	8	5	1	.615	325	228	97	6.9	0.5	7.4	3.8	3.6
Washington Redskins	6	8	0	.429	297	314	-17	-1.2	4.2	3.0	3.6	-0.6
Philadelphia Eagles	3	10	1	.231	241	332	-91	-6.5	2.0	-4.5	-0.9	-3.6
NFC Central												
Minnesota Vikings*	12	2	0	.857	335	143	192	13.7	1.4	15.1	5.9	9.2
Detroit Lions+	10	4	0	.714	347	202	145	10.4	3.7	14.0	7.4	6.6
Green Bay Packers	6	8	0	.429	196	293	-97	-6.9	5.1	-1.8	-2.4	0.6
Chicago Bears	6	8	0	.429	256	261	-5	-0.4	2.6	2.2	0.4	1.8
NFC West												
San Francisco 49ers*	10	3	1	.769	352	267	85	6.1	0.4	6.5	6.4	0.1
Los Angeles Rams	9	4	1	.692	325	202	123	8.8	0.8	9.6	4.4	5.3
Atlanta Falcons	4	8	2	.333	206	261	-55	-3.9	1.6	-2.3	-3.5	1.2
New Orleans Saints	2	11	1	.154	172	347	-175	-12.5	4.6	-7.9	-4.6	-3.3

AFC WILDCARD: THE MIAMI DOLPHINS

Out of the fresh faces to enter the playoffs, besides the Colts and Raiders, were the Miami Dolphins. Established as a team in 1966, Miami endured four years of losing seasons. The year before, the Dolphins had the worst record in the AFL. The team had hoped to capitalize on the season before, in 1968, when the team finished with a 5-8-1 record. However, when 1969 started, the Dolphins struggled from the season's start, losing their first three games before tying the Oakland Raiders and losing their next two games to start the season 0-5-1. After their week seven win over the Buffalo Bills, the Dolphins would end the season with a 3-10-1 record.[2]

2. Guy Beard, "New Look, New Season, New Era-1970 Miami Dolphins," published April 19, 2018, accessed November 1, 2018, https://www.youtube.com/watch?v=pB6H2_-pyeA.

An overhaul was needed for the Miami franchise. The overhaul began at the top by getting a new head coach. That head coach was Don Shula, who guided the Baltimore Colts from 1963–1969, and who had a lot of success coaching competitive Colt teams. Unfortunately, the Colts lost two big games under Shula; the NFL Championship in 1964 and Super Bowl III in 1969. Miami's owner, Joe Robbie, knew he would need a strong coach who would be a stern leader and disciplinarian to get the Dolphins headed in the right direction. Miami was full of talented young players like quarterback Bob Griese and running backs: Mercury Morris, Larry Csonka, and Jim Kiick to power a ball controlled rushing offense. After the 1969 season, Joe Robbie signed Shula to become Miami's second head coach in its short history. As a result of Shula's signing, the team was charged with tampering by the NFL, which forced the Dolphins to give their first-round pick to the Colts. The decision was controversial because of Shula and Robbie's negotiations conducted before and after the official NFL/AFL merger, respectively. Had the negotiations been concluded before the merger, while the NFL and AFL were rivals, the NFL's anti-tampering rules could not have been applied.[3]

If stern and disciplined was what owner Joe Robbie wanted in Shula, he certainly got his money's worth. Shula had worn out his welcome in Baltimore, with the Colts' players breathing a sigh of relief by his departure. However, Miami would welcome him and his abilities as a coach with open arms. The team knew what they were getting in Shula, a tough, stern disciplinarian who had a winning track record and who was relentless on himself and the players in the pursuit of being a winner. Running back Larry Csonka summed up Shula's style of coaching: It dawned on me that I'd better be concentrating every second . . . because the time you least expect it, you're going to get Shula's foot in your rear."[4]

Quarterback Bob Griese knew that getting Shula as their head coach was something special for the team. He remarked: "Shula is a big factor

---

3. Jack Olsen, "The Rosenbloom-Robbie Bowl," *Sports Illustrated* (November 9, 1970), accessed November 5, 2018, https://www.si.com/vault/archive/1970s.

4. Schultz, *The NFL, The 1970 Season and the Dawn of Modern Football* (VA: Potomac Books, 2013), 164.

for us . . . Maybe it's just that he's a winner, and we know it. It gives us confidence."[5]

Shula indeed brought to the Dolphins in 1970 a new attitude. Along with his attitude, the front office made major changes in trading for good veteran players and drafting quality college players to build a solid foundation in Miami. The veterans that were acquired by the Dolphins were: tight end Marv Fleming, wide receiver Willie Richardson, free-agent kicker Garo Yepremian, who was the smallest player in the NFL. The most significant acquisition was wide receiver Paul Warfield from Cleveland. Smooth, agile, and fast, Warfield added instant explosiveness to the Miami offense.[6]

The new draftees in 1970 would be on the team for many years to come: tight end Jim Mandich, who played for the Dolphins until 1977, defensive back Tim Foley who would play for the team until 1980, defensive back Curtis Johnson who would play until 1978, defensive back Jake Scott who would play for the team until 1976, Hubert Ginn who would play for the Dolphins until 1973, and linebacker Mike Kolen, played for Dolphins 1970 to 1977.[7]

With the three running backs that Miami had, Shula groomed them into an explosive running team. The first back was Mercury Morris. Morris excelled as both a running back and as a kick returner. Most of his playing days were spent with the Miami Dolphins. From 1969 to 1971, he backed up Jim Kiick at halfback and served as the Dolphins' primary kickoff return man. In his rookie year of 1969, Morris averaged 26.4 yards per kickoff return, leading the AFL in the kickoff return category with 43 and kickoff return yardage with 1,136.

The next back was the fullback Larry Csonka. Csonka was the number one pick by the Miami Dolphins in the 1968 Common Draft, the eighth player and first running back drafted in the first round. He signed a three-year contract that paid him a signing bonus of $34,000. Csonka's pro career, however, got off to a shaky start. In the fifth game of the 1968

5. Ibid.
6. Beard, "New Look, New Season," accessed November 1, 2018.
7. Ibid.

season against Buffalo, Csonka was knocked out and suffered a concussion when his head hit the ground during a tackle. He spent two days in
the hospital. Three weeks later, against San Diego, he suffered another
concussion, plus a ruptured eardrum and a broken nose. There was talk he
might have to give up football. Csonka missed three games in 1968 and
three more in 1969. As his teammate Nick Buoniconti explained, "There
was some question [after the 1969 season] whether Csonka would ever
play fullback again—not just because of injuries but because he didn't
play well . . . When Shula came in [in 1970], he had to teach Csonka
how to run with the football. He used to run straight up and down, and
Shula impressed upon him that he had to lead with his forearm rather
than his head. Shula and his backfield coach Carl Taseff re-engineered
Csonka to where he became the Hall of Fame player. Csonka emerged as
the offensive leader of the Dolphins."[8]

Over the next four seasons, Csonka never missed a game, and he led
the Dolphins in rushing the next five seasons. Teammate Jim Langer said,
"Csonka had the utmost respect of every player on the team, offense, and
defense." By the 1970s, he was one of the most feared runners in professional football. Standing at 6 ft 3 in (191 cm) and weighing 235 lb (107
kg), he was one of the biggest running backs of his day and pounded
through the middle of the field with relative ease, often dragging tacklers
five to ten yards. He was described as a bulldozer or battering ram. His
running style reminded people of a legendary power runner from the
1930s, Bronko Nagurski. Minnesota Vikings linebacker Jeff Siemon
observed Csonka's style of play after Super Bowl VIII, "It's not the col-
lision that gets you. It's what happens after you tackle him. His legs are
just so strong he keeps moving. He carries you. He's a movable weight."[9]
He rarely fumbled the ball or dropped a pass. He was also an excellent
blocker.

There are many stories abound about Csonka's toughness. He broke
his nose about ten times playing football in high school, college, and the

---

8. Danny Peary, *Super Bowl: The Game of Their Lives* (NY: Macmillan, 1997), 100–101.
9. Mickey Herskowitz, *Purple People Eaten by Dolphins, The Super Bowl: Celebrating a Quarter-Century of America's Greatest Game* (NY: Simon and Schuster, 1990), 46.

pros, causing it to be permanently deformed. What was more remarkable is that Csonka would remain in all these games with blood pouring out of his nostrils. Csonka may be the only running back to receive a personal foul for unnecessary roughness while running the ball. In a game against the Buffalo Bills in 1970, he knocked out safety John Pitts with a forearm shot that was more like a right cross.[10] In a close game against the Minnesota Vikings, in the perfect season of 1972, Csonka was hit in the back by linebacker Roy Winston in a tackle so grotesque it was shown on *The Tonight Show*. Csonka thought his back was broken, and he crawled off the field. Once on the sideline, he "walked it off" and was back in the game in a few minutes. His return to the game was crucial, as the winning touchdown pass to tight end Jim Mandich was set up by a fake to Csonka. He was named the tenth toughest football player of all time in the 1996 NFL Films production *The NFL's 100 Toughest Players*. Dolphins' offensive line coach Monte Clark was asked about Csonka's bruising running style, and he responded, "When Csonka goes on safari, the lions roll up *their* windows." Csonka's 1971 season was also the only year in the 1970s that a running back gained over 1,000 rushing yards without a single fumble.

To complement the hard-running style of Csonka, the Dolphins had running back Jim Kiick. The two became good friends and roommates and were known as Butch Cassidy and the Sundance Kid. The funny thing was that Jim Kiick, a New Jersey native, played for the Wyoming Cowboys in college. He was drafted by the Dolphins in the AFL and played running back from 1968 to 1969. When the leagues merged, he would play for the Dolphins from 1970 through 1977, except for 1975 when he played in the World Football League.[11]

Although not blessed with breakaway speed, the 5 ft 11 in (1.80 m), 214 lb (97 kg) Kiick was a versatile player; in addition to being an effective inside power runner, he was also an excellent blocker and clutch pass receiver. He had over 1,000 yards combined rushing and receiving

---

10. Dave Hyde, *Still Perfect! The Untold Story of the 1972 Miami Dolphins* (Philadelphia: Dolphins/Curtis Publishing, 2002), 89–90.

11. Beard, "New Look, New Season," accessed November 1, 2018.

in each of his first four years. He was often compared to such well-known all-purpose backs as Paul Hornung, Tom Matte, and his boyhood idol, Frank Gifford. Teammate, Jim Langer, described him as "a very heady runner and receiver."[12] He played hurt and rarely fumbled. Kiick once played with a broken toe, a broken finger, a hip pointer, and a badly bruised elbow.[13] He led the Dolphins in rushing in 1968 (621 yards) and 1969 (575 yards) and was selected for the AFL All-Star game both years. His nine rushing touchdowns in 1969 led the AFL, and his 1,155 total yards from scrimmage in 1970 led the AFC and ranked fifth in the NFL. Nick Buoniconti remembers: "Jim Kiick . . . loved the game and loved clutch situations—where he was at his best. When we needed a first down on third-and-4 or 5, he'd get it. We might get the ball to him on a short option because there was no one better coming out of the backfield to catch a pass. I've never seen anyone put moves on like him. He'd get a linebacker to lean one way and then go the opposite way. Even when they'd double team, he'd get open."[14]

Kiick negotiated a one-year $32,000 contract during the 1970 training camp after initially being offered $20,000.

Shula's Miami teams were known for great offensive lines (led by Larry Little, Jim Langer, and Bob Kuechenberg), strong running games (featuring Larry Csonka, Jim Kiick, and Mercury Morris), solid quarterbacking (by Bob Griese and Earl Morrall), excellent receivers (in Paul Warfield, Howard Twilley, and tight end, Jim Mandich) and a defense that worked well as a cohesive unit. The Dolphins were known as "The No-Name Defense," though they had several great players, including defensive tackle, Manny Fernandez and middle linebacker Nick Buoniconti.[15] The five rookies that started on defense: Mike Kolen, Doug Swift, Tim Foley, Curtis Johnson, and Jake Scott meshed well with the veterans to add to the no-names on defense.

As for the season itself, the Dolphins endured several highs and extreme lows. After losing the first game of the season to the Boston

12. Peary, *Game of Their Lives*, 118.
13. John Underwood, "The Blood and Thunder Boys," *Sports Illustrated* (August 7, 1972), 28.
14. Peary, *Game of Their Lives*, 101–102.
15. John Underwood, "Two That Were Super," *Sports Illustrated* (January 10, 1972).

Patriots, it looked like the Dolphins were headed for another dreadful season like the year before. However, the Dolphins would go on to win the next four games, whereby the team was meshing with themselves as a unit and instituting the coaching style of Don Shula.

However, games 6, 7, and 8 would bring a losing spell that rocked the Dolphins' core just as they believed they had become a competitive team. In-game six, the Cleveland Browns, who decided to cross over to become an AFC Team, gave the Dolphins a dosage of tough NFL style football and snapped the Dolphins' win streak by shutting them out 28–0. Game seven was a disaster for Don Shula as he returned to Baltimore. The Dolphins were shut out again two weeks in a row, as Baltimore pounded the Dolphins 35–0. Game Eight should have been a relief for the Dolphins as Philadelphia was not a very good team. The Eagles, however, had enough chutzpah to beat the Dolphins 24–17. At 4–4, things looked bleak for the Dolphins

Then the magic returned to Miami as they won their next six games, including beating the first-place Colts in Miami, to give them a playoff berth at 10–4 for the season.

With the additions of a new coach, new players, and a new attitude, 1970 would start a new era in Miami. They would become the AFC's first Wild Card winner in the realignment era. They would also go to 3 super bowls from 1972–1974, winning titles in 1973 and 1974. Their perfect season of 1972 is still intact after all these years, even with the perfect record of 16–0 by the New England Patriots of 2007, due to the Patriots losing to the New York Giants in Super Bowl 42.

After the season ended, the Dolphins would be slated to play John Madden's Oakland Raiders in the first round of the playoffs.

NFC WILDCARD: THE DETROIT LIONS

When we think of the Detroit Lions in the modern age of football, we think of hard-luck teams that were not very good, or if they did make the playoffs, they would leave in misery after the first round. 1970 might have been the best season ever for the Lions. They were also the first NFC Wild Card team to make the playoffs.

The team was formed in 1929, when they played in Portsmouth, Ohio as the Portsmouth Spartans, hence making them one of the oldest NFL teams in the league. The Lions moved from Portsmouth and played their first season in Detroit in 1934. They started the season off with a 10-game win streak that included 7 shutouts; however, they lost the last three games of the season and finished in second place behind the Bears in the west. In 1935, the Lions had a terrific year finishing with a 7-3-2 record, which was first in the West, and Detroit advanced to the 1935 NFL Championship Game against the New York Football Giants, who were three-time Eastern Conference champions and the defending NFL Champions. The championship game was played at 2:00 P.M. on December 15, 1935, in front of 15,000 fans in Detroit. The Lions won the game 26–7 to win the clubs' first World Championship, which was also a part of Detroit's City of Champions for the 1935–1936 sports season. The Tigers won the 1935 World Series in baseball, and the Detroit Red Wings also captured the 1936 Stanley Cup in hockey.[16]

By the end of the 1930s, most of the players that helped the Lions win a title in 1935 and kept them competitive for the rest of the decade were gone from the team. The 1940s would be a decade of futility for the Lions.

The 1950s would be a turnaround for the team. They would win consecutive championships in 1952 and 1953. Then, in 1957 the team won their last championship. The next decade would see the team fall on hard times. With the new merger, the Lions looked to capitalize on the re-aligned league in 1970.

The 1970 Lions were a high-scoring club with a defense that shut down offenses. The Lions were led by Head Coach Joe Schmidt, who was a great linebacker for the Lions on those great teams in the 1950s. He became the Lions' head coach in 1967 and had slowly improved the team each year. He retired in 1972 with a winning record, the last Lions coach to pull that off. As one of the finest linebackers ever to play the game, Schmidt helped write the book on tough, aggressive, fundamental football. There were no fancy frills for Schmidt, and the Lions were

16. Stateside Staff, "The Year Detroit Became 'The City Of Champions,'" Michigan Radio, accessed November 6, 2018, http://www.michiganradio.org/post/year-detroit-became-city-champions.

created in the image of their coach. They were also built along the lines of the great Packers teams of the Lombardi era.[17] He had two proficient defenders in Alex Karras and Dick Lebeau.

Karras was a stellar lineman who played 13 seasons for the Lions. 1970 would be his last season. Before the season, he was removed as captain of the team in 1970 because he was an outspoken individual who decided to take his issues to the press and who threatened to hold out every season. Many remember Karras on the TV show *Webster* back in the 1980s, as the comical and gentle father. This was in stark contrast during his playing days.

Dick LeBeau was a reliable safety for the Lions and would have nine interceptions in the 1970 season. Like Karras, LeBeau played his entire career as a Detroit Lion, and in 1970, he was in his 12th season. After the 1972 season, he would retire but spend the next 45 years as a head coach and assistant coach for various NFL teams.[18]

The Lions had some truly great players like cornerback Lem Barney, who played college football at Jackson State from 1964 to 1966. He was drafted by the Detroit Lions and played for the Lions as a cornerback, return specialist, and punter from 1967 to 1977. He was selected as the NFL Defensive Rookie of the Year in 1967, played in seven Pro Bowls, and was selected as a first-team All-NFL player in 1968 and 1969. He was inducted into the Pro Football Hall of Fame in 1992 and was one of the greatest cornerbacks in NFL history.[19]

Another great player on that 1970 Lions team was tight end Charlie Sanders, who also would become a Hall of Famer. Sanders was also known as a superior blocker. He was chosen for the Pro Bowl seven times (1968–1971 and 1974–1976). He was the only rookie to be named to the 1969 Pro Bowl, following a season with 40 receptions for 533 yards. Sanders was named to the All-Pro First Team for the 1970 and 1971 seasons, receiving the most votes of any player in both years.[20]

17. Schaefer, *Detroit Lions 1970: A Game-by-Game Guide*, 316–321, Kindle.
18. Schultz, *Dawn of Modern Football*, 120.
19. Mike Goodpaster, "1970 Detroit Lions, What Might Have Been," The Grueling Truth, accessed November 6, 2018, http://thegruelingtruth.net/football/nfl/1970-detroit-lions-might/.
20. Ibid.

In addition to Barney and Sanders, the team was packed with excellent players, including running back Mel Farr, center Ed Flanagan, and linebacker Paul Naumoff, who complemented defensive tackle Alex Karras and cornerback Dick LeBeau on a bruising defense.

The year before, in 1969, the Lions had a great season, going 9-4-1 and proved they could be a factor among the elite teams of the NFL. To do that, they needed to improve their offensive attack. In the 1970 season, they made those necessary adjustments. Even without a clear-cut starter at quarterback, the Lions' attack still blossomed into a steady point-producing outfit. Bill Munson and Greg Landry split the quarterback position. However, Landry played more as the season went on. Both found good runners in Mel Farr and Altie Taylor, followed by excellent receivers in Earl McCullouch, Larry Walton, and Charlie Sanders. The offensive line gave both quarterbacks adequate protection and figured highly in the offense's performance.[21]

The 1970 Lions, ranked second in the NFL in points scored and points not allowed, won their first two games by a combined score of 78–3, and finished the season with the league's second-highest average point differential (10.4), according to pro-football-reference.com. They had the best turnover ratio in the league. Two things stood out in the Lions' 1970 campaign. One, they were the victims of New Orleans' Tom Dempsey's then-record 63-yard field goal, and two, the team produced an impressive five-game winning streak to end the regular season.[22]

The team started fast with a 3–0 record. Their first loss came in week 4 to the Washington Redskins. By November, the Lions were 5–1 and had established themselves as an elite team in the NFC Central. They beat their division rival Bears twice, Green Bay once in a 40–0 blowout, trounced the former NFL Browns, and beat the Bengals, who would win the AFC Central.

Like the Dolphins, a mid-season losing streak put the team in disarray. The mighty Minnesota Vikings beat them 30–17, followed by Tom

---

21. Schaefer, *Game-by-Game Guide*, 16–20, Kindle.
22. Kevin Seifert, "Best Lions Team Ever: 1970," ESPN, accessed November 7, 2018, http://www.espn.com/blog/nfcnorth/post/_/id/13324/best-lions-team-ever-1970.

Dempsey's winning 63rd-yard field goal in a 19–17 loss to the New Orleans Saints, and then again to the purple people eater gang 24–0.

The Lions, however, rebounded, beating an elite 49er team easily 28–7. The 49ers were having a superb year, and the Lions would be one of their only three losses on the season. They then trounced the Oakland Raiders 28–14, who would win the AFC West, then beat the Cardinals and Rams, who were both in contention for a playoff spot all season, and finally the Packers, shutting them out again in the season, this time 20–0.

The Lions achieved their goals in 1970 with a ticket to the playoffs as a wild card team. Their first challenge in the playoffs would be the unpredictable Dallas Cowboys.

DIVISION WINNER: NFC CENTRAL - THE MINNESOTA VIKINGS

When the season started, a return Super Bowl trip was not the biggest thing head coach Bud Grant had to focus on. Finding a quarterback was the main priority. Joe Kapp had left after a contract dispute, and Gary Cuozzo took over. Cuozzo was a career backup, though, in fairness, part of that career involved being the backup to Johnny Unitas with the Baltimore Colts. Cuozzo would become an effective general with excellent strategy as the starting quarterback for the Vikings in 1970.

The Minnesota Vikings' offense featured a running game led by Dave Osborn, who had a mediocre season with 681 yards on the ground but still made the Pro Bowl. At fullback, Bill Brown was a former Pro Bowler, and at age 32, was still productive.[23] The aerial attack for Cuozzo featured wide receivers: Gene Washington, John Henderson, and Bob Grim. Big John Beasley rounded on the receiving corp as the Vikings' tight end.

Though the offensive line did not produce a pro bowler, there was more to this Viking front five than what met the eye. Center, Mick Tingelhoff was an All-Pro in five seasons. Ron Yary, at tackle, was a third-year player and embarking on a Hall of Fame career.[24] With this wall of

---

23. "Minnesota Miss A Perfect Super Bowl Opportunity," The Sports Notebook, accessed November 8, 2018, http://thesportsnotebook.com/1970-minnesota-vikings/.

24. Ibid.

an offensive line, the front five would pave the way for the running and passing attack for the Minnesota offense.

The defensive unit of the Vikings was just an amazing beast in the NFL that year. The defensive line was the best front four in the league. Carl Eller at end and Alan Page at tackle were first-team All-Pros. Gary Larsen was another Pro Bowler on the side. Usually, Jim Marshall at defensive end would be in that group, but at 33, Marshall was starting to show signs of decline and was "only" pretty good, as opposed to one of the game's best.[25] He still would play another eight seasons as one of the purple people eaters. Like the defensive line who could stop the rushing attack by any offense in the league, passing against the Vikings' secondary seemed a monumental task as well. Ed Sharockman at cornerback picked off seven passes in what was then a 14-game schedule. Karl Kassulke was a Pro Bowl strong safety, and Paul Krause was another future Hall of Famer at free safety.[26] The Vikings' defense became the second defense in the history of the NFL to lead the league in fewest points allowed and fewest total yards allowed for two consecutive seasons.

Sweet revenge was on the Vikings' minds to start the 1970 season on September 20, 1970, at Metropolitan Stadium in Minnesota. The team waited nine months for this moment to get another chance at the Kansas City Chiefs, who embarrassed them in Super Bowl IV. Their revenge was cemented with a dominating 27–10 performance over the Super Bowl Champs. In-game two, also at home, the Vikings were dominant again, blanking the New Orleans 26–0. Things started very well for the Vikings to begin the 1970 season.

Going on the road to Wisconsin, and facing the Packers, derailed the team's euphoria after two dominating performances, as the team lost to Green Bay 13–10. The Minnesota defense limited Packer runners to 57 yards in the loss, but the offense failed to get going, which led to the upset by Green Bay. Bud Grant took this loss seriously, and before the team went to Chicago to play the Bears, he told them: "We are now at a

---

25. Ibid.
26. Ibid.

very challenging segment of our schedule."[27] The challenge would be met head-on vs. a stingy Bears defense. But the purple gang won 24–0, in a dominating performance.

Returning home to Metropolitan Stadium, the Vikings pounded the Cowboys 54–13, which was the worst defeat in Cowboys' history. No one was prepared for the breadth and scope of what the Vikings would inflict on Dallas. Sharockman scored off a blocked punt and an interception return in the first quarter alone. The Viking defensive front produced seven sacks. The score was 34–6 by halftime and ended at a stunning 54–13.[28] Bud Grant's team was off and rolling again.

Monday Night Football came to the Twin Cities for the Rams-Vikings game, a rematch of a good divisional playoff game the prior year when Minnesota rallied to win in the fourth quarter. Both defenses ruled this game. Cuozzo connected with Brown on a 17-yard touchdown pass in the first quarter, but neither team broke the end zone for the rest of the night. Minnesota recovered four of seven Los Angeles fumbles, won the rushing battle in yards,146–66, and chiseled out a 13–3 win.[29]

Detroit was not an elite team like the Cowboys or Rams, but the Lions became a very competitive team in 1970. They were 5–1 and tied for first with the Vikings when they hosted Minnesota at old Tiger Stadium on November 1. The first half involved a lot of back-and-forths. Minnesota corner Bobby Bryant intercepted a pass and took it 39 yards to the house. Cuozzo threw a pair of second-quarter touchdowns, one of them a 41-yarder to speedy Gene Washington. The Viking defense was uncharacteristically not dominant in the first half, and the Lions were within 7 points in a 24–17 score at half time. The second half brought that dominating defense out as the Vikings kept the Detroit ground game under wraps. Minnesota got a couple of field goals from Pro Bowler kicker Fred Cox and won 30–17.[30]

27. Randy Fast, "The First Ten Years. 1970 Minnesota Highlights," accessed November 8, 2018, https://www.youtube.com/watch?v=jLD8ot3u_d8.
28. The Sports Notebook, accessed November 8, 2018, http://thesportsnotebook.com/1970-minnesota-vikings/.
29. Ibid.
30. Ibid.

Minnesota kept their focus in a win against the mediocre Washington Redskins by the score of 19–10. However, Detroit lost again, creating a two-game gap in the division race. And the schedule brought the Lions right back the next week, with the rematch in Minneapolis set for November 15.

The Vikings' special teams were usually a core strength for the team in recent years, but the 1970 season saw too many opposing teams returning punts and kickoffs for long gains. The game with the Lions was another example, as a second-quarter kickoff return after a field goal gave Detroit a 10–3 lead. They still led 20–10 in the fourth quarter and were poised to tighten the NFC Central race.

Cuozzo did not have a great game, completing just 13 of 30 passes. But he made them count, getting 228 yards, and he led drives that set up two short touchdown runs from Clint Jones. Minnesota escaped with a 24–20 win. There were five games to go, and the Vikings led the division by three games, and they owned the tiebreaker.[31]

Game ten saw the Packers come to town for a rematch in sub-zero degree weather, where the Vikings won a very lackluster game by a score of 10–3. The game was marked by zero turnovers and zero ball movement either way. The Packers had faded from the race and would finish 6–8, as would the Bears.

Game eleven was the Sunday after Thanksgiving and took the Vikings to Shea Stadium to meet the New York Jets. The Jets, of course, did not have Joe Namath due to injury. But the Vikings would lose their quarterback during the first quarter. Backup quarterback Bob Lee stepped in for Cuozzo. A win would mean the third straight title for the Vikings. But the Jets got the best of them. Lee threw four interceptions in a 20–10 loss. With the loss to the Jets and Cuozzo hurt, many questions surrounded the team as they were about to grasp the NFC Central Division title.

The Chicago Bears came to town on a Saturday game for week 12. Hoping to wrap up the division, and in an era where home-field advantage was determined by rotation rather than merit, that was all that mattered in the regular season. Running back Dave Osborn played his best game

---

31. Ibid.

of the year, rushing for 139 yards on 29 carries. Quarterback Lee stayed away from mistakes, and the Vikings were ahead 16–6 late. However, the special teams' coverage problems resurfaced when Chicago returned a kickoff for a touchdown and made the game interesting, but the defense closed out a 16–13 win. Minnesota was NFC Central champs.[32]

The Vikings then traveled to Boston to play the Patriots after they clinched their division a week before. Their old friend, Joe Kapp, was the quarterback of the Patriots now. The defense intercepted Kapp 3 times and held the runners to 56 yards. Bob Lee still was in for Gary Cuozzo as the Vikings won easily, 35–14.[33]

A trip to Atlanta marked the end of an incredible season for the Vikings. Fred Cox had three field goals to give him the most points in the league for the second year in a row. The Vikings proceeded to blow out the Falcons 37–7 in the season finale.

At 12–2, the Vikings were the best team in the entire NFL. Going into the playoffs, the Vikings were a solid favorite to beat the surging San Francisco 49ers, who had a great season due to quarterback John Brodie having a career year in his 13th season with the 49ers.

NFC WEST - THE SAN FRANCISCO 49ERS

No one expected the San Francisco 49ers to be a contender in 1970. After many years of near misses and disappointments, 1970 was a surprise for San Francisco. For the 1968 season, the 49ers hired as their head coach, Dick Nolan, Tom Landry's defensive coordinator with the Dallas Cowboys. Nolan's first two seasons with the 49ers had gone much the same as the previous decade, with the 49ers going 7–6–1 and 4–8–2. For the 49ers, 1970 held the promise of stability and recovery. After the uncertainty that came with the large turnover on the roster between 1968 and 1969, followed by the rash of debilitating injuries that, ultimately, caused even more turnover, the 49ers entered 1970 much the same team that they had been at the close of 1969 but also, and more importantly, healthy.[34]

---

32. Ibid.
33. Fast, "1970 Minnesota Highlights," accessed November 8, 2018.
34. "49ers Year By Year: 1970," SB Nation (January 2, 2009), accessed November 10, 2018, https://www.ninersnation.com/2009/1/2/707719/49ers-year-by-year-1970.

Things would change in 1970. For one, the team had played at Kezar Stadium for many years, and now the team was slated to move to Candlestick Park, home of the baseball Giants after the season. Candlestick Park gave the 49ers a much more modern facility with more amenities that were easier for fans to access by highway. Another change would be the defense. Unlike the offense that was always respected in the NFL, the defense didn't fare as well for many years. In 1970, the 49er defense surprised most experts by turning in a superb season performance. Coach Dick Nolan platooned and rotated the front four spots and thus kept in men who were not always fatigued in the game. Dave Wilcox excelled at linebacker, and the secondary of Jim Johnson, rookie Bruce Taylor (who won defensive rookie of the year in 1970), Rosey Taylor, and Al Randolph discouraged enemy passers.[35]

As for the offense, it all began with veteran John Brodie. During various years of his NFL career, Brodie led the league in passing yardage, passing touchdowns, least sacked, and lowest percentage of passes intercepted. This year, in 1970, he would become the league MVP. He retired as the third most prolific career passer in NFL history and a two-time Pro Bowler.[36] Brodie had a great cast all around him on offense. This year, the offense blossomed into one of pro football's best with fine seasons from wide receiver Gene Washington, offensive lineman Forrest Blue, and fellow offensive lineman Cas Banaszek.[37] Blue and Banaszek were on a line that was so good that Brodie was only sacked eight times during the whole 1970 season. Also, placekicker Bruce Gossett was acquired from Los Angeles and became the stable kicker the 49ers needed.

The most important aspect of the 49ers was coaching. Coach Dick Nolan was brought in two years earlier and was looked upon being a savior of some sort, due to his success under Tom Landry in Dallas. Nolan played his NFL career as a defensive back with the Giants, Cardinals, and Cowboys, retiring in 1962. He began his coaching career as an assistant under Tom Landry and later attributed all his knowledge about football

---

35. Schaefer, *San Francisco 49ers 1970, A Game-by-Game Guide*, 20, Kindle.
36. "John Brodie wins Jim Thorpe Trophy," *Tuscaloosa News*, Alabama, NEA (December 29, 1970), 9.
37. Schaefer, *Game-by-Game Guide*, 17, Kindle.

to Landry. As a coach, Nolan is credited as being one of the creators of the flex defense. Each of the three years that Nolan coached the 49ers, he took them to the playoffs (1970, 1971, and 1972), and he faced off against his old mentor, Tom Landry, and the Dallas Cowboys, all three times. Each time, he lost. But in 1970, Nolan was recognized for his achievement in San Francisco, winning the coach of the year award.

The year started off good, with a win over the Redskins in week one at home in San Francisco. Quarterback John Brodie showed off his aggressive style of play right away that would last all season, throwing Washington's coach Bill Austin's defensive game plan off. The 35-year-old quarterback made Austin tear up his defensive game plan when he completed 17 of 21 passes for 178 yards in the 49ers' victory. The Redskins went into their opener with plans to blitz frequently. By the second half, they were laying back to gang up on Brodie's receivers, particularly second-year man Gene Washington. "We thought we could throw them off balance, and we could not," Austin said. "It's a calculated risk to blitz, and we had to cover Washington one-one-one."[38] The 49ers would win 26–17.

Week two saw the Browns come into town, Again the most encouraging thing for fans coming out of this game, as in the first, was the strong play of John Brodie. This game saw Brodie throw for three touchdown passes that were vital in lifting the team over the Browns in week 2. The shoulder problem that had given him so many problems during the first half of 1969 appeared to be a non-factor in 1970, as shown in the first two games. And that was good news for the team.[39] The 49ers would beat the Browns in a shootout, 34–31.

The team stumbled in week 3, going on the road for the first time that season and losing a heartbreaker in the fourth quarter of a game against the Falcons in which they had never trailed. The Atlanta Falcons survived a last-ditch effort by the San Francisco 49ers to grab a heart-stopping, come-from-behind 21–20 victory before a sellout crowd of 58,850 in Atlanta Stadium. With six seconds on the clock, the 49ers' Bruce Gossett, a reliable veteran placekicker, lined up for what could be

38. Ibid., 812–834.
39. "49ers Year By Year: 1970," SB Nation, accessed November 10, 2018.

called a "gimme" field goal attempt from the 19-yard line. The Falcons put the rush on but not a hand touched the ball as it sailed wide to the right of the goalposts. Gossett had earlier in the game kicked two field goals of 27 and 43 yards.[40]

San Francisco rebounded, though, by manhandling the undefeated, 3–0 Rams in Los Angeles a week later. John Brodie was as hot as the 106-degree weather on the floor of the Los Angeles Coliseum. He scored one touchdown personally, unleashed a 59-yard scoring pass to Gene Washington, and ex-Ram Bruce Gossett contributed to the downfall of his former teammates with two field goals. A crowd of 77,272 was on hand to watch its hometown heroes go down to defeat for the first time in 1970.[41] And after four games, the 49ers were 3–1 and one game away from matching their win total from a year before.[42]

Week five saw two former 49er players come to town. Quarterback Billy Kilmer and wide receiver Dave Parks led New Orleans into Kezar Stadium. Both would have an impact on the game.

The matchup proved to be competitive throughout the game. The Saints trailed 20–13 and got the ball on the 49ers' 46-yard line with 90 seconds left. Kilmer, who replaced starter Edd Hargett in the fourth quarter, completed four straight passes, the first two to Jim Otis for 11 yards, the last two to Parks for 35 yards. The final pass to Parks was a 13-yard scoring pass with 42 seconds to play that earned the tie. Tom Dempsey kicked the extra point that knotted the score and knocked the 49ers out of first place in the Western Division of the NFC.[43]

The dejected 49ers remained in San Francisco and hosted the Denver Broncos at Kezar Stadium the next week. A shutout effort by the 49er's defensive unit in the second half, which featured a John Brodie pass to John Isenbarger for a 61-yard touchdown and Bruce Gossett kicked two of his four field goals, enabled the San Francisco 49ers to beat the Denver Broncos 19–14 in a rugged defensive struggle.

40. Schaefer, *Game-by-Game Guide*, 317, Kindle.
41. Ibid., 428–448.
42. "49ers Year By Year: 1970," SB Nation, accessed November 10, 2018.
43. Schaefer, *Game-by-Game Guide*, 560, Kindle.

The 49ers would win the next three games, beating Green Bay at home 26–10, traveling to Chicago and beating the Bears 37–16, and then going to Texas and beating the Oilers 30–20.

Game ten in Detroit stopped the 49er winning express dead in its tracks. Lions quarterback Greg Landry overcame brisk winds to fire three touchdown passes and key defensive plays that sparked the Lions' offense. Detroit's defense was stellar and intercepted three John Brodie passes, and recovered a fumble. The Detroit Lions snapped their three-game losing streak with a 28–7 victory over the mistake-prone San Francisco 49ers and remained in the hunt for a playoff spot.

San Francisco would return home to Kezar Stadium for game eleven, to face off against the Rams for first place honors. The 49ers were up by a game in the standings over the Rams, and so this game was very important to both teams in a race to either win the division or chase a playoff berth with a wild card spot. The battle of the California divisional rivals was a disaster for the 49ers on this day. Rams' kicker, David Ray's three field goals in the game and three touchdown runs by running back Willie Ellison enabled the Los Angeles Rams to overcome a 13–6 halftime deficit and secure a 30–13 victory over San Francisco, that put them in a tie for first place with the 49ers in the NFC West. The victory left the Rams and 49ers with identical 7-2-1 records with three games left to play.[44]

Riding a two-game losing streak by very good Detroit and Los Angeles teams, the 49ers were getting weary as the season began to wind down. However, good fortune would smile on the 49ers again, as they beat Atlanta the next week, with a 24–20 victory, and then beat the New Orleans Saints the week after, 38–27.

The season's final game was to be played across the bay in Oakland, San Francisco's main rival in North California. The Raiders were having a good season and were bound for the playoffs in the AFC West. At 9-3-1, having put together the team's best season since 1953, the 49ers needed a win in the final game of the season to wrap up their division and reach the post-season. In the first matchup between the two Bay Area teams, the 49ers brutalized the Raiders, scoring 24 points by halftime

_____

44. Ibid., 1362.

and cruising to a 38–7 victory. For the first time in 14 years, the 49ers were going to the post-season.[45]

Awaiting the 49ers in the first round of the playoffs were the 12–2 Vikings. The game would be played in Metropolitan Stadium, in the tundra of Minnesota. This would not be 49er football weather.

AFC CENTRAL - THE CINCINNATI BENGALS

Out of all the teams that qualified for the playoffs in 1970, none was more shocking or more inspiring than the Cincinnati Bengals. Bruised, battered, and tired emotionally after seven games, the Bengals started 1–6 and was dead last at the halfway point in the AFC Central.

The season began for the Bengals' dismally, with star quarterback Greg Cook on the injury list. He could be seen on the sidelines during games, which left a pessimistic cloud over the club. The year before, Cook was named Rookie of the Year and led the AFL in passing. Cook endured an arm injury that would never heal for the entire 1970 season. Replacing Cook at quarterback was Virgil Carter. Hopes were not high with Carter quarterbacking the Bengals because he was rejected by both the Bears and Bills. For extra added security, Cincinnati also had veteran quarterback Sam Wyche, who was a proven backup but not a superstar.[46]

The first seven games for the Bengals in 1970, was a tale of continuous mistakes, misfires, and awful team chemistry. The long, six-game losing streak wore down the Bengals. Mentally, physically, and emotionally, this team looked they were not going anywhere at that halfway point. It was hard to fathom that a huge turnaround was coming for the Bengals. Even with the dismal record and psyche that was far from optimistic, the team, however, learned valuable lessons in their losses. Quarterback Virgil Carter learned about losing savagely through sacks and miscued passes, which ended up as interceptions. However, he bounced back from these harsh lessons and remain poised and polished for the rest of the half-season. Running back, Paul Robinson would regain his old

---

45. "49ers Year By Year: 1970," SB Nation, accessed November 10, 2018.

46. Grey Beard, "Chronicles of a Champion-1970 Cincinnati Bengals" (April 19, 2018), accessed November 12, 2018, https://www.youtube.com/watch?v=SOEcbXrFSnE.

form, which made him a threat again to the defensive linemen and secondaries in the NFL. Rookie Mike Reid crafted his skills as a defensive tackle and was able to form into a productive defensive bulwark on the line. The secondary was beginning to play as a cohesive unit and stopped getting burned as it had in the first half of the season. Running back Jess Phillips forged a formidable running attack with Paul Robinson. The aerial attack flourished with wide receiver Chip Myers, and the offensive line built a wall on either side of the center. Kicker Horst Muhlmann became an almost automatic three points with his continuous sure-footed field goals. Linebacker Bill Bergey, along with rookies Mike Reid, Ron Carpenter, and Lemar Parrish, spearheaded a defense that gradually improved as the season went on. The tools for victory were painfully forged in this long losing streak.[47]

For six straight games, the Bengals were like an unsolved puzzle. But the pieces were slowly coming together. The season was about to turn around in a big way for the Bengals. Losing was about to give way to winning. Cincinnati was a time bomb ready to explode. That bomb exploded in the second half of the season.

It did not look like the season would be difficult as the Bengals beat the powerful Oakland Raiders in the first game of the season, 31–21. Oakland coach John Madden summed up the game as follows: "There are no excuses; the Bengals are a very good football team . . . This is a game of momentum . . . They had it early in the game, we got it back on some fine pass plays, and they took it back again on that long draw play touchdown (a scampering 78-yard run by back Jess Phillips)." "They took the opportunities we gave them," he said. "And they had the ball most of the time. The defense was excellent and kept giving the ball to the offense."[48]

Sam Wyche got the call at starting quarterback and threw a touchdown but completed less than half of his passes. This was a glaring red flag for the coaching staff, even with the win.

---

47. Ibid.
48. Schaefer, *Cincinnati Bengals: A Game-by-Game Guide*, 49–53, Kindle.

Week two was a disaster for the Bengals when they faced the Lions, who had just blanked the Packers 40–0 the week before. The Lions defense roared against the Bengals, who lost their tiger stripes along the way in this 38–3 loss. Virgil Carter replaced a lackluster Sam Wyche as the quarterback, but that could not spark a rally on offense. This first loss signaled a continuous theme for the next six games for the Bengals.

In the next game, at Cincinnati, Wyche was pulled again as the quarterback as Virgil Carter took the reins to try to come back against the Oilers. The Oilers would win 20–13.

Game four saw coach Paul Brown and his team travel to Municipal Stadium against his former team, the Cleveland Browns. Boos rained down on Paul Brown and his Bengals from the hostile crowd at the dog pound in Cleveland. The game would be a heart breaker for the Bengals, as the Browns stormed back to win 30–27. It was not a very artistic game, but it certainly was not just another game, either. There was a lot of personal pride involved in the first meeting of these new American Football Conference rivals. These two Ohio cities had already become heated rivals, even before they played their first game against each other. Of course, Paul Brown was the catalyst that stirred the passions and animosity for the fans in both cities. Brown was further booed by the Cleveland faithful for failing to congratulate Cleveland coach Blanton Collier after the game. He shrugged the whole thing off. "I talked to Blanton before the game," Brown said. "When the game is over, I get off the field. I have for years. At one time, the NFL ordered us to."[49] Many believed that Brown, who coached the Browns for sixteen years, still held a grudge against Browns' owner Art Modell for firing him. If that were true, Brown would be further incensed as the game ball was given to Modell with this win over the Bengals.

Paul Brown started Virgil Carter instead of Sam Wyche to shake up the offense from the doldrums against the Browns. It seemed to work as Carter connected a perfect 9 out of 9 passes thrown to begin the game with a bang, igniting an offensive attack that was dormant since the opening game of the season. The defense was dominating as Ross Perry

49. Ibid., 443–448.

picked up a fumble and rumbled into the end zone. But the Browns began to click . . . and came back to beat the Bengals 30–27. To Brown, there was no reason to hang his head in shame. The Bengals played tough football in a rowdy and hostile Municipal Stadium in Cleveland.

The Bengals brought their 1–3 record back to Cincinnati, and the hometown faithful at Riverfront Stadium, against the Super Bowl Champion Kansas City Chiefs in game five. Coming into the game, the Super Bowl champions did not want to use quarterback Len Dawson, who was just recovering from a knee injury. There was no other choice for Hank Stram at game time, and the hobbling veteran quarterback's two touchdown passes rallied the Chiefs to a 27–19 over the Bengals.[50]

Game Six saw the Bengals going to RFK Stadium to take on the Washington Redskins. Washington quarterback Sonny Jurgensen threw two touchdown passes to wide receiver Charley Taylor, while Curt Knight added two field goals, as Washington defeated Cincinnati 20–0. It was the first shutout produced by Washington since the Redskins defeated Pittsburgh 30–0 in 1964. It left Washington with a 3–3 record while Cincinnati had won only one of six games.[51]

Game seven saw the team travel to Pittsburgh, where a quarterback controversy was brewing in the steel city. A frustrated rookie, Terry Bradshaw, vowed he wouldn't play second fiddle to Terry Hanratty after the 1970 season. This controversy didn't stop the Steelers from beating the lowly Bengals.

Pittsburgh defeated the Cincinnati Bengals 21–10 in the first-ever meeting between the new rivals and the first *Monday Night Football* game for both teams. But it was Terry Hanratty, coming off the bench, who bailed out the Steelers in the fourth quarter. He threw a touchdown pass and then led his Steelers to another score.[52] The Bengals, now at 1–6, looked like a team that was broken and done for the season. With the team's morale at an all-time low, they failed to see any sort of blue sky

---

50. Ibid., 603.
51. Ibid., 762.
52. Ibid., 878.

on the horizon. Fans and the media, alike, could never predict what was about to happen. A time bomb was ticking.

Game eight saw that time bomb go off at War Memorial Stadium in Buffalo. Rookie Lemar Parrish returned a kickoff return for 95 yards for a touchdown, then ran back a blocked field goal for 83 yards. Parrish also intercepted a pass and spearheaded a hungry secondary firing on all cylinders. The defensive unit stopped the Bills offensive unit and forced a fumble for a score by lineman Royce Berry. That was his second fumble return of the year. Sweet revenge was on the mind for quarterback Virgil Carter, who was discarded by Buffalo. The team scored 43 points, most in Bengals' history, and beat the Bills 43 to 14. Carter got his revenge, and the Bengals got a much-needed win, with fireworks as a bonus.

Both coaches had their own opinions on how the Bengals won this shocker in Buffalo. Cincinnati coach Paul Brown thought the 95-yard kickoff return by rookie cornerback Lemar Parrish broke the game between the Bengals and the Buffalo Bills wide open. Buffalo coach John Rauch said his club was still in the game after the return, but it was Parrish's 83-yard return off a blocked field goal that made the difference.[53]

The Bengals returned home to Cincinnati to face the Browns again for the second and last meeting of the season in week nine. Revenge was on the Bengals' minds as they wanted vindication from the 30–27 heartbreak loss to the Browns earlier in the season.

The Browns came to town tied for the division lead as the Bengals still were dwelling in the cellar. Quarterback Virgil Carter showed his quick legs by running for 110 yards on 9 carries, including a 77-yard run, although he fumbled the ball. When injured quarterback Cook ran the offense in the previous year, the Bengals relied on the bomb for an offensive attack. With Carter as the quarterback, he was more versatile than Cook or Wyche, and his mobility gave him another dynamic to make plays that had defenses guessing. In this rematch, he certainly had the Browns guessing. Carter ate them up. The 14–10 win was a personal one for Carter, as he was now seen as a star in the NFL. This game cemented his star power.

53. Ibid., 1011.

Paul Brown twirled his hat above his head, jumped in the air, and dashed off the field like a happy schoolboy. The Bengals had just knocked off the Cleveland Browns 14–10, and it was one of the most significant moments of his life. "This was my best victory," Brown said later in the dressing room after the roar of a record 60,000 fans at Riverfront Stadium had died down. "It sure makes it feel like it was worthwhile coming back."[54]

The man who had been fired as coach of the Browns nearly eight years before had come back to defeat his old team, and it was Brown who was laughing loudest when the game was over. "Are you talking about your best victory of 1970?" a listener asked the Bengals coach. "I'm talking about my best victory," Brown said emphatically, meaning it was the highlight of a 36-year coaching career.[55]

"Everyone was aware of Coach Brown's situation," pointed out quarterback Virgil Carter. We were going out there trying to die for the guy. We know how he feels personally."[56] Brown wanted to win this game badly, and the team knew it. Remarkably the Bengals came back to win after the Browns had jumped to a 10–0 lead. The victory put the Bengals in the thick of the race for the Central Division crown in the AFC.

Week ten saw the Pittsburgh Steelers come to town for the last matchup between the two teams this season. Virgil Carter solved Paul Brown's quarterback concerns, but Steelers' coach Chuck Noll was not that fortunate to see any concerns regarding Carter. Riding his star power, the young Carter ran and passed the Cincinnati Bengals to their third straight victory, 34–7 over the black and gold. "I'm very pleased with Virgil. He's doing really well," Brown said after Carter fired touchdown strikes of 53 and 10 yards to Bob Trumpy and Eric Crabtree and ran four yards for another score. Carter's daring play and a young, aggressive defense had the Bengals deadlocked with the Steelers at 4–6, one game behind Cleveland.[57]

54. Ibid., 1156.
55. Ibid., 1160.
56. Ibid., 1165.
57. Ibid., 1290–1295.

The Bengals remained home for week eleven and welcomed the boys from the bayou, the New Orleans Saints, to town. The Bengals picked up their fourth straight win, a 26–6 romp over New Orleans. With the win, Cincinnati took a piece of a three-way tie in the Central Division of the American Football Conference, after Pittsburgh downed Cleveland 28–9 to give each team a 5–6 record.

The Bengals traveled west to San Diego for game twelve against the Chargers. One of the most memorable highlights in this match-up saw Bengals' defensive back Lemar Parrish recover a fumble, and also, return a punt for 79 yards for a touchdown. Quick strikes by Virgil Carter to the receivers also made room for the running game as the Bengals won 17–14.

There was something magical happening in Cincinnati. Even before the dismal 1–6 start, the Bengals were picked to finish in the cellar. Now, Paul Brown watched his team clinch at least a tie for the division title by defeating the Houston Oilers 30–20 in week thirteen. Unlike the first time these two teams played, miscues and misfortune in the turnover department seemed to switch to the Oilers this time.

Excitement was in the air for the Bengals because a win against the Patriots would seal them winning the AFC Central Division. Coach Paul Brown warned the Bengals to forget about the playoffs for now because the one remaining game was with Boston, a team they had never beaten. "We have yet to beat Boston since we've been in business," Brown said. He recalled a 33–14 loss in 1968 and a 24–14 loss in 1969.[58]

The standings showed the Bengals at the top with a 7–6 record. Their rival, the Cleveland Browns, were right behind them with a record of 6–7. For Cincinnati, they had to win or tie against the Patriots to win the AFC Central. A 7–7 deadlock between the two Ohio clubs would send the Browns into the playoffs because of a 4–2 record in division play. The Bengals divisional record was at 3–3. While the Bengals were at home to host the Patriots, Cleveland was on the road in Denver to play the Broncos.

Game fourteen was played at the friendly confines of Riverfront Stadium, where home cooking hopefully would propel the Bengals to

---

58. Ibid., 1716–1720.

division winners. A record-breaking crowd of 60,157 poured in to see if the Bengals could lock up a playoff berth with a win over the Boston faithful. The fans were treated to a Bengals romp over the Patriots 45 to 7. Paul Robinson had three touchdown runs. Sam Wyche was put in as quarterback and sparkled. Every aspect of the Bengals game shined. The fans went wild after the game, with their team making it into the playoffs.

For fourteen weeks, the Bengals clawed and scratched their way through the division to the top. Even with star quarterback Greg Cook out of action for the season, and the team's dismal start, the Bengals miraculously stormed into the playoffs. Coach Paul Brown was excited in many ways with the outcome for his Bengals after the 1970 regular season. His team had played hard, tough, injured, and surmounted a comeback that no one could have seen coming. He also delighted in finishing ahead of his old team, the Cleveland Browns, in a race for first place in the Central Division. This team had depth and lots of it.

Now, Cincinnati would need that magic once more, as they faced a significant challenge in the first round: The Colts from Baltimore.

AFC WEST - THE OAKLAND RAIDERS

1970 was the year of George Blanda. At 43, he performed miracles that players half his age could never do. The old man, playing in his 21st season of pro football, made a specialty out of pulling games out of the fire at the last second as he saved five games in a row with late heroics (He filled in for the injured Daryle Lamonica at quarterback and threw three touchdown passes to beat Pittsburgh 31–14. He kicked a 48-yard field goal with three seconds left to tie Kansas City 17–17. He kicked a 52-yarder to beat Cleveland 23–20 in the last three seconds. He came off the bench to drive the Raiders to the winning touchdown in a 24–19 victory over Denver. And he kicked a field goal with four seconds left to beat San Diego 20–17.). All these Blanda "miracles" helped Oakland take first place in the AFC West.[59]

Blanda also had a tremendous supporting cast around him that made the Oakland Raiders a powerhouse in the newly constructed AFC West.

---

59. John Schaefer, *Oakland Raiders 1970: A Game-by-Game Guide*, 17–25, Kindle.

Daryle Lamonica (aka "The Mad Bomber") was still proficient at quarterback, along with a rookie named Ken Stabler. Stabler would eventually become the heir to Lamonica, as the Raider's starting quarterback, who helped the Raiders win their first Super Bowl in 1977. All three quarterbacks combined would throw for more than 3,000 yards in the 1970 season.

At running back, the Raiders had fullback Hewritt Dixon, who powered his way through defenses to rush for 861 yards. They also had Charlie Smith, who rushed for 681 yards, and Marv Hubbard, the third back who rushed for 246 yards. All these running backs had a stellar net gain avg of over 4.0 per rush, which made the Raiders' rushing attack just as potent as their prolific aerial attack with Lamonica and Blanda.[60]

The receiving core of the Raiders was one of the best in the NFL that season. Warren Wells, Rod Sherman, and Fred Biletnikoff were speedy, sure-handed, wideouts who could make the big plays. Tight end Raymond Chester was an extra weapon for receiving and blocking when needed.

The coach was the legendary John Madden. Al Davis hired Madden as linebackers coach for the AFL's Oakland Raiders in 1967. Madden helped the team reach Super Bowl II that season with a bruising style of play that the defense exhibited during the season. A year later, after Raider's head coach John Rauch resigned to take the head coaching position with the Buffalo Bills, Madden was named the Raiders' head coach on February 4, 1969. At the age of 32, Madden became professional football's youngest head coach at that time. Under Madden's leadership, the Raiders had the best record in the AFL at 12-1-1. According to former Raiders coach Dennis Allen, John Madden was arguably the best Oakland Raiders coach in the history of the team

In his first year at the Raiders' helm, Madden earned American Football League Coach of the Year honors as he led the Raiders to the AFL Western Division title. In fact, under Madden's guidance, Oakland never experienced a losing season. Madden's Raiders made eight playoff

---

60. 1970 Oakland Raiders, Pro Football Reference, accessed November 14, 2018, https://www.pro-football-reference.com/teams/rai/1970.htm.

appearances. These teams played smash-mouth football and had endurance. An example of this endurance was shown in a 37–31 six-quarter
AFC Divisional Playoff win over the Baltimore Colts in 1977. Perennial
winners, the team never finished with fewer than 8 wins in the then-14
game season (8-4-2 in 1970 and 1971).[61]

Madden's dedication is well summed up in his own words: "Coaching isn't work. It's more than a job. It's a way of life . . . no one should
go into coaching unless he couldn't live without it . . . Football is what I
am. I didn't go into it to make a living or because I enjoyed it. There is
much more to it than just enjoying it. I am consumed by football, totally
involved. I'm not into gardening . . . or any other hobbies. I don't fish or
hunt. I'm into football."[62]

The 1970 season would not start on a good footing for the black
and silver, as they took on the Bengals in week one in Cincinnati. The
Raiders were surprised by a tight-knit Bengals squad and lost 31–21. For
the Raiders, this was the first time since 1964 that a Raiders team lost
its first game to start the season. However, in defeat, a star emerged in
rookie tight end Raymond Chester, who had three catches for 89 yards
on the day.[63]

Game two in San Diego saw the Chargers' quarterback John Hadl
fire two touchdown passes in the fourth quarter, and Oakland's George
Blanda missed a 32-yard field goal attempt with nine seconds left in
the game as the San Diego Chargers and Oakland Raiders battled to a
tie.[64] The Raiders' offense was in full throttle and ran up 27 points, but
the defense could not hold the lead, and the score ended in a tie at 27.
Blanda's missed field goal would be one of the few times in the season he
would fail.

Game three saw the Raiders travel to tropical and wet Miami to face
the Dolphins. Despite a torrential downpour during the Saturday night
game, which turned the Orange Bowl into a mini lake, the Dolphins

61. "John Madden," Pro Football Hall of Fame, accessed November 14, 2018, https://www.profootball
hof.com/players/john-madden/biography/.

62. Ibid.

63. Schaefer, Game-by-Game Guide, 137, Kindle.

64. Ibid., 174.

overcame a last-minute surge by Oakland, and they beat the Raiders for the first time in their franchise history, by a score of 20–13. A record crowd of 57,140 popped open umbrellas and sat through it all until victory was in hand by the home team. Many people even waited until the last Dolphin player had trotted into the dressing room before the Orange Bowl started to clear.[65] The Raiders' offense was just as unpredictable as the weather, and luck was not with the black and silver this fateful day. The glaring image of hard-luck was exemplified by Raider running back Charlie Smith, who ran for a 68-yard touchdown, but a penalty wiped it out. Oakland was now 0-2-1.

Still, without a win in the first three games, the Raiders returned home to Northern California to take on the division-leading Denver Broncos in the season opener in Oakland. The fourth game of the season saw the Raider's offensive line making big holes for the running game to flourish, while quarterback Daryle Lamonica threw four touchdown passes and set up another one with a 51-yard bomb to get downfield. The Raiders roared past the Broncos 35–23. However, victory was marred by all-pro cornerback Willie Brown, who injured his shoulder on an interception.

Week five saw the Washington Redskins visiting northern California to play the Raiders. For the first three games, it looked like the Raiders were the sleeping volcano of the NFL. The week before, that sleeping giant awoke. In this game, the volcano continued to erupt, this time on *Monday Night Football*, to a nationwide television audience. Sonny Jurgensen and the Redskins' air game was shot down by the Raiders' defensive backs, Kent McCluen, and Nemiah Wilson. The defensive line and the linebackers stifled Washington's running game and short passing attack. On offense, Raider's running back Dixon ran wild, chalking up 164 yards, behind the stellar blocking of the offensive line. The running game opened up the passing attack for Daryle Lamonica, as the Raiders won 34 to 20.[66] Lamonica finished the night with 11 touchdown passes

---

65. Ibid., 307.

66. Lafayette Cathey, published on April 12, 2016, "1970 Oakland Raiders Challenge of the 70s," accessed November 16, 2018, https://www.youtube.com/watch?v=Fu1o9heRpZQ.

on the season, including seven in his last two games. The Raiders were now rolling down the right track.

Game six was against the Pittsburgh Steelers. This would be the first time the two clubs would ever meet, and it would set the stage for a fierce rivalry for the next decade. The Raider defense shut down Terry Bradshaw and the Pittsburgh offense. Daryle Lamonica hurled a 37-yard heroic bomb to Raymond Chester for a touchdown. But Lamonica's day would be short-lived as he suffered a muscle spasm in his back and was forced to leave the contest early in the first quarter.[67] That brought in the old man, George Blanda, who came off the bench to throw a touchdown strike to Raymond Chester. Later, Blanda threw a dump-off pass to Chester, who ran it in for a touchdown from long yardage, An old veteran and a rookie, wreaked havoc on the Steelers. In the end, the Raiders dominated the Steelers, winning 31–14. When questioned later about his decision to start Blanda over Kenny Stabler, Madden said he went with Blanda instead of Ken Stabler because "you have to go with experience." Madden looked like a genius when Blanda quickly put the Raiders in front to stay as he teamed up with Warren Wells on a 44-yarder to make it 14–7 with 9:10 left in the half.[68] The Raiders would sail smoothly for the rest of the game. With the win, the Raiders were slowly climbing to the top of the AFC West.

Game seven saw the Raiders take on the World Champion Chiefs, battling for first place. The Chiefs got out to an early lead in the game, but the Raider's defense was good that day and slowed the Kansas City express down. In a see-saw battle throughout the game, the Chiefs came back to lead the Raiders 17–14 in the late 4th quarter. Then all hell broke loose. The controversy started when Len Dawson, protecting that 17–14 lead, scrambled to Oakland's 29 on a third-and-11 play. At that point, the Chiefs quarterback was clobbered by big Ben Davidson of Oakland, who piled on Dawson. A brawl ensued as the teams collided in a fury. Penalties were called on both sides, wiping out that first-down run. This whole debacle showed the national television audience that the Oakland

67. Schaefer, *Game-by-Game Guide*, 760, Kindle.
68. Ibid., 769.

Raiders and Kansas City Chiefs brought their bitter rivalry to the new NFL, and all their old animosity remained. The national television audience and 51,334 fans at Kansas City were left mystified by the strange sequence of action in the last minutes of the Chiefs' wild, fight-marred melee with the Raiders in the latest meeting of the old American Football League combatants.[69] After the brawl was over, the Raider defense took command. Then, with 46 seconds to go, Daryle Lamonica drove the offense downfield, and with 8 seconds left on the clock, old George Blanda was called upon to kick a long 48-yard field goal. He did not fail. The game ended in a surprising 17–17 tie.

Game eight saw the Raiders come home to Oakland to play the Cleveland Browns for the first time. Late in the fourth quarter, Cleveland led 17 to 13. Then near-disaster happened: Lamonica was injured on a hit in the Raiders' end zone after throwing an incomplete pass. Madden, once again, brought the old man in to save the day. Like a story that never gets old, George Blanda was tapped once more to be the savior and to perform his magic. However, Blanda miscued when he threw an interception, which gave the Browns an extra three points with a field goal. But Blanda was just warming up. Staying cool as a cucumber, old man Blanda led the Raiders again to pay dirt. With 4:11 on the clock, he started a Raiders drive at the Oakland 31, and eight plays later connected with Warren Wells on a 14-yarder for the tying touchdown. Most teams would just be happy with a tie. But not the Raiders. Not the season of Blanda, the wizard.

Kent McCloughan, who shared game ball honors with Blanda, came up with a big play as he picked off a Bill Nelsen pass and returned it to the Browns' 40 with 34 seconds left. A sack and a penalty sent the Raiders back. With no time outs and 12 seconds left, the Raiders hurriedly lined up, and Blanda hit running back Dixon at the sidelines for a nine-yard gain to the Browns' 46 with the clock stopped at three seconds.[70] Then Madden made the call to have the old man kick it from 52 yards. The old man calmly lined up behind the holder, Ken Stabler, and booted

---

69. Ibid., 899.
70. Ibid., 1050.

one straight through from 52 yards for the ballgame. The magical season continued for both Blanda and the Raiders.

Blanda was even calmer about his heroics to the press. "I feel good about it," said the graying veteran, "because it was a ballgame we had to win. All of them are important in this division." And important it was. The win left the Raiders ahead of Kansas City by a one-half game with a 4-2-2 record in the Western Division of the American Football Conference.[71]

Game nine saw the Raiders take on the Denver Broncos again, the last matchup between the two teams for the season. Denver rallied and led 19–17 late in the game. Mile High fans were already celebrating by the confetti seen on the field and the goal post. The familiar script continued when Lamonica injured his shoulder again, and old man Blanda came in for some late-game heroics. Blanda took over and drove the team downfield. A touchdown strike to Fred Biletnikoff sealed it for the Raiders 24–19.[72] The unbelievable, the fantastic, the comeback kids; these were some of the names that were beginning to define this 1970 Raiders team with their heart palpitating wins.

Week ten saw the Raiders come home to Oakland for their second and last match up for the season with the San Diego Chargers. These Raiders were on a heroic seven-game stretch without a loss, and now they were anticipating that streak to continue against the visiting San Diego Chargers. The script was the same as the last few games. The Raiders came from behind to tie up the score at 17. Oakland was hanging from the cliff again in another 4th quarter drama that put Daryle Lamonica in the spotlight. Daryle Lamonica was chased out of the pocket and ran to the Chargers' 30-yard line and out of bounds. The clock ran down to 7 seconds, and old George Blanda was called on to do it again. Blanda hit the field goal giving the Raiders another last-second victory.[73] The Raiders would have little time to savor their latest great escape because they had to turn around in four days and play in Detroit on Thanksgiving Day.

71. Ibid., 1058.
72. Cathey, "Oakland Raiders Challenge of the 70s," accessed November 16, 2018.
73. Ibid.

Game eleven was played on Thanksgiving Day in Detroit at Tigers Stadium. On this day, the surging Lions were hungry for more than turkey. This was no longer the pushover Lions of the past. These Lions played dominant football as if they were let out of a cage with a ravenous appetite. The Lions' Greg Landry, starting only his third game of the season, fired three touchdown passes and kept Detroit alive with his running ability as the Lions came from behind to beat the Oakland Raiders 28–14. The Raiders were stopped cold by the Lions' defense and ended their express of miracle wins. But this was only temporary, as more magic awaited the Raiders next week in New York City against the Jets.

The Raiders flew into New York City for a date at Shea Stadium, in Queens, to take on the Jets. The Jets led 13 to 7 in snowy conditions late into the 4th quarter. Cornerback Willie Brown intercepted the ball with 38 seconds remaining. Memories from the *Heidi* game surfaced, which was played back in 1968 when national television switched the Jets-Raiders to the regularly scheduled program of the movie *Heidi*. The network assumed wrongly that the Jets would win and switched its broadcast to the movie. What television audiences missed was one of the greatest comebacks ever in pro football, as the Oakland Raiders scored twice in 20 seconds to pull the rug out from under the Jets.

Now, two years later, with 38 seconds left and the Jets up 13–7, another miracle was needed.

For the first time in their series of spectacular finishes, veteran substitute quarterback George Blanda was not the Raiders' miracle worker this time. Blanda did kick the extra point, which meant the margin of victory, but it was a tumbling catch of a deflected pass, thrown by Daryle Lamonica, by flanker Warren Wells in the end zone with only one second remaining, that was the decisive score. And with a second left, George Blanda hit the extra point to seal it by a score of 14–13 for the Raiders.[74]

The Oakland Raiders and Kansas City Chiefs were used to squaring off in key battles. But few of their previous meetings carried the weight of this one in-game thirteen of the season. The old American Football League rivals went into this nationally televised Saturday game

---

74. Schaefer, *Game-by-Game Guide*, 1629, Kindle.

with identical 7-3-2 records. The winner would clinch the AFC's West Division title, while the loser would fall behind the 8–4 Miami Dolphins in the wild-card standings. "This game Saturday could mean everything to us," Chiefs quarterback Len Dawson said earlier in the week. "The loser might not make the playoffs." Added Raiders coach John Madden: "Lose this one, and you'll be home for Christmas."[75]

Would another heroic scene be set up as was throughout the season?

There would be no heroics needed. The Raiders played mistake-free football. Running back Mike Hubbard bowled his way through the Chiefs defense in an eye-opening performance. Then the game plan for Madden was to not only barrel over the Chief's defense but go over them in the passing attack from Lamonica. When it was all over, the final score was 20–6 in favor of Oakland. The Raiders had won the Division for a record-breaking four years. Madden was hoisted onto his team's shoulder and carried out.

The Raiders and Chiefs still could finish tied for first in the division, but Oakland's record in the games played between the two teams, at one win and one tie, would make the Raiders the champions.

"All we can do now is hope for a break," muttered Chiefs coach Hank Stram, in the deadly quiet of the losers' dressing room. "They did nothing different; they simply played a great football game."[76] The break for the World Champions would never come.

For the Oakland Raiders, the last game against San Francisco was not as important as it was for the 49ers. This was the greatest day in the quarter-century history of the much-maligned San Francisco 49ers, and a gifted quarterback named John Brodie. Brodie and his gang had to win. After it was announced that the Los Angeles Rams had clobbered the New York Giants 31–3, the only way to the division championship and the Super Bowl playoffs, by the 49ers, was a win or tie against the Bay Area rival Raiders. The Raiders, already division champs for the fourth

---

75. Ibid., 1736–1758.
76. Ibid., 1788.

straight year, were primed for the opportunity of killing off the 49ers, and wrecking their hopes for a first pennant since their birth in 1946.[77]

The weather in Oakland was not kind to the players, or the playing field, as the rains swirled around Oakland. Oakland General Manager Al Davis deemed the game "no big deal for us."[78] Good thing there wasn't a big deal, as the San Francisco 49ers routed the Raiders 38–7. This clinched the NFC West and a playoff spot for the 49ers, who had a very surprising year.

The Raiders regrouped and awaited the Miami Dolphins to visit them for the first round of the playoffs.

The eight teams were set to play in the new playoff format that featured a wild card in each conference. More excitement from this vintage year was due to come.

---

77. Ibid., 1891–1896.
78. Ibid.

11

THE PLAYOFFS

The new playoff format began on December 26, 1970, the day after Christmas. Cincinnati would go to Baltimore to play the Colts in the AFC, and Detroit would go to Dallas to play the Cowboys in the NFC.

AFC FIRST ROUND - CINCINNATI BENGALS VS. BALTIMORE COLTS - DECEMBER 26, 1970

On paper, this game looked like a mismatch from the start. The Bengals were still considered a new franchise, with only its third year in existence and no playoff experience. Besides, the Bengals had glaring issues before the game. Quarterback Virgil Carter was playing hurt with a broken hip, busted lip, and gashed tongue.[1] Carter was so beat up; he could not eat solid food for a week and dropped ten pounds before the game. The specially designed rib protector he would wear would hinder his mobility, but not his throwing arm. With Carter playing injured, the Bengals would have to rely more on the running game.

Coach Paul Brown remained humble for the opportunity to play in the playoffs, even with an injured quarterback and underdog status, against a mighty opponent in the Colts. Brown indicated that: "When you realize that the Rams or Kansas City didn't get a chance to play . . .

---

1. Schultz, *The NFL, Year One*, 166.

we were flattered to get into this game."[2] In 1967, Brown had predicted a winner in Cincinnati in five years when he took over the team, so he was two years ahead of time.

As for the Colts, they were hungry all season. That hunger intensified as they readied themselves for the Bengals in the first round of the playoff. The season went well enough for Baltimore, and they rebounded from a subpar season the year before. The need to avenge Super Bowl III still hung over the team, and they were playing with a determination that seemed almost obsessive. Unlike the Bengals, the Colts were an experienced playoff team that had been through this exciting and nerve-racking time before. They, of course, failed to take home a single trophy during the 1960s. The NFL Championship game of 1964 saw the rise of the Colts to an elite status in the NFL, in only coach Don Shula's second year of coaching the team. The Baltimore faithful were disappointed seeing their Colts lose to the Browns. More demoralizing for the Colts was the embarrassing loss to the Jets two years earlier in Super Bowl III.

Entering the playoffs, the Colts had concerns of their own with their quarterback's health, like their opponents. Johnny Unitas had an injured right shoulder, which worried the Colts' coaching staff, in that Unitas might not be up to par to play against the Bengals. Unitas, however, would play the game like there was nothing wrong with him.

When it was game day, the temperatures fell below the freezing mark in Baltimore. The Bengals' offense also was ice cold as they were stonewalled by the Colts' defense, who came ready to play. Realizing that Cincinnati would have to rely more on a running game due to Virgil Carter's injuries, the Colts studied films on the Cincinnati offense. As told by Baltimore Ray May: "We knew from watching films that their running game had to work against us if they were going to succeed . . . if their running game doesn't go, then their passing doesn't either."[3] On this game day, the Colts permitted the Bengals past midfield only twice while stopping their offense with their dominating defense. Cincinnati's running game was stopped cold, and Virgil Carter only completed eight

2. Ibid.
3. Ibid., 167.

of his 21 passing attempts for 93 yards and an interception. The Colts defense gave up only 46 yards rushing and limited the Bengals offense to only 139 total yards for the whole game.

Like the Bengals, the Colts also wanted to institute running the ball as their primary offensive game plan. Rookie, Norm Bulaich, bowled over the frozen Bengals' defense and ran for 116 yards on twenty-five carries. With the ability to move the ball on the ground, the Colts' running game paved the way for the passing game to get into the end zone twice. Even though John Unitas completed only six of seventeen passes, two were touchdown strikes of 45 and 53 yards in the first quarter and fourth quarter.[4]

In the end, the Bengals' Cinderella season and the seven-game winning streak were stopped in the cold in Baltimore, losing to the Colts 17–0. "A fantastic job," Colts' head coach Don McCafferty said in summing up the overall performance. "We respected Cincinnati's speed, and I think we did a good job of stopping their runs and rollouts."[5]

As for the Bengals, quarterback Virgil Carter said of the game: "the Bengals were 'just the victim of a stronger team.' We couldn't get any momentum going. We came in here thinking we could win if we played well. We beat some other teams no one expected us to beat. But they (the Colts) didn't make any mistakes."[6] Besides, Bengals' coach Paul Brown commented, "the Colts are big and mature, and when it gets down to the end of the season for the money, it takes the same kind of people to play them . . ."[7]

Overall, the Colts played a good game against Cincinnati. The Colts, who were a touchdown favorite, thoroughly outclassed the Bengals. With the win, the Colts extended their winning streak to five in a row while running their 1970 record to 12-2-1 as they played before their first home non-sellout crowd in 52 games. Fifty-one thousand one hundred twenty-seven spectators attended Memorial Stadium, with temperatures in the low 30s and wind up to 30 miles an hour. The stadium was not

4. John Schaefer, *Baltimore Colts 1970: A Game-by-Game Guide*, 1863, Kindle.
5. Ibid., 1893.
6. Ibid., 1906.
7. Ibid.

filled due to the weather, with about 9,000 below capacity.[8] With the win, the Colts would await the victor of the Dolphins and Raiders, which would be played the next day on December 27th, for the first American Football Conference Championship game.

NFC FIRST ROUND - THE DETROIT LIONS VS. THE DALLAS COWBOYS - DECEMBER 26, 1970.

Both the Dallas Cowboys and the Detroit Lions entered the first-round game with 10–4 records. The game was played at the historic Cotton Bowl, on Dallas's home turf. The weather wasn't horrendous, as the temperature was a moderate 35 degrees with mild winds. Neither the weather, nor the teams, nor the fans, could predict the outcome of this bizarre football game. Not even a touchdown was scored by either opponent. Only a safety and a field goal by Dallas was needed to do the Lions in.[9]

The Lions didn't even play a penalty ridden game, committing only one in the entire game. However, they did get chewed upon the ground, as Dallas rushed for 209 yards compared to Detroit's dismal amount of 76 yards. The Lions averaged less than three yards per rush. Dallas's workhorse was the enigmatic Duane Thomas, who carried the ball 30 times for 135 yards. His backfield-mate Walt Garrison added 72 yards on 17 carries.[10]

The only scoring came on Dallas' Mike Clark's 26-yard field goal, and, of course, the Lions suffered the embarrassment of having Dallas' George Andrie and Jethro Pugh sack quarterback Greg Landry in the end zone to make the final score 5–0.[11]

Both Lion's quarterbacks were horrible on this day. Detroit's Greg Landry and Bill Munson combined to go 7-for-20 for 92 yards with an interception. For Dallas, quarterback Craig Morton was worse, going 4-for-18 for 38 yards with one interception. Both defenses shut down the other team's offense. The Cowboys' defense won the battle it had to,

---

8. Ibid., 1910.
9. Barry Werner, "In 1970, Lions-Cowboys produced one of the rarest results in NFL History" (December 16, 2016), accessed November 28, 2018, https://www.foxsports.com/nfl/story/1970-lions-cowboys-produced-one-rarest-results-nfl-history-122216.
10. Ibid.
11. Ibid.

because shutting down quarterback Greg Landry was the key to winning this grudge match. And Dallas did that. Not only did the Cowboy defense hold Lions quarterback Greg Landry to 48 passing yards, but they also contained his running, as Landry was an excellent running quarterback. During the season, Landry had averaged 10 yards per carry and gained 350 yards. However, in this game, Landry was limited to only 15 yards rushing.[12]

The Lions barely crossed midfield all day, but they had one last gasp drive in them. Bill Munson had replaced Landry to shake things up. Munson led a gallant effort in another against-the-clock, frantic drive late in the 4th quarter.

The Lions crept closer to the Cowboys' goal line. They made it to around the 35-yard line. The drive finished unexpectedly, when Munson's pass to Earl McCullouch near the 20-yard line was a tad high, and the ball went off Earl's fingertips, and was intercepted by Dallas' Mel Renfro.[13] That sealed the shutout and the game for the Cowboys. Renfro told a CBS affiliate years later, "[The Lions] were marching down the field, and everybody was thinking we are going to lose the big one again. Fortunately, inside the 20-yard line, I was able to get the interception. It was a great relief."[14]

Of course, Renfro was alluding to the fact that Dallas lost the big games for the last four years. To the Dallas Cowboys, their fans, and the coaching staff, it was indeed a relief.

Dallas Cowboys coach Tom Landry could have hung out his shingle and become a resident swami. "Defense," Landry had preached long and loud, "controls the playoffs."[15] "You saw the zero today," Landry said of the fierce trench warfare between the Lions and Cowboys. "We played the best defense we ever have in a crucial game." The victory extended the Cowboys' defensive string of not allowing a touchdown to 21 quarters.

---

12. Ibid.

13. Greg Eno, "How The 1970 Detroit Lions Broke A Seven Year Old's Heart," Bleacher Report, May 7, 2009, at https://bleacherreport.com/articles/169762-how-the-1970-detroit-lions-broke-a-seven-year -olds-heart, accessed November 28, 2018.

14. Werner, "Lions-Cowboys," accessed November 28, 2018.

15. Schaefer, *Game-by-Game Guide.* 2002, Kindle.

"Anytime you can go that many quarters, you have a tremendous defensive unit," Landry said. "It's the best we've played in quite a few years," said game-saving cornerback Mel Renfro.[16]

Renfro also remarked that the league saw the Dallas cornerback position as a weakness to the defense. But that interception to seal the game was a bit of redemption by Renfro. "They've always felt like that cornerback spot was our weakness," Renfro said. "And with me over there, I guess they think it's pretty well plugged."[17]

The game was played in an old school way. Stellar defense by both teams, followed by a punishing run attack. However, the Dallas Doomsday defense did their job holding back Detroit's running game, which was the No. 2 rushing team in the National Football Conference behind the Cowboys. On this day, Detroit was held to just 76 yards on the ground.

Even in defeat, the 1970 season for the Lions is considered one of their best seasons ever. Hall of Fame cornerback Lem Barney maintained that if the Lions could only have gotten past the Cowboys, they would have won the Super Bowl. Sadly, for a franchise with few great memories, this playoff contest didn't add anything to Lions' lore.

Dallas had finally gotten the monkey off their back with a playoff win. The team had survived, which was a significant accomplishment for a team that had lost the big games for four years. There had to be work done with the offense, but overall, Landry was satisfied with the victory. He summed it up in a nutshell: "This was the biggest win we ever had . . . I think the problem we had with winning big games is behind us now."

Up next, Dallas would have to play the winner of the Vikings-49ers match up for the NFC Championship.

NFC FIRST ROUND - THE MINNESOTA VIKINGS VS. THE SAN FRANCISCO 49ERS - DECEMBER 27, 1970

As the Dallas Cowboys gathered around their televisions sets to watch this matchup between the Vikings and the 49ers, they believed, like everyone else, that the Vikings would meet them in the NFC Championship.

16. Ibid., 2002–2005.
17. Ibid., 2010.

San Francisco was a fresh face to the playoffs, spearheaded by the league MVP quarterback John Brodie, but the Vikings had the best record in the league at 12–2. The Vikings not only gave up the fewest scoring points in the league but ranked second behind the 49ers in scoring.[18] Also, the Vikings were on a mission, trying to avenge their embarrassing loss to the Chiefs in last year's Super Bowl. They were thirsting for victory, and they had an advantage in this game, which was their home turf. The Vikings were accustomed to playing in the icy, friendly confines of Metropolitan Stadium's tundra, where they had yet to lose a game in two years. Minnesota thought they would have a psychological advantage over the 49ers by playing in the cold. Even though there was no snow, and the game was played in clear conditions, along with a dry field to play on, the temperature that day was only ten degrees above zero. However, it felt like negative six degrees with the wind chill.[19] There were, however, some icy parts on the playing field. This included ice on both end zones. Another thing going for the Vikings is that they had playoff experience, whereas the 49ers were ten years removed from any playoff appearance.

In the first quarter, it looked like Minnesota would have the advantage as predicted, when safety Paul Krause ran 22 yards after he picked up a fumble by the 49ers' Ken Willard, out of the air, and scored the games' first touchdown.[20]

The 49ers regrouped and found their stride when their MVP quarterback figured out how to deal with the playing conditions. "It took us a while to find out where the icy spots were," he said, "but when we did, I called the plays and ran the patterns so we wouldn't get into them."[21]

Defensive back Bruce Taylor set up both San Francisco scores with stellar field positions. In the first period, he returned a punt 30 yards to the Vikings' 27. John Brodie then passed to Dick Witcher for 24 yards and the tying touchdown. Taylor's next return got to near midfield, which set up a 40-yard field goal by kicker Bruce Gossett. This put the 49ers up 10–7 going into the half.

18. Schultz, *The NFL, Year One*. 168–169.
19. Ibid. 169.
20. John Schaefer, *San Francisco 49ers 1970: A Game-by-Game Guide*, 1933, Kindle.
21. Ibid., 1903–1924.

Both defenses clamped down in the second half, which turned the game into a war of attrition that neither team got far on offense. The next score came in the 4th quarter by San Francisco when Bruce Taylor returned a punt 29 yards to the Vikings' 14. Running back Ken Willard gained 13 yards in two plays, but he failed to get into the end zone on two more running plays. The 49ers did score when Brodie ran over from the one-yard line for the decisive touchdown with only 80 seconds left to play.[22]

Vikings quarterback Gary Cuozzo, who completed nine of 27 attempts for 146 yards, couldn't complete anything in the second half until after the 49ers had a 17–7 lead late in the 4th quarter. Then he hit on five of six tries, including the Vikings' futile last-second touchdown pass to Gene Washington for 24 yards.[23]

Brodie was able to hit on 16 of 32 passes for 201 yards and had no interceptions. Although he had some issues on the ice, Brodie guided the 49er offense to victory. After the game, Brodie responded to the win by stating: "What might have made my task easier was that the 49ers ran 'a simple offense,' and the Vikings 'a simple defense.' We knew what they were going to do, and they knew what we were going to do," he said, "so it came down to execution. Our defense sure did."[24]

Brodie was indeed correct in his observance. The 49er defense stymied the Vikings offense and held them in check all day until the last second touchdown strike at the end of the game. Although both teams said the frigid temperature did not hamper their ball-handling, there were eight fumbles in the game, five by the 49ers, who lost the ball three times. San Francisco picked off two of Minnesota quarterback Gary Cuozzo's passes and recovered two of Minnesota's three fumbles to offset those.[25]

The 49ers beat a superior opponent and dealt the Vikings their first loss in the first round of the playoffs in three years. The 49ers would now meet the Dallas Cowboys in the first-ever NFC Championship game.

As for the Vikings, they remained an elite team throughout the 1970s. Quarterback Fran Tarkenton returned to the team in 1972, and

22. Ibid., 1937.
23. Ibid., 1946.
24. Ibid., 1924.
25. Ibid., 1942.

the Vikings would play in three more Super Bowls, but lost to the Dolphins in 1974, Pittsburgh in 1975, and to the Raiders in 1977.

Vikings coach Bud Grant achieved much for the franchise during his tenure with the Vikings, and that was highlighted by the four trips to the Super Bowl. He never won it all, and this 1970 team might have been his best shot. The 1969 team had been heavily favored in Super Bowl IV, but that was due to the public for underrating the Chiefs and the old AFL. In future years, Minnesota was simply not as good as its opponents in the AFC.

What makes the 1970 season particularly harsh for Minnesota, was that if they would have beaten San Francisco, their next opponent would have been Dallas, the same team they had beaten by 41 points during the season. With their dominant run throughout the season, there was no reason to think that Minnesota would have won the Super Bowl if they had just gotten there.[26]

AFC FIRST ROUND - THE MIAMI DOLPHINS VS. THE OAKLAND RAIDERS - DECEMBER 27, 1970

The Miami Dolphins and Oakland Raiders would begin their fierce rivalry in the AFC for the upcoming decade starting in 1970. John Madden became the Raiders head coach in 1969, a year before Shula took the reins in Miami, and both coaches had immediate success. Going into the game, the Raiders already had playoff experience for the last three years, and Don Shula's Dolphins propelled themselves into the 1970 playoffs in his rookie year as their coach. This first meeting between the two clubs would usher in the rivalry, as both teams remained on top of the AFC throughout the 1970s. The two Hall of Fame coaches would eventually face each other in the regular season four times, with each team winning two. They would also meet in the playoffs three times, with Madden getting the better of Shula twice.[27]

---

26. "Minnesota Miss A Perfect Super Bowl Opportunity," The Sports Notebook, accessed November 8, 2018, http://thesportsnotebook.com/1970-minnesota-vikings/.

27. Jerry Knaak, "Three Raiders vs. Matchups For Three Different Decades," accessed November 29, 2018, https://raiders.exposure.co/three-raiders-vs-dolphins-matchups-for-three-different-decades.

The AFC Divisional playoff game between the two teams took place on December 27, 1970. The Oakland Raiders, winners of the AFC West with an 8-4-2 record, hosted the Miami Dolphins, who had gone 10–4 to place second in the AFC East. This qualified Miami as a wild card entry. Even though Miami had a better record, the wild card traveled to the division winner.

There were 54,401 fans in attendance on a damp day at the Oakland-Alameda County Coliseum, and the field was extremely muddy. The Dolphins had the first possession, failed to gain much yardage, and eventually punted. Oakland then moved well with Hewritt Dixon and Charlie Smith running the ball, and Daryle Lamonica completed a pass to Fred Biletnikoff for 12 yards on a third-and-two play. But the drive stalled at the Miami 16, and the Raiders came up empty when George Blanda's 23-yard field goal attempt hit the goal post and bounced away.[28]

Miami put together a promising drive in response. Larry Csonka had a pair of five-yard runs, and halfbacks Mercury Morris and Jim Kiick handled most of the running load, while Bob Griese completed three passes. A Griese pass to wide receiver Howard Twilley for 14 yards and a pass to Kiick for 15 to convert third downs moved the Dolphins into Raider's territory. But Miami failed to get on the board when kicker Garo Yepremian was wide on a 24-yard try for a field goal.

The teams traded punts as the game headed into the second quarter. Miami got a break when the defensive end Bill Stanfill recovered a Smith fumble at Oakland's 19. Two plays later, Griese passed to Paul Warfield for a 16-yard touchdown. Yepremian added the extra point, and the Dolphins led by 7–0.

The teams exchanged punts until things got moving for Oakland, who were on offense with 4:35 remaining in the first half. The Raiders' offense drove 62 yards downfield to score a touchdown. This drive included quarterback Daryle Lamonica completing a third-and-six pass to Raymond Chester for 21 yards, which took the Raiders to the Miami 37.

28. Keith Yowell, "1970: Big Plays Lift Raiders Over Dolphins in AFC Divisional Playoff Game" (December 27, 2015), accessed November 29, 2018, https://fs64sports.blogspot.com/2015/12/1970-big -plays-lift-raiders-over.html.

Then Lamonica converted another third down successfully, with a throw to Biletnikoff for 11 yards. Another completion to Biletnikoff in the end zone was good for a 22-yard touchdown. Blanda kicked the point after to tie the score.[29] The teams went into halftime even at 7–7.

The Raiders took the kickoff to start the third quarter and advanced deep into Miami territory. Full back Marv Hubbard ran six times for 22 yards, and Lamonica completed two third-down passes, one to Smith for nine yards and one to Chester for 26 yards. But facing second-and-goal at the two, Smith fumbled again, and Jake Scott recovered for the Dolphins at their own 10-yard line.[30]

Bob Griese immediately got the offense going for the Dolphins with a pass to Warfield for 24 yards and, after two short running plays, Griese connected with Kiick for nine yards on a third-and-six play. But luck would run out on the Dolphins, as Griese was then sacked for a 12-yard loss by Raiders' tackle Tom Keating and then by defensive end Tony Cline. With the two sacks, it seemed that the black and silver's defense shook up Griese because two plays later, Griese threw an interception on a third-and-19 play. That interception was picked off by cornerback Willie Brown, who returned the pick 50 yards for a Raider touchdown. Blanda added the point after to give Oakland a 14–7 lead.[31] This is how the score would remain going into the 4th quarter.

The Dolphins had the ball as the contest moved into the fourth quarter. A 12-yard run by Morris got the ball to the Oakland 40, and Griese passed to Warfield for 16 yards. The Miami drive, however, stalled at Oakland's 17. Miami kicker, Yepremian, failed to get extra points for the Dolphins by missing a field goal, whereby the ball was kicked to the left of the goal pole on a 24-yard field goal attempt.[32] The ball sailed wide to the left of the goal pole.

Oakland struck back quickly. Hubbard ran for four yards and halfback Pete Banaszak fumbled on the next play, which Raiders' tackle Harry Schuh had recovered but had the Raiders facing a third-and-12

29. Ibid.
30. Ibid.
31. Ibid.
32. Ibid.

situation. On third down, Lamonica, anticipating a blitz, threw long for wide receiver Rod Sherman, who pulled the ball in at the Miami 45 and went the distance for an 82-yard touchdown. Blanda's extra point put the home team up by 21–7.[33]

The Dolphins came back with a long drive of 69 yards in eight plays. A personal foul on the Raiders erased a sack, and Griese completed a throw to receiver Willie Richardson for 23 yards. Kiick ran for 13 yards on the next play, and Griese again connected with Richardson, this time in the right corner of the end zone for a seven-yard touchdown. Yepremian's conversion again made it a seven-point game.[34]

However, time was running out on the Dolphins. They were unable to recover an onside kick that went out of bounds, and, following a short Oakland possession, they got the ball back at their 13 with 2:28 left on the clock. Morris ran for four yards; two passes fell incomplete, one of which was intended for Warfield and knocked away by linebacker Gus Otto, and on fourth down, a toss to Kiick came up a yard short. The Raiders were able to run out the clock and won by a final score of 21–14.[35]

Oakland had the edge in total yards (307 to 242), although the Dolphins had more first downs (16 to 12) and ran more plays (63 to 52). The Raiders also turned the ball over twice, to one miscue suffered by Miami. The Raiders committed the only four penalties of the game. Both placekickers had difficulty on the muddy field as Miami's Yepremian missed both of his field-goal attempts and Blanda missed one.[36]

Daryle Lamonica completed 8 of 16 passes for 187 yards and two touchdowns with no interceptions. Fred Biletnikoff had three catches for 46 yards and a touchdown, and Rod Sherman, with his one long scoring reception, led the Raiders with 82 receiving yards. Marv Hubbard topped the rushers with 58 yards on 18 carries.[37]

---

33. Ibid.
34. Ibid.
35. Ibid.
36. Ibid.
37. Ibid.

For the Dolphins, Bob Griese was successful on 13 of 27 throws for 155 yards, and two touchdown passes with one interception returned for a score. Jim Kiick gained 64 yards on 14 rushing attempts and caught four passes for 34 yards. Paul Warfield gained 62 yards on his four receptions that included a touchdown. Larry Csonka was held to 23 yards on 10 carries, and Mercury Morris contributed 29 yards on 8 attempts.[38]

"I'm proud of the way our people came back," Raiders coach John Madden said after the victory . . .[39] "Our season came to a screeching halt right now," said losing coach Don Shula . . .[40] Up next for the Raiders would be the Baltimore Colts for the AFC Championship.

AFC CHAMPIONSHIP SUNDAY - JANUARY 3, 1971

The game between the Baltimore Colts and the Oakland Raiders was setting up to be a war of giants. Both teams had been dominant during the 1960s. Oakland lost Super Bowl II to the Packers, and the Colts lost Super Bowl III to the Jets. Like Baltimore, Oakland was looking to get back to the Super Bowl. Oakland certainly had good chances and good teams to get back to the Super Bowl. The Raiders had three years of consecutive playoff appearances, making this the fourth consecutive year. The Colts were trying to regain some of that old Baltimore magic. The loss of Super Bowl III, and the dismal season before, was in the rearview mirror now for Baltimore. They were in the first AFC championship game, led by their stellar defense, and two experienced quarterbacks piloted their offense in Unitas and Morrall. Baltimore hoped to keep the express rolling after their win over Cincinnati and the strategy that propelled the team forward to success all season long.

The transition to the AFC, from being an NFL team in the former league proved successful for the Colts. But their tenure in the NFL was far from forgotten by both the media and fans when it came to this matchup against the Raiders. Even Oakland coach John Madden believed this to

---

38. Ibid.
39. John Schaefer, *Oakland Raiders 1970: A Game-by-Game Guide*, 2048, Kindle.
40. Ibid., 2057.

be true by stating: "This will be like the American Football League vs. the National Football League."[41]

Whether it was years of frustration among both teams, a war of words ensued against each other before the game was even played. Spearheaded by the Raider's managing partner Al Davis, his statements against the Colts had the look of a confident Raiders team, but it came out sounding quite arrogant. Al Davis's confident stance trickled down to his players, who also believed that a Raider win was imminent. Cornerback Willie Brown remarked: "When Unitas looks across the line of scrimmage Sunday, he's going to see the best defense in football, no matter what anyone says. For a long time, we weren't playing as a unit. But now we are."[42]

Brown's remarks were bold for a team that finished with an 8-4-2 record and would play a Colts team that went 11-2-1. Word got out that the Raiders were planning to ship all its football equipment directly from Baltimore to Miami for the Super Bowl. Colts defensive tackle Bubba Smith recalls: "[Raiders' defensive back] George Atkinson told me, yeah, we are going to go right here to Miami . . . I said: What, you guys are going to the game? You got tickets? Because we're going to beat the hell out of you."[43]

The animosity between the two teams wasn't the only cold thing. Two days before, a snowstorm hit Baltimore, and the emergency crews had to clear five inches of snow at Memorial Stadium. This left only bare field that was frozen dirt and dust, that kicked up from the turf from the swirling winds.

The Colts were no strangers playing on the field labeled "the dirt bowl," as head coach Don McCafferty called it. Because of the lack of grass, only the end zones and the center of the field were painted with logos for game time. Memorial Stadium, like many other stadiums, housed a baseball team as well. The Orioles had torn up the playing surface throughout the 1970 season and even won the 1970 World Series on this dirt field. The Colts tried to get the grass back in shape by

41. Schultz, *The NFL, Year One*, 172.
42. Ibid.
43. Ibid.

re-sodding, but the sod never took, and the field remained barren. Like the Vikings in the first round, who thought the cold would be advantageous, the Colts believed that the barren field was advantageous to them over any visiting opponent, even the overconfident Raiders.

On game day, as the Colts came out of their locker room and onto the field, Al Davis watched the team take the field and exclaimed: "So those are the Colts . . . I hate the Colts. Just getting this far isn't enough. We've got to beat them."

The Baltimore faithful were out in the stands. Fifty-six thousand three hundred sixty-eight fans showed up at Memorial Stadium to root on their beloved Colts. Mounds of hard snow filled the end zones, gray from Baltimore's omnipresent smog, even on a day of clear skies and no wind. Signs festooned the stands—KILL, BUBBA, KILL, LOVE OUR COLTS, and LEAKY ROOF? CALL LIBERTY ROOFING.[44]

The game was billed as a quarterback duel between the great Johnny Unitas vs. Daryle Lamonica, aka "The Mad Bomber." The excitement was overwhelming for both clubs and their fans. However, Super Bowl III still hung over the Colts and their fans in this championship contest. "God, that memory hurts," said Carroll Rosenbloom, the Colts' contentious owner. "But maybe it toughened us. I used to puke before every game, and now I don't anymore." Indeed, in the moments before the opening kickoff, Rosenbloom was—well—blooming with good cheer. "Hey," he said to Al Davis, who was watching a redheaded teen-ager throwing back practice field-goal balls, "That kid throws better than any of our quarterbacks." Davis sniffed, "Oh, yeah?" The kid was Al's son, but you got the distinct impression he would prefer a Unitas.[45]

The first half of the game was a lackluster affair. The Colts marched down the field in the first quarter and kicker, Jim O'Brien hit a 16-yard field goal. In the second quarter, the Colts scored again on a Norm Bulaich 2-yard rush to put the Colts up 10–0. To make matters worse for Oakland, their quarterback Daryle Lamonica, had to leave the game

44. Robert Jones, "To Kill A Memory That Still Hurts," *Sports Illustrated* (January 11, 1971), accessed November 30, 2018, https://www.si.com/vault/1971/01/11/554232/to-kill-a-memory-that-still-hurts.
45. Ibid.

due to a groin injury after being hit by the Colts' Bubba Smith. With Lamonica out, the old man, George Blanda, took over, as he did so many times during the season, for the Raiders. The Raiders were hoping the 43-year-old Blanda still had that magic left in his magician's hat that he performed throughout the season. It now came down to a battle of the elderly in the quarterback position; 37-year-old Unitas vs. 43-year-old Blanda in what would be appropriate for an old timer's game rather than the AFC Championship.

Blanda showed some of that magic with flair and did indeed strike back after a roughing-the-kicker penalty moved the ball closer to the field goal posts. Blanda kicked a 48-yard field goal to send the teams into the locker room with a 10–3 lead by Baltimore.

Baltimore had controlled the ball throughout the first half, and Oakland didn't get a first down until their third play of the second quarter—but when Blanda & Company returned to the field, a feeling of insecurity began to imbue the Colts. "We were just waiting for the Cinderella finish," admitted John Mackey, the Colts' tight end. "The Cinderella Man was in there, and his tricks were working." Pushing for the touchdown that tied the score at 10–10, Blanda used all the tricks up his voluminous sleeve. Hitting Warren Wells and Fred Biletnikoff, he flooded the Baltimore zones deep and short, eye-faked defenders out of their coverage and generally made ninnies of the Colts in a nine-play, 80-yard drive, which ended with a 38-yard pass to Biletnikoff.[46]

With Blanda performing his miracles again, there was a feeling of that Raider magic surrounding Memorial Stadium. But the Colts shook off that Raider mystique and struck back. Baltimore marched down the field, and Jim O'Brien kicked a 23-yard field goal to put the Colts ahead 13–10. The Colts defense then stiffened and held Blanda and the Raiders in check. Unitas went to work again from his own 35. The Colts quarterback, whose career appeared at an end during the 1968 season when arm problems plagued him, now was in rhythm like the old days. Unitas hit Hinton for 13 yards, and then Jefferson for 11 and then 13 yards to bring the ball to the Oakland 11. Unitas then called on Bulaich

---

46. Ibid.

for a reverse play, and the rookie from TCU careened around left for 11 yards to score a touchdown for a 20–10 lead with 1:28 left in the third period.[47]

Blanda, however, wasn't finished either. He hit the rookie tight end, Raymond Chester, with a 35-yarder and Wells for 38 yards as the Raiders pushed the Colts backward. Then he finished off the 80-yard drive with a 15-yard scoring toss to Wells. Wells was hit hard in the end zone, dropping the ball, but under the rules, it was a touchdown as soon as he gained possession and crossed the goal line. However, the Colts' fans didn't see it that way, and snowballs were heaved from the stands as the teams lined up for the conversion.[48]

With Baltimore leading now, just 20–17, Unitas got the clincher just three plays later, heaving the crucial pass down the left side to Ray Perkins. Defensive back Wilson seemed to misjudge the ball, and when it came down, Perkins was there, and Wilson was some five yards away. Perkins, a four-year veteran who had scored only one previous touchdown during the season, raced the remaining 45 yards to score.[49] "It was bump-and-run, recalled Perkins, and Wilson expected me to make a sharp outside cut for the first down. Instead, I kept going." Wilson moved out, then in, like a man in a revolving door during the flight of the ball. Unitas laid the pass right into Perkins's hands, and he galloped into the end zone for the clinching touchdown. It was another of McCafferty's weekly specials, this one having the descriptive title of "Double Bow-Out pattern."[50] Perkins' touchdown sealed the Raiders' fate as the Colts beat Oakland 27–17 and punched their ticket to Super Bowl V representing the newly formed American Football Conference. When the final gunshot rang out, the Colts carried their rookie coach off the field in celebration of returning to the Super Bowl.

After the game, 15-year veteran John Unitas even received praise from the defeated Raiders for his play. "I have not seen No. 19 (Unitas)

47. John Schaefer, *Baltimore Colts 1970: A Game-by-Game Guide*, 2060, Kindle.
48. Ibid., 2060–2064.
49. Ibid., 2064–2069.
50. Jones, "To Kill A Memory," accessed November 30, 2018.

play better this year," Raiders coach John Madden said. "He kept hitting those open guys."

"Unitas," said defensive back Willie Brown, "threw the ball as well as he ever has."[51]

Colts' McCafferty was humbled in the win. "It was an uneasy win," McCafferty admitted. "The only breath I took was with 29 seconds left." With a big grin on his old-shoe face, he added, "It was just great. Amen to that."

Rosenbloom could only agree. "This game kicks the genius coach theory into a cocked hat," he said with a scarcely veiled reference to Don Shula, the Baltimore coach who was lured to Miami. He also added: "What did Mac do? He only took a team that looked like nothing last year, a team riddled with dissension and often hurt this season, and turned it into a champion. Here's a man who has no inner sanctum, no pretensions, no assistants—only associates. Everyone gets the credit but McCafferty. He is just a splendid man. What's more, he brought the fun back into the game of football for me."[52]

"This is as big if not bigger than playing in the 1969 Super Bowl," defensive tackle Billy Ray Smith said. "No one thought we could do it."[53] Norm Bulaich had a great day rushing for 71 yards on 22 carries, and scored two touchdowns on the ground. He was wearing a grin of his when the gun sounded ending the game. "How do you like that?" he said dazedly. "A rookie, and I'm in the Super Bowl." Those Colts who were there in Super Bowl III realized full well, from their experience, that the name of the season is three good games, back-to-back to back.[54] They had one more game to fulfill this prophecy. Winning Super Bowl V.

The 1970 Baltimore Colts earned their trip to Miami again, and a chance to get the $15,000 a person prize money, and the Super Bowl trophy. Perhaps the demons of Super Bowl III could be exorcised. Colts' linebacker Mike Curtis remarked, "Our '68 team executed far better than

51. Schaefer, *Game-by-Game Guide*, 2034–2038, Kindle.
52. Ibid.
53. Ibid., 2073.
54. Jones, "To Kill A Memory," accessed November 30, 2018.

this one. But we might have learned something from the trip to Miami that year. Maybe we won't relax as much as we did then."[55]

NFC CHAMPIONSHIP SUNDAY - JANUARY 3, 1971

San Francisco was the site for this title game for the NFC crown, with the winner going on to play the Colts in Super Bowl V. After a surprise win over the Vikings at frozen Metropolitan Stadium, in the first round of the playoffs, the 49ers now played host to the Dallas Cowboys. It also marked the end of an era for the 49ers, as they would play their last game at Kezar Stadium and move to the bigger Candlestick Park for the 1971 season.

With the up and down season the Cowboys had, coach Tom Landry readily admitted he thought his team's chances of reaching the big money game of the Super Bowl was a flat zero just six short weeks earlier.[56] Yet these same Cowboys persevered and now prepared to do battle with the 49ers for the NFC Championship. Yet the specter of losing the big games for the last four years still haunted the Cowboys. The title battles against Green Bay in 1966 and 1967 proved to the Cowboys that Green Bay was still the best of the best during those two seasons. With those losses to the Packers, Dallas still had to wait for glory, even though they came a long way since their humble beginnings as a franchise back in 1960. But glory faded, as the club failed to get past the first playoff round in the next two years, both in 1968 and 1969. Like the Colts, the aura of losing the big one was still present in the Dallas psyche.

As for the 49ers, there were no haunting memories that plagued the team like their opponents. There was excitement in the city by the bay, as folks were walking around with buttons in San Francisco saying, "I've got 49er fever."[57] San Francisco quarterback John Brodie, however, took a more nonchalant attitude towards the game. "What's all the excitement? It's just another football game. You can't make more of it than

---

55. Schultz, *The NFL, Year One*, 173.

56. John Schaefer, *Dallas Cowboys 1970: A Game-by-Game Guide*, 2121, Kindle.

57. William N. Wallace, "49ers Rated Over Cowboys," *New York Times* (January 3, 1971), accessed December 1, 2018, https://www.nytimes.com/1971/01/03/archives/49ers-rated-over-cowboys-brodie-key -man.html.

that."[58] Brodie's laid-back attitude probably surprised most people since Brodie had been a loser more often than a winner in his 14 seasons with the 49ers.

The 49ers led the NFL in scoring, thus racking up the most points by any team for the 1970 season. Their offense was a juggernaut, spearheaded by a dangerous aerial attack led by the MVP Brodie. But the Cowboys had their Doomsday defense, who coming into this game, didn't give up a single touchdown in 21 quarters.[59] The 49ers had a similar style of defense as the Cowboys, due to head coach Nolan designing his defense in the likeness of his mentor Landry. With the Cowboys' offense being unpredictable, the 49ers knew Dallas would depend on its defense. This was shown in the recent games played by Dallas, especially with a rare 5 to 0 victory over a Lions team that had a high-octane offense that ran out of gas against the Doomsday defense in the first round of the playoffs. "They must be good," said Brodie. "The defenses will win or lose this game."[60]

The 49ers focused on stopping Duane Thomas, the rookie runner who gained 135 yards against Detroit the past Saturday. The Cowboys were a running team, partly by choice, because of players like Thomas who can gain good yards on the ground, and partly by necessity because of Craig Morton's poor passing.[61]

There were 59,625 in attendance on a cool and clear day at Kezar Stadium. The 49ers threatened first when Brodie threw to Gene Washington for 42 yards, but the wide receiver couldn't maintain his footing and went down at the Dallas nine. San Francisco missed out on a sure touchdown when Brodie misfired on a pass to an open fullback Ken Willard in the end zone, and the home team had to settle for a 16-yard Bruce Gossett field goal.[62] The game settled into a defensive struggle for the remainder of the first half. The Cowboys moved the ball more effectively

---

58. Ibid.
59. Ibid.
60. Ibid.
61. Ibid.
62. Keith Yowell, "1971: Cowboys Beat 49ers For The NFC Championship," This Date In Football, (January 3, 2013), accessed December 1, 2018, https://fs64sports.blogspot.com/2013/01/1971-cowboys -beat-49ers-for-nfc.html.

but couldn't put points on the board until Mike Clark, who missed from 40 yards in the opening period, kicked a 21-yard field goal in the second quarter. The score was just 3–3 at halftime.[63]

The teams traded punts to start the third quarter, at which point the game turned on two interceptions. San Francisco, starting its next possession at its 21-yard line, lost ground when Brodie was sacked by the linebacker, Dave Edwards, for a seven-yard loss. With Cowboys' defensive end Larry Cole pressuring Brodie on the next play, Brodie tried to throw the ball away, but middle linebacker Lee Roy Jordan made a shoestring interception. Dallas had the ball at the San Francisco 13, and on the next play, Duane Thomas cut toward the sideline and broke three tackles on the way to a touchdown.[64]

On San Francisco's next series, Brodie threw long for Gene Washington, but cornerback Mel Renfro picked it off at the Dallas 19 and returned it 19 yards. The Cowboys proceeded to advance 62 yards in nine plays for another touchdown on a five-yard pass from Craig Morton to running back Walt Garrison. Along the way, Garrison, playing despite suffering a sprained ankle in the first quarter, ran for 12 yards and then gained 23 yards on a screen pass to the San Francisco 29. A Morton pass intended for Bob Hayes was overthrown, but 49er safety Mel Phillips was flagged for pass interference, setting up the touchdown throw.[65]

The 49ers came back with an impressive 73-yard drive in eight plays that ended with Brodie throwing to tight end Dick Witcher for a 26-yard touchdown.

In the next series, the 49ers nearly got a big break when Thomas fumbled, but wide receiver Reggie Rucker recovered the ball to retain possession for the Cowboys, which gave them a first down. Dallas then drove to the San Francisco 17 but came up empty when Clark's 24-yard field goal try sailed wide.[66]

The 49ers got no closer than the Dallas 39 in the time remaining, and in that instance, a pass intended for Witcher was broken up by

63. Ibid.
64. Ibid.
65. Ibid.
66. Ibid.

cornerback Herb Adderley. Then, Gossett missed a 47-yard field goal attempt. The Cowboys, playing near error-free football, held on to win by a score of 17–10.[67]

Dallas had the advantage in total yards (319 to 307), with 229 yards of that total coming on the ground as the Cowboys attacked the less-experienced side of the 49ers' defense by running to the right. They also had the edge in first downs (22 to 15), ran more plays (75 to 61), and held onto the ball for almost ten more minutes than the Niners. The 49ers gave up the two big third quarter turnovers while Dallas turned the ball over once.[68],

Duane Thomas had an outstanding performance as he rushed for 143 yards and a touchdown on 27 carries and caught two passes for 24 more yards. Walt Garrison contributed 71 yards on 17 rushing attempts and was also the team's leading receiver with three catches for 51 yards and a score. Craig Morton completed just 7 of 22 passes for 101 yards and a touchdown with none intercepted. Only one pass was completed to a wide receiver (Reggie Rucker for 21 yards).[69]

For the Cowboys, history didn't repeat itself when they battled the 49ers. With a tremendous running game powered by rookie Duane Thomas and gutsy Walt Garrison, Dallas beat the favored 49ers and finally made it to the Super Bowl.[70] Landry declared the victory over the 49ers must take the "loser onus" off his Cowboys, although he pointed out quickly, "there is one game left."[71]

"This is the way we have played all season," Landry said. "We ran well, and we played good defense."

"It's all so fantastic, so unbelievable," Morton gushed. Indeed, given the Cowboys' previous big-game flops and their missteps during the 1970 season, it did seem hard to believe that Dallas would be competing for a championship. But Tom Landry's crew had come of age, and

---

67. Ibid.
68. Ibid.
69. Ibid.
70. Schaefer, *Game-by-Game Guide*, 2140, Kindle.
71. Ibid., 2144.

the franchise that would soon become known as "America's Team" had turned a corner.[72]

Losing coach Dick Nolan said his team's inability to stop Thomas made a big difference. "He is an excellent runner," Nolan said. "With his ability and the rest of their running game, he becomes a big weapon for them. We met a good team, and we lost."[73]

The 49ers would be back in the playoffs for the next two seasons, but only to lose to these same Cowboys in the 1971 NFC Championship game and again in the divisional round in 1972. Nolan would never be able to beat his teacher and mentor, Tom Landry, in the playoffs. Landry would remain the "master" of his pupil to Nolan. Thus, the 49ers would have to wait until 1981 to make the playoffs. This time the team was coached by Bill Walsh, who would win three Super Bowls for San Francisco.

Landry looked ahead to the Super Bowl match-up against the Colts on January 17, 1971. "Baltimore's offense will provide much the same challenge as did the 49ers," reasoned Landry after the game. Landry believed quarterbacks John Brodie of the 49ers and Johnny Unitas of the Colts presented similar problems. "Brodie was fabulous this season, and I think I aged 20 years in the second half," he declared as he breathed a sigh of relief that his team won. "When you play Baltimore, you're playing another great pro in Unitas. Baltimore, like San Francisco, is a passing team with great receivers. They'll give us about the same challenge as did the 49ers."[74]

The planning for Super Bowl V was underway. Baltimore and Dallas, two franchises with the aura of crushing defeats in past big games, would take center stage in Miami. One would go home a champion. The other would again be branded as the team who could not win the big one and would have to "wait another year."

---

72. Ibid., 2169–2173.
73. Ibid., 2161.
74. Ibid., 2144–2148.

12

SUPER BOWL V: PRELUDE TO THE GAME

THE COLTS

Trying to forget their disastrous trip to the Super Bowl in Miami in 1969, the Colts did everything differently this time. Everyone felt that bad luck still hung over the Colts since the loss in Super Bowl III, even with punching their ticket to Super Bowl V. This negative aura put a superstitious nature over Baltimore. They tried not to follow in their footsteps from two years before. The Colts flew from frigid Baltimore to south Florida ten days before the game on a different airline, stayed at a different site (a country club rather than a beachfront hotel), and practiced in a different field. The Colts were motivated by two factors. First, vindicating themselves for their loss to the Jets in Super Bowl III. Second, proving to the pro football world that they could win the big game without the "genius" of Don Shula.[1]

Hard hitting defensive end, Bubba Smith, recalled the Colts' attitude two years earlier. "We walked out of the hotel that morning (of Super

---

1. "1970: Super Bowl V - Dallas Cowboys vs Baltimore Colts," *Golden Football Magazine*, accessed December 3, 2018, http://goldenrankings.com/SuperBowl5-A.htm.

Bowl III) like the Jets were going to be too scared to show up. The Jets stole our pride and everything else. We have to get it back."[2]

Time magazine had this to say in its preview of the game about the Colts: "The Colts are a plodding and unspectacular team, which reflects, in part, the unobtrusive personality of their first-year head coach." One Colt who attracted attention from the media was tight end John Mackey, the president of the players' association and leader of the strike that shut down training camps back in August. He was asked if the three-day walkout improved the relationship between players and owners. "Yes and no. Some things have been solved, and some things haven't. In two weeks, after the Pro Bowl in Los Angeles, we'll have a meeting and decide where we're going." He refused to discuss player-owner matters any further. "I've got a game to get ready for." But he did respond to a question about how much the loss to the Jets motivated the Colts. "I think of sitting around at halftime of that game two years ago, and how bad it was, how unprepared we were . . . I dropped a few passes in that game, but I'm not haunted by them . . . I was low, man, real low for five, six months. I remember feeling like I wanted to dig a hole and hide until the next season started."[3]

Earl Morrall was also asked if he endured any lingering effects from his poor performance in Super Bowl III. He responded: "That was the biggest game of my life, and it didn't turn out too well. I've tried to shrug it off, but I just can't. I keep thinking about it, and I still get flashbacks, remembering all the bad things and all the turning points. I've replayed in my mind that whole game over and over again. The interceptions, the flea-flicker, the whole mess. Now that I'm back at the Super Bowl, I'll be returning to the scene of the crime. I guess there is no way I can escape it."[4]

Morrall wrote in his 1971 autobiography: "I was somewhat dejected as the day of the game (Super Bowl V) drew near. I figured that I was

---

2. Ibid.
3. Ibid.
4. Ibid.

going to be a spectator, that I wasn't going to get a chance to play unless things went badly for us or we managed to get way ahead."[5]

Reporters also wanted to talk to Johnny Unitas, who had gained a (deserved) reputation for being curt with the press. He agreed to two sessions early in the week and seemed to enjoy them. Unitas's image contrasted sharply with that of Joe Namath, the hero of the AFL for leading the Jets to victory in Super Bowl III. John was considered a model citizen—family man, businessman, crew cut, quiet, calculating team leader. Namath cultivated his playboy image—long hair, a different knockout young lady on his arm each time he was seen in public, flinging passes with abandon. However, unknown to the public, Unitas was burdened with personal problems that would culminate in his wife filing for divorce five days after Super Bowl V. John also admitted after the Super Bowl that he had suffered from headaches ever since the Cincinnati playoff game.[6]

THE COWBOYS

As for Dallas, they arrived a week before the game and moved into their lodging and training sites in Fort Lauderdale, where the Jets had prepared two years earlier. Unlike the Colts, who had their wives with them, the Cowboys were not allowed to speak to their wives, who fended for themselves in South Florida.[7]

The Cowboy who made the most splash nationwide when he spoke to the press was Duane Thomas, who already had a reputation for being "different." Asked if he felt pressure as a rookie as he approached the Super Bowl, Duane replied, "I don't believe in pressure. But this is the ultimate game; how can you not feel pressure? No, it isn't . . . It's not the ultimate game? If this was the ultimate game, they wouldn't be playing it again next year."[8]

In its preview of Super Bowl V, *Sports Illustrated* called the Cowboys "a team without a quarterback." The upcoming game was painted as Johnny Unitas vs. the Dallas defense. Craig Morton was asked if he minded

---

5. Ibid.
6. Ibid.
7. Ibid.
8. Ibid.

Coach Landry calling all the plays. Morton replied: "Tom started calling the plays because he thought I'd gotten too conservative. Also, he thought maybe I was being affected by the static we were getting from the fans. And we won that game, so he called them the next week, too. And we kept winning, so you don't change a winning combination . . . our philosophy right now on offense is not to make mistakes, control the ball. We have a great running game going, so we stay with it. We've won seven in a row, and I've had two interceptions in those seven games, no fumbles."[9]

One Cowboy who was especially excited to be in the Super Bowl was rookie safety, Charlie Waters who said: "A year ago this time, I was sitting in a frat house at Clemson, watching the Super Bowl game on television. I had just had shoulder surgery. I was so convinced something like this was out of my reach that I didn't even bother to dream about it."[10]

Years later, linebacker Chuck Howley looked back at Super Bowl V and said: "We acted like it was just another game, but it wasn't. It was the Super Bowl. We wanted to win it, but I don't know if we had the urgency we needed in a game of that magnitude."[11]

Tight end Pettis Norman later pointed to the two-week layoff between the NFC Championship Game and the Super Bowl as a factor in how Dallas played in the big game: "The 49er championship game was better from an emotional standpoint than the Super Bowl. First of all, there was a two-week lag time. To me, you lose some edge when you wait like that, and then you try to get it back. We went to the Orange Bowl in Miami, and the atmosphere was not quite real. It was kind of boring. You get tired of going through thousands of interviews, posing for pictures, this and that."[12]

THE BALTIMORE EXPERIENCE

With Baltimore, a former NFL team, representing the AFC, Super Bowl V lacked the excitement of that old David vs. Goliath mentality with a great rivalry in the upstart junior league (AFL) vs. the establishment

9. Ibid.
10. Ibid.
11. Ibid.
12. Ibid.

(NFL), which the first four Super Bowls had. Without that old AFL-NFL rivalry storyline, Super Bowl V lacked a compelling story. The past four Super Bowls had interesting storylines; Super Bowl I marked the inaugural showdown between the two champions from each league to see who was the more dominant league, Super Bowl II was Packers' coach Vince Lombardi's swan song, and Super Bowl III was Joe Namath's outlandish prediction, which became a reality, and put the AFL in a more respectable light. Super Bowl IV marked the end of the AFL, and the Chiefs gave the AFL square footing with the NFL with two Super Bowl victories apiece.[13]

With this lack of a compelling story, the Colts sensed this and came to Miami feeling unloved and unappreciated. Colts' center Bill Curry spoke about the mood felt by the Colts: "We came into a new league this season, and nobody wanted to see us win the championship . . . and they still don't."[14] Colts defensive tackle Billy Ray Smith (who would retire after Super Bowl V) said, "I don't want to win one for the old AFL. I want to win one for . . . the Colts. This will be my last game . . . why shouldn't I feel that way? We've been in the AFC for one season—how in hell can the league identify with us, and vice-versa? We're still the Colts the Jets beat to a lot of people in the league. Nobody's sending us telegrams this year."

John Unitas was blunter: "My only allegiance is to Baltimore."[15]

DALLAS DIGS IN

For Dallas, Tom Landry made some changes in his offensive lineup during the week of the big game. Calvin Hill, a forgotten man in the last two months, was running with the first team in practice drills. Duane Thomas moved over to fullback in place of Walt Garrison, who came out of the 49ers game with a badly twisted ankle, to go along with the strained knee and chipped collarbone he already had.[16]

Landry and his staff gave the offensive players a 45-page notebook with the game plan to combat the Colts' ever-changing defenses. However,

---

13. Schultz, *The NFL, Year One*, 178.
14. "Dallas Cowboys vs Baltimore Colts," *Golden Football Magazine*, accessed December 3, 2018.
15. Ibid.
16. Ibid.

once the game began, the play-caller on the sideline, Landry himself, would start eliminating plays. Offensive coach Jim Myers reflected on strategy regarding game plans: "You find out quickly what's going to work against their defenses, and then you throw out what won't work. The process of elimination. When you settle on what is going to work, you keep repeating it. That's the big factor, to repeat and repeat and repeat."[17]

Landry was asked if his team was handicapped by the "can't win the big one" syndrome. Landry explained: "This season, we've laid that one to rest. We won tough games over Green Bay, Cleveland, Detroit, and San Francisco, when a loss would mean we were out of it. That idea might have been a problem at one time, though I doubt it. But it's certainly not now."[18]

The day before the game, Landry announced he was starting Garrison at fullback despite all his injuries: "Garrison has been improving each day . . . right now, he's 75% of himself, but by game time, we feel he should be close to 100%. We're going to go with him. He has been limping, but when he has the ball under his arm, he runs hard."[19]

Landry implied that who started on offense was unimportant, as he believed the defense would control the game. Going into the game, Landry was dead on that defense won the last four Super Bowls. Landry was confident in his Doomsday defense, which had ranked in the top three in rushing defense dating back to 1965, that they could stop the Colts' running game. Baltimore had no outside runners with Norm Bulaich, a power runner at halfback, and less-than-fleet full-back Tom Nowatzke. Landry's game plan was to make Unitas beat them through the air.[20]

Dallas reporter, Steve Perkins, was treated to an inside look at the Cowboys' analysis of the Colts' offense. When Perkins asked backfield coach Ermal Allen, "You think Dallas can handle Unitas?"

---

17. Ibid.
18. Ibid.
19. Ibid.
20. Ibid.

In response, Allen invited Perkins to his hotel room, where he showed a diagram he had made while watching some films of the Colts. His chart showed where each pass Unitas had thrown traveled on the football field. Circled numbers indicating completed passes were almost all clustered in the middle of the field, with just four completions near the sidelines. "Is his arm gone?" Perkins asked.

Ermal replied, "I don't know anything about his arm. I just know he throws to the middle."[21]

In addition to his elbow and shoulder miseries, Craig Morton also battled a case of laryngitis that, fortunately, cleared up by game time. Also, Morton had a disturbing experience on the morning of the Super Bowl. While walking along the beach by the team's hotel, he saw Duane Thomas sitting there on the curb with his head down. Morton recalled: "He looked zonked. I don't know what he was on, but it scared the hell out of me. I mean, here was a guy who was supposed to be my main man this afternoon. Well, he got back to the hotel, and before the kickoff, he gave me this big wink, so I knew he was all right, I guess." Linebacker Steve Kiner, who shared an apartment with Thomas, admitted in later years that the two of them smoked pot. He also said they talked about taking mescaline before the Super Bowl.[22]

A SUPER BOWL WITH AN IDENTITY CRISES

Sportscaster Howard Cosell remarked, "The event lacks tradition . . . yet it ranks with a heavyweight championship [boxing] fight, and the World Series as one of the three super events in American sport."[23]

Nevertheless, the game had been sold out for weeks, except for 1,000 tickets that would be available to walk-up customers. The NFL office announced that tickets for the end zone sold faster at $15 each, more than they had three years earlier at $6 each for the Packers-Raiders Super Bowl in the same stadium. Public Relations Director Don Weiss said, "We could have sold 100,000 tickets for this game if we had the room."[24]

---

21. Ibid.
22. Ibid.
23. Schultz, *The NFL, Year One*, 178.
24. "Dallas Cowboys vs Baltimore Colts," *Golden Football Magazine*, accessed December 3, 2018.

With many having the feeling that this upcoming Super Bowl lacked the drama of past Super Bowls, with colorful characters and two separate league rivalries, there were underlying storylines for both the Colts and the Cowboys entering Super Bowl V. Both were frustrated in losing the big ones in the past. Both had unspectacular seasons, where neither team showed dominance over the other.

For Baltimore, the Colts had undergone three significant changes since they were upset by the New York Jets in Super Bowl III. Ernie Accorsi saw firsthand why the Colts needed to make changes when he took the job as press manager: "When I got to Baltimore in late winter 1970, I was astonished at the whole mental state of that organization. They had not recovered from Super Bowl III still. First, they had a new coach, 49-year-old Don McCafferty, who was promoted from an offensive assistant position when Don Shula took the head coaching job with the Miami Dolphins after the 1969 season. Baltimore also had a new general manager, Don Klosterman. (More Dons than a Mafia convention!)"[25]

A disciple of Paul Brown, Shula was once described as respected as a tactician, but never popular with the players. When he left, defensive end Bubba Smith said, "Fine, maybe we'll get a coach now who'll treat us like human beings instead of dogs. Like many players, Bubba didn't like being yelled at."[26]

Nicknamed "Easy Rider" by the players, McCafferty was the antithesis of Shula—easy-going, friendlier, tolerant of individuality as long as the player produced on the field. Fortunately, McCafferty inherited a veteran team that disciplined itself and did not need micromanaging. As told by Bubba Smith, "McCafferty is beautiful, man. He doesn't holler at all. He's human, too. The other night he sat in on a poker game the guys were having. Shula never did anything like that. McCafferty sits right down, wins a $50 pot, and then leaves . . . As a coach, he's never tried to fool us about anything. He just lays it on the line. He hasn't got any set way, and everybody on this team will go out and break his neck for the guy."[27]

---

25. Ibid.
26. Ibid.
27. Ibid.

Colts owner Carroll Rosenbloom, who demanded and got a number 1 draft pick from Miami in compensation for their signing Shula, praised McCafferty after Baltimore beat Oakland to win the 1970 AFC crown. Besides praising his new head coach, Rosenbloom vented some of his bitterness toward his previous coach: "That kicks the genius coach theory into a cocked hat. Mac took a team that looked like nothing last year (8-5-1), a team riddled with dissension and often hurt this season, and turned it into a champion. Here is a man who has no inner sanctum, no pretensions, no assistants—only associates. Everybody gets the credit except McCafferty. He is just a splendid man. What's more, he brought the fun back into the game of football for me.[28]

Earl Morrall was interviewed about the change in head coaches and had this to say about the situation: "After Shula defected to Miami . . . I was a bit apprehensive. I thought the easy-going, sweet-tempered McCafferty might be too lenient and that some of the guys would take advantage of him. But it never happened. McCafferty held the team in firm control all the way. The methods he used were different. Whereas Shula might scream at a player for making a mistake, McCafferty would have a private chat with him."[29]

Thirty-seven-year-old Johnny Unitas had taken back the starting quarterback role from Earl Morrall after the failed campaign of 1969. Unitas would have his best season in five years, in 1970. The numbers didn't show an elite status for Unitas when compared to his youthful days. The Colt legend threw a paltry 2,213 yards that year and finished the season with a career-low 51.7% completion rate. Unitas also threw more interceptions (18) than touchdowns (14). Still, he was Mr. Clutch in the playoff games against Cincinnati and Oakland. When Unitas's shoulder injury flared up, Morrall replaced him for most of three games, two early in the season, and Earl's redemption victory against the Jets in the season finale.

On a more positive note, Colts' center Bill Curry summarized the mystique of Johnny Unitas over the team.

28. Ibid.
29. Ibid.

Unitas would come in—of course, his track record had a lot
to do with it—and there was something about being in a
huddle with him with a minute and 45 seconds left, and you
needed a touchdown, and you were back on your 20-yard
line. Everybody would look over at that famous crooked nose
with the scar down it. He sort of blinked his eyes behind the
bar on his helmet, and you'd know you were going to get a
touchdown. And we would. It was all so matter of fact with
him. There was very seldom a pep talk. He might say to
Jimmy Orr or Roy Jefferson, 'What ya got? Can you get him
on an up? Can you beat him on an out? Is he playing you
inside? Okay, let's try it out this time.' He'd stick his head in
the huddle and call the play, boom. He assumed that we were
going to keep a pass rush off of him and that if we did, we
were going to win the game. He might say, "Let's go. Keep
them out, okay?" It was all very laconic—just straightforward
business. "Let's go do it. Here we go."[30]

During the 1970 campaign, Unitas enjoyed throwing to two young,
fast wide receivers in 23-year-old Eddie Hinton and 27-year-old Roy
Jefferson. The pair finished 1–2 on the club in receptions and yardage,
combining 91 catches and 1,482 yards. However, the offense took a hit
when the Colt running game took a hit—literally and figuratively—
when veteran halfback, Tom Matte, injured a knee in the second game.
He spent the rest of the season as a backfield coach. Norm Bulaich took
his place and led the team with 426 yards to relieve some of the pressure
on Unitas.[31]

The offense got the job done, but it wasn't the strength of this Colts
team. Baltimore's defense was where the team excelled. Eight starters from the 1968 NFL champions' defense returned and helped the
Colts finish second in the AFC in the least points allowed, trailing the

30. Ibid.
31. Ibid.

Dolphins by only six points. The credit for this defensive juggernaut was due to ex-coach Don Shula. Shula had revamped the Colts' pass defense the year after the Super Bowl loss. Working with defensive back Bobby Boyd (who became an assistant coach for the Colts in the 1969 season), Shula devised a strategy to combat the short passes that Joe Namath had used so effectively in Super Bowl III. The Colts called it the double zone, but in later years it became known as the cover 2. The strategy worked like this: The cornerbacks and linebackers defended the short passes, while the safeties dropped to guard against the bomb. Boyd later recalled, "Nobody else in the league was using it. Teams didn't know how to attack it. He credited the 1970 NFC Championship in part to its effectiveness."[32]

The Colts also had a new place-kicker for 1970, rookie Jim O'Brien. Defensive Tackle Walt Michaels had done all the kicking since 1964. But he missed a 27-yard field goal in Super Bowl III and then hit just 45.2% of his field-goal attempts in 1969. So, Michaels was cut at the end of the 1970 preseason. O'Brien recalled: "The fact that I was competing in camp with a popular player made things a bit difficult for me with some of the veterans. Michaels was one of their buddies, and here comes this young kid. They were older and very conservative, and most of them were married, and here I was, young and single and feeling my oats, so to speak. I exuded a lot of confidence, and probably that was seen as my being brash or cocky. Also, I let my hair grown an inch longer than anybody else's."[33]

Nicknamed "Lassie" by defensive tackle Billy Ray Smith, O'Brien helped win over his teammates when he booted a 19-yard field goal in the final seconds to beat San Diego 16–14 on opening day.

The Dallas Cowboys had endured five years of frustration as they entered the 1970 season. They lost two years in a row to the Packers in the NFL title game, the first at home in 1966 and the second in the "Ice Bowl" at Green Bay in '67, with both games not decided until the final seconds. After losing to the Browns in the Division Playoffs each of the

---

32. Ibid.
33. Ibid.

next two seasons, Dallas was referred to as "Next Year's Champions," but not in a flattering way.[34]

The year after the first Cleveland loss, Landry told the players that he wanted even more dedication, more seriousness, more hard work. No kidding around at practices, which were strictly business. Following the second season-ending Cleveland loss, Landry decided to take a different approach for the 1970 season—involve the players more. So, he mailed each player a lengthy questionnaire about every aspect of life as a Cowboy. After analyzing the questionnaires (probably with the help of a computer since the Cowboys were the pioneers of pro football in using the new machines for scouting and talent evaluation), Landry made some modifications in his coaching staff. He changed Ermal Allen's designation from Backfield Coach to Special Assistant and charged him with breaking down films of opponents. Twenty-six-year-old Dan Reeves, still on the active roster, was made Running Backs Coach. The Offensive Line Coach, Jim Myers, was in effect made the offensive coordinator, a term not used yet. Landry also tightened up discipline in a few ways, such as not allowing players to lay their helmets down during practices. The team watched films of the previous games on Monday and had Tuesdays off instead of the other way around. More importantly, Landry decided there would be less reliance on big plays such as the bombs to wide receiver Bob Hayes, labeled "The World's Fastest Human" after winning two gold medals at the 1964 Olympics. Instead, more emphasis would be placed on the running game.[35]

Adding to Landry's challenge for 1970 was the underlying bitterness among the veteran players had against General Manager Tex Schramm's refusal to bring their salaries up to the league average. Even though the team had been one of the best in the NFL for years, the Cowboy players were not paid well. In particular, the veterans resented Schramm's attitude that asking for a raise was a sign of greed before free agency. The players thought Schramm should exhibit more loyalty toward them for their contributions to the team. Running back Duane Thomas, the club's

34. Ibid.
35. Ibid.

#1 pick in the 1970 draft, was shocked to learn that he was making more as a rookie than defensive tackle Jethro Pugh, a six-year veteran. The black players, like Pugh, figured out that Schramm paid more to white players than black players. Calvin Hill noticed that none of the black stars were offered endorsement or commercial opportunities. Middle linebacker Lee Roy Jordan recalled: "Most of us were unhappy with the money we were making. The Cowboys were making a fortune . . . It was a problem for us to accept why we were winning and doing as well as we were, while we were the second-lowest-paid team in the league."[36]

Defensive back Mel Renfro also chimed in and remarked: "We were hearing that other teams and other players were making good money. We were hearing this from the opposing players. The word was getting out that there were some guys out there making good money, and they didn't have half the success the Dallas Cowboys were having. I heard that Larry Wilson of the Cardinals was making almost $100,000, and I was making $35,000. And I had the same credentials as Larry Wilson."[37]

The Cowboys voted strongly to go on strike at the beginning of training camp to get better pension benefits. Of course, the strike fizzled out right before the season began.

Even with these issues floating around, Landry questioned the hearts of his players. At the beginning of training camp, the coach announced that he was establishing minimum performance levels, position by position. Any player who failed to attain the required level would lose his starting job. One of the first casualties of the new approach was Bob Hayes. The wide receiver, entering his fifth season with the club, had failed to show up regularly for the mandated off-season training program and therefore didn't have the physical fitness to meet his performance requirements. However, Hayes was certain that the real reason he was being benched was that he entered the season playing out his option and had publicly complained about Schramm's low salaries. Hayes' demotion also provoked charges of racism because Dennis Homan, a slower white guy, took Bullet Bob's job. Landry ultimately reinserted Hayes in the starting lineup in the

36. Ibid.
37. Ibid.

Thanksgiving Day game against Green Bay, which Landry said afterward was "the best game I've ever seen Bob Hayes play."[38]

A few weeks before the season began, Dallas made a trade that gave them the best secondary in the NFL. They traded two second-line players to the Packers for cornerback Herb Adderley, a starter on all five of Vince Lombardi's championship teams of the 1960s. To make room for the nine-year veteran, Cornell Green moved to the strong safety position. Combined with Mel Renfro, the trio had played in 14 Pro Bowls among them. However, fitting in would be hard for Adderley, as he liked to play a liberal style of defense that bordered taking the risk of leaving the receiver open on a pass play. In an era of bump-and-run technique that the AFL popularized, Adderly liked to play off the line of scrimmage. He would trick the quarterback into thinking his man was open, then accelerate to the ball and knock it down or intercept. Adderley's theatrics did not sit well with Landry. Landry's defense utilized zone defense coverage. Adderly remembered: The kind of defensive scheme Dallas used always went against my basic philosophy. In Green Bay, we played about 90% man-to-man. I had the freedom to line up where I want to . . . I never felt comfortable playing the Dallas type defense. Even when I would make a big play or an interception, it seemed I was out of position or something. I just never really got the feel for it. And I think Landry recognized the difficulty I was having because, on some occasions, he would allow me to just go ahead and play man-to-man while we were supposed to be in some other kind of coverage.[39]

Adderley credited Mel Renfro with teaching him a great deal about the Dallas coverage scheme. Renfro remembered: "Herb brought a lot of attitude with him. He knew how to win. They (Green Bay) won when they weren't even that good. But Lombardi knew how to win, and he (Adderley) brought a little of that attitude with him. He screamed at us in the locker room a couple of times, and no one had ever done that. Coach wouldn't scream at us, but Herb did, and he got our attention."[40]

---

38. Ibid.
39. Ibid.
40. Ibid.

Like the Colts, the Cowboys would hang their hat on their veteran defense. Nine of the starters on that side of the ball had played at least five seasons, and four of those had survived eight or more campaigns. Landry continued to polish his "Flex" defense based on the "Umbrella" defense he had learned from Steve Owen with the Giants and taught as Giants' defensive coordinator in the late '50s. The Flex was a 4–3 defense with one down tackle and one down end "flexed" a few feet off the line of scrimmage in a zigzag pattern. The idea was to give each flexed lineman an extra second to see the flow of the play before attacking. Landry also sets his ends and tackles in gaps between the offensive linemen. That made it more difficult to option-block. He asked each down lineman to control the gap they were assigned. The three linebackers were asked to do the same. Landry was willing to reduce his defense's chance of throwing a running back for a loss to decrease the chance of giving up a big gain.[41]

A SEASON OF UPS AND DOWNS

Midway through the 1970 schedule, the Cowboys seemed to have no chance at making the playoffs despite Landry's changes on both sides of the football. First, the season started with a quarterback controversy and never got resolved. Landry benched Craig Morton, his starter in 13 games in 1969, because Craig had not returned from his off-season shoulder surgery in better shape. So, Roger Staubach, the Naval Academy graduate in his second season with the club after completing his military obligation, started the first two games of the regular season until Morton's shoulder soreness abated. Staubach was too emotional and instinctive for Landry's taste in quarterback style of play. Landry felt Staubach was too quick to call an audible when he was daunted by a defensive setup that confused him. Staubach's movement from the pocket worried Landry because he felt that his concentration was broken on the receivers by leaving the pocket. Landry preferred a quarterback like Morton, who was an extension of his computer-like brain. For Staubach, he was an older player at 29 years old. He lacked the experience needed to run an

41. Ibid.

offense due to his service for four years in the Navy. Staubach hated the dual quarterback set up and planned to ask for a trade when the season ended. Morton also disliked sharing the position, and it got to his head. He lost so much confidence that he started seeing a hypnotist during the season.[42]

Along the way, one of Landry's goals for the season was met in their running game. The quarterback position was suspect, with Morton and Staubach's dual roles, and not surprisingly, Dallas ranked in the middle of the league in passing yardage. Their running game, however, was tops in the league. Even though he didn't start until the fifth game, the leading runner was enigmatic rookie Duane Thomas with 803 yards. Next was the 1969 Associated Press's NFL Offensive Rookie of the Year, Calvin Hill, who gained 577 yards, despite spending time in the hospital because of an infected blister on his foot and then a broken toe. The reliable full-back, Walt Garrison, added 507 yards. Garrison was the only Dallas Cowboy who was a real cowboy. During the off-season, he competed on the rodeo circuit. He was also an Oklahoma State Cowboy during his college football career.[43]

Despite two games in which they were torched for 54 by Minnesota and 38 points by the Cardinals, the Cowboys finished 4th in the NFC in the least points allowed by their Doomsday defense. Also, Dallas was known for its special teams, which were manned by speedsters who would start on other clubs. Between a power running game, a stonewall defense, and a stellar special teams, Dallas felt their time had come.

FAKE TURF

Another interesting pre-game issue was the turf the two teams would play on. Back in 1969, the turf was real grass at the Orange Bowl. But in 1970, the Orange Bowl was among the first stadiums to utilize the new poly turf surface, which was a rising trend in new baseball and football stadiums. Poly-Turf was manufactured by the company American Bil-trite. It was one of three different types of artificial grass used in stadiums

---

42. Ibid.
43. Ibid.

at the time, along with Tartan Turf and AstroTurf. When Poly-Turf was installed at the Orange Bowl, its impact on the game was huge. The playing surface became faster, enabling running backs and receivers to make quick cuts.[44] "When I first got on it, I felt super-fast," said former Miami Dolphin running back Jim Kiick. "But then I started thinking, what do the fast guys feel like?"[45]

The Miami Dolphins quickly used Poly Turf to their advantage. Players like receiver Paul Warfield and running back Mercury Morris thrived on the surface. Both players were quick on any surface, but they were almost impossible for defenses to contain on Poly Turf. Another characteristic of Poly-Turf was its ability to absorb heat. At times playing conditions became unbearably hot. "It was difficult. It was hard because the heat reflected off the artificial turf," Kiick said. "There were times when the temperatures were 130 degrees on the field."[46]

While the Dolphins were used to playing and practicing in the hot climate of South Florida, visiting teams often wilted on the Poly-Turf. Both the Cowboys and the Colts would have to deal with the nuances that the poly turf surface posed for Super Bowl V. It was the first Super Bowl played on this surface. With the trend of Poly Turf, commissioner Pete Rozelle predicted that the artificial surface would replace natural grass in all the stadiums in years to come. But disturbing evidence had started to accumulate that the Poly Turf surface caused an increase in injuries, which stopped the poly turf trend dead in its tracks. By 2013, most stadiums resorted back to natural grass due to its softer surface.

A MEDIA BLITZ

Curt Gowdy did the TV play-by-play, and Kyle Rote provided commentary for NBC television. Jay Randolph and Al De Rogatis handled the radio call. Bill Enis served as a sideline reporter for both TV and radio. A 30-second commercial cost $72,000.[47] The NBC television coverage

44. Miami Southpaw, "Ghosts of the Orange Bowl: Poly Turf" (August 23, 2009), accessed December 4, 2018, http://miamisouthpaw.blogspot.com/2009/08/ghosts-of-orange-bowl-poly-turf.html.

45. Ibid.

46. Ibid.

47. Ibid.

included a camera in a blimp circling over the stadium for the entire game. A record audience would tune in for the fifth straight year (39.9 ratings and a share of 75).[48] Miami was not part of this record audience due to blackout restrictions in the contract between the NFL and NBC. A lawsuit aimed at lifting the television blackout of the Super Bowl in the Miami area was put forward but was dismissed four days before the game. The judge ruled that the court had no authority to lift the blackout.[49]

Outside the Orange Bowl before kickoff, scalpers were hawking $15 tickets for as much as $100, but the supply was greater than the demand. "The scalpers took a beating today," said a Miami policeman. They ended up selling them at face value a half hour before the kickoff.

The pregame show did not have a tough act to follow the debacle in New Orleans the previous year. Dallas's own Tommy Loy played "The Star-Spangled Banner" as a trumpet solo. The only glitch was the Air Force jets that were supposed to buzz the stadium during the national anthem arrived two minutes after it ended.

As the designated home team, Dallas was forced to wear its blue jerseys for the Super Bowl under rules in place at the time, which did not allow the home team its choice of jersey color, unlike the regular season and playoff games leading up to the Super Bowl. Dallas had not worn its blue jerseys at home since 1963, as Cowboys general manager Tex Schramm opted to have the team wear white at home to present fans with a consistent look. The Cowboys wore their blue jerseys twice during the 1970 season, losing 20–7 at St. Louis in week four and winning 6–2 at Cleveland in week 13. The designated home team was first allowed its choice of jersey color for Super Bowl XIII, allowing the Cowboys to wear white vs. the Pittsburgh Steelers.

Vice President Spiro Agnew, a Colts fan since the team began playing in Baltimore in 1953, attended the game. Agnew was Governor of Maryland before his election as Richard Nixon's running mate in 1968. Nixon was a huge football fan and had a vacation home in Key Biscayne, approximately ten miles from the Orange Bowl.

---

48. "Dallas Cowboys vs Baltimore Colts," *Golden Football Magazine*, accessed December 3, 2018.
49. Ibid.

Kickoff for this game was at 2:00 P.M., making it the earliest starting time in the Eastern time zone in Super Bowl history, and one of only three Super Bowls to start in the morning for viewers in the Pacific time zone (the others were Super Bowl VI in New Orleans and Super Bowl X in Miami).

13

SUPER BOWL V: THE GAME

Super Bowl V is one of those games many people tend to forget, or maybe they want to forget it due to its sloppy play by both teams. Negative things have been written about it for the last 50 years. Many called this game "the Blunder Bowl," "the Stupor Bowl," and even the "Blooper Bowl," as there were eleven turnovers in the game, seven by the winning team. Even with all those mishaps, the game itself was the closest Super Bowl game played since its inception four years earlier. It also was the first Super Bowl whereby a winner was not readily apparent with a quarter to play and made for an exciting and entertaining game. The game was decided in the last seconds.[1]

After a back and forth start to the game with no scoring between the Colts and Cowboys, John Unitas set the tone for a mistake-riddled game by throwing an interception to Dallas Linebacker, Chuck Howley. Howley, who made a diving, juggling catch of the poorly thrown ball, returned it to the Baltimore 46, where Unitas made the tackle.[2] Dallas had the opportunity to drive well into Colts territory, but penalties hindered the Cowboys' drive, and they were forced to punt. On the punt, Dallas caught a huge break. Another miscue by Baltimore happened when the

1. John Schaefer, *Baltimore Colts 1970: A Game-by-Game Guide*, 2197, Kindle.
2. Tex Maule, "Eleven Big Mistakes," *Sports Illustrated* (January 25, 1971), accessed December 6, 2018, https://www.si.com/vault/1971/01/25/542218/eleven-big-mistakes.

punt returner Ron Gardin coughed up the ball. Speedy special team and defensive back Cliff Harris recovered a fumble deep in the Colts' territory. Harris, the backup safety who made his mark on special teams, was known as "Captain Crash." Colts' punt returner Ron Gardin recalled the play: "There was nowhere to hide. All I could think of was what my mother would think. She doesn't know that much about football, but she would know I had done something stupid."[3]

Dallas, however, could not get a touchdown despite starting at the Baltimore 9-yard line. They had to settle for a Mike Clark field goal to go up 3–0.[4] Meanwhile, the Colts were having no success at all trying to run. Their aerial game was grounded as well, as they were having no success at all trying to pass, either. Dallas' Doomsday defense had stifled the Baltimore offense on both fronts. Clark's field goal would be the only scoring of the first quarter, and the score would have Dallas up 3–0 going into the 2nd quarter.

In the 2nd quarter, Dallas' offense got rolling again, as quarterback Craig Morton tossed a 47-yard pass to speedy receiver Bob Hayes. On that play, Morton threw one of his few good passes in the game. The pass was hurled down the sideline to Hayes, but it did not look like Hayes would catch it. However, Morton's pass was on the money, and Hayes came up with the ball in miraculous fashion because he was caught between two Colts' defenders, Charlie Stukes and Jerry Logan, who sandwiched Hayes in double coverage.[5] That play got the Cowboys deep into Baltimore territory, to the Baltimore 12-yard line. The Colts defense seemed rattled and over-eager after that play and committed a penalty for roughing Morton. This moved the ball even closer for Dallas. The Colts' defense regrouped, and they pushed Dallas back out of touchdown range by sacking Morton when he hesitated in throwing a pass by Baltimore tackle, Billy Ray Smith. On the play, Smith had engulfed Morton, who threw the ball at offensive guard Blaine Nye, who was conveniently nearby but was an ineligible receiver. Morton was called for

3. "Dallas Cowboys vs Baltimore Colts," *Golden Football Magazine*, accessed December 3, 2018.

4. Lootmeister, "Super Bowl V Review," accessed December 6, 2018, http://www.lootmeister.com /superbowl/v.php.

5. Maule, "Eleven Big Mistakes," accessed December 6, 2018.

intentionally grounding the ball, which cost Dallas 15 yards back with a loss of a down. The Cowboys' offense could not get in the end zone, but Clark kicked a 30-yard field goal to make it 6–0 in favor of the Cowboys.

With the ball back in Baltimore's offense, the Colts finally got some good fortune, but on a play that was not only not part of the game plan but a further indication of how the game was going. Unitas was having all kinds of issues against Dallas' Doomsday defense up until this play. The rush of the Dallas front four was making Unitas hurry his passes, which were haphazardly thrown for in-completions. Doomsday's linebackers were dropping off into Unitas's passing lanes to secure zone coverage, and the Cowboy defensive backs clung tenaciously to Baltimore's receivers. After the Dallas kickoff, the old man, Unitas, went back into the huddle to guide the Colts' offense. He threw two passes. Both were incomplete. Then he threw the third pass. This one was intended for wide receiver Eddie Hinton. The pass, however, was far over Hinton's head. To grab the pass, Hinton jumped high and managed to touch the ball with his fingertips, deflecting it toward Cowboys' defensive back Mel Renfro, who also seemed to touch it with his fingertips. The ball bounced in the air, finally came to rest in the sure hands of a surprised Colts' tight end John Mackey, who scored to complete a 75-yard touchdown play.[6] Mackey describes the catch: "That play was not in my game plan. The ball was thrown to Hinton, and I thought it was going to be intercepted. But then it was tipped around. I don't know by whom, and it landed right in my arms, and I did my 9.1 to the end zone."[7]

Cowboys' middle linebacker Lee Roy Jordan describes how he saw it: "I thought Mel was going to intercept the ball until I saw Hinton tip it over his head. I saw Mackey run on into the end zone, but I didn't think anything about it. I figured it was all illegal. Then I saw the official signaling a touchdown . . ."[8]

6. Ibid.
7. "Dallas Cowboys vs Baltimore Colts," *Golden Football Magazine*, accessed December 3, 2018.
8. Ibid.

Cowboys cornerback Herb Adderley recalled: "Hinton deflected the ball; there's no question about it . . . I kept complaining to the official, but he told me to shut up. He just said Blue (Dallas) touched the ball, but he never said who did it.[9]

Cowboys' safety Charlie Waters was the closest to Mackey when he caught the ball and might have run down the ball carrier if he hadn't been screaming at the officials that it was an illegal catch after the ball touched two straight offensive receivers. However, the officials let the play stand because Renfro (presumably) deflected the ball after it hit Hinton's hands, making Mackey's catch legal.

Renfro recalled that "somebody touched the ball . . . I don't think I did."

If Renfro, or perhaps Cornell Green, had not touched the ball, the pass would have been ruled incomplete, since two offensive players cannot handle the ball as receivers unless a lateral is involved.[10]

Mackey admitted: "I wasn't the primary receiver . . . My job was to go deep to clear the zone, and Hinton cuts in under me. It's what we call an individual to the flanker. Now it's an individual to the flanker to the tight end."[11]

Years later, Mel Renfro talked further about the play. "The refs said the ball touched me. Which it could have, I suppose. But I had no sensation of touching the ball. That was my right hand, the hand that was messed up when I punched the mirror back at Oregon. That was the hand I have no feeling in those three fingers. I have no feeling in that finger, and if it hit my finger, that's the finger that it hit."[12]

NFL Films' highlights of Super Bowl V showed the touchdown pass twice, including once in slow motion. The announcer says to look closely, and you can see the ball change direction slightly after hitting Renfro's hand.

Whatever that play was intended to be, or what happened, it gave the Colts six points on that miscue, which is all they got since their

9. Ibid.
10. Maule, "Eleven Big Mistakes," accessed December 6, 2018.
11. Ibid.
12. "Dallas Cowboys vs Baltimore Colts," *Golden Football Magazine*, accessed December 3, 2018.

extra-point attempt was blocked when Tom Nowatzke missed his man to guard, leaving the score tied 6–6. It was just the way things went in this game. Everything became suspect to miscues.

Despite their errors, Baltimore was even with Dallas. But not for long, as the Colts made another blunder. John Unitas decided to scramble when his receivers were covered and fumbled as he was hit. Dallas recovered on the Colts' 28-yard line.

When Dallas took over, Morton, under a blitz, hit Dan Reeves with a short pass that Reeves converted into a 17-yard gain. Then Morton threw another short pass, this one to Duane Thomas, who ran it in for a touchdown. The Cowboys were back on top 13–6.

Baltimore got the ball back, but misfortune struck the Colts again. In the next series, Unitas, dropping back to pass, was smashed by George Andrie, and the ball fluttered into Mel Renfro's hands for yet another interception. Unitas suffered a hairline fracture of his rib cage on the play and left the game for good. But this set the stage for the redemption of Earl Morrall, the goat of the Colts' Super Bowl debacle against the Jets two years ago.[13] Morrall recalled: "Johnny had to come out. Suddenly the whole thing was in my lap. I didn't think about what had happened before (Super Bowl III). I didn't have a chance to. My mind was filled with formations and plays we could use to beat the Dallas defense."[14]

In the first play Morrall handled the ball; he threw a perfect pass to Eddie Hinton for 26 yards. Then he hit Roy Jefferson on a similar pass play pattern for 21 more. Just like that, Earl Morrall had the Colts on the Dallas two-yard line and was poised to score. With the end zone within reach, the Colts' and their fans believed a touchdown or surely a field goal at worse was possible to add on extra points. But in this blooper of game, anything was possible. This strange aura surrounded the game, like a dark cloud. Morrall sent running back Norm Bulaich into the line for the next three plays and wound up going nowhere. The Colts remained on the two-yard line due to the stubborn will of the Doomsday defense. With 21 seconds left in the half, Morrall called time out and trotted over

13. Maule, "Eleven Big Mistakes," accessed December 6, 2018.
14. "Dallas Cowboys vs Baltimore Colts," *Golden Football Magazine*, accessed December 3, 2018.

to the sideline to confer with Head Coach Don McCafferty. Since the Colts were trailing by seven points, a field goal would put them inside touchdown range and was the only call. But McCafferty deferred and gambled on the risk of getting a touchdown. The coach called for a pass to tight end Tom Mitchell. On the play, Morrall faked to Nowatzke and threw over the middle to Mitchell, but it was too high. Morrall recalls: "On our last try, I decided to go to the air, calling a play that's listed as "119 weakside end delay" in the Colt playbook, a pass with Tom Mitchell as the primary receiver. Mitchell threw a block at linebacker Chuck Howley, but as he tried to slide off, Howley stayed with him. Mitchell, in trying to struggle free, got his feet tangled with tackle, Jethro Pugh's, and half stumbled. The Dallas front four was pressing me now, and I had to throw. I purposely lofted the ball to give Mitchell an extra second to regain his momentum, but he never did. The pass went incomplete."[15]

The Colts wound up with nothing for Morrall's heroics but a half-time rest to mull matters over.[16] Morrall remembered: "As I went off the field, I got a sickening flashback of our first Super Bowl game, a sort of taped replay of the last minute or so. We hadn't scored now. I figured I was in for a lot of sleepless nights during the coming year."[17]

Landry told reporters that the Cowboys felt very confident at half-time, being up 13–6. For Baltimore, according to Bubba Smith, coach McCafferty told the Colts: "The defense has played great ball. It has hung in there and done a great job. Continue to hang in there, and the breaks will start to go our way. No ranting or raving. No discouragement. No fight talk. Just plain sense."[18]

The Southeast Missouri State College band entertained at halftime, and Anita Bryant sang the "Battle Hymn of the Republic."

After the halftime show, many expected that these two quite good football teams would settle down to their game plans without bloopers and correct their mistakes in the first half. That just didn't happen. Error-prone football was still the prescription in the second half on this day.

15. Ibid.
16. Maule, "Eleven Big Mistakes," accessed December 6, 2018.
17. Ibid.
18. "Dallas Cowboys vs Baltimore Colts," *Golden Football Magazine*, accessed December 3, 2018.

Dallas kicked it off to the AFC's top kick-off return man, cornerback/ returner Jim Duncan. Duncan gathered the ball in and fumbled it. Dallas recovered the fumble at the Baltimore 31-yard line.

Coach Tom Landry had forsaken the forward pass as a weapon after the first half and relied on smash mouth strategy with the running game. Dallas quarterback. Craig Morton handed off five times to his running backs, who drove to a first and goal on Baltimore's two-yard line. Then came a play that is one of the most famous, or infamous, in Super Bowl history. On 1st-and-Goal, Duane Thomas smashed off the left tackle but fumbled when he was hit just short of the goal line by Colt's safety Jerry Logan. The ball disappeared into a pile of players. Defensive tackle Billy Ray Smith yelled, "Colts ball!"

Line judge Jack Fette, whose view was obscured by the back judge Hugh Gamber, signaled that Baltimore had recovered, even though Cowboys' Dave Manders came up from under the pile with the ball. The official scorer awarded the recovery to Baltimore cornerback Jim Duncan, who fumbled the ball on that earlier kickoff to put the Colts deep in a hole. To him, this was glorious redemption.[19]

Duncan, after the game, recalled: "I came up to meet the play, was knocked on the ground, and there the ball was. I was surprised as hell to see it lying there. I was fighting someone for possession of it, but I got there first . . . I owed one for fumbling the kickoff."[20]

But Billy Ray Smith, the one who yelled "Colts ball" to the officials, also claimed recovery: "All I know is that, when Ray May hit the ball carrier, the ball bounced loose, and I fell on it. (Smith later admitted that he never had the ball.)"[21]

Cowboys' Jim Manders was adamant that he recovered the fumble: "It rolled right under me, and I got up and handed it to the ref. I couldn't believe it when he said it was the Colts' ball."[22]

Cowboys guard John Niland (#61) observed: "I know Manders recovered it. I was right there on the ground next to him. There was no

19. Ibid.
20. Ibid.
21. Ibid.
22. Ibid.

way it should have been Baltimore's ball. Some officials just came running in from left field and made the call."[23]

Craig Morton recalled: Before they were unpiled, Dave Manders was right on top of the ball. I screamed to the line judge on my side, "call the first thing! Call it, you son of a bitch."[24]

But Line Judge, Fette told them, "One more word out of either of you, and you're both out of the game!"[25]

Manders further asserted his belief that he recovered the ball: "It was the most clean-cut recovery of a fumble I had ever been involved in for all my playing days . . . It is so frustrating because he (Fette) came in from the right side and could not see anything, and he makes that call in an instant. He was going on Billy Ray's "we got it. we got it!"[26]

Bubba Smith later admitted that the Cowboys should have gotten the call because they did recover the ball, but that Billy Ray Smith . . . "had conned that official right out of the Super Bowl," by yelling "We got it, we got it," which confused the refs.[27]

Running back Duane Thomas went to the bench and cried for fumbling the ball. According to one reporter who got to know him, during that third quarter of Super Bowl V, he decided not to talk to the media.

A bad omen hung over the Cowboys after that debacle. Coach Landry admitted after the game: "After that, . . . it was all errors for us . . . That was the turning point . . . If we'd scored there, they would have been 14 points back. And the ball would have to bounce around three or four times for them to get that many points."[28]

Having dodged a major bullet but backed up to their goal line, the Colts offense began to surge forward. They drove past midfield but couldn't penetrate the Doomsday defense any further than the Cowboys' 35-yard line. This set up a 52-yard field goal attempt by kicker Jim O'Brien. And again, another head-shaking moment occurred. The field

23. Ibid.
24. Ibid.
25. Ibid.
26. Ibid.
27. Ibid.
28. Schaefer, *Game-by-Game Guide*, 2229–2233, Kindle.

goal attempt fell short and was downed by Baltimore center Tom Goode at the 1 after Dallas safety Mel Renfro had a strange mental lapse and chose not to field the ball. So, the Colts had flipped the field from their 1 to the Dallas 1. Renfro later indicated: "I can't second guess myself. I thought the momentum (of the kick) would take it into the end zone. On second thought, maybe I should have picked it up."[29]

The Cowboys had to punt after the Colts held Dallas in their territory. John Unitas, heavily taped up after being x-rayed in the locker room when he was knocked out of the game in the second quarter, warmed up on the sideline. But McCafferty stuck with Morrall.

Morrall moved the Colts downfield primarily on a pass to Nowatzke that carried 45 yards. The quarter ended with the Colts on the Dallas 11, and a 3rd and 6 was upon the Colts' offense. The 3rd quarter ended, still with a score of 13 to 6 in favor of the Cowboys.

As the 4th quarter started, the Colts were looking to score on 3rd and 6, and Morrall could taste the end zone after that drive downfield gave the Colts an aura of confidence from the momentum. Morrall got the snap and moved back to pass. He saw running back Norm Bulaich open momentarily in the end zone and threw the ball. But Cowboys' linebacker, Chuck Howley, intercepted the pass for a touchback in the end zone. That was the Colts' 5th turnover of the game. Once again, a major error prevented the Colts from scoring any points. As Howley remembered: "I was covering a down-and-in, and the ball was right there. I couldn't help but catch it. I was just having fun. That's what I did when I played the game."[30]

The Colts' defense prevailed once more and held the Cowboys, who punted the ball to the Colts' 18-yard line. Morrall then drove the Colts' offense downfield. Morrall threw a 3rd down pass in another sloppy play that was incomplete due to avoid being sacked by the safety blitz. However, the Colts were saved when Dallas committed another penalty, this one for defensive holding, which gave the Colts an automatic 1st down

---

29. Maule, "Eleven Big Mistakes," accessed December 6, 2018.
30. "Dallas Cowboys vs Baltimore Colts," *Golden Football Magazine*, accessed December 3, 2018.

at the Dallas 39-yard line. With all the turnovers, bad luck, and sloppy play, the next turnover was a real doozie.

It happened on a play you might diagram in the dirt during a backlot game of touch football. On the drive, Morrall lateraled the ball to Sam Havrilak, a halfback who was once a quarterback for Bucknell. Havrilak was supposed to lateral the ball back to Morrall, who would then throw a pass to Hinton at the flag that marks the corner of the field at the end zone.

Morrall got the ball to Havrilak as planned, but Jethro Pugh, the big Cowboy tackle, was between Morrall and Havrilak when Havrilak was supposed to throw the ball back. So Havrilak looked down the field, saw the tight end, Mackey open, and threw the ball at him. Colts' Hinton cut in front of Mackey and caught it, and headed for the goal line. Hinton recalled: "I could see the end zone in front of me . . . I was trying to work my way there when all of a sudden, someone knocked the ball out of my hands from behind. I tried to get to it, but someone tackled me, and I couldn't reach it."[31]

What happened was that strong safety, Cornell Green, had hooked the ball out of Hinton's grasp, and Renfro had tackled him. The ball, meanwhile, was squirting over the goal line, where a bevy of Cowboys and Colts took turns not recovering it until it had trickled beyond the end zone. The officials ruled it a touchback, giving the Cowboys the ball on their 20-yard line. That was Baltimore's seventh disaster.[32]

In a reprise of a play he botched in Super Bowl III, two years before, Morrall saw Deja Vu, except this time the play worked. The defensive gem by Green stripping the ball when pay dirt was near just cemented the strange aura of the game. Hinton further recalled: "Oh, that end zone was just right there in front of me, and I figured all I had to do was step in. Man, I sure didn't know anyone was around me. That guy (Cornell Green) just came up behind me and punched the ball out of my hands. I couldn't believe it. I could have made the recovery, too, but someone was on top of me, and I couldn't get up."

---

31. Maule, "Eleven Big Mistakes," accessed December 6, 2018.
32. Ibid.

On the Colts sideline, linebacker Curtis was discouraged. All these turnovers and misfortunes to the end zone deprived Baltimore too many times and late in the game, it seemed like it was a hopeless task to just score. Curtis believed, "That one hurt. After that, I figured it was all over for us."[33]

The Colts' discouragement became a glimmer of hope when the Cowboys committed a blooper of their own. Almost immediately, Craig Morton, under pressure, threw a pass intended for Walt Garrison that was tipped by Jim Duncan and intercepted by safety Rick Volk. Volk carried the ball down to the Dallas three-yard line. Volk recalled: "We were in a zone defense as usual, and I was just playing my area . . . We had all their wide receivers covered. Garrison came out of the backfield and down the middle . . . There's a lot of luck involved in those tips. And all day I was thinking we didn't have any luck on our side, but I've changed my mind now."[34]

Defensive end Roy Hilton, whose hard rush caused the errant throw by Morton, said: "I got a good rush on Morton. I thought I should have slapped the ball down, but he threw high to get it over my arms."[35]

Just like that, the Baltimore defense allowed their inept offense to tie the game. Two Nowatzke plunges later, the Colts scored. Jim O'Brien attempted the point after, and the Colts held their breath. The point after was good, and now the score was knotted up.

With neither offense able to mount a sustained drive, many of those at the game and watching on TV started thinking about overtime. One guy in the press box exclaimed, "My God, if this goes into overtime, we'll be here till Monday."[36]

Playing conservatively deep in their territory, the Colts ran the ball three times: Nowatzke for 4 yards, Nowatzke for 1, and Bulaich for 0. That took them to the two-minute warning. With overtime looming, Colts' Punter David Lee booted a punt for 38 yards to the Cowboys' Hayes, who went out of bounds as he caught it at the Colt 48.[37]

33. "Dallas Cowboys vs Baltimore Colts," *Golden Football Magazine*, accessed December 3, 2018.
34. Ibid.
35. Ibid.
36. Ibid.
37. Ibid.

Seeing an opportunity with the clock ticking down, the Cowboys tried to take advantage of their excellent field position to get into field goal range, rather than take this into overtime. Running back Duane Thomas took a pitchout to the right, but Colts' Bubba Smith pulled him down for a one-yard loss. Then the Colts' Fred Miller broke through and sacked Morton for a loss of 9 yards. However, a holding penalty was called on Dallas. Preferring to put the Cowboys further away from field goal range even though they would get the down back, Colts' Coach McCafferty took the penalty to put the ball on the Dallas 27. That made it 2nd-and-31 for Dallas. Rather than run out the clock and go to overtime, Dallas tried to get back into Colt territory. Morton faded back and threw downfield for Dan Reeves. But with Hinton looming over him, Morton threw a little high. The ball went through the hands of the leaping Reeves and into Colt Mike Curtis's waiting arms, who returned it 13 yards to the Dallas 28 with 0:59 on the clock. In the blink of an eye, the Colts were within range to kick the winning field goal.[38]

Coach Tom Landry, who took away the play calling from Craig Morton during the season, revealed after the game that Morton called the play that resulted in Curtis's interception. With so little time remaining, there was no opportunity to work the tight end-shuffle to send in the next call. However, Landry said he thought Craig made the right call because: ". . . we were in our two-minute drill at the time . . . We were not thinking about running out the clock. We were going for the win. I'd hate to think that we had a minute to go and not go out to win the game . . . I wanted him to throw the one pass and, if it was complete, throw another. If incomplete, we run the ball on third down, punt, and take our chances in sudden death."[39]

Curtis explained how he was in the right place at the right time: "I drift back and play alongside the safeties and look for crossing patterns. When Jerry(Logan) saw Reeves come into his zone, he went for the tackle . . . The ball came off Reeves's hands and just hung up there. When I grabbed it, I almost squeezed the air out of it. The first thing I

---

38. Ibid.
39. Ibid.

thought about was a fumble. I didn't want to be the goat. I gave 'em my old fullback moves."[40]

Taking no chances, Morrall ran Bulaich twice for a total of 3 yards. The Colts let the clock run after the second-down play to 0:09 and called timeout. Kicker Jim O'Brien, who won the season's opening game with a field goal on the last play, had a chance to do it in the final game. First, though, Dallas finally took a timeout.

As the final minute wound down, O'Brien said his teammates "kept telling me not to be nervous, to stay calm. They said the score was tied and that even if I missed, we'd beat them in sudden death." O'Brien didn't like kicking on artificial turf. He said the day before the game: "When I kick a football, I like to take a divot, and on artificial turf, you can't get one. Your foot kind of gets jammed up. It doesn't feel right as you kick."

Colts public relations director Ernie Accorsi had a haunting memory, "The day before the game, we were practicing, and he [O'Brien] was having trouble kicking on the turf . . . I hope they're not counting on me tomorrow. Well, who else are we going to count on?[41]

During the Colts timeout, Morrall, the holder for field goal kicks, went to the sideline. "[Coach]McCafferty grabbed me . . . Talk to him, Earl," he said, motioning toward Jim O'Brien. "Keep him calm."

O'Brien was in a frenzy. "Let's go, Earl," he said. "Let's get out there."

"O'Bie," I said, "we've got plenty of time."

"Which way's the shouting. He's going to miss," yelled another.

"Let's go! Let's go!" O'Brien shouted. "Put the ball down!"

Kneeling there, I turned to O'Brien. "We're O.K., O'Bie," I said. "There's plenty of time."[42]

The snapper, veteran Tom Goode, had been acquired by the Colts late in the year for just such an occasion. This would be the last game of his career.

Goode's snap was perfect, as was Morrall's placement. O'Brien booted the 32-yarder straight through the uprights. Morrall recalled: I watched

---

40. Ibid.
41. Ibid.
42. Ibid.

him (Goode) grip the ball. "I watched it right into my hands. I put it down. O'Brien's foot boomed through. I could tell by the sound that it was a solid hit. I lifted my head to watch. I swear my heart had stopped beating. It was no hard end-over-end kick; it kind of sailed, traveling a crazy path, first heading for the right post but then looping back toward the middle to clear the bar by several feet. I was frozen. I couldn't move. I just knelt there for a second or two. Then I saw O'Brien jumping up and down, and the realization of what had happened hit me . . . We had won the Super Bowl. I leaped into the air."[43]

O'Brien said the yelling did not bother him. "I was accustomed to such things because in practice, Billy Ray Smith does the same sort of things to help improve my concentration. He screamed louder than the Cowboys did . . . on the kick: I knew it was good when it came off my foot. You could tell by the way it felt. When I looked up there, it was a little to the right (of center). It was the most beautiful picture I ever saw."[44]

O'Brien confessed some nervousness before the field goal attempt but insisted he had known it would happen all along. "My mother said so," he announced. "She's an astrologer, and she told me there was no way we could lose. I believed her—she's good enough to do astrology for a fee—although she wouldn't tell me how it was going to happen. I guess she didn't want to make me nervous."

But O'Brien's occult powers had provided a clue on that. "I had this dream all week," he said straight-faced. "I could see a field goal going over to win the game, but I couldn't tell who kicked it. It could have been Mike Clark of Dallas, or it could have been me. I never knew. I guess I kept waking up too soon."[45]

Dallas linebacker Chuck Howley (who won the Sport Magazine MVP award for his play in the Super Bowl) received a new car for his two interceptions and a fumble recovery—the first time a defensive player won the award. Considering the nature of this game, with its bloopers that looked more like a comedy show of errors, even the award for MVP

---

43. Ibid.
44. Ibid.
45. Schaefer, *Game-by-Game Guide*, 2215–2220, Kindle.

was as surprising as it was comical being awarded to a member of a losing team. It is still the only time it has been given to a member of the losing team. That's how preposterous the play on the field was by the Colts, that none of them were worthy of an MVP trophy.

Each Colt player earned $15,000 and a ring for the victory, while each Cowboy took home $7,500 for the loser's share of the Super Bowl money.

Super Bowl V was now in the books. The Colts had won. But the win seemed more relief than redemption due to the heart in your mouth way the game was played. Instead of feeling that they had avenged the loss two years earlier to the Jets in Super Bowl III, the team just felt they survived and could have lost with all their turnovers. They did not have that glorious feeling of a champion. They felt they got lucky, and they knew it. That didn't close the old wounds still left by the bitterness of Super Bowl III. Center Bill Curry admitted:

"Super Bowl V evokes for me a sense of not carrying our share of the load . . . It was not the redemption we desperately sought for what went on before. It was my most mixed sense of achievement in my career."[46]

His teammate Bubba Smith remarked that he was depressed as he walked off the field: "I knew I was supposed to be feeling good . . . but I wasn't feeling that way because I was supposed to look at my other ring from Super Bowl III."[47]

The whole aura of the game confused both players, coaches, and fans alike. Even the feeling of being Super Bowl champs was more of a dull and dazed effect on the Colts players rather than the joy and jubilation it should have been. The Blunder Bowl had etched its dark cloud over the inaugural season of 1970. What should have been a season to remember for the ages ended in a Super Bowl that has been long forgotten or frowned upon but for a footnote in NFL history.

---

46. Schultz, *Dawn of Modern Football*, 191.
47. Ibid.

14

SUPER BOWL V, THE POST GAME

The general reaction of the public to Super Bowl V was one of disgust. The media dismissed the game as an abomination to professional sports, as both teams were far from "super" that day to earn the right to raise the Vince Lombardi trophy. The NFL renamed the trophy the "Vince Lombardi trophy," after the master coach himself, who died before the season. To compare either of these teams in the same sentence with the great Lombardi would be ludicrous. Super Bowl V is looked upon by fans and the media alike as one of the worse championships played not only in football but in all sports.[1]

Tex Maule reflected upon the mood of the game as he wrote in his *Sports Illustrated* column: "Perhaps the game should be called the Blunder Bowl from now on. The Baltimore Colts are the new world champions, but they won their first Super Bowl by default, not design. They defeated the Dallas Cowboys 16–13 on a field goal by rookie Placekicker Jim O'Brien with five seconds remaining, one of the few plays of the day that worked as it was supposed to."[2]

---

1. Schultz, *Dawn of Modern Football*, 190.
2. Maule, "Eleven Big Mistakes," accessed December 6, 2018.

"The Blunder Bowl" would stick as the name for Super Bowl V in the American conscience from then on. Other sportswriters got in on the insults thrown at that game.

Wells Twombly, a notable sportswriter for the *San Francisco Examiner*, remarked: "It was supposed to be a great spectacle . . . instead, the result was pure slapstick humor."[3]

And in the column, "Ray on Sports," Ray indicated, "The game was an artistic mess, and it looked as if neither team was going to be able to erase that losing stigma, or if either was even capable."[4]

That stigma turned to blame, but with so many blunders, who was the culprit? Either team could have either won that won or lost it with any of those bloopers made. Naturally, fingers pointed to Cowboys' quarterback Craig Morton. His stats were awful that day, throwing 12 complete passes out of 26 attempted, for 127 yards, with a touchdown pass but three interceptions, that comprised of the four turnovers made by the Dallas Cowboys. Many suggested that if there were a competent quarterback who ran the offense; the scales would have tipped in Dallas's favor. Back up Dallas quarterback Roger Staubach said: "Against Baltimore, all we had to do is have a halfway good passing game." Staubach was right on the passing perspective as only one pass was caught by a Dallas receiver all day.[5]

Cowboys' defensive tackle Bob Lilly ripped off his helmet and sent it flying halfway down the field. In his autobiography, Lilly wrote this about hurling his helmet: "I was just so disgusted with the way we had played, and to lose in the final seconds was the straw that broke the camel's back. I just lost it. What made matters even worse is that a rookie from the Colts brought my helmet back to me and said, "Mr. Lilly, here's your helmet." I felt about an inch tall."[6]

3. Schultz, *Dawn of Modern Football*, 190.
4. Ray on Sports, "NFL, Super Bowl V, The Blunder Bowl," accessed December 9, 2018, http://rayonsports.com/nfl-super-bowl-v-the-blunder-bowl/.
5. Schultz, *Dawn of Modern Football*, 189.
6. "1970: Super Bowl V - Dallas Cowboys vs Baltimore Colts Part 2," *Golden Football Magazine*, accessed December 8, 2018, http://goldenrankings.com/SuperBowl5-C.htm.

Lilly also reiterated: "To lose as we did was the lowest point of my career . . . The Ice Bowl, the Cleveland games, they were bad. But the Baltimore game was the worst I ever felt."[7]

Part of the blame was directed at the realignment of the league for the 1970 season. Longtime sports columnist Bob Oates of the *Los Angeles Times* wrote: "It is not easy to explain why such an important event should be poorly played, but the seeds were laid long ago . . . The Colts won the championship of the NFL's inferior American Football Conference without much offense. Unitas made a few big plays, and with the defense he had, it was enough."[8]

Players on both sides were interviewed on their take on the game.

IN THE COLTS LOCKER ROOM

Coach McCafferty cited the two tipped interceptions as the keys to the Colts' victory. "Both were big plays, giant plays actually, but you have to call Curtis's interception the turning point. That's the one which won it for us."[9] McCafferty mentioned two notable strategies he used during the game:

- On his decision to go for it on 4th-and-Goal at the end of the 1st half: "If we had lost, it would have been the worst call I made this year. If it had worked, I would have been a hero."[10]
- On Morrall finishing the game: "I knew Unitas was available, but I stuck with Earl because Earl was doing a fine job, and I saw no reason to change."

As for Earl Morrall, he admitted he wasn't sure he would lead his team to victory. "I just kept wondering if it was going to be 1968 all over again—all those missed opportunities . . . Without question, our defense won the game for us. But when you consider everything that was riding on that kick, you have to give a lot of credit to Jim. That's a lot

7. Schultz, *Dawn of Modern Football*, 189.
8. Ibid., 190.
9. "Dallas Cowboys vs Baltimore Colts Part 2," accessed December 8, 2018.
10. Ibid.

of pressure for a rookie to be under . . . Heck, that's a lot of pressure for anyone to be under, including me, and I've been around a long time."[11]

Morrall said in his autobiography: "Some people say my experience in the 1971 Super Bowl suggests great irony, or that it represents sweet atonement or at least poetic justice. I guess any one or all of these could apply . . . My wife says it's like the ending of a fairy tale. It is—but it's more. Someone upstairs played a big part in it."[12]

John Unitas remarked: "I'm happy for Earl. He did a fine job. I did not mind not going back to the game. That was the coach's decision. Earl was down in the dumps after our other Super Bowl, and it was great that he could come back."[13]

The Colts awarded one game ball to Coach McCafferty and the other to O'Brien, who carried it around with him wherever he went, even putting a clean towel over it. On his winning kick, O'Brien indicated: "It made me cry, and I usually don't cry very much. He said he hit the ball solidly—in fact; it was the only solid kick he had all day."

Asked about feeling pressure, O'Brien answered:

"You know I didn't think that much about the kick . . . I knew I might get myself in trouble if I did. Of course, it was obvious that we were going to run the clock down and go for the field goal, so that last-minute could have been a long one if I started worrying about it . . ."[14]

Billy Ray Smith, who nicknamed Jim O'Brien "Lassie" because of his long hair, praised the rookie. "That kid sure ain't no dawg. He may wear his hair a bit funny, but he's a winner, that's for sure."

On his retirement: "It's all over now. I just won $15,000. And see this blood on my pants? You ask me whose blood this is? My blood. This is my last game. What can I possibly do after this—come back here and have the coaches run me out?"[15]

Defensive tackle Fred Miller: "We were ready for overtime, even expected it, but knew we were holding the high cards. It's been like this

11. Ibid.
12. Ibid.
13. Ibid.
14. Ibid.
15. Ibid.

all year and just climaxed today. We have had to struggle, but we refused to give up."[16]

Middle linebacker Mike Curtis made an admission. "Man, I didn't think there was any way we would win this game. Maybe I shouldn't say that, but the way things were going, that's the way I felt. But then this epitomizes our entire season . . . I mean, it's appropriate that we should win the big one in a game like this because this is the way we've played all season. There have been so many times that I couldn't tell you how we won, but we did it . . . just like today."[17]

Strong safety Jerry Logan summed up his feelings this way. "I've been here three times, and it is about time I come away with one of them (titles)."

Years later, tight end John Mackey said, "The best team I ever played on lost the Super Bowl. The worst team I ever played on won it."[18]

IN THE COWBOYS LOCKER ROOM

According to a Baltimore writer who went to the Dallas locker room: There was no gnashing of teeth . . . and no one wept openly. None of the players threw a helmet against the wall or shouted obscenities. This was a scene the Cowboys have played over and over again, and they are masters at it. Only Craig Morton seemed visibly shaken, and he had a right to be.

Looking like he had aged several years overnight, Coach Tom Landry said he didn't say much to the players when they arrived in the dressing room after the game.

"I tried to say something, but there's not much you can say. It was all there, and we lost it . . . There was never a point where we didn't think we were going to win it. That's what makes it so tough to take . . . We beat ourselves. The fumble and two interceptions killed us . . . This hurts pretty badly. We fought hard to get here. You couldn't play defense any better than we were playing today. We've been playing like that for weeks, and everything went right for us. But this time, we did, and it still wound

---

16. Ibid.
17. Ibid.
18. Ibid.

up wrong . . . Although we weren't hitting passes, we were moving the ball . . . We were moving fine in the third quarter until [Duane]Thomas fumbled on the 1. If we had gone in to score then, we came out with a 20–6 lead. They would have had an awful lot of catching up to do."[19]

Asked if this loss hurt worse than the losses to Green Bay for the NFL title in '66 and '67, Landry replied: "They may take it harder, but I can't see them letting down. They came back a long way to get here. We fought as hard as we know how, but we just didn't put it together at the right times today."[20]

On the play of his quarterback Landry indicated: "I never considered taking Morton out for Staubach. We seemed to be controlling the ball and felt no reason to change."[21]

As for quarterback Craig Morton, he spoke so softly; reporters had to strain to hear him. In his response to reporters: "When you are down like I am, what do you do? I guess you just have to start all over again next year . . . This game was a great challenge for me. People had been critical of my performances in the past, and there was a great chance to answer that criticism. But I just didn't do it. I thought we had the game under control, and we did what we wanted to do. I probably should have completed a few more passes . . . We just made too many mistakes. Their defense didn't do anything we didn't expect. They shut down our run. In the second half, I didn't know what they did, though maybe they changed upfront . . . I wasn't the worst quarterback on the field. Look at what happened to Unitas. They were lucky to win, or he would have been the goat."[22]

Reporters wanted to talk to Duane Thomas, especially about the crucial fumble at the goal line, but he dressed quickly and left before the press was let in. Decades later, Thomas still resented being cast as the scapegoat as he explained: "Tom got on me about losing the game. How about Dan Reeves? He tipped the damn ball into Mike Curtis's hands for the interception. At least I scored a touchdown in the game."[23]

19. Ibid.
20. Ibid.
21. Ibid.
22. Ibid.
23. Ibid.

As for MVP winner linebacker Chuck Howley he remarked: "I'm glad I won the Most Valuable Player award because it's a tribute to the entire defensive team. It's a great honor, but I would much rather we be world champions . . . I'm not a sarcastic guy, but something like all this sure leaves you shaking your head. I guarantee you I thought we were ready to go right on winning when we got here. We were loose and happy all week long, just like we had been in our last seven games. We felt good. And nothing changed when we took the field today. We went into the game, and it went just like we thought it would. We were well prepared for the Colts. We forced them into errors and had it going our way. We could have had it all locked up earlier, but we also could have won it at the end by getting a couple of first downs and kicking a field goal . . . What can you say? It's not much to be the leftovers . . . Freak plays beat us. I don't feel like we were beaten. I feel like we won, but they got the title."[24]

Middle linebacker Lee Roy Jordan on the tipped pass to Mackey for a touchdown: "I hate bad enough to lose on things they do to your defense but to give up a touchdown on something like that is incredible . . . We played well . . . but we had the breaks go against us. When you play to win, and it doesn't work out, all you can do is get ready for next year . . . I don't have any complex about this game, and I'm not going to take any lip about it. We're coming back. I hate to tell 'em, but we are."[25]

Dan Reeves blamed himself for the killer interception that set up the winning field goal: "The ball simply went through my hands. How high was it? High enough to catch. I got no excuse. You get paid for catching the hard ones. I don't remember anything ever hurting so much or costing so much. What hurts is having your defense play as great as ours did and lose. But I'm sure our defensive players would tell you we're a 40-man team. We got here as a team, and we've been winning as a team, and we lost as a team . . . This was the biggest game we ever played. I just wish we could have won it. What hurts most was giving up points on two tipped plays . . . It's bad enough to lose but to just give it to them."[26]

---

24. Ibid.
25. Ibid.
26. Ibid.

Defensive tackle Bob Lilly remarked: "I don't have any feelings right now. I wish I didn't even have to go to the west coast for the Pro Bowl. I'm so fed up. I wish I didn't even have to think about football anymore . . . We were hurt by three deflected passes. They picked off two of ours to set up their last 10 points, and they got their first six on a ball tipped by their guy . . . But that's football."

But Lilly didn't think any of the tips were the biggest plays: "When Thomas fumbled on the 1, it cost us pretty heavily. If he had held the ball, and we scored another touchdown, it would have been a different game from then on. I really couldn't see them getting a lot of touchdowns the rest of the way. I figured 17 points would win it before the game. As it turned, it would have."[27]

Lilly had considered retiring if the Cowboys won Super Bowl V. A pal gave him a Cuban cigar to enjoy after winning the championship. When Dallas lost, Bob brought the cigar back to Dallas and kept it on ice for safekeeping in hopes that he could light it after Super Bowl VI.

Offensive Guard John Niland praised the defense: "They did a terrific job. But in the final analysis, this game is a team effort, and it's a team loss . . . We got field goals when we should have had touchdowns. Overall, our offense didn't do well. We had some good plays at the time, but we were erratic. I don't think the Colts defense built up any momentum. A mistake here and a mistake there gave them a lift. That's momentum going against you, but it wasn't created by them."[28]

Free safety Charlie Waters thought Dallas got the raw end of the officiating: "We made our breaks, and the officials made theirs (the Colts'). Every time we would stop them, we would be called for interference. Every time we started moving, we would get called for holding. I just can't accept that."[29]

Years later, Assistant Coach Ray Renfro recalled an incident on the bus ride back to the hotel. "You know when I got really angry at Craig? On the bus ride back to the hotel. My wife and I were sitting there crying

---

27. Ibid.
28. Ibid.
29. Ibid.

our eyes out, and I looked back, and he was back there, goosing to his girlfriend and laughing . . . That's when I got angry at Craig."[30]

Reflecting on Super Bowl V years later, Walt Garrison said: "Our goal at the start of the season (1970) was to go to the Super Bowl, and we did. But I think we wasted all our energy on the playoffs and then relaxed and forgot what we were doing there."[31]

A few days after the game, an Associated Press article announced that Super Bowl V attracted the largest television audience ever to watch a single sports event. According to NBC, the game was seen in 31,670,000 homes by an audience of 64 million people. But the gripes about the game continued. In New York, the NFL office received more than 500 complaints about the officiating in the Super Bowl, and many fans began suggesting that instant replay be used to review calls.

Later that January, Lee Roy Jordan gave the talk at a January football banquet in Alabama where he played for Bear Bryant: " We had to play against sixteen men. One official made five or six calls against us himself. I was very upset with the officiating. In the second half, every time we broke up a pass or made a long gain on third down, I looked up and saw a flag."[32]

From all the bad plays, turnovers, miscues, and terrible officiating, Super Bowl V to this day is far from revered. Typically, history has a way of being kinder to a particular person or subject as the years move on. In this case, it didn't. All that can be said is that the real difference in the game was that the Colts got away from their mistakes and the Cowboys paid for theirs.[33]

Many who were part of the game reflected on the turnovers and that it might have been the style of play that contributed to the blunders, rather than the fault of the players. Earl Morrall said, "It was a physical game. I mean, people were flying into one another out there."[34]

---

30. Ibid.
31. Ibid.
32. Ibid.
33. Schaefer, *Baltimore Colts 1970: A Game-by-Game Guide*, 2247, Kindle.
34. Bill McGrane, "A Mad, Mad, Mad Super Bowl," in *The Super Bowl: Celebrating a Quarter-Century of America's Greatest Game*" (NY: Simon and Schuster, 1990).

Jim O'Brien wrote, "It was a hard-hitting game . . . It wasn't just guys dropping the ball. They fumbled because they got the snot knocked out of them."[35]

Said Coach Tom Landry: "I haven't been around many games where the players hit harder. Sometimes people watch a game and see turnovers, and they talk about how sloppy the play was. The mistakes in that game weren't invented, at least not by the people who made them. Most were forced."[36]

Bubba Smith refused to wear his Super Bowl ring due to the sloppy play that day. To him, Super Bowl III was not vindicated with the Super Bowl V win.

On a more positive note, Coach Don McCafferty was the first rookie coach to win a Super Bowl until George Seifert, many years later with the San Francisco 49ers. McCafferty was in the shadow of Don Shula's departure all season, and the victory liberated him from that shadow. He had done what Shula could not: bring a Super Bowl victory to Baltimore.

For the city of Baltimore in 1970, it was the place to be if you were a sports fan. The Orioles won the World Series earlier in October, and now the Colts joined them in giving the city a second championship, this time in football.

Even if the city of Baltimore celebrated, respect was not a word to describe the game. It was evident that respect was lacking when Dick Young, the eminent New York historian, said, "This one was so bad, (President Richard) Nixon didn't call either team."[37]

35. Danny Peary and Jim O'Brien, "Super Bowl V," in *Super Bowl: The Game of Their Lives* (NY: Macmillan, 1997), at Super Bowl, the game of their lives : Peary, Danny, 1949- : Free Download, Borrow, and Streaming: Internet Archive

36. McGrane, "Mad Super Bowl."

37. Schaefer, *Game-by-Game Guide*, 2256, Kindle.

15

THE IMPACT OF THE
1970 SEASON

The first season in the newly merged NFL left a tremendous impact on the game and set the events in motion to which we know the game as it is today. Super Bowl V was the springboard to what would become a major sporting event bonanza that every football fan waits for every year. With the merger, there were no more two different leagues playing for superiority. The thought that Super Bowl V had no underlying storyline as the previous four Super Bowls was quickly wiped away as shown by fan interest by the attendance records set at Miami for the game and the television audiences who viewed the game. Fans eventually acclimated to the American Football Conference (AFC) and the National Football Conference (NFC) of the new NFL, with the victors of those conferences fighting it out at the end of each season. The two-week gap between the conference championship games allowed suspense to build as the media presence grew dramatically. By 1974, the event had grown to such proportions that Norman Vincent Peale declared that if Christ were alive, "he'd be at the Super Bowl."[1]

---

1. Robert Flegler, "The History of the Super Bowl," The American Historian, accessed December 12, 2018, https://tah.oah.org/content/the-history-of-the-super-bowl/.

From a financial standpoint, the NFL outdid its competitors in baseball, basketball, and hockey, especially to see who would be the champion.
While viewership for the World Series, NHL, and NBA Finals are highly
dependent on whether large-market teams or major stars participate or
not, the Super Bowl's ratings are almost unaffected by these factors. The
NFL's revenue-sharing arrangement allows small-market teams to remain
competitive and even become national brands.[2]

The coming decade known by many pro football historians and fans
as the "Super Seventies" truly lived up to its name, after the 1970 season.
The game experienced tremendous growth during those ten years. All
three networks (ABC, NBC, and CBS) all had major contracts to televise
pro football games. *Monday Night Football* became a staple in primetime
on Monday Night, which still exists after 50 years. With these television
contracts, the NFL found a financial partner that would help grow the
game. From being a localized sport in a specific geographical location,
television expanded the game into the national pastime. With the expansion of football into other markets, merchandising and advertising went
with the game into these new territories. Many advertisers were more
than happy to pay top dollar to promote their products during Sunday
afternoons and Monday nights, knowing full well most of the nation was
watching the games and would be tempted to buy what they were selling.

Even with television expansion into other markets, overall attendance
at regular season and postseason games increased in many of the league's
cities each year, and the Super Bowl became an undeclared national holi-
day. Just six years later after the merger, the NFL was high in demand and
expanded in 1976, with franchises in Tampa Bay and Seattle.[3]

The 1970s changed the NFL in many ways. Owners started to see the
money pour in from all the revenue earned from attendance of games,
the television contracts, and the merchandise sold. But while the owners'
pockets were being filled, the players themselves wanted more of a share.
They wanted higher salaries, and because of this, there were two-player

2. Ibid.

3. Joe Zagorski, *The NFL in the 1970s* (Jefferson, NC: McFarland & Company, Inc., 2016), 82–85, Kindle.

strikes. "No freedom, no football," was the chant, and the decade ushered in free agency, where teams would bid for marquee players. Competition from the World Football League only furthered the continuity of the brand in the NFL, as well as trying to break the monopolistic hold that the NFL had on the game.[4]

New and increasingly modern stadiums also started to expand the NFL landscape. The multi-purpose stadium serviced both football and baseball teams in 17 cities. Although many fans thought these stadiums lacked any character and were cookie-cutter carbon copies of one another, the crowds still came out to see the game. Luxury boxes were created, and better seating for the fans put those old stadiums like War Memorial Stadium in Buffalo out to pasture. It was outdated and irrelevant to the game.

The popularity of pro football was well documented by NFL films. Founder and owner Ed Sabol and his son Steve pioneered the filming of games, and after the merger, NFL Films grew to massive proportions. Before there was cable tv to give us the rundown of the scores and action, programs, such as *This Week in Pro Football* or *NFL Game of the Week*, were the backbone of NFL Films' television schedule. Today, NFL Films is the primary vehicle by which the game has become popular.[5]

The 1970s saw the players vie for the limelight. Gone were the days when there was a protocol for behavior from the players. Players now were more colorful, using emotional expressions such as dancing when they scored a touchdown in the end zone. As NFL films captured the action, film crews would also pan the sidelines for team reactions to a play. It was now in style to see the players mug for the camera to raise a number one gesture with their index finger or smile into the camera to say, "hi mom." Superstars also saw opportunities elsewhere in movies and on tv commercials. Running back O.J. Simpson from the Buffalo Bills became a speaker for the rental car company Hertz, while Pittsburgh Steelers defensive lineman Mean Joe Greene became a spokesperson for the soft drink Coca Cola.

---

4. Ibid., 67.
5. Ibid., 122.

Old style coaching vs. new style coaching emerged. Visions of Vince
Lombardi as a stern disciplinarian and strategist were given way to a new
breed of coaches: the nice guy, the father figure, the player's coaches.
Rookie coach Don McCafferty of the Colts exemplified this nice guy
approach and was a stark contrast to his predecessor, Don Shula, who
was well steeped in the old harsh coaching style. But McCafferty's nice-
guy image was rewarded with hoisting the Vince Lombardi trophy for
the 1970 season. Baltimore Colts defensive end Bubba Smith once
claimed rookie head coach John McCafferty "was such a nice guy, that
you didn't want to play bad and disappoint him, to a point where he
could lose his job."[6]

Coaches like Tom Landry still were seen as a pillar of the old coaching styles. Landry rarely showed emotion and was a disciplinarian and
strategist throughout. When 1977 rolled around, and his players started
to show their expressions on the field, Landry had to let it go. That Dallas
team won the Super Bowl that year.

John Madden set few rules for his Oakland squads. They were a colorful bunch with names such as "Snake, Foo, and Dr. Death." This team's
distinctive personality that set it apart from all others of the 1970s was
the perception that this was a group of outlaws and rebels who thumbed
their noses at convention. Add to this the fact many were castoffs from
other teams for behavioral or other issues, and you had a truly volatile
band of misfits.[7] But somehow, the affable John Madden, who was the
perfect coach for this team, was able to take this group of irrepressible
"adults" and mold them into a feared, championship football team. This
was a hard-partying and hard-practicing team even with all of the pranks
the players pulled while preparing for the season. It was a fun-loving and
wild group of men who John Madden somehow molded into winners.
Partially he did it by letting them have their fun and treating them like
men but making sure that they practiced and played hard. While they
might have been a wild, fun-loving bunch, they also loved football and

6. Ibid., 204.
7. Douglas C. Baker, "The 1970s Oakland Raiders, Tales From The Dark Side," Bleacher Report (March
27, 2011), accessed December 13, 2018, https://bleacherreport.com/articles/646766-the-1970s-oakland
-raiders-tales-from-the-dark-side.

wanted to win. The Raiders would win Super Bowl XI over the Vikings in 1977.[8]

Playing styles were also changing. Most offenses favored a brutal rushing attack like Miami with Larry Csonka, Jim Kiick, and Mercury Morris to propel their offenses. It was old school football that led the Packers a decade before to their many Championships. The further innovation of strategy in the offense to the passing game made the mid-to late 1970s a huge time for a change in the NFL. The "shotgun" offense was revived by Dallas head coach Tom Landry in 1975 (he called it the "spread formation"), and it helped to open up the passing game by positioning the quarterback several yards behind his center. Once he caught the center's snap, the quarterback would have more time to read the opposing defenses and more time to throw the ball. Landry realized the pro game by the end of the decade was leaning more to a wide-open style of play, where throwing the ball became increasingly prevalent. Most teams today employ some version or another of the shotgun, a testament to Landry's vision.[9]

The NFL Rules Committee grew too. Comprised of some coaches, front office people, and referees, they saw a need for innovation and change to make the game more exciting and safe at the same time. Here is a rundown of the rule changes after the 1970 season:

1972

The inbounds lines or hash marks were moved nearer the center of the field, 23 yards, 1 foot, 9 inches from the sidelines.

The method of determining the won-lost percentage in standings changed. Tie games previously not counted in the standings were made equal to a half-game won and a half-game lost.

1973

A jersey numbering system was adopted, April 5: 1–19 for quarterbacks and specialists, 20–49 for running backs and defensive backs, 50–59 for centers and linebackers, 60–79 for defensive linemen and interior

---

8. Ibid.
9. Zagorski, *NFL in the 1970s*, 217, Kindle.

offensive linemen other than centers, and 80–89 for wide receivers and tight ends. Players who had been in the NFL in 1972 could continue to use old numbers.

1974

Sweeping rules changes were adopted to add action and tempo to games: one sudden-death overtime period was added for preseason and regular-season games; the goalposts were moved from the goal line to the end lines; kickoffs were moved from the 40- to the 35-yard line; after missed field goals from beyond the 20, the ball was to be returned to the line of scrimmage; restrictions were placed on members of the punting team to open up return possibilities; roll-blocking and cutting of wide receivers were eliminated; the extent of downfield contact a defender could have with an eligible receiver was restricted; the penalties for offensive holding, illegal use of the hands, and tripping were reduced from 15 to 10 yards; wide receivers blocking back toward the ball within three yards of the line of scrimmage were prevented from blocking below the waist.

1976

Owners adopted the use of two 30-second clocks for all games, visible to both players and fans to note the official time between the ready-for-play signal and snap of the ball.

1977

A 16-game regular season, 4-game preseason was adopted to begin in 1978.

A second wild-card team was adopted for the playoffs beginning in 1978, with the wild-card teams to play each other and the winners advancing to a round of eight postseason series.

Rule changes were adopted to open up the passing game and to cut down on injuries.

Defenders were permitted to make contact with eligible receivers only once; the head slap was outlawed; offensive linemen were prohibited from thrusting their hands to an opponent's neck, face, or head; and wide receivers were prohibited from clipping, even in the legal clipping zone.

1978

The NFL continued a trend toward opening up the game. Rules changes permitted a defender to maintain contact with a receiver within five yards of the line of scrimmage but restricted contact beyond that point. The pass-blocking rule was interpreted to permit the extending of arms and open hands.

1979

NFL rules changes emphasized additional player safety. The changes prohibited players on the receiving team from blocking below the waist during kickoffs, punts, and field-goal attempts; prohibited the wearing of torn or altered equipment and exposed pads that could be hazardous; extended the zone in which there could be no crackback blocks; and instructed officials to quickly whistle a play dead when a quarterback was clearly in the grasp of a tackler."

The 1970s saw pro football grow to all kinds of proportions, and it all started with that one vintage season of 1970. With all the gripes of the merger, a Super Bowl debacle, and squabbles in the front office, 1970 proved to be the spark that lit the flame for the NFL's future. The 1970 season changed pro football forever. A new league, new divisions, new rivalries, more money, more television coverage, more attendance records, and a new decade put pro football on the dawn of the modern era.

EPILOGUE

POST-1970 PLAYOFF TEAMS

For the Dallas Cowboys, vindication came the next year from the disheartening loss to the Colts in Super Bowl V. It was the year the Dallas Cowboys had waited for since they became a significant force in the league since 1966. As in the previous season, Dallas had a quarterback controversy, as Roger Staubach and Craig Morton alternated as starting quarterback (in a loss to the Bears in game 7, Morton and Staubach alternated plays). The Cowboys were 4–3 at the season midpoint.[1] But in the eighth game of the season, head coach Tom Landry settled on Staubach. With Staubach manning the Cowboy offense, he contributed to the team's success for the rest of the season. The Cowboys won their last seven regular-season games to finish with an 11–3 record, and Staubach would win the Bert Bell Award as the player of the year.[2]

In the playoffs, Dallas traveled to frigid Minnesota to play the Vikings in the divisional round of the playoffs, who also had a stellar 11–3 record like the Cowboys. The Cowboys beat the Vikings 20–12 at Metropolitan Stadium and traveled back home to Dallas to face the San Francisco 49ers in the NFC Championship. As they did the year before, Dallas beat the

1. "Cold Hard Football Facts: The Dandy Dozen: 12 best passing seasons in history." Archived from the original on July 9, 2012, accessed December 14, 2018, https://web.archive.org/web/20120729042325/http://www.coldhardfootballfacts.com/Articles/Archive_3224_The_Dandy_Dozen:_12_best_passing_seasons_in_history.html.
2. Strasen, *Cowboys Chronicles*, 85.

49ers again, this time by a score of 14–3 to advance to the Super Bowl. In the Super Bowl, they dominated the rising AFC champs, the Miami Dolphins, who made the Super Bowl in only the second year of Don Shula's tenure as head coach. The final score was Cowboys 24 Miami 3. The Cowboys would remain a powerful force for the next decade, going to three more Super Bowls in the 1970s and winning one more.

As for the Baltimore Colts, they fell off the ranks of being an elite team by the end of the decade. Citing friction with the City of Baltimore and the local press, Carroll Rosenbloom traded the Colts franchise to Robert Irsay on July 13, 1972, and received the Los Angeles Rams in return. Under the new ownership, the Colts did not reach the postseason for three consecutive seasons after 1971. After the 1972 season, starting quarterback and legend Johnny Unitas was traded to the San Diego Chargers. Earl Morrall was gone, too. Morrall went to the Dolphins, where he reunited with Don Shula and won the Super Bowl in 1972 and 1973. Following Unitas's departure, the Colts re-built their team and made the playoffs three consecutive seasons from 1975 to 1977, losing in the divisional round each time. In 1977, the Colts playoff loss came in double overtime against the Oakland Raiders. The game was famous because it was the last playoff game for the Colts in Baltimore and is also known for the Ghost to the Post play. It refers specifically to a 42-yard pass from Ken Stabler to Dave Casper, nicknamed "The Ghost" after Casper the Friendly Ghost, that set up a game-tying field goal in the final seconds of regulation in double-overtime for the AFC divisional playoff game. These consecutive playoff teams that the Colts had featured 1976 NFL Most Valuable Player Bert Jones at quarterback, and an outstanding defensive line, nicknamed the "Sack Pack." However, the Colts never returned to glory in Baltimore and moved away to their current hometown in Indianapolis in 1984.

The Minnesota Vikings remained a powerhouse for many years to come. In 1972, quarterback Fran Tarkenton returned to the team, and he guided the Vikings to three more Super Bowl appearances, only to lose them all. Like the Bills in the 1990s, the Vikings have the dubious distinction of losing four Super Bowls. Bud Grant remained as the Vikings coach until 1983, took a year off, and returned to coach the Vikings in 1985. After that season, Grant retired. When he left the game, Grant was ranked as the eighth most successful coach in NFL history with an overall record of 161 wins, 99 losses, and 5 ties. Even now, he remains the most successful coach in Vikings history. During his tenure with the Vikings, he led the Vikings to four Super Bowls, eleven division titles, one league championship, and three NFC conference championships.[3]

No team that played in the 1970s was more successful than the Pittsburgh Steelers. Coach Chuck Noll learned from the master himself, head coach, Sid Gillman when he was a defensive line coach for seven years with the Chargers. Noll's most remarkable talent was in his draft selections, by which he built the premier team of the 1970s. Noll drafted: "Mean" Joe Greene in 1969, Terry Bradshaw and Mel Blount in 1970, Jack Ham in 1971, Franco Harris in 1972, and Mike Webster, Lynn Swann, John Stallworth, and Jack Lambert in 1974. According to the NFL Network, 1974 was the best draft class in the history of the NFL with Webster, Swann, Stallworth, & Lambert all in the Hall of Fame, and all four won four Super Bowl championships. This group of players formed the base of one of the greatest teams ever in NFL history, along with one of the best defensive lines, which was nicknamed "The Steel Curtain."[4]

The Miami Dolphins quickly rose to the top of the NFL with the hiring of coach Don Shula. On what looked like a gradual buildup through years of cultivating talent, 1970 was a surprising season for the Dolphins. They came from nowhere and made the playoffs as the AFC's first Wild Card team. The next year, they became AFC champs, and they went to Super Bowl VI, only to lose to the Dallas Cowboys. The loss didn't deter Shula or his team, and they stormed back the next year to win the Super Bowl in the 1972 season (with a perfect 14–0 season), and they repeated as champs winning the Super Bowl after the 1973 season. They

3. Brian Marshall, (1998). "BUD GRANT: PURPLE AND BLUE, THROUGH AND THROUGH". Professional Football Researchers Association. Archived from the original on April 3, 2007, accessed December 14, 2018.

4. "Chuck Noll," Pro Football Hall of Fame, accessed December 14, 2018, https://www.profootball hof.com/news/chuck-noll-1932-2014/.

remained a powerhouse throughout the 1970s, and Don Shula remained the Dolphins' coach until 1995.

Once John Madden became coach of the Oakland Raiders in 1969, he would continue a winning tradition in Oakland from their surprising appearance in Super Bowl II. Under Madden, the Raiders would become one of the most successful teams in the NFL. From 1973–1975, the Raiders suffered three AFC Championship losses but would fight back to win Super Bowl XI in 1977, for their first-ever NFL title. Madden led the Raiders to 10 consecutive winning seasons but left in 1979, at the age of 43, to pursue a career as a television commentator. Tom Flores, the first-ever Hispanic head coach in NFL history, took over Madden's position. In 1980, starting quarterback Dan Pastorini broke his leg and was replaced by a number-one draft pick, Jim Plunkett, who was drafted by the Patriots back in 1971. Plunkett revived his career in Oakland and led the Raiders to an 11–5 record and their first wild card berth. The Raiders swept their opponents in the playoffs, which led them to a match-up between the Philadelphia Eagles in Super Bowl XV. The Raiders defeated the Eagles 27–10, becoming the first wild card team to win a Super Bowl. They would win another Super Bowl three years later in Super Bowl XVIII when they beat the Washington Redskins 38–9.[5]

Under Paul Brown's guidance, the Cincinnati Bengals continued to grow as a team after the 1970 season. With that remarkable run to get into the playoffs in 1970, the Bengals were poised to go further in the realigned league. Brown's tenure as coach of the Bengals would last five more seasons. He retired after the 1975 season but continued to serve as general manager until he died in 1991.[6]

In 1971, the Bengals selected Ken Anderson, a quarterback from little-known Augustana College, in the third round of the draft. For the next 16 seasons, Anderson was the key man of the Cincinnati offense and a four-time AFC individual passing champion. Cincinnati won its

5. "Oakland Raiders History," Ticket City, accessed December 14, 2018, https://www.ticketcity.com/oakland-raiders-tickets/oakland-raiders-history.html.

6. "Cincinnati Bengals, Team History," Pro Football Hall of Fame, accessed December 14, 2018, https://www.profootballhof.com/teams/cincinnati-bengals/team-history/.

second AFC Central championship in 1973 and a wild-card berth in the 1975 playoffs in Brown's final year as coach. The Bengals missed the playoffs for the next five seasons but won big in 1981, the year the Bengals unveiled their new uniforms with tiger-striped helmets, jerseys, and pants. With Forrest Gregg as the coach, Cincinnati won the AFC Central with a 12–4 record and defeated San Diego 27–7 in the AFC championship game. However, they lost the Super Bowl XVI showdown with the San Francisco 49ers, 26–21.[7] Cincinnati would also meet the 49ers in Super Bowl XXIII, where ex Bengal quarterback Sam Wyche was now the coach. Wyche and his Bengals would lose to his mentor, Bill Walsh, and the San Francisco 49ers, in one of the most spectacular finishes in Super Bowl history, by a score of 20–16.

Many argue that the 1970 Detroit Lions might have been the best Lions team ever, even without winning a championship. This notion remains intact, even though the Lions of the 1950s won three NFL championships. Lions cornerback Lem Barney remarked that a win over Dallas in that 5–0 divisional game would have led to the Lions winning the Super Bowl. They might have had a good chance since Minnesota lost to the 49ers in the divisional round. Minnesota had beaten the Lions twice in the season, but Detroit beat the 49ers in the 10th week of the season, 28–7 at home in Detroit. The Lions might be the biggest "what if" of all the teams that made the playoffs for 1970.

----

7. Ibid.

BIBLIOGRAPHY

#43 Cliff Harris, Safety, 1970-1979. Dallas Cowboys.com, at https://www.dallascowboys.com/team/ROH-Cliff-Harris.

1963 Baltimore Colts Statistics & Players. Pro Football Reference, at https://www.webcitation.org/6KwWCUXYP?url=http://www.pro-football-reference.com/teams/clt/1963.htm.

1970 Dallas Cowboys. Pro Football Reference, at https://www.pro-football-reference.com/teams/dal/1970.htm.

1970 Los Angeles Rams. Pro Football Reference, at https://www.pro-football-reference.com/teams/ram/1970.htm.

1970 New York Giants. Pro Football Reference, at https://www.pro-football-reference.com/teams/nyg/1970.htm?redir.

1970 Oakland Raiders. Pro Football Reference, at https://www.pro-football-reference.com/teams/rai/1970.htm.

1970 St. Louis Cardinals. Pro Football Reference, at https://www.pro-football-reference.com/teams/crd/1970.htm.

1970: Super Bowl V - Dallas Cowboys vs Baltimore Colts. Golden Football Magazine, at http://goldenrankings.com/SuperBowl5-A.htm.

1970: Super Bowl V - Dallas Cowboys vs Baltimore Colts Part 2. Golden Football Magazine, at http://goldenrankings.com/SuperBowl5-C.htm.

"49ers Year By Year: 1970." SB Nation. January 2, 2009, at https://www.ninersnation.com/2009/1/2/707719/49ers-year-by-year-1970.

"A Brief History of Football," at http://www.historyoffootball.net/.

Al's Wingman. "The Business of the Raiders' is Business." October 4, 2008, at http://alswingman.blogspot.com/2008/10/al-davis-fires-his-head-coach-even.html.

Arnold, Geoffrey C. (November 16, 2017). "NBC's 'SkyCam' will provide Madden-like view of tonight's Titans-Steelers game," at https://www.oregonlive.com/nfl/index.ssf/2017/11/nbcs_skycam_will_provide_madde.html.

Baker, Douglas C. "The 1970s Oakland Raiders, Tales From The Dark Side." March 27, 2011. Bleacher Report, at https://bleacherreport.com/articles/646766-the-1970s-oakland-raiders-tales-from-the-dark-side.

"Baltimore Colts: Team History." The Pro Football Hall of Fame, at https://www.profootballhof.com/teams/indianapolis-colts/team-history/.

Banks, Don. *Forty-Five Years after last AFL season, rivalry with NFL still resonates.* Sports Illustrated, at https://www.si.com/nfl/2014/11/12/afl-history-kansas-city-chiefs-oakland-raiders.

Beard, Gary. *The Decline and Rise of the Dallas Cowboys, 1970 Highlights.* Published on June 18, 2018, at https://www.youtube.com/watch?v=aaxLuYN73-U.

Beard, Guy. *New Look, New Season, New Era-1970 Miami Dolphins.* Published on April 19, 2018, at https://www.youtube.com/watch?v=pB6H2_-pyeA.

Bedford Wynne, Jr. Find A Grave. September 19, 2010, at https://www.findagrave.com/memorial/58907002/bedford-shelmire-wynne.

Belock, Joe. *Super Bowl III: Joe Namath leads NY Jets to arguably the biggest upset in history over Baltimore Colts.* New York Daily News. December 20, 2013, at http://www.nydailynews.com/sports/football/super-bowl-iii-namath-jets-shock-baltimore-colts-16-7-article-1.1553628.

Bob Hayes Bio. Dallas Cowboys Fan Club.com, archived from the original on October 19, 2010.

Bock, Hal. *Oakland romps past Houston, 40-7; meets Packers in Super Bowl Jan. 14.* Youngstown Vindicator, Ohio. Associated Press (January 1, 1968).

Brown, Maury. *A Look Back On The First ABC Monday Night Football On Its 45th Anniversary.* Forbes. September 21, 2015, at https://www.forbes.com/sites/maurybrown/2015/09/21/a-look-back-on-the -first-abc-monday-night-football-on-its-45th-anniversary/#13d8bc6d111c.

Browns' Blanton Says He's Retiring This Year. Rochester Sentinel. December 2, 1970.

"Camp and His Followers: American Football 1876–1889." Professional Football Researchers Association, at OHIO TIGER TRAP (profootballresearchers.org).

Cannizzaro, Mark. *New York Jets: The Complete Illustrated History.* MVP Books. Minneapolis (Copyright, 2011).

Cantor, George. *Paul Brown: The Man Who Invented Modern Football,* Triumph Books. Chicago, Illinois (Copyright, 2008).

Carlson, Michael. *George Blanda: American footballer who played in the NFL at the age of 48.* Independent. December 3, 2010, at https://www.independent.co.uk/news/obituaries/george-blanda-american-foot baller-who-played-in-the-nfl-at-the-age-of-48-2149823.html.

Carroll, Bob. *When The Grass Was Real.* Simon and Schuster. New York (Copyright, 1993).

Carter, Bob. *Rozelle Made The NFL What It Is Today.* ESPN, at http://www.espn.com/classic/biography/s /rozelle_pete.html.

"Chuck Noll." Pro Football Hall of Fame, at https://www.profootballhof.com/news/chuck-noll-1932-2014/.

"Cincinnati Bengals, Team History." Pro Football Hall of Fame, at https://www.profootballhof.com/teams /cincinnati-bengals/team-history/.

"Cold Hard Football Facts: The Dandy Dozen: 12 best passing seasons in history." Archived from the original on July 9, 2012, at https://web.archive.org/web/20120729042325/http://www.coldhardfootballfacts .com/Articles/Archive_3224_The_Dandy_Dozen:_12_best_passing_seasons_in_history.html.

Cross, Duane. *The AFL, A Football Legacy, Part 2.* CNN/SI (January 22, 2001), at http://www.remembertheafl .com/CNNSIAFLStoryPartII.htm, accessed on September 28, 2018.

Dallas and Twin Cities get NFL franchises; AFL declares war. Milwaukee Journal, press dispatches. January 29, 1960, at p.11, Part 2.

Dallas Cowboys. Pro Football Hall of Fame, at https://www.profootballhof.com/teams/dallas-cowboys /team-history/.

"Dallas Eleven Changes Made." New York Times, March 20, 1960.

"Dallas Lands Six Players." Milwaukee Sentinel, UPI, March 16, 1960.

Describing "The Innovator."' The Sporting News, archived from the original on December 1, 2005.

Dickey, Glenn. *Just Win, Baby: Al Davis & His Raiders.* Harcourt. New York (Copyright, 1991).

Doyle, Jack. *"I Guarantee It. Joe Namath."* December 23, 2009, at PopHistoryDig.com/Topics/JoeNamath/.

Ellerbee, Bobby. "September 21, 1970... 'ABC *Monday Night Football'* Debuts" Eyes of a Generation... Television's Living History, September 21, 2014, https://eyesofageneration.com/september-21-1970 -abc-monday-night-football-debutsmost-think-this-was-a-m/.

Eno, Greg. "How The 1970 Detroit Lions Broke A Seven Year Old's Heart." Bleacher Report. May 7, 2009, at https://bleacherreport.com/articles/169762-how-the-1970-detroit-lions-broke-a-seven-year-olds-heart.

Eskenazi, Gerald. *Tex Schramm Is Dead at 83; Builder of 'America's Team.',* New York Times. July 16, 2003, at https://www.nytimes.com/2003/07/16/sports/tex-schramm-is-dead-at-83-builder-of-america-s-team .html.

ESPN Sport Science at espngo.com.

Eyes of a Generation, September 21, 1970. ABC *Monday Night Football,* at http://eyesofageneration.com /september-21-1970-abc-monday-night-football-debutsmost-think-this-was-a-m/.

Fast, Randy. "The First Ten Years. 1970 Minnesota Highlights," at https://www.youtube.com /watch?v=jLD8ot3u_d8.

Felser, Larry. *Birth of the New NFL: How the 1966 NFL/AFL Merger Transformed Pro Football.* Lyons Press. Kindle edition.

Flegler, Robert. "The History of the Super Bowl." The American Historian, at https://tah.oah.org/content /the-history-of-the-super-bowl/.

Fleming, Frank. *The Baltimore Colts*. Sports Encyclopedia, July 5, 2002, at http://www.sportsecyclopedia. com/nfl/balticolts/baltcolts.html.

————. *The Dallas Cowboys*, Sports Encyclopedia. July 11, 2002, at www.sportsecyclopedia.com/nfl/dallas /cowboys.html.

Ford, Mark. *54, 40 or Fight Canada's 1954 War With the NFL*. THE COFFIN CORNER: Vol. 24, No. 4 (2002), at https://web.archive.org/web/20101218180121/http://profootballresearchers.org/Coffin _Corner/24-04-946.pdf.

Foss, Joe. The Telegraph. January 3, 2003, at https://www.telegraph.co.uk/news/obituaries/1417707/Joe-Foss .html.

Franco, Roberto and Andrade, Jose. *Why Does No One Remember Joe Kapp, the NFL's First Mexican American Super Bowl Quarterback?* Remezcla. September 29, 2017, at http://remezcla.com/features/sports /joe-kapp-nfl-latino-pioneer/.

Frommer, Harvey. *When It Was Just A Game, Remembering The First Super Bowl*. Taylor Trade Publishing. Lanham, Maryland (Copyright, 2015).

George Blanda. Hall of Fame, at http://www.profootballhof.com/players/george-blanda/.

Goodpaster, Mike. "1970 Detroit Lions, What Might Have Been." The Grueling Truth, at http: //thegruelingtruth.net/football/nfl/1970-detroit-lions-might/, accessed on November 6, 2018.

Gregory, Sean. *The Football Game That Changed It All*, Time Magazine. December 29, 2008, at http: //content.time.com/time/specials/packages/article/0,28804,1868793_1868792_1868802,00.html.

Grey Beard. published on April 19, 2018. "Chronicles of a Champion-1970 Cincinnati Bengals," at https: //www.youtube.com/watch?v=SOEcbXrFSnE.

Gruver, Ed. *The American Football League a Year-By-Year History*, 1960-1969. McFarland, North Carolina (Copyright, 1997).

Guest, J. Conrad. *The Lions Were Sunk By a 63 Yard Field Goal*. Detroit Athletic Company. December 29, 2012, at https://www.detroitathletic.com/blog/2012/12/29/tom-dempsey-63-yard-field-goal/.

Hank Stram. Pro Football Hall of Fame, at http://www.profootballhof.com/players/hank-stram/.

Hensley, Stephen. "NFL Competitors 1926-1975." Professional Football Research Association, at https://web.archive.org/web/20060319233552/http://www.footballresearch.com/articles/frpage. cfm?topic=nfl-comp

Herskowitz, Mickey. *Purple People Eaten by Dolphins. The Super Bowl: Celebrating a Quarter-Century of America's Greatest Game*. Simon and Schuster. New York (Copyright,1990).

————. *The Foolish Club*. Pro Football Weekly (1974), at https://web.archive.org/web/20070605071618 /http://www.kcchiefs.com/media/misc/5_the_foolish_club.pdf.

Hyde, Dave. *Still Perfect! The Untold Story of the 1972 Miami Dolphins*. Dolphins/Curtis Publishing. Philadelphia, Pennsylvania (Copyright, 2002).

Jackson, Kevin, Merron, Jeff & Schoenfield, David. *100 Greatest Super Bowl Moments*. ESPN, at http://www .espn.com/page2/s/superbowlmoments50.html, accessed on October 2, 2018.

John Brodie wins Jim Thorpe Trophy. Tuscaloosa News, Alabama, NEA, December 29, 1970.

"John Madden." Pro Football Hall of Fame, at https://www.profootballhof.com/players/john-madden /biography/.

Jones, Robert. *To Kill A Memory That Still Hurts*. Sports Illustrated. January 11, 1971, at https://www.si.com /vault/1971/01/11/554232/to-kill-a-memory-that-still-hurts.

Kansas City Chiefs. Chiefs History, at https://web.archive.org/web/20070823170852/http://www.kcchiefs .com/history/70s/.

Kansas City Chiefs. Wayback Machine, at http://www.kcchiefs.com/history/60s/.

Knaak, Jerry. *Three Raiders vs. Matchups For Three Different Decades*, at https://raiders.exposure.co /three-raiders-vs-dolphins-matchups-for-three-different-decades.

Lafayette, Cathey. published on April 12, 2016. "1970 Oakland Raiders Challenge of the 70s," at (3) 1970 Raiders - YouTube.

Lootmeister. "Super Bowl V Review," at http://www.lootmeister.com/superbowl/v.php.

————. "Super Bowl IV Review," at http://www.lootmeister.com/superbowl/iv.php.

MacCambridge, Michael. *America's Game... The Epic Story of How Pro Football Captured A Nation*. Random House. New York (Copyright,2004).

Maraniss, David. *In throes of winter, a team in disarray is reborn."* Milwaukee Journal Sentinel. Milwaukee, Wisconsin (September 14, 1999).

Maraniss, David. *When Pride Still Mattered, A Life of Vince Lombardi.* Simon & Schuster. Reprint edition, New York (September 3, 2000).

Marshall, Brian. (1998). "BUD GRANT: PURPLE AND BLUE, THROUGH AND THROUGH." Professional Football Researchers Association. Archived from the original on April 3, 2007.

Maule, Tex. "Eleven Big Mistakes," *Sports Illustrated.* January 25, 1971, at https://www.si.com /vault/1971/01/25/542218/eleven-big-mistakes.

McGrane, Bill. "A Mad, Mad, Mad Super Bowl," The Super Bowl: Celebrating a Quarter-Century of America's Greatest Game." Simon and Schuster. New York (Copyright,1990).

Miami Southpaw. "Ghosts of the Orange Bowl: Poly Turf." August 23, 2009, at http://miamisouthpaw .blogspot.com/2009/08/ghosts-of-orange-bowl-poly-turf.html.

Miller, Jeff. *Going Long.* The McGraw-Hill Companies. New York (Copyright, 2003).

Miller, Norm. *Super Chiefs Wreck Vikings, 23-7.* New York Daily News. December 21, 2003, at http://www. nydailynews.com/sports/football/super-bowl-iv-super-chiefs-wreck-vikings-23-7-article-1.1552249.

"Minnesota Miss: A Perfect Super Bowl Opportunity." The Sports Notebook, at http://thesportsnotebook. com/1970-minnesota-vikings/.

"NFL founded in Canton." NFL Pro Football Hall of Fame. January 1, 2005, at http://www.profootballhof .com/news/nfl-founded-in-canton/.

"NFL: Super Bowl V, The Blunder Bowl." Ray on Sports, at http://rayonsports.com /nfl-super-bowl-v-the-blunder-bowl/.

"NFL TV: A History," at http://www.kenn.com/the_blog/?page_id=5533.

"Oakland Raiders History." Ticket City, at https://www.ticketcity.com/oakland-raiders-tickets/oakland-raiders-history.html.

Olsen, Jack. *The Rosenbloom-Robbie Bowl.* Sports Illustrated, November 9, 1970, archived at https://www .si.com/vault/archive/1970s.

Patoski, Joe Nick. *The Dallas Cowboys... The Outrageous History of the Biggest, Loudest, Most Hated, Best Loved Football Team in America.* Little Brown and Company. Boston, Massachusetts (Copyright 2012).

Peary, Danny. *Super Bowl: The Game of Their Lives.* Macmillan. New York (Copyright, 1997), at Super Bowl, the game of their lives : Peary, Danny, 1949- : Free Download, Borrow, and Streaming : Internet Archive

Peary, Danny. *"Matt Snell, Super Bowl III, Super Bowl: The Game of Their Lives."* Macmillan. New York (Copyright,1997), at Super Bowl, the game of their lives : Peary, Danny, 1949- : Free Download, Borrow, and Streaming: Internet Archive.

Peary, Danny, Jim O'Brien, *"Super Bowl V,"* Super Bowl: The Game of Their Lives, Macmillan, NewYork (Copyright, 1997), at Super Bowl, the game of their lives : Peary, Danny, 1949- : Free Download, Borrow, and Streaming: Internet Archive

Pluto, Terry. *Fumble: The Browns, Modell, & the Move.* Cleveland Landmarks. Cleveland, Ohio (Copyright, October 1, 1997).

Professional Football is Born. History.com, at https://www.history.com/this-day-in-history /professional-football-is-born.

Rappoport, Ken. *The Little League That Could, A History of the American Football League.* Taylor Trade Publishing. Lanham, Maryland (Copyright, 2010).

Remembering "The Kick," at avoyellestoday.com. Avoyelles Journal. Bunkie, Record. Marksville Weekly. Archived from the original on January 4, 2015.

Rowen, Lindsay. *How The Super Bowl Got Its Name.* The Christian Science Monitor. January 29, 2015, at https://www.csmonitor.com/USA/Sports/2015/0129/How-the-Super-Bowl-got-its-name.

"Sammy Baugh: The Greatest Overall Football Player Of All Time." March 15, 2009. Bleacher Report, at https://bleacherreport.com/articles/139513-sammy-baugh-the-greatest-football-player-of-all-time.

Sanders, Craig, and Jasinski, Laurie E. *Lamar Hunt.* Handbook of Texas Online, at http://www.tshaonline. org/handbook/online/articles/fhu99.

Schaefer, John. *Baltimore Colts 1970: A Game-by-Game Guide.* Kindle edition.

———. *Cincinnati Bengals 1970: A Game-by-Game Guide.* Kindle edition.

———. *Dallas Cowboys 1970: A Game-by-Game Guide.* Kindle edition.

———. *Detroit Lions 1970: A Game-by-Game Guide.* Kindle edition.

———. *Oakland Raiders 1970: A Game-by-Game Guide.* Kindle edition.

———. *San Francisco 49ers 1970: A Game-by-Game Guide.* Kindle edition.

Schramm, Tex. *How It Happened.* Sports Illustrated. June 20, 1966, at https://www.si.com/vault/1966/06/20/608557/heres-how-it-happened.

Schultz,Brad. *The NFL, Year One, The 1970 Season and the Dawn of Modern Football.* Potomac Books. Virginia (Copyright, 2013).

Season 1970. Pro Football Reference, at https://www.pro-football-reference.com/years/1970/index.htm

Seifert, Kevin. *Best Lions Team Ever: 1970.* ESPN, at http://www.espn.com/blog/nfcnorth/post/_/id/13324/best-lions-team-ever-1970.

Shrake, Edwin. *After Foss, A Hotter War.* Sports Illustrated. April 18, 1996, at https://www.si.com/vault/1966/04/18/614489/after-foss-a-hotter-pro-war.

Shuck, Barry. *When Al Davis Tried to Sabotage The NFL.* SB Nation, at https://www.bigblueview.com/2017/12/2/16721994/when-al-davis-tried-to-sabotage-the-nfl.

Silverman, Steve. *Vince Lombardi Felt Intense Heat in Super Bowl I.* CBS. January 25, 2017, at https://newyork.cbslocal.com/2017/01/25/lombardi-pressure-super-bowl-i/.

Smith, Brandon J. "Football Origins, Growth, and History of the Game." The People History, at http://www.thepeoplehistory.com/footballhistory.html, accessed on September 17, 2018.

Stateside Staff, "The Year Detroit Became 'The City Of Champions,'" Michigan Radio at http://www.michiganradio.org/post/year-detroit-became-city-champions, accessed on November 6, 2018.

Strasen, Marty with White, Danny. *Cowboys Chronicles, A Complete History of the Dallas Cowboys.* Triumph Books, Chicago, Illinois (Copyright 2010).

Strother, Shelby. *It came with a Guarantee," The Super Bowl: Celebrating a Quarter-Century of America's Greatest Game.* Simon and Schuster. New York (Copyright, 1990).

Super Bowl IV, Hank Stram, NFL FILMS, NFL - 1970 - NFL Film - Super Bowl IV Memories - Chiefs VS Vikings - Coach Stram's Miked On Sideline, at https://www.youtube.com/watch?v=Jd0EMw7YMWI.

Super Bowl IV, Super Bowl I-X Collector's Set. NFL Productions, LLC. 2003.

The Chancellor of Football. *Super Bowl V Champion 1970 Baltimore Colts.* Taylor Blitz Times at https://taylorblitztimes.com/2014/05/18/super-bowl-v-champion-1970-baltimore-colts/.

The Dallas Morning News, January 29, 2007.

Tom Landry. Wikipedia, at https://en.wikipedia.org/wiki/Tom_Landry.

Tom Landry. Biography.com. April 2, 2014, at https://www.biography.com/people/tom-landry-9372692.

Top Ten Single Season Defense: Honorable Mention, at https://taylorblitztimes.com/tag/1968-baltimore-colts/.

Underwood, John. *The Blood and Thunder Boys.* Sports Illustrated. August 7, 1972.

———. *Two That Were Super.* Sports Illustrated. January 10, 1972.

Vaccaro, Mike. "*Monday Night Football* debut 50 years ago began a a television revolution" *New York Post,* September 21, 2020, https://nypost.com/2020/09/21/monday-night-football-debut-50-years-ago-began-a-tv-revolution/.

Wallace, William N. *49ers Rated Over Cowboys.* New York Times. January 3, 1971, at https://www.nytimes.com/1971/01/03/archives/49ers-rated-over-cowboys-brodie-key-man.html.

Weiner, Evan. Super Bowl XLV, *Vince Lombardi Wanted No Part Of The Super Bowl.* February 3, 2011, at http://thesportdigest.com/2011/02/super-bowl-xlv-vince-lombardi-wanted-no-part-of-the-super-bowl/.

Werner, Barry. "In 1970, Lions-Cowboys produced one of the rarest results in NFL History." December 16, 2016, at https://www.foxsports.com/nfl/story/1970-lions-cowboys-produced-one-rarest-results-nfl-history-122216.

Yowell, Keith. "1970: Big Plays Lift Raiders Over Dolphins in AFC Divisional Playoff Game." December 27, 2015, at https://fs64sports.blogspot.com/2015/12/1970-big-plays-lift-raiders-over.html.

———. "1971: Cowboys Beat 49ers For The NFC Championship." This Date In Football. Published on January 3, 2013, at https://fs64sports.blogspot.com/2013/01/1971-cowboys-beat-49ers-for-nfc.html.

Zagorski, Joe. *The NFL in the 1970s* McFarland & Company, Inc., Publishers. Kindle edition (2016).

INDEX

A

Accorsi, Ernie, 254, 278
Adams, Bud, 25–28, 46, 65
Adderley, Herb, 73, 151, 245, 260, 269
AFL-NFL, 1, 41, 44, 69, 71–72, 74–75, 78–81, 83, 92, 122, 139, 251
Agnew, Spiro, 264
Akron Pros, 11
Alabama, 38, 43–44, 203, 289
Alabama, University of, 43
Albert, Frankie, 19
All-American Football Conference ("AAFC"), 18–21, 23, 89
Allegheny Athletic Association, 9
Allen, Dennis, 215
Allen, Ermal, 100, 252–53, 258
Ameche, Alan, 91
Ameche, Don, 19 152, 246
American Biltrite, 262
American Broadcasting Company ("ABC"), 3–4, 30–31, 44–45, 107, 111–14, 125, 128, 130, 142, 292
American Football Conference ("AFC"), 1–3, 72, 79, 84, 94, 107, 111, 120, 122, 124, 127–30, 132, 135, 146, 166, 171, 173, 180, 185–88, 193–94, 197–98, 206–7, 209, 212–214, 216, 218, 220, 222, 224, 227, 232–33, 236, 239–40, 250–51, 255–56, 272, 283, 291, 299–302
American Football League ("AFL"), 1–3, 17–18, 24, 26–59, 61–70, 72, 74–77, 79–87, 90, 92–94, 96, 101, 103, 106–8, 111–12, 125, 127, 129, 133–34, 136, 173, 176, 181, 186, 188–90, 192–93, 207, 215, 219, 221, 232, 237, 249–51, 260
American Professionl Football Association ("APFA"), 11
Anderson, Donny, 78

Anderson, Ken, 301
Andrews, Billy, 114, 128
Andrie, George, 100, 153, 227, 270
Arledge, Roone, 113
Arrington, Rick, 184
Astrodome, 177
Astro-Turf, 263
Atkinson, George, 237
Atlanta, 48–49, 67, 81, 101, 107–8, 122–23, 156, 188, 202, 204, 206
Atlanta Falcons, 67, 122–23, 156, 188, 202, 204–5
Augustana College, 301
Austin, Bill, 204

B

Bakken, Jim, 155
Baltimore, 1–4, 19–22, 38, 55, 70, 72–73, 80–82, 89–91, 93–95, 97, 107–8, 118, 122, 127, 130, 139, 142, 148, 170–83, 185–87, 189, 194, 198, 214, 216, 224–26, 236–41, 246–47, 250–52, 254–56, 264, 266–68, 270–76, 281–83, 285, 290, 294, 299
Baltimore Colts, 1–4, 22, 38, 70, 72–73, 80–84, 89–95, 97, 107, 118, 122–23, 127, 138–40, 142, 147–48, 167, 170–89, 194, 198, 214, 216, 224–27, 236–42, 246–49, 251–57, 261, 263–64, 266–78, 280–84, 287–90, 294, 298–99
Baltimore Orioles, 89, 178, 237, 290
Banaszak, Pete, 79, 234
Banaszek, Cas, 203
Barney, Lem, 196–97, 229, 302
Bartle, Harold Roe, 102
Baugh, Sammy, 16–17, 308
Bearcats, University of Cincinnati, 173
Beasley, "Big" John, 198
Belden, Bob, 154

Bell, Bert, 14, 23, 25–28, 31, 111, 298
Bell, Bobby, 37
Belmont Stakes, The, 89
Bengtson, Phil, 181
Bergey, Bill, 208
Berkeley, 117, 120
Berry, Raymond, 90–91
Berry, Royce, 211
Bert Bell Award, 111, 298
Berwanger, Jay, 14
Beverly Hilton Hotel, 46
Bidwill, Charles, 25
Bidwill, Stormy, 60
Biletnikoff, Fred, 215, 220, 233–35, 239
Birmingham, Alabama, 33
Blackout Home Games, 23, 128, 165, 264
Blanda, George, 36, 110–11, 118, 130, 134, 214–16, 218–21, 233–35, 239–40
Blooper Bowl, The, 266
Blount, Mel, 300
Blue, Forrest, 73, 203, 302
Blunder Bowl, 1, 266, 280–82
Boston, 7, 16, 18, 28, 32–33, 35, 42, 49, 66, 70, 72, 107–8, 133, 161, 176–77, 187, 193, 202, 213–14
Boston College, 33, 301
Boston Red Sox, 33
Boston University, 32–33
Bowman, Ken, 70
Boyd, Bobby, 75, 257
Boyer, Bill, 26
Braase, Ordell, 83, 93
Bradshaw, Terry, 210, 218, 300
Brandt, Gil, 52
Brees, Drew, 118
Brian's Song, 109
Briscoe, Marlin, 184
Brocklin, Norm Van, 81
Brodie, John, 55, 65–66, 122, 136, 202–6, 222, 230–31, 242–44, 246
Bronx, The (Borough of NYC), 22, 159

Brooklyn (Borough of NYC), 16, 18–21, 50
Brooklyn Dodgers, 21, 113
Brooklyn Horsemen, The, 18–19
Brown, Bill, 198, 200
Brown, Paul, 19, 36–37, 42, 70, 125–26, 132, 186, 209–14, 224–26, 254, 301–2
Brown, Willie, 217, 221, 234, 237, 241
Bryant, Anita, 271
Bryant, Bobby, 200
Bryant, Paul "Bear," 38, 44, 289
Buchanan, Buck, 37
Buck, Jack, 113
Bucknell University, 275
Budde, Ed, 37
Buffalo, 11, 20, 28, 32, 34–35, 42, 52–55, 59, 70, 72, 107–9, 123, 181–82, 184–85, 187–88, 191–92, 211, 215, 293
Buffalo Bills, 28, 32, 35, 42, 52, 70, 72, 109, 123, 181–82, 184–85, 187–88, 192, 207, 211, 215, 293, 299
Bulaich, Norm, 171, 174–75, 185, 226, 238–39, 241, 252, 256, 270, 274, 276, 278
Buoniconti, Nick, 42, 70, 191, 193
Burk, Adrian, 118
Busch Memorial Stadium, 154
Butkus, Dick, 44
Butler, Cannonball, 156

C
California, 56, 74, 79, 93, 116, 117, 120, 206, 217
California, University of, 117, 120
Camp, Walter, 8
Canadian Football League, 7, 116–117, 119
Candlestick Park, 203, 242
Cannon, Billy, 29, 44
Cannonball Butler, 156
Canton, Ohio, 11
Canton Bulldogs, 11
Capitol Division, The, 104, 108
Cappelletti, Gino, 176
Card-Pitt ("Carpets"), 15
Carlisle School, The, 11
Carothers, Hamilton, 56

Carpenter, Ron, 208
Carter, Virgil, 207, 209, 211–13, 224–26
Case, Harold, 33
Casper, Dave, 299
Cassidy, Butch, 192
Celler, Emmanuel, 63–64
Central Broadcasting Station ("CBS"), 3, 21, 23, 30, 44–45, 76, 78, 106, 112–13, 228, 292
Century Division, The, 108
Cheeseheads, 163
Chester, Raymond, 215–16, 218, 233–34, 240
Chicago, 11–15, 17–18, 23, 25, 39, 44, 76, 97, 107–9, 155, 183, 188, 199, 201–2, 206
Chicago Bears, 12–14, 17–18, 23, 25, 36, 39, 44, 76, 97, 176, 183, 188, 195, 197, 199–201, 206–7, 298
Chicago Cardinals, 11–12, 15, 21, 25–26
Cincinnati, 3, 36, 67, 70, 107, 109, 125–26, 131–32, 166, 173, 186–87, 207–14, 216, 224–26, 236, 249, 255, 301–2, 304
Cincinnati, University of, 173
Cincinnati Bengals, 67, 70, 125–26, 131–32, 166, 186–87, 197, 207–14, 216, 224–26, 301–2, 304, 306, 308
Clark, Mike, 153–154, 160, 163, 166, 227, 244, 267–68, 279
Clark, Monte, 192
Clarke, Frank, 101
Clemson University, 250
Cleveland, 2, 11, 18–21, 36, 53, 66, 72–73, 80–81, 83, 91–92, 94, 103–5, 107–8, 113, 118, 124–28, 135, 149, 152, 165–66, 187, 190, 194, 209–10, 212–14, 219, 252, 258, 264, 283
Cleveland Browns, 2, 20, 36, 42, 53, 66, 72–73, 80–81, 84, 91–92, 94, 103–5, 113–14, 118, 124–28, 135, 149–50, 165–66, 187, 194, 197, 204, 209–14, 219, 225, 257
Cleveland Indians, 11, 126
Cleveland Panthers, 18
Cline, Tony, 234

Coastal Division, The, 92, 94, 108, 170
Collier, Blanton, 124, 209
Collins, John, 33
Columbia University, 8
Columbus Panhandles, 11
Coogan's Hollow, 34
Cook, Greg, 207, 211, 214
Cornish, Frank, 182
Cosell, Howard, 113–14, 142, 253
Cotton Bowl, The, 33, 40, 78, 101, 103, 105, 122, 156, 158, 161–64, 166, 227
Covington & Burling, 56
Cox, Fred, 200, 202
Cox Broadcasting Corp., 49
Crabtree, Eric, 212
Crosby, Bing, 19
Csonka, Larry, 189–93, 233, 236, 295
Cuban Cigar, 288
Culp, Curley, 37
Culver Military Academy, 24
Cuozzo, Gary, 86, 91, 156–57, 198, 200–2, 231
Curry, Bill, 93, 251, 255, 280
Curtis, Mike, 83, 171, 180, 241, 276–77, 283, 285–86
Czechoslovakia, 15

D
Dallas, 1–4, 24–28, 31, 33, 37, 41, 43, 52, 54–55, 57–58, 60–64, 70, 72–73, 76, 78, 90, 95–98, 100–5, 107–9, 113, 121–22, 127, 137, 141, 145–46, 149–50, 152–58, 160–68, 188, 198, 200, 202–4, 224, 227–29, 231–32, 242–47, 249–52, 257–60, 262, 264, 266–72, 274–79, 281–82, 285, 288, 294–95, 298, 300, 302
Dallas Cowboys, 1–4, 31, 33, 43, 52, 54, 58, 61, 64, 70, 73–74, 76, 78, 90, 95–98, 100–5, 113, 121–22, 127, 137, 141, 145–47, 149–69, 188, 192, 198, 200, 202–4, 224, 227–29, 231, 242–47, 249–54, 257–59, 261–64, 266–77, 279–83, 285, 288–89, 298–300

Dallas Cowboys Cheerleaders, The, 97
Dallas–Fort Worth, 101
Dallas Rangers, 97
Dallas Steers, 97
Dallas Texans, 26–27, 33, 36–37, 41, 43, 72, 90, 96, 101
Daniels, Clem, 79
Davidson, Ben, 130, 218
Davidson, Cotton, 36
Davis, Al, 37, 41, 50–52, 54, 57, 64–67, 69, 134, 215, 223, 237, 238
Davis, Henry, 121
Davis, Willie, 73, 100
Dawson, Len, 36–37, 42, 72, 85–87, 130, 158, 175, 210, 218, 222
Dayton Triangles, 11
Decatur Staleys, 11–12
Dempsey, Tom, 115–16, 144, 197–98, 205
Denver, 25, 27, 32–33, 35, 37, 39, 107, 109, 188, 205, 213–14, 217, 220
Denver Broncos, 32–33, 39, 188, 205, 213, 217, 220
De Rogatis, Al, 263
Detroit, 12, 14, 85, 107–8, 112, 115, 120, 123, 144, 169, 187, 194–96, 200–1, 206, 220–21, 224, 227–29, 243, 252, 302
Detroit Heralds, 12
Detroit Lions, 14, 112, 115, 123–24, 144, 149, 169, 187–88, 192, 194–98, 200–1, 206, 209, 221, 227–29, 243, 302
Detroit Red Wings, 195
Detroit Tigers, 195, 221
Dickey, Glenn, 50
Ditka, Mike, 155
Dixon, Hewritt, 80, 215, 217, 219, 233
Dobbs, Glenn, 19
Donovan, Artie, 90
Doomsday Defense, 104, 153–54, 158, 163, 165, 229, 243, 252, 262, 267–68, 270, 273
Dorrow, Al 36
Dowler, Boyd, 75
DuMont Television Network, 22, 111–112

E
Eaton, Scott, 121
Edwards, "Big" Bill, 17–18
Edwards, Dave, 165, 244
El Dorado, Arkansas, 24
Eller, Carl, 84, 199
Ellison, Willie, 206
Enis, Bill, 263
Ewbank, Wilbur Charles "Weeb," 38, 80–81, 90–91, 170

F
Farr, Mel, 197
Faulkner, Jack, 37
Fenway Park, 33–34
Fernandez, Manny, 193
Fette, Jack, 272–73
Field-Goal, 235, 238, 257, 297
Flanagan, Ed, 197
Fleming, Marv, 190
Florida, 1, 170, 247, 249, 263
Foles, Nick, 118
Foley, Tim, 190, 193
Forte, Chet, 113
Foss, Joe, 30–31, 43, 46–50, 53, 57, 309
Franklin Field, 152
Friedman, Benny, 12

G
Gabriel, Roman, 55, 65–66
Gamber, Hugh, 272
Gardin, Ron, 171, 174, 180, 267
Garland, Boots, 100
Garrett, Carl, 176
Garrett, Mike, 85, 87, 130
Garrison, Gary, 174
Garrison, Walt, 150–51, 153–54, 164, 174, 227, 244–45, 251–52, 262, 276, 289
Gaubatz, Dennis, 93
Gehrig, Mrs. Lou, 19
Georgetown University, 109–10
Georgetown University Hospital, 109–10
Gerela, Roy, 177
Gibbs, Joe, 37
Gifford, Frank, 78, 113, 193
Gillman, Sid, 37, 173, 300
Ginn, Hubert, 190
Gogolak, Pete, 53–55, 59–60, 67, 160
Goode, Tom, 274, 278–79

Gossett, Bruce, 203–5, 230, 243, 245
Gowdy, Curt, 113, 263
Grabowski, Jim, 78, 181
Graham, Otto, 19
Grambling State University, 40
Grange, Harold "Red," 12, 17–18
Grant, Bob, 178
Grant, Bud, 38, 86, 129, 139, 157, 198–200, 232, 299–300
Grantham, Larry, 38
Great Lakes Naval Center, The, 19
Green, Cornell, 151, 260, 269, 275
Green Bay, 70, 72–75, 77–80, 84, 92, 98–99, 103–5, 107–8, 112, 123–24, 164, 168, 180–81, 188, 197, 199, 206, 242, 252, 257, 260, 286
Green Bay Packers, 17, 23, 70, 72–80, 92, 98–99, 103–4, 110, 112, 162–64, 180–82, 188, 196, 198–99, 201, 209, 236, 242, 251, 257, 260, 295
Greene, "Mean" Joe, 293, 300
Gregg, Forrest, 73, 302
Grey Cup, The, 119
Gridiron, 8
Griese, Bob, 143, 182–83, 189, 193, 233–36
Grim, Bob, 198
Guthrie, Grant, 182

H
Hadl, John, 174, 216
Halas, George, 13, 28, 36, 39, 76, 97
Halas, Mugs, 60, 76, 97
Hall of Fame, 22, 37–38, 77, 90, 125, 151, 191, 196, 198–99, 229, 232, 300
Ham, Jack, 300
Hammond Pros, 11
Hanratty, Terry, 210
Hargett, Edd, 205
Harris, Cliff, 151, 154, 156, 158, 267
Harris, Franco, 300
Hart, Jim, 121
Hart, Phil, 63–64
Harvard Stadium, 176
Harvard University, 8, 33

Hash Marks, 13, 295
Havrilak, Sam, 275
Hawkins, Ben, 153, 159
Hayes, "Bullet" Bob, 100, 103, 151, 153–54, 158–60, 165–66, 168, 244, 258–60, 267, 276
Heatherton, Joey, 165
Heffelfinger, William "Pudge," 9
Heidi Game, The, 221
Heisman Trophy, 14, 29, 44, 102
Henderson, John, 85, 198
Hendricks, Ted, 171, 185
Hererra, Efren, 100
Hershey, Pennsylvania, 90
Hertz Rental Car Company, 293
Hill, Calvin, 105, 150, 152–55, 157–58, 251, 259, 262
Hill, Jerry, 181, 183
Hill, Winston, 93
Hill School, The, 24
Hilton, Barron, 27–28, 53, 58, 276
Hilton, Roy, 276
Hinton, Eddie, 171, 176, 182, 184, 239, 256, 268–70, 275, 277
Holmes, Robert, 175
Homan, Dennis, 259
Hope, Bob, 19
Hopkins, Roy, 177
Hopkins School, The , 8
Horn, Don, 181–82
Hornung, Paul, 73, 77–78, 193
Houston, 3, 25–27, 29, 34, 36, 53, 55, 57, 79, 96, 107–8, 138, 161, 166, 168, 177, 188, 213
Houston Oilers, 27, 29, 34, 36, 43, 65, 79, 84, 166–68, 177, 188, 206, 209, 213
Howard, Chuck, 113
Howley, Chuck, 146, 250, 266, 271, 274, 279, 287
Howsam, Bob, 25–26, 47
Hubbard, Marv, 215, 234–35
Hubbard, Mike, 222
Huff, Sam, 98
Hughes, Howard, 112
Hunt, L. H., 33
Hunt, Lamar, 24–29, 33, 37, 39–41, 43, 46, 58, 61, 63–66, 70–71, 90, 96, 101, 133
Hutson, Don, 17

I

Indianapolis, 61, 98, 172, 299
Irsay, Robert, 172, 299
Isenbarger, John, 205

J

Jackson, Keith, 113, 128, 142
Jackson State University, 196
Jeannette Athletic Club, 9
Jefferson, Roy, 171, 175, 177, 183, 239, 256, 270
Jeppesen Stadium, 34
Jim Thorpe Trophy, The, 203
Johnson, Charley, 177
Johnson, Curtis, 190, 193
Johnson, Jim, 203
Johnson, Ron, 121, 154, 160
Jones, Bert, 172, 299
Jones, Clint, 201
Jones, Ed, 100
Jones, Homer, 114, 128
Jordan, Henry, 73
Jordan, Lee Roy, 155, 163, 167–68, 244, 259, 268, 287, 289
Jurgensen, Sonny, 66, 210, 217

K

Kalsu, Bob, 109
Kanicki, Jim, 121
Kansas City, 26, 37, 40, 43, 57, 64, 68, 70, 72, 74, 76–77, 83–87, 102, 107, 109, 118, 122, 128–30, 139, 157–58, 171, 174–75, 188, 199, 210, 214, 218–21, 224
Kansas City Chiefs, 26, 37–38, 40, 64, 68, 70, 72, 74–77, 83–85, 87–88, 102, 118–19, 122, 128–30, 139, 157–59, 162, 174–76, 188, 199, 210, 218–19, 221–22, 230, 232, 251, 307, 309
Kapp, Joe, 84, 86, 116–20, 138, 177, 179, 198, 202
Karras, Alex, 100, 196, 197
Kassulke, Karl, 87, 199
Keating, Tom, 234
Kemp, Jack, 36
Kennedy, John F., 40, 102
Kent State University, 170
Kentucky Derby, The, 89
Kezar Stadium, 34, 56, 203, 205–6, 242–43

Kiick, Jim, 189–90, 192–93, 233–36, 263, 295
Kilmer, Billy, 205
Kiner, Steve, 253
King, Jr., Martin Luther, 39, 44
Klosterman, Don, 254
Knight, Curt, 210
Kolen, Mike, 190, 193
Kramer, Jerry, 73
Krause, Paul, 85, 199, 230
Kuechenberg, Bob, 193

L

Lake Erie, 126
Lambeau Field, 78
Lambert, Jack, 300
Lamonica, Daryle, 79, 111, 136, 214–15, 217–22, 233–35, 238–39
Landry, Tom, 37, 73, 97–100, 102, 104, 137, 145, 149–59, 162–64, 167–69, 197, 202–4, 206, 221, 227–229, 242–43, 245–46, 250–52, 258–62, 271–73, 277, 285–86, 290, 294–95, 298
Lane, MacArthur, 121–22
Langer, Jim, 191, 193
Lanier, Willie, 37
Larsen, Gary, 84, 199
Lassie, 174, 257, 284
Latrobe YMCA, 9
LeBaron, Eddie, 101
Lebeau, Dick, 196–97
Lee, Bob, 201–2
Lee, David, 276, 289
LeVias, Jerry, 177
Lilly, Bob, 156, 167, 169, 282–83, 288
Liscio, Tony, 158
Livingston, Dale, 163, 181
Lockhart, Spider, 121
Logan, Jerry, 171, 178–79, 181, 184, 267, 272, 277, 285
Lomardi, Marie, 110
Lombardi, Vince, 59–60, 72–78, 80, 86, 98, 105, 109–110, 146, 152, 196, 251, 260, 281, 294
Longo, Tom, 121
Looney, Don, 17
Los Angeles, 18–19, 22–23, 27, 29, 31, 33, 46, 53, 55, 65, 70, 91–92, 107–9, 113, 121–23,

165, 172, 188, 200, 203, 205, 206, 222, 248, 283, 299
Los Angeles Chargers, 33, 37, 53
Los Angeles Dons, 23
Los Angeles Memorial Coliseum, 33
Los Angeles Rams, 22–23, 29, 31, 33, 55, 65, 70, 91–92, 121–24, 165–66, 172, 176, 188, 198, 200, 205–6, 222, 224, 299
Los Angeles West Coast Wildcats, 18
Louisiana State University ("LSU"), 29
Luckman, Sid, 118
Lurtsema, Bob, 121

M

Mackey, John, 91, 93, 182-84, 239, 248, 268, 269, 275, 285, 287
Madden, John, 69, 135, 194, 208, 215, 216, 218, 219, 222, 232, 236, 241, 294, 301
Maitland, Jack, 171, 177, 178
Manders, Dave, 99, 272, 273
Mandich, Jim, 190, 192, 193
Manning, Peyton, 118
Mara, Wellington, 54, 55, 58, 59, 76
Marchetti, Gino, 90, 91
Marchibroda, Ted, 172
Marshall, George Preston, 40, 96
Marshall, Jim, 84, 85, 199
Maryland, 89, 264
Massachusetts, 176
Massillon Tigers, 11
Matte, Tom, 91, 171, 174, 179, 193, 256
Maule, Tex, 281
May, Ray, 225, 272
Mayflower Trucks, 172
MCA, Inc., 49
McCafferty, Don, 94, 140, 170–71, 174–76, 185–86, 226, 237, 240–41, 254–55, 271, 274, 277–78, 283–84, 290, 294
McCloughan, Kent, 219
McCluen, Kent, 217
McCullouch, Earl, 197, 228
McGah, Ed, 69
McGill vs. Harvard, 8

McGraw, John, 11
McMillan, Ernie, 122
McNeil, Clifton, 160
Memorial Stadium, 118, 174–75, 179, 183, 226, 237–39, 293
Mercein, Chuck, 78
Mercer, Mike, 174
Meredith, "Dandy" Don, 96–97, 101–5, 113, 142, 161
Methodist University Mustangs, 33
Miami, 1, 3, 20, 37, 42, 49, 52, 65, 67, 79, 89, 94–95, 101, 107–8, 125, 140, 143, 152, 170, 172, 179–80, 182–83, 187–90, 192–94, 216, 222–23, 232–35, 237, 241–42, 246–47, 250–51, 254–55, 263–65, 291, 295, 299, 300
Miami, University of, 37
Miami Dolphins, 42, 52, 67, 94, 120, 125, 140, 143, 170, 172, 179–80, 182–183, 187–194, 197, 216–17, 222–23, 227, 232–36, 254, 257, 263, 299–301
Miami Seahawks, 20, 89
Michaels, Walt, 257
Miller, Marvin, 109
Milwaukee, 180
Minneapolis, 27–28, 201
Minneapolis-Saint Paul, 27
Minnesota, 25, 28, 40, 83–87, 91, 101, 107–8, 116, 118–20, 123, 129–30, 139, 156–58, 165, 168, 174, 177, 179, 187–88, 191–92, 197–202, 207, 229–32, 262, 298–99, 302
Minnesota Lakers, 25
Minnesota Vikings, 28, 38, 83–87, 91, 101, 116–19, 123, 129, 139, 156–58, 165, 174–75, 179, 187–88, 191–92, 197–202, 207, 229–32, 238, 242, 295, 298–300
Missouri State College, 271
Mitchell, Lydell, 172
Mitchell, Tom, 271
Modell, Art, 36, 42, 53, 55, 59–60, 124, 126–28, 209
Monday Night Football, 3–5, 107, 111–15, 122–23, 125–28,

130, 135, 142, 161, 167, 174, 181, 200, 210, 217, 292
Montgomery, Arthur, 49
Moore, Lenny, 90
Morabito, Tony, 60
Morrall, Earl, 81–83, 93, 138, 140, 171–72, 175–76, 180, 185, 193, 236, 248, 255, 270–71, 274–75, 278, 283–84, 289, 299
Morris, Mercury ,189–90, 193, 233–36, 263, 295
Morton, Craig, 105, 141, 150, 155–64, 166, 168, 227, 243–45, 249–50, 253, 261–62, 267, 270, 272–73, 276–77, 282, 285–86, 298
Moseley, Mark, 153, 184
Most Valuable Player ("MVP"), 38, 82–83, 86, 91, 122, 146, 203, 230, 243, 279–80, 287
Muhlmann, Horst, 208
Muncie Flyers, 11
Municipal Stadium, 102, 125–26, 128, 157, 165, 209–10
Munson, Bill, 197, 227–28
Murchinson, Jr., Clint, 57, 61, 95–96
Myers, Chip, 208
Myers, Jim, 252, 258

N

Nagurski, Bronko, 14, 191
Namath, Joe, 38, 43–45, 80–83, 93, 114, 123, 125, 128, 135, 178, 185, 201, 249, 251, 257
Nance, Jim, 176
National Broadcasting Company ("NBC"), 3, 21–22, 31, 44–45, 47–49, 67, 76, 106, 112–13, 263–64, 289, 292
National Football Conference ("NFC"), 1–3, 73, 94, 106–7, 120–23, 136, 144–46, 149, 155, 158–60, 162, 164, 166, 168, 187–88, 194, 197–98, 201–2, 205–6, 223–24, 227, 229, 231, 242–43, 246, 250, 257, 262, 291, 298, 300
National Football League ("NFL"), 1–5, 7, 9, 12–18, 20–21, 23–29, 31–50, 52–57, 59, 61–67, 69, 70, 72–74, 76–77, 79–84, 86–89, 91–95,

97–100, 103–9, 111–12, 114, 116–18, 120–21, 126, 129, 133–34, 139, 149–52, 154, 156, 161–63, 165, 170–74, 176, 179, 183, 185–87, 189–90, 192–97, 199, 202–3, 208–9, 211, 215, 217, 224–25, 227, 230, 236–37, 242–43, 250–51, 253, 256–58, 260, 262, 269, 280–83, 286, 289, 293, 295–97, 299–302

Naumoff, Paul, 197

Navy, 102, 262

Neely, Ralph, 99

Nelsen, Bill, 125, 219

Newark Bears, 18

New England, 33–35, 119, 194

New England ("Originally Boston") Patriots, 28, 32–35, 42, 49, 66, 70, 72, 119, 176–77, 179, 187, 194, 202, 213–14, 301

New Jersey, 192

Newman, Jack, 86–87

New Mexico, 96

New Orleans, 67, 70, 107–8, 115, 122–23, 129, 188, 197–99, 205–6, 213, 264–65

New Orleans Saints, 67, 70, 108, 115, 122–23, 144, 188, 198, 205–206, 213

New York, 4, 11, 14, 17–19, 21–23, 27, 33–35, 37–38, 42–44, 48, 50, 53, 55–56, 58–64, 72–73, 76, 79–84, 89, 90, 92, 101, 107–8, 113, 118–21, 123, 125, 127, 138, 147, 149, 153–54, 159, 164, 166, 167, 170, 172–73, 178, 185, 187–88, 194–95, 201, 221–22, 254, 289–90

New York Giants, 11, 14, 17, 22–23, 33–34, 37–38, 42–43, 53–56, 65, 69, 72–73, 76, 90, 98, 101, 107–8, 120–21, 123, 149, 153–54, 159–60, 162, 164, 166, 172, 188, 194–95, 203, 222, 261

New York Jets, 4, 38, 42–44, 48, 53, 56, 58, 79–84, 90, 92–93, 107, 113, 118, 123, 125, 127, 128, 138, 142, 170, 173, 178–79, 185–87, 201,

221, 225, 236, 247–49, 251, 254–55, 264, 270, 280

New York Titans, 27, 34, 38, 42, 81

New York Yankees, 16, 18, 20, 89

NFL Films, 71, 86–87, 114–15, 129, 192, 269, 293

NFL Strike, 109

Nielsen Ratings, The, 114

Niland, John, 151, 272, 288

Ninowski, Jim, 66

Nitschke, Ray, 73

Nixon, Richard, 110, 264, 290

Nolan, Dick, 145, 202–4, 243, 246

Noll, Chuck, 37, 92, 212, 300

Noonan, Karl, 183

Norman, Pettis, 168, 250

Nowatzke, Tom, 171, 184, 252, 270–71, 274, 276

Nye, Blaine, 167, 267

O

Oakland, 28, 34–35, 37, 42, 50, 53, 55–56, 58, 69, 79–80, 84, 107, 109–11, 124, 129–30, 135, 187–88, 194, 198, 206, 208, 214–23, 232–36, 238–40, 255, 294, 299, 301

Oakland Alameda County Coliseum, 233

Oakland Raiders, 34–35, 37, 42, 50, 53, 56, 58, 65, 69, 79–80, 84, 110–11, 124, 129–30, 134–36, 187–188, 194, 198, 206, 208, 214–23, 227, 232–41, 294–95, 299, 301

Oates, Bob, 283

Ohio, 8, 10–11, 19, 36, 38, 125, 128, 195, 209, 213

Ohio State University, 38

Oklahoma, 25, 262

Olympics, 103, 258

Oneida Football Club, 7

Orange Bowl, The, 1, 79, 83, 182, 216–217, 250, 262–64

Oregon, 269

Orr, Jimmy, 256

Osborn, Dave, 86, 198, 201

Otto, Gus, 235

Otto, Jim, 34–35, 235

Owen, Steve, 261

O'Brien, Jim, 147–148, 173–74, 177–78, 181–82, 184–85,

238–39, 257, 273, 276, 278–79, 281, 284, 290

P

Pacoima, Los Angeles, 117

Page, Alan, 84, 91, 199

Palm Springs, California, 93

Palo Alto, 56

Parilli, Babe, 36, 82

Parks, Dave, 205

Parrish, Lemar, 208, 211, 213

Pastorini, Dan, 301

Pate, Lloyd, 184

Paulson, Dainard, 38

Peale, Norman Vincent, 291

Pecan Bowl, The, 165

Pennsylvania, 9–10, 15, 24, 90

Percival, Mac, 183

Perkins, Don, 96–97, 101, 104–5, 150

Perkins, Ray, 181, 185, 240

Perkins, Steve, 252–53

Perry, Ross, 209

Philadelphia, 3, 14–15, 17–18, 21, 72, 107–8, 152–53, 158–59, 162, 188, 192, 194, 301

Philadelphia Eagles, 14–15, 17, 21, 72, 152–53, 158–59, 162, 183–84, 188, 194, 301

Philadelphia Quakers, 18

Phillips, Jess, 208

Phillips, Mel, 244

Phil-Pitt Steeler-Eagles ("Steagles"), 15

Phipps, Mike, 125

Piccolo, Brian, 109

Pittman, Ralph, 63–64

Pitts, Elijah, 77

Pitts, Frank, 88, 175

Pitts, John, 192

Pittsburgh, 2–3, 9, 14–15, 37, 92, 94, 101, 103, 107–8, 111, 121, 126, 171, 188, 210, 212–14, 218, 232, 264, 293, 300

Pittsburgh Pirates, 14

Pittsburgh Steelers, 2, 14–15, 92, 94, 101, 107, 111, 126, 188, 210, 212, 218, 264, 293, 300

Plunkett, Jim, 301

Poland, 15

Polo Grounds, 34

Poly-Turf, 1, 262–263

Portsmouth Spartans, 13–14, 195

Preakness Stakes, The, 60, 89
Princeton University, 7–8, 18
Pugh, Jethro, 100, 227, 259, 271, 275
Purple People Eaters, 84, 156, 198–200, 307
Pyle, C.C., 17, 18

Q

Queens (Borough of NYC), 34, 221

R

Radio Nord, 95
Randolph, Al, 203
Randolph, Jay, 263
Rauch, John, 79, 211, 215
Ray, Bill, 74, 181, 185, 225, 240–41, 251, 257, 267, 272–73, 279, 282, 284, 288
Ray, David, 206
Reeves, Dan, 55, 59, 70, 104, 258, 270, 277, 286–87
Reid, Mike, 208
Reinsch, Leonard, 49
Renfro, Mel, 102, 151, 158, 160, 168, 228–29, 244, 259–60, 268–70, 274–75, 288
Rentzel, Lance, 151, 153–54, 159, 164–66
RFK Stadium, 162, 210
Rhode Island, 35
Rhodes, Willard, 27
Rice University, 34
Richardson, Gloster, 175
Richardson, Willie, 93, 190, 235
Riddell Sporting Goods, 14
Riverfront Stadium, 3, 126, 131, 210, 212–13
Robbie, Joe, 189
Robinson, Brooks, 178
Robinson, Dave, 73, 214
Robinson, Johnny, 37, 85, 175
Robinson, Paul, 207–8, 214
Robustelli, Andy, 100
Rochester, 11, 119
Rochester Jeffersons, 11
Rock Island Independents, 11, 18
Rock-pile, The, 32
Rooneys, The, 60
Roosevelt Administration, The, 32
Rosenbloom, Carroll, 55, 59–60, 70, 94, 172, 180, 238, 241, 255, 299

Rote, Kyle, 263
Roy, Alvin, 100
Rozelle, Pete, 23, 29, 31–32, 43–45, 48–49, 54–55, 57–59, 64–67, 70–71, 76, 94, 111–112, 115, 133, 263
Rucker, Reggie, 166, 244–45
Rutgers University, 7, 8

S

Sabol, Ed, 86, 114, 293
Sabol, Steve, 114, 293
Sack Pack, The, 299
Salinas, California, 116, 119
Sanders, Charlie, 196–197
San Diego, 37, 53, 58, 72, 107, 109, 123, 130, 173–75, 188, 191, 213–14, 216, 220, 257, 299, 302
San Diego Chargers, 53, 58, 65, 72, 123, 173, 174, 176, 188, 213, 216, 220, 299, 300
San Francisco, 20–21, 34, 53, 55–56, 58, 60, 65, 69, 107–8, 122–23, 145, 187–88, 202, 204–6, 222–23, 229–32, 242–44, 246, 252, 282, 290, 298, 302
San Francisco 49ers, 23, 53, 55–56, 60, 65, 69, 122–24, 136, 145, 149, 187–188, 198, 202–7, 222–23, 229–31, 242–46, 250–251, 290, 298–99, 302
Santa Fe, New Mexico, 116
Santos, Gil, 34
Sayers, Gayle, 109
Schachter, Norm, 78
Schenectady, New York, 21
Schmidt, Joe, 144, 195
Schmitt, John, 42
Schramm, Tex, 31, 54, 64–66, 70, 96–98, 103, 107, 133, 161, 258, 259, 264
Schuh, Harry, 234
Schultz, Brad, 74
Scott, Jake, 182–83, 190, 193, 234
Scully, Vin, 113
Seattle, 27, 67, 292
Seattle Seahawks, 27, 67
Seifert, George, 290
Seiple, Larry, 182
Septien, Rafael, 100
Sharockman, Ed, 199, 200

Shaw, Dennis, 182, 184
Sheraton-Carlton Hotel, 63
Sheraton Hotel, 63
Sherman, Allie, 121
Sherman, Rod, 215, 235
Shula, Don, 80–82, 91–94, 98, 140, 143, 152, 170–72, 179, 180, 182–83, 189–91, 193–94, 225, 232, 236, 241, 247, 254–55, 257, 290, 294, 299–301
Siemon, Jeff, 191
Simpson, O.J., 293
Sinkwich, Frankie, 19
Skoglund, H.P., 47
Skorich, Nick, 124
Smith, Billy Ray, 178, 205, 241, 251, 257, 267, 272–73, 279, 284
Smith, Bubba, 142, 171, 173, 237–39, 247, 254, 271, 273, 277, 280, 290, 294
Smith, Charlie, 215, 217, 233
Smith, Jackie, 122
Snead, Norm, 153, 159, 184
Snell, Matt, 38, 82–83, 308
Songin, Butch, 36
South Dakota, 30, 46, 119
Southeast Missouri State College, 271
Southern Methodist University ("SMU"), 37, 96
Spadia, Lou, 55–56, 58–60
Spalding Brand "J5-V.15" Football, 77
St. Louis, 3, 25, 38, 60, 102, 107–8, 113, 121–23, 149, 154–55, 157, 159–61, 164, 166–67, 169, 188, 264, 303
St. Louis Cardinals, 38, 60, 102, 113, 121–23, 149, 155, 157–58, 161–62, 167, 188, 198, 203, 259, 262
Stabler, Ken, 215, 218–19, 299
Stagg, Amos Alonzo, 99
Stalin, Josef, 15
Stallings, Larry, 122
Stallworth, John, 300
Standlee, Norm, 19
Stanfill, Bill, 233
Stanford University, 120
Stanley Cup, 195
Starr, Bart, 73, 78, 104, 116, 181–82

Star-Spangled Banner, 264
Staubach, Roger, 102, 141, 150, 152–58, 161, 168, 261–62, 282, 286, 298
Steadman, Jack, 26, 28, 40
Stenerud, Jan, 37, 85, 175
Stockholm, Sweden, 11
Stram, Hank, 37–38, 68, 86–88, 129, 210, 222
Stukes, Charlie, 267
Stupor Bowl, The, 1, 266
Sullivan, Billy, 49, 62, 66, 70, 273
Summerall, Pat, 44
Super Bowl, The, 1–4, 6, 26, 38, 40, 68, 71, 73–77, 79–86, 90, 92–94, 99, 103, 105–7, 110, 116, 118–20, 122, 127, 129, 137–39, 142, 146–52, 157, 163, 167, 169–75, 178–80, 185, 189, 191, 194, 198–99, 210, 215, 222, 225, 229–30, 232, 236–38, 240–42, 245–54, 257, 263–67, 269–73, 275, 279–82, 284–85, 288–292, 294–95, 297–302
Swann, Lynn, 300
Swift, Doug, 193

T

Tampa Bay Buccaneers, 67, 292
Tarkenton, Fran, 121, 154, 160, 231, 299
Tartan Turf, 263
Taseff, Carl, 191
Taylor, Altie, 197
Taylor, Bruce, 203, 230–31
Taylor, Charley, 210
Taylor, Jim, 36, 73, 77–78
Taylor, Lionel, 36, 39
Taylor, Otis, 37, 86, 88, 130
Taylor, Rosey, 203
TCU, 16, 240
TCU Horn Frogs, 16
Texas, 16, 24, 27, 34, 41, 73, 78, 96, 166, 206
Texas Christian University ("TCU"), 16
The Dick Cavett Show, 114
The Steel Curtain, 300
Thomas, Duane, 150–51, 158, 162, 164, 227, 243–46, 249,

251, 253, 258, 262, 270, 272–73, 277, 286, 288
Thomas, Emmitt, 37
Thorpe, Jim, 11, 203
Three Rivers Stadium, 3, 126
Thursday Night Football, 5
Tiger Stadium, 112, 200
Tingelhoff, Mick, 198
Titans-Steelers, 21, 303
Tittle, Y. A., 118
Topping, Dan, 19, 20
Tripucka, Frank, 36
Tulane Stadium, 115
Twombly, Wells, 282

U

Unitas, John, 38, 81–82, 90–91, 116, 139, 171–85, 198, 225–26, 236–41, 246, 249, 251–53, 255–56, 266, 268, 270, 274, 283–84, 286, 299
United States Naval Academy, 102, 261

V

Vietnam, 109
Volk, Rick, 171, 181, 276

W

Waller, Charlie, 173
Walsh, Bill, 246, 302
Walton, Larry, 197
Warfield, Paul, 125, 183, 190, 193, 233–236, 263
War Memorial Stadium, 32, 34, 184, 211, 293
Warwick, Hotel, The, 64
Washington, 16, 20, 22, 27, 37, 40, 56, 59, 63, 66, 96, 103, 107–8, 110, 117, 162, 164, 168, 188, 197–98, 200–1, 203–5, 210, 217, 231, 243–44, 301
Washington, University of, 27
Washington Redskins, 16, 22, 40, 66, 96, 103, 110, 162, 164, 188, 197, 201, 204, 210, 217, 301
Waters, Charlie, 151, 250, 269, 288
Webster, Alex, 121, 160, 300

Webster, Mike, 300
Webster (Television Show), 196
Wehrli, Roger, 122
Weiss, Don, 253
Welles, Orson, 33
Wells, Lloyd, 215, 218–19, 221, 239–40
Wells, Warren, 215, 218–19, 221, 239–40, 282
Werblin, Sonny, 42–44, 48–49, 53, 55, 58, 67
West, Charlie, 85
Wilcox, Dave, 203
Willard, Ken, 230–231, 243
Williams, Edward Bennett, 59
Williams, John, 171
Williams, Travis, 78
Williams, Willie, 121
Williamson, Frank, 75
Wilsmer, Max, 27
Wilson, Ben, 78
Wilson, George "Wildcat," 18
Wilson, Larry, 122, 259
Wilson, Nemiah, 217, 240
Wilson, Ralph, 42, 52–55, 62, 70
Wilson "Duke" Football, 77
Winner, Charley, 155
Winter, Max, 25–28, 47
Wisconsin, 73, 199
Wismer, Harry, 42, 46
Witcherm Dick, 230, 244
Wolfner, Violet, 25
Wolfner, Walter, 25
Wolman, Jerry, 60
Wood, Willie, 73
Work Progress Act, 32
WRGB, 21
Wright, Rayfield, 99, 151, 154
Wrigley Field, 14
Wyche, Sam, 207–9, 211, 214, 302
Wynne, Bedford, 95–96
Wyoming Cowboys, 192

Y

Yale University, 8–9
Yankee Stadium, 22, 159
Yary, Ron, 198
Yepremian, Garo, 190, 233–35
Young, Dick, 290

ABOUT THE AUTHOR

Ian Kahanowitz is a lawyer who specializes in tax law. He is also a historian who concentrates on American sports in the 20th century. His book *Baseball Gods In Scandal: Ty Cobb, Tris Spreaker, and The Dutch Leonard Affair* was a finalist for SABR's Lawrence Ritter Award in 2020. Ian resides in North Attleboro, Massachusetts, with his wife, Ann-Marie, and his twin sons, Jacob and Ryan.

Made in United States
North Haven, CT
23 May 2022